CHILD
DEVELOPMENT
An Individual
Longitudinal
Approach

Leland H. Stott

THE MERRILL-PALMER INSTITUTE

CHILD
DEVELOPMENT

An Individual
Longitudinal
Approach

HOLT, RINEHART AND WINSTON, INC.
New York   Chicago   San Francisco   Toronto   London

Photographs on jacket, title page, and
facing all chapter openings by Suzanne
Szasz. The children shown are not
the case-study twins.

PREFACE

This book is an outgrowth of some twenty years of teaching and re-search in the related fields of Child Development and Family Relationships. The prime objective in writing has been to offer to the student of child development a somewhat different approach to the subject matter with the conviction that it can contribute in a special way to his understanding and appreciation of what the growing child is like.

Experience and observation indicate that the most effective and rewarding approach to understanding human development is to study the established principles and concepts in direct relation to the actual courses traversed by real individual children on their way to adulthood.

In the particular setting of this writing, direct and more or less continuous contact was maintained through the years with some thirty families and their growing children. Developmental records were kept on each child and these measurements and observational data were incorporated into the total family account of happenings, interaction patterns, and relationships. These family records constitute an invaluable learning resource. Their use in teaching, and as a "laboratory" facility for students, constitute the experiential background for writing this book.

We do realize, of course, that in the majority of settings in which courses in child development are offered actual developmental and family records are not available for direct study. This book attempts to compensate to some extent for that lack. It begins with a brief sketch abstracted from the records of a particular family, highlighting its unique features as a setting for growing children and outlining briefly the developmental courses pursued by each of the family's twins, Paul and Sally, the first-born. The data from the records of these two children and their family are then used throughout the book to illustrate principles of development and methods of representing those principles graphically, and to suggest wherever possible relationships between specific aspects of development and family influences and other environmental factors. Finally, Appendix C offers brief abstracts of the developmental and family records of two *other* children for students' laboratory use.

The uniqueness and individuality of the human being are emphasized throughout the book. Development is, very broadly, change —any change and all changes that take place in the living individual from conception to death. These changes are manifest in the structure of the physical organism or in its functioning, or both. All development, structural and functional, is the result of organism-environment interchange and interaction. The book points out specific instances of developmental acquisition in the lives of the twin subjects in which the principle of interaction is clearly evident.

Many people have contributed in various ways to the point of view and approach here offered, and to the actual production of this book. The work to a considerable degree is based largely upon the framework of my course manual, *The Longitudinal Study of Individual Development,* published by The Merrill-Palmer Institute in 1955. Hence, acknowledgments are due to a number of earlier members of the Institute faculty and administration who contributed in many ways. I wish to express special appreciation and thanks to Dr. Pauline Park Wilson Knapp, President, to Dr. William W. McKee, Vice-President, and to Dr. Irving Sigel, Chairman of Research, for use of the space and facilities of the Institute and for the privilege of having access to the files of the longitudinal research series. Dr. S. Idell Pyle has long been a supporter of the project and has offered many invaluable suggestions.

I acknowledge with much appreciation the very significant contribution of Dr. Dale B. Harris who read the entire manuscript. His criticisms and suggestions were exceedingly helpful. Mrs. Irene Zak who typed the manuscript, and assisted in many other ways, deserves much credit and my thanks. Family 695 and the twins, Paul and Sally, who, of course, must remain anonymous willingly gave permission for the special use made of their record files. To them I am especially grateful. And finally, to my wife I give much credit and express here my deep appreciation for her forbearance and her help and encouragement throughout the period of my concentration on this work.

Detroit, Michigan   L. H. S.
January 1967

CONTENTS

PART I

Introduction

Prologue

A lusty yowl of protest signaled the end of eighteen hours of strain and anxiety for the 695s. They had just become a family of three; they were no longer only two. But they were not three for long! A somewhat less lusty voice began mingling with the stronger one. Their first born now had a little sister—3 pounds lighter, and 10 minutes younger. They were now already a family of four. Thus began the life of Paul and Sally, twins.

Their parents, Tom 695 and Margaret White, first met in a working situation. They were associated as colleagues in the employ of an architectural firm, Tom as an architect and Margaret as a model draftsman. They thus became acquainted as two professional people. Their affection for each other developed out of common interests and aspirations, a shared sense of equal status as professional colleagues and mutual respect and admiration as persons.

Tom 695 was born of Armenian parents. His father was a native of Smyrna, Turkey and his mother of Istanbul. They had been married while still in their teens by family arrangement, as was the Armenian custom. During the Armenian uprising against the Turks, the young husband became a political refugee and the couple was forced to flee to Cairo where they lived for a number of years. There in Cairo their first child, a daughter, was born. When it became possible, the family moved back to Smyrna to live and to work with the paternal family.

Tom, the only son of the family, was born in 1910 in his ancestral home. There he lived his first 18 months.

Some months after Tom's birth, his father came to the United

States, and a year later he sent for his wife and her two young children to join him in New York. With them came his wife's mother and her three younger children. The family settled and became established in New York.

Tom thus grew up in the big city. As he progressed through the city public school system, he early became interested in architecture. Graduating from high school, he obtained employment with an architectural firm and while working there full time he attended night school at Columbia and New York Universities. In this way he gained a thorough preparation for his life's work by incorporating practical experience with his academic training.

In 1935 Tom 695 and one of his friends won an international competition for the design of a stock-exchange building in Teheran, Persia, and they went to Persia as guests of the Persian government to supervise the construction of the building. Upon arrival in Persia, however, they discovered that the site of the proposed building was inappropriate. They proceeded to convince the Shah to build at a new site, which entailed the demolition of a vast slum area. By the time the slum area was cleared, the available funds for the building were exhausted. So the stock-exchange building never materialized. However, during their two years in Persia they did build a bank and several residences. Before returning to the United States, Tom was able to visit many of his relatives in the Near East.

Back in New York in 1938, Tom began working for the N-B-G firm on their World's Fair exhibit. In that situation he met his future wife. Margaret White, in many respects had a background markedly different from that of the man she was to marry. Her father was born in a small town in Ohio, and her mother was a native of Idaho. Both sides of her family were of English extraction. Margaret's grandmother White was a "wisp of a woman" weighing only 90 pounds; her grandfather was described as a "blusterous pioneer" of 200 pounds. While Margaret's mother was still a child, the family moved to Minnesota. There she grew up and attended school.

Out of normal school, this young woman began teaching art and physical culture in a city school system. While thus employed she met and married another teacher. Margaret was the second of their two children. She and her older brother thus grew up in an American school-teacher family.

When Margaret was 4 years old, the White family moved to the city where Margaret continued her schooling through three years at the University. She then worked for a time as an assistant in the University's nursery school and later as a scientific illustrator for the zoology department.

In 1936, Margaret's brother, after receiving his Ph.D. in geology, went with his wife to Washington, D.C., for the winter. Margaret decided to go with them. While in Washington she worked as a free-lance artist. In the fall of 1937 she went to New York to work and to finish her studies for a degree at Columbia University. In 1938 she obtained employment with N-B-G as a model draftsman. Thus began a new phase in the lives of Tom and Margaret, two people with widely different ethnic and experiential backgrounds, but still with much in common upon which to build a life together and establish a family. They were married in New York in 1940.

In 1942 they moved West. Tom had won a national competition for the design of a university student center, and the move was made in order that he might supervise the construction of the building. By this time, of course, wartime restrictions on building materials were in effect, hence the university could not proceed with the new building. As an architect, however, Tom 695 experienced a series of successes and continued to grow in prestige.

Their twins, Paul and Sally, were born on September 1, 1943. Paul at birth weighed 8 pounds 5 ounces, while Sally, born 10 minutes after Paul, weighed only 5 pounds 9 ounces. Mother and babies remained in the hospital for thirteen days, during which time they were cared for according to the regular routine of the hospital. The babies were brought regularly to their mother to be nursed, as pre-scribed by the physician. During this period of "recovery," the babies, as is usual, lost some of their birth weight, but by the end of their stay in the hospital they were very nearly at their respective birth weights.

For some time prior to the birth of the babies, the mother, as a result of reading and discussing with her obstetrician and others, had seriously considered following the so-called self-demand feeding regime. Upon returning home with her babies, in consultation with the pediatrician and with the support and encouragement of her husband, Mrs. 695 undertook to breast feed her two babies "on demand." For the first two or three weeks this proved to be a difficult and taxing experience. There was at first, of course, no regularity in the babies' demands to be nursed, either day or night. There was much interruption of the mother's rest. Sometimes both babies de-mand feeding at the same time. And to nurse two babies at once proved to be especially difficult and relatively unsatisfactory to both mother and babies.

After this first adjustment period, however, a pattern of regularity gradually began to emerge in the nursing demands of each infant. By the end of their fourth week of self-regulation their feedings were very largely confined to the hours from 6 A.M. to 10 P.M. After another four or five weeks they were regularly "settling" for three feedings in each twenty-four hours—at around 9 A.M., at midday, and 6 P.M. or 7 P.M.

In general, Mrs. 695 experienced much "gratification and fulfillment" in her experience of breast feeding her babies. Early in this experience also there came to clear focus certain temperamental differences between Paul and Sally, even as nursing infants, as well as definite differences in the mother's affective reactions to these differences.

The babies were first put to breast when they were only 12 hours old. From the first, Paul's sucking was immediate and strong and firm. The mother's reaction to his first nursing was "one of deep satisfaction and fulfillment," and this reaction on her part continued to characterize her experience with Paul throughout the whole nursing period to the time of weaning.

Sally, on the other hand was smaller and weaker, and in the beginning she required a different care regime than did Paul. She was brought regularly in to her mother, as was Paul, at feeding time. At her first experience at breast, however, her grasp was so tight as to cause her mother sharp discomfort. With some slight improvement, this unpleasant aspect of her nursing time continued. Also it was difficult to know when Sally was in need of food, for she cried often during this early period after she was fed and sometimes during feeding. She would arch her back and cry and sometimes refuse to suck for several minutes. And during this whole procedure, when she did nurse she caused her mother considerable pain. During this same period Sally was very slow in releasing to sleep. She sometimes would cry for half an hour or more at night before she could relax and go to sleep.

The parents naturally became quite concerned about the whole situation of Sally's feeding and sleeping. They, of course, consulted their physician. They soon came to feel strongly that Sally needed more of a sense of being loved, a stronger sense of security. They now realized that, because she was "so tiny" in comparison to Paul, they perhaps had refrained from holding and handling her quite as much as they had her brother. Furthermore, Sally seemed less responsive than Paul and so perhaps had been talked to more and played with less.

Out of their concern for Sally, the parents decided to make a concerted effort to give her the kind and amount of attention they now felt she needed. They began to be very careful to divide their attention equally between the babies when they both were present. Since Paul went to sleep more readily, after he was asleep they would give Sally a little extra attention and fondling. Her father would carry her over his shoulder and play with her for a few minutes before she was taken to her crib. She responded especially to this sort of attention from her father.

This change in the amount of attention and stimulation Sally received apparently had the desired effect. She soon was able to relax more readily and go to sleep. She began to show obvious signs of being more responsive and happier. Her nursing also changed for the better, and her mother soon began to experience real satisfaction in nursing her. Mrs. 695 soon began to feel "the same close bond with her daughter as with her son."

So the twins came through their period of complete dependency. They were healthy babies, free from serious illness. Weaning procedures were instituted gradually and without pressure or strain. At about their seventh month, milk in a cup was introduced, which they soon began to take without difficulty. Both babies came gradually not to want the breast. By age 10 months they were completely weaned.

As was noted earlier, there were, from the beginning, some interesting temperamental differences between Paul and Sally. Sally became an "outgoing, gay and friendly" preschooler, quick in movement and generally aggressive. Paul, by contrast, showed more "imagination and understanding" than his sister. He made friends more slowly, but came to "accept people wholeheartedly when he was ready to trust them." He was slower learning to walk than Sally. Very early, at 4 months of age, Paul began to chew his toys and suck his tumb. His thumb sucking continued through much of his preschool period. Sally also bit and chewed on her toys at around 6 months of age, but she never sucked her thumb.

As they were nearing the end of their nursery school period an interesting situation developed in their relationship which is probably related to their contrasting temperaments. Paul, who had previously given up his thumb sucking, rather suddenly reverted to the habit. The nursery school staff felt that this probably was in part Paul's reaction to Sally's "increased outgoingness and making friends independently" of him. A teacher commented that "Sally and her friend delight in teasing and excluding Paul from their play. 'Only girls can do this . . . Only girls can come here.' They whisper secrets to each other. Sally is the instigator, and she sees it as a joke, but Paul takes it seriously and resents it." Apparently as a result of this ostracizing behavior of his sister, Paul began to ask to stay home from school.

The twins' parents took care to provide for them a rich and challenging variety of experiences. They had their own records and they greatly enjoyed playing them. Many books and other appropriate literature were provided. Paul (age 4 years), on one occasion, became absorbed in examining the pictures in a professional journal article on construction methods, and his father sat down with him and explained the process explicitly. This fascinated and delighted the child. He had been doing a great deal of paper cutting and construction. He characteristically would become so absorbed in such activities that he would resist going out to play. On a number of occasions he got up very early to work on some construction project before breakfast.

One frequent visitor in the home wrote: "the mother is warm and affectionate, yet she helps the children to be independent. They dress themselves. The parents provide maximum opportunities for the children's development. The mother takes them to the puppet show, to the library where they borrow many books, and to the office to visit their father. On the way to school in the car, and also before naps and bed, she tells them stories."

The father also frequently would tell each of them a bedtime story in his or her own room. This they enjoyed greatly.

Mr. 695 was the cello player in a local chamber-music group, and on many occasions this group played in the 695 home. Paul, particularly, enjoyed this very much.

Perhaps largely as a result of their culturally rich home environment as well as high endowment in intellectual potentiality, both children were precocious in their speech development. They consistently scored high on mental tests.

At age 5 years, the twins became members of a "recreational club" for kindergarten-age children. This club was one of a series designed to maintain regular weekly contact and observation of the children of the "longitudinal" research series after they had left the nursery school and had entered the public schools. The following are excerpts from a summary of their first year in the club:

> Paul needs challenging experiences. He has good ideas and exceptional ability to organize, and carry through activities. Self-contained and self-sufficient. Although he does not shun them, he does not seek out other children except his sister. In games he is often the last one to be "it," as he is too shy to call out that he wants to be chosen.

> His activity and interest spans are very long and he seeks little aid or praise but becomes deeply engrossed in his work. He follows through with an activity with a great deal of imagination.

> Paul (in the club situation) has a very good relationship with Sally, who is very warm and outgoing. She seems to bring out more aggressive behavior in him.

Later, when the children were 10 years of age the following comments were made:

> Paul doesn't seem to push or drive himself. He gets along well with the group but is usually not involved in the group activity. His is a more individualistic role. His organizational ability seems more directed toward materials than people. He is likely, however, to be the leader when the group is small and there are few adults present. He doesn't visibly have the semblance of the leader, but seems to be doing what he wants to do and other children fall in with him.

During the twins' later childhood and adolescence, the 695 home continued to adapt itself to the changing needs of the family members. On occasions when special school or church events necessitated unusual preparatory activities, or extra space in the living room for preparation of materials, there continued to be family flexibility and a willingess on the part of those not involved to be "inconvenienced," temporarily and without undue disruption of normal family functions.

Thus Paul and Sally passed through their adolescence and approached the responsibilities of young adulthood.

CHAPTER 1

Developmental Concepts and Definitions

It is a curious fact that the nature of children and of childhood is not easy to grasp from the viewpoint of the adult. It would seem that a parent, sensing his responsibility and his need to understand his children, might gain greatly from a review of his own experiences in growing up. The facts, however, seem to be that, as we leave our childhood behind us, we have in reality passed through the various phases of growing up without realizing what was taking place gradually and imperceptibly day by day. Each of us has his sense of identity —the sense of being the same person all along without really sensing change, and so, as an adult, one is likely to look upon the world of childhood as a stranger, with wonder, and with no immediate basis for understanding. In the words of Fraiberg (1959):

> It is only in the minds of adults that childhood is a paradise, a time of innocence and serene joy. The memory of the Golden

Age is a delusion for, ironically, none of us remembers this time at all. At best we carry with us a few dusty memories, a handful of blurred and distorted pictures which often cannot tell us why they should be remembered. This first period of childhood, roughly the first five years of life, is submerged like a buried city, and when we come back to these times with our children we are strangers and we cannot easily find our way. (p. ix)

Historical Conceptions of Child Nature and Development

And so it has been throughout ages past. Philosophers and students of human nature have pondered the problems of childhood and of the nature of the transition from childhood to adulthood. Children *are* human beings. The child must somehow be like the adult who is trying to deal with him, yet he is so different. Just what is the nature of childhood? What happens to change the newborn infant into a child, an adolescent, an adult, an aged person? The metamorphosis takes place so gradually, so imperceptibly that one cannot discern its nature, yet the gulf between the infant and the adult is enormous. Throughout the course of this change, nevertheless, individual identity persists. With all the changes from the infant to the adult, thirty or fifty years later still the same individual exists.

Different philosophical positions regarding the nature of "human nature" and human existence have prevailed from time to time, and these have dominated the thinking about what children are like and how they develop. Always, these views have involved the question of the relative importance of the inherited make-up versus the influences of the environment. In earlier times, only one of these factors, was usually emphasized. The prevailing conception tended to be either one of biological determinism or of environmental (situational) determinism.

Biological Determinism

During the first few centuries A.D. in the Christian world, the idea developed that mortal man is by nature evil. Being "born in sin," he cannot be other than sinful. The individual's task, therefore, if he was to be redeemed, was to triumph over (overcome) the flesh. From this point of view, the child, born in sin as he was and not having lived to overcome his mortal impurities, became an object for particular attention. He possessed, by very nature, all of the traits of mortal man, man's moral weaknesses and tendencies to do evil.

PREFORMATIONISM   If the infant, being very small, possesses all of the traits and characteristics of mortality, he must possess them in miniature. The theory thus developed that the newborn infant was to be regarded as a miniature adult. Indeed, even at the moment of conception the individual was thought to begin his existence completely preformed in miniature.

Development from this medieval point of view was thought to be purely quantitative in nature. It is merely a process of increase in physical size and in magnitude of traits and perverse tendencies that are there from the beginning. This preformationistic conception of human development was reflected in the art of that age. Phillippe Aries (1962), French student of the history of family life, described that period of medieval art as follows:

> Medieval art until about the twelfth century did not know childhood or did not attempt to portray it. It is hard to believe that this neglect was due to incompetence or incapacity; it seems more probable that there was no place for childhood in the medieval world. An Autonian miniature of the twelfth century provides us with a striking example of the deformation which an artist at that time would inflict on children's bodies. The subject is the scene in the Gospels in which Jesus asks that little children be allowed to come to Him. The Latin text is clear; *parvuli*. Yet the miniaturist has grouped around Jesus what are obviously eight men, without any of the characteristics of childhood; they have simply been depicted on a smaller scale. In a French miniature of the late eleventh century the three children brought to life by St. Nicholas are also reduced to a smaller scale than the adults, without any other difference in expression or feature. A painter would not even hesitate to give the naked body of a child, in the few cases when it was exposed, the musculature of an adult. (p. 33)

Since in the medieval view of childhood children are not qualitatively different than adults, they were forced to behave according to adult standards and in terms of the acceptable patterns of behavior of the era. The literature of that time contained many anecdotal records of extremely severe and cruel beatings of children by "righteous" parents who interpreted every slight infraction of rules and every failure to obey orders or to perform according to arbitrary, parent-imposed standards as acts of perversity and from which the child must be purged.

No understanding of the nature of immaturity or of the need for immature expression existed. Hence, there was little sympathy for or toleration of behavior natural to and appropriate for children. The idea that "children should be seen but not heard" is a fairly common contemporary remnant of this conception of child nature. The concepts of innate ideas, prenatal mentation, and racial instincts are, in reality, preformationist concepts.

PREDETERMINISM   A somewhat different view of the nature of children and how they develop was elaborated some two centuries ago by the French philosopher Rousseau. According to his conception, the child is not already preformed in detail in the reproductive cell or at birth, but, rather, a complete blueprint and pattern for his development is set and predetermined by heredity at conception. Development thus was thought of as consisting of the "unfoldment" of this design. Children were fundamentally good, and the function of the environment, therefore, was to protect rather than to purge. The developing personality is to be fostered in its unfolding. Nothing must interfere with the process. Parents and teachers were charged with the responsibility of allowing and encouraging the natural tendencies and inclinations of the child to develop without interference.

As an explanation of the assumed regularity and inevitability with which the predetermined developmental pattern, in each case, was presumed to be carried out when not interfered with, Rousseau and his followers proposed the idea that the course of individual development paralleled that of the species through the various stages of its evolution. A hundred years later this doctrine of *recapitulation* was elaborated and refined by G. Stanley Hall. Because of Hall's prestige and the completeness and clarity with which he elaborated his view of human development, it became widely accepted. However, as developmental data accumulated and as relationships between the biological and the cultural aspects of development were more carefully examined, Hall's system of parallelisms no longer constituted an acceptable theory of ontological development.

Environmental Determinism

In the history of thinking about human development there have also been theories in which environment was emphasized as the all-important factor. In contrast to the theories of biological determinism, the child from this general point of view was regarded as highly pliable and "modifiable," like the "blank slate" (*tabula rasa*) of John Locke, to be written upon by environmental influences.

Lamarck, a French zoologist and evolutionist in the early part of the nineteenth century was an influential promulgator of the extreme environmentalist doctrine. He is better known, however, for his view that new traits and characteristics may become established in the individual through the influence of the environment and may be then transmitted genetically to offspring. Thus, in Lamarck's thinking, the environment was the crucial factor in phylogenetic as well as ontogenetic development.

The environmental philosophy has dominated much of the recent thinking and practice in the education and upbringing of children.

> The humanistic movement in philosophy and education has consistently championed the environmentalist position that, given proper conditions of nurturance, man's developmental potentialities are virtually unlimited in scope or direction. Implicit in this optimistic appraisal is (a) the belief that "human nature" is essentially amorphous and can be molded to whatever specifications man chooses to adopt as most compatible with his self-chosen destiny, and (b) unbounded confidence in the possibility of attaining this objective through appropriate educational procedures. (p. 38 in *Theories and problems of child development,* 1958, Grune & Stratton, Inc., by permission)

Extreme behaviorism under the leadership of J. B. Watson (1928) was strongly environmentalist, stressing in more psychological terms the *tabula rasa* emphasis with a rejection of the idea of inherent developmental designs and predispositions.

Currently, child development researchers strongly emphasize the importance of stimulation in early infancy. There is a suggestion that infant learning capacity (functional development) is much greater than has hitherto been recognized and that under appropriate conditions of stimulation and by means of simple experimental procedures this inherent learning capacity can be mobilized at an earlier age.

Interactionism

The essential roles of both endogenous (innate) and environmental factors in individual development are, of course, generally recognized today. Organism-environment interaction, it is assumed, underlies all developmental change. Even in such "biological" processes as cell proliferation and differentiation in the growth of the embryo, the essential role of the environment is recognized by biologists. The pattern of pressures, stresses, and pulls of gravity is different for different portions of the rapidly forming organism. This sort of environmental influence in interaction with the genetic determiners is presumed to bring about the differentiation of cell groups to form specialized tissues, organs, and parts of the body.

Functional development in the child, likewise, is generally understood as resulting from a continuous encounter between the child with his endogenous capacities and predilections and his environment. The importance of an understanding of child nature as it changes in quality as well as in quantity is emphasized. Of equal importance, of course, is environmental nurturance and guidance.

The Nature of Development

Child development as a scientific field has contributed significantly to our understanding of children and, in a general sense, of how they develop. But there is still much not yet well understood. Human development is a broad and complicated field, which, for its adequate exploration, must be entered separately by a number of scientific disciplines, each with its kit of tools, concepts, and approaches and each viewing the phenomena to be studied from its own particular level of observation.

Development, of course, means *change* through the process of living through time. The phenomena for study, then, common to all the various scientific approaches, are change phenomena. But developmental processes in the living human being are not open to easy observation. The physical anthropologist, from his level of observation for example, can see and measure change that the processes of development have brought about. He can measure and record the various physical attributes and dimensions of the body periodically, each set of observations separated from the preceding one by a specific interval of time. Then by comparing his observations he can describe precisely in quantitative terms the changes that have taken place, but he has not really observed development as such. The same is true for the physiologist, the psychologist, the sociologist, and so on. Each can observe the direction and measure the magnitude of change that has taken place in a given interval of time and at a particular stage of development, but the actual process of development cannot be seen.

Undoubtedly the nearest approach to the actual observation of the fundamental processes of development is being made by the biochemist in collaboration with the geneticist. Their techniques converge upon the very beginnings of individual life and the elemental life processes.

In our present study of individual development we shall have to content ourselves with observations and measurements made at a number of grosser levels of observation (for example, those of the physical anthropologist, the developmental psychologist, the psycho-

analyst, and the specialist in education) at different levels of development. Our present knowledge of child development is based essentially
upon data obtained at these levels of observation.

We have already stressed the continuity and the "process" nature
of development and the fact that only the products, or outcomes, of
the processes of development can be observed. We can note that
change has taken place because things are different from time to time.
The child is larger now than he was a month ago. But developmental
change can be noted not only in the child's physical being (the structure) but also in the functioning of that structure.

Structural Development

In an organism as complex as the human being, the various aspects
and manifestations of development are numerous, interrelated, interdependent, and difficult, if not impossible, to differentiate clearly. In
the study of physical-growth phenomena, however, it has proved
useful theoretically, at least, to identify and describe two main aspects
of developmental change.

GROWTH   Growth, first of all, involves the obvious changes
in bodily dimensions. During infancy and childhood the body steadily
becomes larger, taller, and heavier. The rate of growth in the various
parts of the body, however, is not the same, in either an absolute or
a relative sense. Growth, therefore, necessarily involves changes in
body parts as well as in over-all stature and weight. All of these
changes are *quantitative* in nature. They are readily measurable in
terms of standardized quantitative units. Growth is the subject of
Chapter 2.

MATURATION   Along with and intimately related to the gross
bodily changes which we call growth, there also occur changes in the
inner structure and organization of parts, organs, or tissues, not in
the sense of the incremental addition to what is already there but
rather in the sense of new and qualitatively different elements or
features being incorporated. These less evident structural changes are
discrete, discontinuous, and qualitative in nature and involve primarily the inner structures of the body. Changes in the brain during
early childhood are largely maturational in nature. These changes
consist not in cell proliferation which result in dimensional change,
but in further organization, extension, and interrelating of nerve cells
already present, making ready for functioning of a progressively
higher order.

INSEPARABILITY OF GROWTH AND MATURATION   It must be emphasized, however, that these two aspects of physical change (development) are indeed but *aspects* of the same basic phenomenon. In an over-all sense, growth (quantitative stature change) also has qualitative aspects. One can, to be sure, measure quantitatively the lengths of all the segments of the body and describe them in those terms, but in total pattern the change cannot be adequately described except qualitative terms. The body of the 6-year-old, for example, is not only larger but also *different* in general appearance, in proportionality, in quality, than it was when he was 6 months old (See Figure 2.1).

Likewise, when the development of a structure such as the skeleton is assessed in qualitative terms and referred to as maturation, growth is also involved. As we shall see in a later chapter, the very process of bone maturation produces quantitative change (change in over-all size of the organism). Growth and maturation are different aspects of physical development, but they are not separable in any real sense. Some physical developmental phenomena can be measured with quantitative measuring scales. These changes we call growth. Others cannot adequately be assessed in quantitative terms. Qualitative changes involving new features, new parts, new relationships, and new qualities are called maturational changes, not growth. Growth and maturation are different aspects of the complex process of physical development.

PRENATAL DEVELOPMENT   The marvel of physical development begins some 267 days before birth. The union of the female and the male reproductive cells creates a new organism, "a creature with a unique growth potential and developmental design" (Baller, 1962, p. 149). That single-cell organism becomes immediately active in preparation for the first cell division. During the first month of its individual existence this tiny organism has already grown to some 10,000 times its original size. It has grown and it has also matured.

> The total journey from a speck of watery material to a seven-pound, nineteen-inch-long human being takes 267 days and is a marvel of refinement. One change prepares the way for the next, and the plan, for all its subtlety, is marked by an incredible accuracy, both in running true to form and in staying on schedule. (Thoms and Blevin in Baller, 1962, p. 166)

In the very beginning the process is entirely one of growth. The growth process is well under way several days before the tiny bit of protoplasm finds its way down one of the Fallopian tubes to the uterus, a distance of only about two inches. By the time of the sixteen-cell stage (even at this early stage differentiation is beginning), a qualitative change is taking place. An outer layer of cells, flatter in form, begins to envelop the inner mass of roundish cells.

During approximately the first week after conception this tiny ball of cells floats freely and passively in the uterine fluid. At about that time, however, it contacts the wall of the uterus, whereupon a rather dramatic change takes place in its behavior. It becomes "aggressively" active, and within a short time it has completely imbedded itself in the wall of the uterus. It has also sent out tiny processes called villi which have intermingled with the blood-rich tissue of the uterine wall and which, by osmosis, are beginning to absorb the oxygen, carbohydrates, proteins, and minerals necessary for survival and further growth. The new organism has now become a true parasite.

With the establishment of a source of oxygen and a food supply, both growth and maturation continue at a rapid pace. Cell layers are further differentiated. One end of the embryo becomes established as the head. At the beginning of the third month it is still little more than an inch in length but already body parts and organs are beginning to differentiate. The tiny organism is now entering a very critical period of its existence. Qualitative changes are now of vital importance. The organs and vital body parts are rapidly forming and so are especially vulnerable to the influence of any noxious chemical substances that may be present in the mother's blood. These substances can be absorbed along with the nutrients and oxygen. The various malformations to which the human organism is subject are thus brought about during this *organogenetic* period, a period of vital qualitative change (maturation) as well as of rapid growth.

Now the baby-to-be is called the fetus. It has its own independent nervous system and circulatory system. The fetal blood stream and the maternal blood stream simply exchange materials within that remarkable organ, which in a sense, is shared by mother and fetus —the placenta.

During the remaining months of the prenatal period, growth is rapid and qualitative changes continue to take place. Although there is some exercise of muscle contraction, along with much organic functioning, the period is primarily one of physical development in which the relation between its two aspects, growth and maturation, is clearly evident.

Functional Development

The functional manifestations of development are, of course, the subject matter of developmental psychology. Functioning generally begins when the structure is developmentally *ready* to function.

Muscle tissue begins exercising its contractile function early in the prenatal period and as the various organs and specialized tissues are formed they begin the activity for which they are specialized. This initial exercise, furthermore, brings about change in the function itself, which we call learning.

A large portion of this book is concerned with learning in this broad sense. The development of patterns of overt activity consists of processes of motor learning. The child, for example, does not walk instinctively. He must learn to walk in spite of the fact that as a human being it is "natural" for him to walk. He learns to walk by perfecting an intricate coordination of sensory, nervous, and muscular functioning. And this is accomplished through exercise and practice.

The same is true of the effective use of the hands in reaching, grasping, and manipulation. It is upon these two complex basic patterns of motor functioning—bipedal locomotion and reaching-prehension-manipulation—that the myriad of specialized overt behavior patterns are superimposed. One learns in the course of a lifetime an almost endless variety of skills involving the agility of the feet and the intricate coordinations of eye and hand.

The development of the so-called higher functions is likewise a matter of learning. Even intelligence, which is basically one's over-all effectiveness in total functioning, is achieved through learning. One is effective in meeting the problems of life to the extent to which he has been able to acquire through exercise the necessary abilities and skills.

Among the facilities necessary for general effectiveness in life as a human being are, of course, vocal speech and the related communicative skills. It is presumed that man is unique among living forms in his ability deliberately, and with intent, to convey to and receive from others meanings and information by means of sound and other symbols. Equally unique is his ability to represent and to mentally manipulate objects and situations not actually present that can be perceived immediately. This tremendously important thinking function is a product of learning from experience.

The quality and the richness of one's affective life (his emotions) are very largely dependent upon learning from experience in interpersonal relationships. As we shall see, according to considerable evidence, one's ability to receive from, as well as to give to, another genuine love depends very largely upon the amount and the quality of interactive experience one has had with a nurturing person during the critical period of babyhood.

Finally, the quality of uniqueness and identity, the individuality of one's total functioning, that pervasive quality we call personality one gains by virtue of learning. We learn to be kindly or timid or hostile or empathetic or cowardly or cruel as we grow from babyhood and interact with others and experience the world around us.

Development: A Resultant of Interchange

At this point we must emphasize the implicit fact that development, both structural and functional, results from the interaction or interchange between organism and environment. This, of course, means that the congenital constitutional and temperamental nature of the individual at birth is an important immediately predisposing factor and that one's nature, as it is constantly modified through development, continues to be a factor always in interaction with the environment, affecting further development. Obviously, without a nurturing environment no development would take place in the fertilized ovum. It is equally true that, even though an emotional pattern or speech facility or a trait of personality is learned, the processes through which learning occurs can take place only through interchange between the individual and his environment.

The Assessment of Developmental Change

The study of development always involves measurement or some other appraisal procedure. In some instances measurement has constituted a rather involved problem.

As we have already noted, physical development presents two aspects, or orders, of change: changes in measurable amount (growth), and changes in kind or quality (maturation). The same is true of the functional aspect of development. In some instances, status or progress in learning can be appraised quantitatively in terms of standard units. The child at age 6 years, for example, can run *faster*, jump *farther*, use *more* words, than he could when he was 3 years old. These are quantitative changes. But the quality and the character of this child's walk at age 3 years is very different than it was at age 9 months, and no standard scale can measure or portray adequately that difference. That change is qualitative in nature.

But here again, there are changes in quality and kind also involved in the child's increase in running speed and in the size of his vocabulary. And likewise, there are measurable changes in amount involved in the smoothness and grace of his walk at age 6 years as compared with his tottering, insecure amble at age 9 months. Magnitude changes in functioning can be distinguished from changes in quality and character of functioning, but again, the two aspects of development are inseparable.

We have no words that are consistently used to designate these two different aspects of behavioral change comparable to the terms growth and maturation with reference to organismic change. In certain instances, however, common usage has made the term growth seem appropriate with reference to functional change. Very often, for example, increase in intelligence is referred to as mental growth. Furthermore, as a rule no distinction is drawn between changes in amount and changes in kind in mental development.

Appraisal of Change in Kind or Quality

As we have already indicated, when development appears as change in kind, that is, when the change consists of a series of qualitatively different events, or features, or "stages," it is not then amenable to measurement by use of any standard scale of units. Other means must be devised for the appraisal of this sort of development. In this connection the concept of stages becomes useful. Changes in kind usually follow one after another in a fixed sequence. When such an invariable sequence of events or stages is observed, that sequence can be made the basis for the assessment of an individual's status with reference to that particular line of development.

A number of such developmental sequences have been established and are commonly used in the assessment of physical development. The use of certain of these sequences is the main concern of Chapter 3, which deals with maturation.

Functional changes, however, most frequently are not open to direct observation. For that reason relatively few attempts have been made to appraise functional development in terms of sequential stages. The area of gross physical activity—the so-called motor functions—of course, is the exception. Bodily acts and changes in the quality of their execution can be observed and recorded. Such functions as the use of the hands in reaching, grasping, and manipulating objects, and the locomotor functions have been studied and useful developmental sequences have been established. Chapter 5 deals with these functions in some detail.

Other areas of functional development, which perhaps involve to a greater extent the so-called higher mental processes, such as the acquisition of speech and other social skills, are subject to study and appraisal in their quantitative aspects, as well as in terms of developmental sequences (see Chapter 9).

The Psychological Functions

Functions other than those involving observable bodily activity are usually not amenable to quantitative measurement. Mental activity or an emotional experience, for example, cannot be observed directly or measured with any standard scale. However, the objective outcomes and behavioral manifestations of these hidden processes often can be observed. These outward aspects, moreover, often change in kind and quality with development in general. The measurement problem thus becomes one of noting these observable changes and, when possible, ordering them into their natural, invariable sequences as they occur in individual development.

DEVELOPMENTAL SEQUENCE IN MENTALITY　An outstanding example of this approach is Piaget's (1952, 1960) analysis of the development of intelligence. Piaget states that the course of mental development involves four major periods, each in turn being a further development of the one preceding it, yet each being characterized by features that are new. This view of mental development is perhaps most clearly seen in the first, or sensorimotor, period, which he sees as consisting of six stages. The whole period is regarded as one of continuous change in the sense that new features, different from yet growing out of the previous situation, emerge in an invariable sequence. This proposed sequence is discussed in some detail in Chapter 6.

A PSYCHOANALYTICALLY DERIVED SEQUENCE　Another even more famous example of an observed sequence in psychological development is the series of stages in psychosexual development which has been observed and formulated by the psychoanalytic school of psychology (Erikson, 1950; Munroe, 1955; Waelder, 1960).

First of all, development, according to psychoanalytic theory, is definitely the outcome of processes of interaction between the biologically given and the environment. Freud consistently insisted that all functioning, including neurotic behavior, has a constitutional basis. "It is the therapeutic technique alone that is purely psychological; the theory does not by any means fail to point out that neuroses have an organic basis" (Freud, 1905, p. 113).

Freud discerned a sequence of stages in the personal (psychosexual) development of the individual. The descriptions of these stages, however, particularly as to their psychological implications, have been elaborated by certain of Freud's followers. The emergence of each stage is presumed to coincide with a particular level of organismic maturation. This level usually involves the beginning of functional readiness of a particular structure or organ system. Accordingly, the sequence is established through a process of continuous development, but since each stage in the sequence is the expression of further structural maturation, its basic nature is qualitatively different than the preceding one.

Thus the first in the sequence, the *oral* stage, coincides in its onset with the profound immaturity and complete dependency of the newborn when the need for frequent and immediate relief from the pain of an empty stomach and the sensual pleasure and gratifications of sucking are paramount in experience. It is a time when the sense of well-being and of trust in the outside or the pain of hunger and the sense of alarm and of distrust of a nondependable outside can be an important predisposing factor in psychological development.

The maturation of the sphincter musculature, which allows voluntary control of the eliminative processes, marks the beginning of the *anal* stage. It is a time when the beginning of an implicit sense of autonomy on the part of the child coincides with the beginning of pressure from the outside for control of elimination thus giving rise to possible conflict between the two opposing tendencies of "holding on or letting go." Again the predominating quality of the interaction between the child and the outside can have important developmental implications with respect to these tendencies (Erikson, 1950).

Further general maturation combined with increased social sophistication causes the child to become more generally sensitive to bodily stimulation and to begin more consciously to seek the pleasures of bodily contact with his mother, the one who has given him comfort and gratification from the beginning. His erogenous zones, including his genital organs, become especially responsive to close contact with his mother as she administers to his bodily needs. Thus a lively "infant sexuality" develops, and in the case of the male child, the mother is the "object" of his love. In the phallic stage of emotional development, according to Freudian theory, the little boy wishes to replace his father as his mother's lover, desires incest relations with his mother, and wishes for the death of his father as a rival. This period of the so-called Oedipus complex is a period full of stress and emotional conflict and the sense of guilt. The little girl, of course, goes through a series of changes and experiences comparable to those of the male child, but different in detail.

The conflicts and distresses of the phallic stage are normally dealt with through the psychological mechanism of repression. Unholy desires, conflicts, and guilt feelings are banished from consciousness, and there develops a general amnesia for the experiences of that period. Thus begins the relatively long *latency* period. During latency any further maturation of the genital system is delayed. Physical development generally is quantitative in nature; the child just grows larger. In its functional aspect, change is largely quantitative, also; the child gains more strength, more speed of movement, more agility. The latency period is also a time of rapid informational learning. Many skills, manual, intellectual, and social are acquired. In general, it is a period relatively free from conflict and of tremendous acquisition of knowledge and skills.

The last of the five childhood stages of psychosexual development, the *puberal*, or *genital*, stage is clearly ushered in by the rather dramatic upsurge in growth and maturation known as the adolescent growth spurt. This is a period of transition when new developmental features come into being, when a physiological reorganization within takes places, and when the child might experience some bewilderment and difficulty in reestablishing a sense of self-identity. According to psychoanalytic theory, the child experiences reawakening and resurgence of much of the repressed material: strivings, wishes, and desires that are presumed to characterize the earlier phallic period. These five stages, then, constitute a fixed sequence to which the development of a particular child might be referred.

Age Equivalents

Before a developmental sequence (such as Piaget's) can be used for purposes of appraising individual developmental status, age equivalents of those stages must first be determined. The age equivalent of a particular stage is simply the average age at which children reach that particular stage. A set of age equivalents corresponding to a series of stages can be made to function as a scale for individual assessment. A fuller discussion of this method of "measuring" qualitative change is found in Chapter 3.

Individuality in Developmental Pattern

In the individual longitudinal study of development the fact that every individual is different from every other in over-all pattern of development becomes strikingly clear. We shall mention here two important respects in which individuals differ. First, children differ widely in general developmental pace. That is to say some children develop faster, generally, and reach their adult status earlier than others. This is particularly evident in their physical growth and maturation. Since growth in stature is a manifestation of the development of the skeleton, the processes of skeletal maturation are of interest in this connection (Bayley, 1943). This matter is discussed in Chapter 3.

The relation between the general rate of physical growth and psychological development and adjustment has been the subject of a number of studies. Such relationships become especially significant during the early stages of adolescence. Of necessity, the child revises his self concept, and often also his feelings about himself, as his childish body makes its transition to the proportions and contours of the adult form. During this period he is acutely aware of his body and is very sensitive to any deviations it may take from the usual and the expected. Hence, being a "fast grower" or a "slow grower" can be a factor of importance in the personal and emotional adjustments during this period. The results of one study of slow growing, as compared with fast growing, adolescent boys indicated that the former "are more likely to have negative self-conceptions, feelings of inadequacy, strong feelings of being rejected and dominated, prolonged dependency needs and rebelious attitudes toward parents" (Mussen and Jones, 1957, p. 255). A comparable study of adolescent girls suggested that rate of physical maturity tends to be a factor affecting their adjustments to a lesser degree but in the same direction as with boys (Jones and Mussen, 1958).

Intraindividual variation in developmental level is a second aspect of development in which children differ rather widely. Indeed, it is another aspect of individuality. One child, for example, may be slow in walking but learn to talk months earlier than average; another child might achieve these functions in the inverse order. Whenever status measurements are made on a series of changing attributes, the developmental profile is always irregular and the pattern of irregularity is different for every individual. Likewise, when developmental progress of each of these various traits is plotted over time (chronological age), the resulting growth curve always differs to a greater or lesser degree from each curve of each other trait. And again, the degree of developmental discordance varies from individual to individual. The research literature suggests a negative relationship between developmental discordance and psychological adjustment (Millard, 1957; More, 1953; Olson, 1937).

The Importance of Individual Study

The intensive longitudinal study of the changing characteristics— physical and psychological—of an individual child is one valuable appoach to an understanding and appreciation of the principles of human development. In such a study we are able to see growth in its true perspective and in relation to some of the conditioning factors. Certain meaningful relationships between one phase of development or one set of circumstances and the next, relationships which are difficult to discern in other types of study, may clearly come to light in the longitudinal view.

Longitudinal orientation is personalistic rather than statistical or normative. Records and direct observations assemble numerous facts regarding the course of a child's developmental changes and associated behavior trends, interests, and abilities. These facts should be examined and interpreted in terms of their interrelationships. To be sure, the quantitative measurements and test results also should be examined against the background of previously established standards and norms for purposes of appraising developmental status and progress. But primarily we must come to see the child under study as a total and uniquely integrated personality, a being who is constantly changing (developing) according to his own individual developmental pattern. We must also discern, whenever possible, the relation between the facts of the individual child's development and his behavior, his feelings, his private meanings, and his social adjustments. G. W. Allport (1942) has stressed the importance of the individual-study approach:

> Not until we are prepared to dwell upon the unique patterning of personality, and to concede that lawfulness need not be synonomous with frequency of occurrence in a population, and to admit that prediction, understanding, and control are scientific goals attainable in the handling of one case and of one case alone—not until then are we in a position to assess the full value of personal documents. (p. 64)

> Acquaintance with particulars is the beginning of all knowledge—scientific or otherwise. In psychology the font and origin of our curiosity in, and knowledge of human nature lies in our acquaintance with concrete individuals. To know them in their natural complexity is an essential first step . . . psychology needs to concern itself with life as it is lived, with significant total-processes of the sort revealed in consecutive and complete life documents. . . . If each personality harbors laws peculiar to itself; if the course of causation is personal instead of universal, then only the intensive ideographic study of a case will discover such laws. (pp. 56–57)

The purpose of this book is to suggest a course of study in child development based upon the longitudinal point of view and also to provide a useful guide for individual study. Appendix C contains rather complete abstracts of two longitudinal record files. One or both of these can be used for study and analysis. (They contain recorded observations of behavior, physical measurements, interviews, questionnaire material, and psychological test results.) Situations where developmental records and observational reports are available and where the child and his family are also accessible for first-hand observation may preferably be used as the basis for study.

A two-fold objective of developmental understanding may be sought by the student. Through actual use he can test, critically evaluate, and compare the methods, special techniques, and devices that have been developed in various research centers for studying individual growth and development (as well as the family situation and other significant aspects of the developmental habitat). At the same time, the student may gain a greater appreciation of the phases and stages through which a growing child passes and the obstacles and problems encountered as one grows toward maturity.

SELECTED READING SUGGESTIONS

Allport, G. W. *The use of personal documents in psychological science.* New York: Social Science Research Council, 1942.

Anderson, J. E. Child development: an historical perspective. *Child Develpm.,* 1956, **27,** 181–196.

Breckenridge, Marion E., and E. Lee Vincent. *Child development.* Fifth ed.; Philadelphia: Saunders, 1965. (Read Chapter 1, Some general principles of development.)

Harris, D. B. *The concept of development.* Minneapolis: University of Minnesota Press, 1957.

Smith, G. M. A simplified guide to statistics for psychology and education. Third ed.; New York: Holt, Rinehart and Winston, Inc., 1962.

PART II

Organismic Development

CHAPTER 2

Growth:
The Quantitative Aspect
of Developmental Change

One of the most striking things about children is the rapidity with which they grow. Striking as it is, this aspect of development is so obvious that we tend to take it for granted. Yet, as we shall see, this continuous change in dimensions, though obvious and commonplace, is not as simple as it seems, and, together with other aspects of development, it may have tremendously important implications in the life of the developing individual.

Status and Progress

One of the problems of growth is the adequate assessment of the developmental status reached by the individual child at a particular point in his life. An assessment of the child's developmental profile, which depicts his individuality and idiosyncracies, is invaluable in making his behavior more comprehensible and meaningful. By comparing the various aspects of a status profile with what has been found to be typical and thus expected in a child of the same age, much valuable information useful in his guidance can be gained. Is the child progressing developmentally at a satisfactory rate? In which respects is he at the expected level? In which is he ahead or behind "schedule"?

In individual studies, also, the significance of individual variation is best realized. No two developmental profiles are alike in total pattern. Each has its peculiarities, its uniqueness. In such studies the whole concept of what is "normal" is re-examined, and much of the concern about being different from the average is lessened. A heightened respect for individuality is fostered.

Another reason for consideration of the status evaluation is that the child's developmental progress can be evaluated and plotted. Development obviously is continuous. Strictly speaking, an individual is never exactly the same from one moment to the next. Life itself is a process of change; nevertheless, in our efforts to understand what is happening continuously we attempt to look intensively at a particular "stage" of development in its various aspects as if the process of change were suddenly brought to a halt to allow inspection of the situation at that point in time, just as one might examine a single frame from a motion picture film. By examining a series of such "stills," certain facts can be deduced about the processes that have gone on between them.

Genetic and Environmental Factors

It is also important, then, to study the course of individual development in its different aspects throughout the complete development cycle. One must begin with a look at the beginnings of individual existence.

As previously noted (Chapter 1), amazing growth changes have already taken place before the child is born into the external world. The human organism begins with the union of two minute reproductive cells, the ovum of the mother and the spermatozoon, or sperm, contributed by the father. Each of these original germ cells contains in its nucleus all of the hereditary factors coming from its donor. Biological hereditary is thus determined in each new individual at his conception.

But from the moment of conception the environmental factor also plays its essential role. An appropriate and favorable intrauterine environment is a necessary condition for development. Through the interaction of these two sets of factors, hereditary and environmental,[1] change in magnitude begins. A series of cell divisions takes place resulting in the formation of two cells, then four, eight, sixteen, and so on, a process which eventuates in the billions of cells that make up the infant at birth. Thus the organism changes from a minute bit of protoplasm, scarcely visible without magnification, to a complex, functioning individual, perhaps 19 or 20 inches long and weighing around 7 pounds at the time of birth. This aspect of change, this increase in size and weight, before birth and throughout the "developmental period," and to some degree through life, is *growth*.

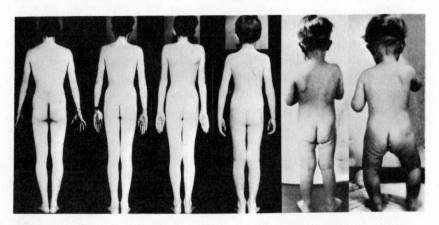

Figure 2.1

Changes in body proportions with growth, shown with photographs of the same boy at six ages, all adjusted to the same height. From Bayley (1956), p. 48, by permission.

Not only does the organism as a whole get taller and heavier, but the various parts and segments change in their relative dimensions. The head early in the growth of the fetus, for example, grows more rapidly than the rest of the body, but as development continues the trunk and limbs grow relatively more rapidly so that the proportions of the total body length taken up by these parts also change (see Figure 2.1).

Development always is complex. Body-growth changes are only one aspect of total development. Together with other developmental changes, they make ready for functioning the particular structures involved and so facilitate the functioning of the total organism. This

[1] Chapter 13 contains a fuller discussion of these two factors of development.

chapter describes growth, the aspect of change that is quantitative in nature and, therefore, is amenable to direct measurement.

The Complexity of Growth

At the naïve level of analysis of gross physical growth, each successive assessment of status differs only quantitatively from the one preceding it, and the change is expressed simply as the addition of more of the same quantitative units of measurement of over-all weight and height. Students of physical growth, however, are much more analytical in their studies (Krogman, 1956). The fact that total weight and total height increase with time is only a sample of the many dimensional changes that take place in the developing human organism. As mentioned earlier the relative length and weight of the different portions of the body change markedly. Krogman also directs his attention to the structures that constitute or determine total height and total weight (pp. 25–30). Wide individual variations are found in the measurements of the various component structures as they relate to different body types.

Much that was earlier assumed to be true about the course and the complexity of structural development based upon cross-sectional studies has proved to be of limited value in the understanding of individual development. It is a mistake now to assume that we have a completely adequate knowledge of human growth, which, on the surface, appears to be a simple matter of quantitative measurement. Much is yet to be learned about complex beneath-the-surface processes involved in what appear to be simple changes in dimensionality.

Some extremely important relationships between the physical and other aspects of development have been observed and appraised. Certain of these relationships are described in Chapter 3. There are, however, many possible connections between variations in structural development and psychological functioning yet to be investigated.

The Dimensions of Growth

Growth, as defined herein, is quantitative bodily change which takes place with increasing age. It is increase[2] in size. But size, of course, is not a simple dimension. Along with the over-all vertical dimension, height or stature, the width or the horizontal circumferences of the

[2] When the complete life span of the individual is to be considered, "growth" defined as change, may involve *decrease* as well as increase in size.

different body segments, as well as their relative length, obviously would be involved in a complete assessment of body size. In practice, however, the two over-all indexes of size most commonly used are total height and total body weight.

THE COURSE OF GROWTH IN HEIGHT Growth in terms of successive measurements of height is commonly represented graphically in two ways. One of these is the simple growth curve in which height measurements are plotted against age. The other way is to plot the *gain* or *increase* in height from age to age.

In Figure 2.2 the course of growth in height of Paul 695[3] is shown in terms of total height (A) and in terms of successive increments of gain (B). These curves are typical and correspond closely in form to other published height-growth curves (Stolz and Stolz, 1951; Tanner, 1961). Normally there are two periods of rapid growth. The first comes during infancy, roughly the first 2 or 3 years of life. After the baby has made his initial adjustment to extrauterine life, growth accelerates to a rapid pace. The *rate* of growth during this period, however, gradually decreases. By age 4 years usually the rate of increase has become stabilized and remains fairly constant during the period of childhood.

Within a considerable range of variation, the second period of rapid growth corresponds roughly with the early teen years (ages 10 to 15). This is the so-called adolescent growth spurt. Again, the rate of increase gradually lessens until the final leveling-off point—an individual's terminal height—is reached.

The course of growth in height in girls is quite similar in general pattern to that in boys. There are, however, some interesting sex differences in timing of the various phases of growth, particularly of the adolescent growth spurt. During early childhood, the average height of boys is somewhat greater than that of girls. Girls, however, tend to catch up with the boys and, for a short time before the beginning of the growth spurt, they become slightly taller on the average than boys. Girls also tend to reach their spurt of growth at ages 10 to 12 years—approximately 2 years earlier than boys. They also begin leveling off and reach their terminal height at an average age of about 16 years. Boys generally continue to grow for another 2 years, reaching an average terminal height of 5 feet 8 or 9 inches. Girls, on the average, end up some 5 inches shorter than boys.

[3] Throughout this book the developmental records of Paul, his twin sister Sally, and their family (No. 695), selected from the files of the Merrill-Palmer Longitudinal Series, is used to illustrate the principles of development and to demonstrate the use of the various graphing techniques and devices. Paul's growth data from birth to age 17 years 8 months are given in Table 2.3.

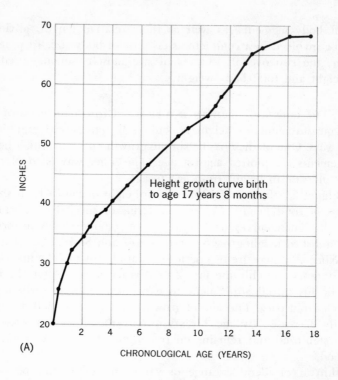

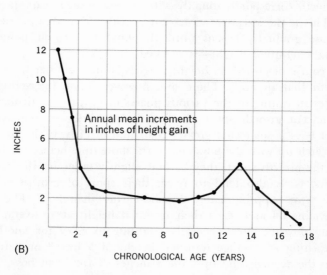

Figure 2.2

Growth in height of Paul 695.

The factors underlying these changes in rate of growth and the sex differences in rates and timing are not well understood in their details. It is quite clear, however, that increases in secretions of the endocrine glands and changes in pattern and balance of endocrine functioning play an exceedingly important role at the time of the dramatic growth changes at adolescence. It is also clear that the triggering of these changes in endocrine functioning is very largely under genetic control.

Body growth in weight Weight is a very useful comparative index of body size and body type. Much has been learned also about human growth from group and population studies of weight measurements, along with measurements of stature. In the longitudinal study of individual children in relation to their individual environments, weight becomes an especially significant measurement variable because of its susceptibility to the influence of such factors as physical health and nutritional adequacy, as well as emotional and other factors of psychological well-being.

As a single indicator of the course of biological development, however, weight is not as useful as height because of the former's instability and wide variability. Growth in height is nonreversible because progress in height is based primarily upon developmental changes in the bony framework of the body. A child normally never loses height but he can, and often does, lose weight for short periods of time. Progress in weight gain alone as an indicator of growth progress clearly has its limitations, but when weight measurements are plotted in combination with height measurements a very useful index of growth progress, as well as of body size and body type, is provided.

Patterns of Growth in Discrete Body Tissues

Although human development in general is a well coordinated and integrated system of processes, the various tissues and organs of the body do not all follow the same developmental time schedule. Growth in over-all body size generally follows the pattern of acceleration and deceleration depicted in Figure 2.2A. Certain tissues and organ systems, however, follow quite different schedules of growth. Figure 2.3 shows the generalized course of body growth (C) in comparison with growth in three other more specialized types of tissue. These curves are plotted in terms of percentage of adult status at age 20. Curve A represents the generalized growth changes in the lymphoid tissue of the thymus gland, tonsils, intestinal lymph masses, and so on. As is indicated in the figure, this type of tissue taken as a whole reached nearly twice its adult mass at the time of the adolescent growth spurt, then rather promptly began its period of decrease to the normal adult level.

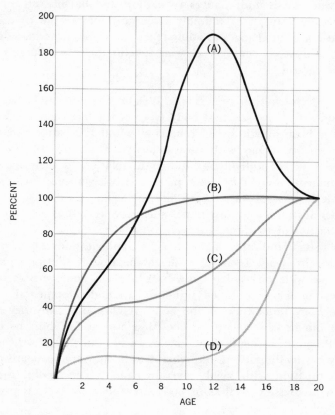

Figure 2.3

Growth curves of different parts and types of body tissues.
(A) Lymphoid type: thymus, lymph nodes, intestinal lymphoid masses. (B) Neural type: brain tissue, dura, spinal cord, certain dimensions of the head. (C) General type: body as a whole, external dimensions (except head), respiratory and digestive organs, musculature as a whole, skeleton as a whole. (D) Genital type: testes, ovary, epididymus, uterine tube, prostate, urethra, seminal vesicles. Adapted from Harris (1930), p. 193, by permission. Copyright 1930 by the University of Minnesota.

The nervous tissue of the brain (B), on the other hand, increases in size at a much more rapid rate during early childhood than does the body in general. The development of the brain is discussed in more detail in Chapter 3. Curve D represents the growth of the reproductive organs, internal and external. Early growth of these organs is very slow, and during the period of childhood there is little if any increase. During early adolescence, however, growth is very rapid. This rather wide diversity in relative rate and timing of growth in different body tissues and organ systems may be seen as an important aspect of the over-all coordination and regularity of biological development.

The Use of Growth Norms

Crude measurements of body size by themselves have no meaning. It is only when such measures are seen in relation to standards of reference that they become meaningful. The standard, or reference point, in the case of a quantitative measurement is usually some index of central tendency, such as the arithmetic mean or the median for the population of which the child is a member. A measure of variation within the population is also essential for the adequate appraisal of an individual child.

A number of well-known studies of physical growth have provided sets of norms (average measurements and indexes of variation) based on the particular sample of children used in each case (Baldwin, 1921; C. M. Jackson, Paterson, and Scammon, 1930; R. L. Jackson and Kelly, 1945; Krogman, 1948, 1957; Meredith, 1935, 1948). Since the children involved in these studies were representative of different sections of the United States, of different eras or periods of time, and of different segments of the population, their respective normative values vary considerably in magnitude. It is important, therefore, to note the source of the normative value and to use discretion in the interpretation of any particular child's measurements. For immediate purposes we have derived a set of average weights and heights with measures of variation (see Tables 2.1 and 2.2), based upon the Iowa growth data (Jackson and Kelly, 1945). The Iowa norms are based upon the study of some 1500 boys and 1500 girls, mostly from the higher economic and educational levels of the Iowa population. It was believed that the Iowa City data set a standard of growth that approaches the optimum.

In order clearly to see how such standards give meaning to actual individual measurements the student should examine the measurements of Paul 695, in Table 2.3, in relation to the Iowa standards in Table 2.1. Note, for example, that when Paul was 6½ years old he was 46.2 inches tall and weighed 52.8 pounds. The Iowa group of 6½-year-olds, with which Paul could reasonably be compared, aver-

Table 2.1

**Median Weights (with Sixteenth and Eighty-fourth Percentiles)
and Mean Heights (with Standard Deviations) for the Iowa
Samples of Boys[a]**

AGE	WEIGHT			HEIGHT	
YEARS-MONTHS	POUNDS	16TH PERCENTILE	84TH PERCENTILE	INCHES	SD
Birth	7.5	6.6	8.3	20.0	0.7
0-1	9.8	8.7	9.3	21.6	0.7
0-2	12.3	11.0	13.8	23.0	0.8
0-3	14.3	12.8	15.8	24.2	0.8
0-6	18.3	16.3	20.3	26.8	0.9
0-9	21.2	18.8	23.4	28.5	1.0
1-0	22.8	20.8	25.6	30.0	1.0
1-6	25.0	23.6	29.0	32.6	1.0
2-0	28.5	25.9	31.8	34.6	1.1
2-6	31.0	27.6	34.4	36.3	1.4
3-0	33.3	29.4	37.0	37.8	1.5
4-0	37.7	32.9	42.0	40.7	1.5
5-0	42.0	37.5	46.5	43.2	1.6
6-0	46.0	40.7	51.0	45.7	1.6
6-6	48.0	43.5	54.0	46.8	1.8
7-0	50.8	45.5	57.5	48.0	2.0
7-6	53.5	47.5	61.0	49.2	2.0
8-0	56.8	50.0	65.0	50.2	2.2
8-6	60.0	52.0	69.0	51.5	2.3
9-0	63.0	54.7	72.7	52.5	2.4
9-6	65.9	57.0	76.8	53.5	2.4
10-0	69.6	60.0	81.0	54.5	2.4
10-6	73.0	62.7	85.2	55.4	2.5
11-0	76.0	65.2	89.8	56.4	2.5
11-6	79.8	68.0	94.0	57.2	2.5
12-0	83.5	71.0	99.0	58.2	2.7
12-6	87.5	74.0	104.0	59.3	2.7
13-0	92.7	78.0	110.5	60.5	3.1
14-0	105.5	87.0	125.0	62.9	3.5
15-0	119.9	98.0	139.0	65.0	3.5
16-0	130.2	110.0	147.0	67.0	3.0
17-0	137.5	119.0	152.0	68.0	2.4
18-0	142.7	125.0	156.0	68.5	2.5

[a] *These values were derived from the Iowa normative growth curves (Figures 2.2, 2.3, and 2.4), based on measurements made at the Iowa Child Welfare Station by R. L. Jackson and Kelly (1945).*

aged 46.8 inches tall and their median weight was 48.0 pounds. Paul's measurements thus begin to take on meaning.

Any raw measurement or quantitative score of an individual child, if it is to have meaning, must always be seen in comparison with a standard of reference, that is, with a value that represents the group or population of which the child is a member or to which he is comparable.

Table 2.2

**Median Weights (with Sixteenth and Eighty-fourth Percentiles)
and Mean Heights (with Standard Deviations) for the Iowa
Samples of Girls[a]**

AGE	WEIGHT			HEIGHT	
YEARS-MONTHS	POUNDS	16TH PERCENTILE	84TH PERCENTILE	INCHES	SD
Birth	7.5	6.5	8.5	19.7	0.7
0-1	8.7	7.7	9.8	21.2	0.8
0-2	11.0	9.5	12.2	22.5	0.8
0-3	13.0	11.0	14.3	23.6	0.8
0-6	17.0	14.8	18.7	26.2	0.9
0-9	19.4	17.2	21.6	27.8	0.9
1-0	21.3	19.0	24.2	29.3	1.0
1-6	24.6	22.4	27.4	32.0	1.0
2-0	27.3	25.0	30.1	34.3	1.2
2-6	30.0	27.0	32.8	36.0	1.4
3-0	32.4	29.4	35.5	37.5	1.4
4-0	37.0	33.6	41.5	40.3	1.4
5-0	41.1	36.7	46.0	42.9	1.5
6-0	45.2	39.8	49.5	45.3	1.6
6-6	47.2	42.0	53.0	46.5	1.7
7-0	50.0	44.0	56.3	47.6	1.8
7-6	52.5	46.0	59.8	48.8	1.9
8-0	55.5	48.2	63.2	49.8	2.0
8-6	58.0	50.5	67.0	51.0	2.1
9-0	61.4	53.0	71.5	52.0	2.3
9-6	64.3	56.0	76.0	53.0	2.5
10-0	68.0	58.4	81.5	54.1	2.5
10-6	71.7	61.9	89.0	55.3	2.5
11-0	76.0	65.0	93.5	56.5	2.5
11-6	81.0	68.8	100.0	57.9	2.6
12-0	87.0	73.0	106.0	59.0	3.0
12-6	92.0	78.0	112.0	60.3	2.8
13-0	99.0	83.7	117.7	61.4	2.8
14-0	107.5	93.2	127.5	62.9	2.1
15-0	113.3	100.0	133.0	63.4	2.0
16-0	116.0	103.0	135.5	63.5	2.3
17-0	117.5	105.5	136.0	63.5	2.3
18-0	118.0	107.0	135.0	63.5	2.4

[a] *These values were derived from the Iowa normative growth curves for girls, based
on measurements made at the Iowa Child Welfare Station by R. L. Jackson and
Kelly (1945).*

Plotting Progress in Growth:
Simple Growth Curves

A second concern in the study of individual development is to explore
and plot developmental progress throughout its course. This can be
done by comparing a series of views of status in relation to the time

Table 2.3

Growth Data (Height and Weight Measurements) for Paul 695
from Birth to Age 17 years 8 months

AGE	WEIGHT (POUNDS)	HEIGHT (INCHES)
Birth	8.3	20.0
3 days	7.8	20.0
13 days	8.3	20.5
0-2	11.3	22.5
0-3	12.4	23.4
0-6	16.5	25.8
0-8	21.7	27.1
0-9	21.3	27.8
1-1	25.0	30.1
1-6	28.3	32.3
2-1	31.8	34.1
2-7	33.1	35.9
3-1	36.5	37.8
3-7	37.0	38.8
4-6	40.6	41.2
5-7	43.3	43.5
6-6	52.8	46.2
7-6	57.3	49.0
8-6	64.8	51.3
9-3	68.4	52.5
10-3	74.9	54.6
11-3	88.0	57.1
11-9	91.7	58.1
12-3	102.5	59.4
12-9	113.3	61.4
13-3	119.3	63.6
13-9	132.3	64.9
14-2	130.6	66.0
16-2	147.0	67.7
17-8	147.7	67.9

intervals between them. The observer then can make inferences about what has happened, that is, about the processes that have been going on in these intervals.

Chapter 1 stated that there are a number of methods, along with appropriate graphing devices and techniques, that have been developed for longitudinally studying individual growth from recorded measurements. Behind each technique is its rationale. In some instances the underlying assumptions have been questioned and certain theoretical difficulties arise in their use and interpretation. Certain of them have features in common, each has certain advantages and limitations, and each, within its limitations, has proved useful in practice.

The simplest and most obvious way of depicting growth progress is to plot raw weights and stature measurements against chronological age. As we saw earlier, these simple growth curves show relative rates of growth for different ages as well as the general course of growth with its fluctuations and irregularities.

A set of forms prepared by the staff of the Iowa Child Welfare Station facilitates the plotting of growth curves of stature and weight (Jackson and Kelly, 1945). These forms contain growth curves based upon the Iowa growth data referred to earlier. There are, in all, six forms—three for boys and three for girls. These six sheets thus present, in graphic form, the complete set of norms derived from 13,500 height observations and 11,000 weight observations made upon some 3000 boys and girls from birth to age 18 years.

The three forms for boys are shown in Figures 2.4, 2.5, and 2.6. They represent average growth in boys (1) during the first year of life, (2) from birth to age 6 years, and (3) from 5 to 18 years, respectively. The upper half of the sheet, in each case, shows the curve of increase in weight in terms of average (median) weights at each successive age level. Also curves based upon measures of variation about the average (16th and 84th percentile) are plotted. The curves in the lower portion of the sheet, in each case, similarly represent the norms for height. Note, however, that the average-height curves are drawn from mean values and the deviation curves represent −1 and +1 standard deviation units below and above the mean.[4]

In using these sheets for portraying growth progress, we plot the individual child's measurements against the corresponding chronological ages (directly on the form), using the scales provided. We can then directly compare the individual curves with the existing normative curves.

As the authors of these devices point out, much information can be read from the plotted growth curves (Jackson and Kelly, 1945). In the first place, the graphic picture shows the individual's course of growth in height and in weight separately and the average or expected path of growth in height and in weight, and comparisons can be easily made. Then, by examining the level of the height-age curve in relation to the weight-age curve at corresponding points, a clear appraisal of body build as well as relative size can be made.

On Figures 2.4, 2.5, and 2.6, for example, we have plotted the growth progress of our subject Paul from birth to age 17 years 8 months. From these curves alone we can gain a fairly accurate impression of the relative size and body build of this boy at any point in

---

[4] The mean and the median are both loosely referred to as averages. The median is the 50th percentile—the score or measurement that divides the group in half when ranked in order of size of score. The mean is the simple arithmetic average. See Appendix A for a further discussion of mean and median.

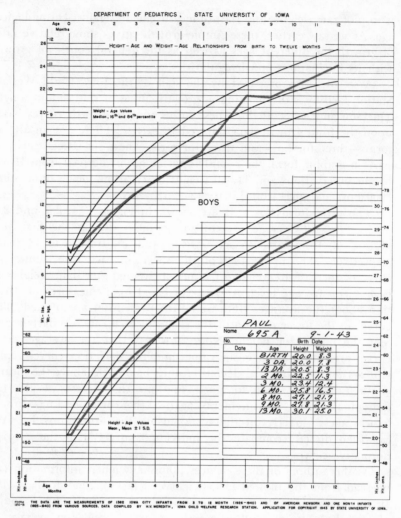

Figure 2.4

The Iowa growth curves with data plotted for Paul 695 during his first year of life. Used by permission.

his development. Changes in body build and relative size from time to time are also readily seen.

The fact that height growth remains more stable than weight may be seen in these graphs. Weight is more readily influenced by environmental factors and by variations in nutritional status and health than is height. Note the clarity of this variation in the curves covering the first 12 months. Although Paul was a somewhat smaller-than-average baby during his first 6 months (and he continued to be

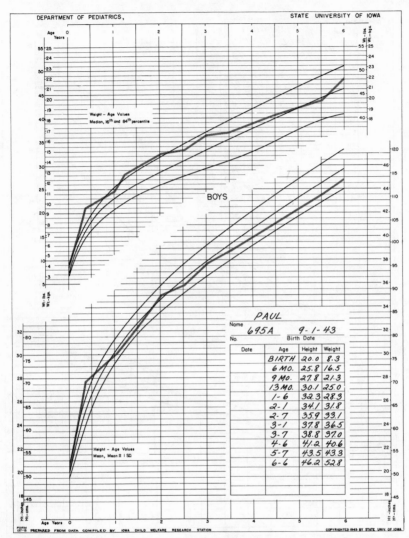

Figure 2.5

The Iowa growth curves with data plotted for Paul 695 during his first 6 years of life. Used by permission.

shorter than average), at 8 months he was considerably heavier than average. From that point on, with some fluctuations in weight status, he tended to be heavy for his height.

The puberal growth spurt is particularly evident in Paul's growth curves. At 12 years of age he was close to the Iowa mean in height but considerably above the median in weight. At that point he began to gain status in height as well as in weight, until age 14 he would

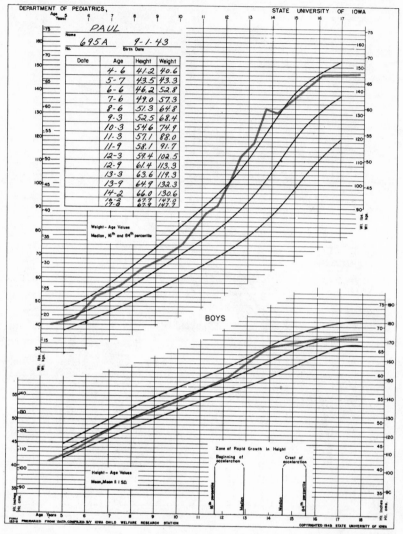

Figure 2.6

The Iowa growth curves with data plotted for Paul 695 from
ages 5 years to 18 years. Used by permission.

have been among the taller 17 percent of the Iowa boys and approximately among the heaviest 10 percent. Thus during his puberal period
he fit the pattern of the "fast grower," and, like fast growers generally,
he leveled off rather abruptly toward his terminal height and weight.
He showed relatively little increase in height after age 16.

A disadvantage of this simple-growth-curve method of plotting in
terms of raw measurements is that different aspects of growth cannot

be plotted together for direct comparison. Weight must be plotted separately from height because their scale units are qualitatively different and in no sense equivalent. The two curves, of course, can be drawn in close proximity, as in Figures 2.4, 2.5, and 2.6 thus facilitating comparisons in terms of their respective group norms, but basically the two curves are of two different orders and are not directly comparable.

The Grid Technique for Appraising Growth[5]

In 1941 Norman C. Wetzel developed a device for depicting graphically the longitudinal growth of individual children in terms of changes in body size and shape. This device, known as the "Wetzel Grid" (see Figure 2.7), is a chart of growth that can be read directly from the age period between 2 and 18 years. It consists of two distinct but related divisions, each with a different purpose and function. The left portion consists essentially of two logarithmic scales. One of these, the vertical axis, is the weight scale; the other, the horizontal, is the height scale. Running diagonally across the form from the lower left is a set of parallel lines that demarcate seven principal "physique channels." These channels, "taken crosswise, cover a range of physique (body build) from the obese to the extremely slender type, and channel-wise, a range of development from infancy to maturity" (Wetzel, 1941, p. 1195).

The Physique-Channel System

The assumption underlying the channel construction of the Wetzel Grid is that in normal, healthy growth height and weight tend to keep pace with each other througout the grow period. To the extent to which this stable relationship holds for a given child, his growth progress when plotted on the Grid's channel system (left-hand portion of the form) will follow consistently the particular physique channel that is "natural" for him. Wetzel states the significance of up-channel progress as follows:

> Healthy developmental progress continues in an established channel as though this were a preferred path; channel width

[5] Much of the present explanation of the structure of the grid forms and the method of interpreting the growth of an individual child when it has been plotted on these forms has been extracted from Wetzel's original articles (1941 and 1946). The reader is referred to these articles for Wetzel's complete explanation of the meaningfulness of the technique and for his own illustrations of growth curves of individual children, which of necessity have been omitted from this explanation.

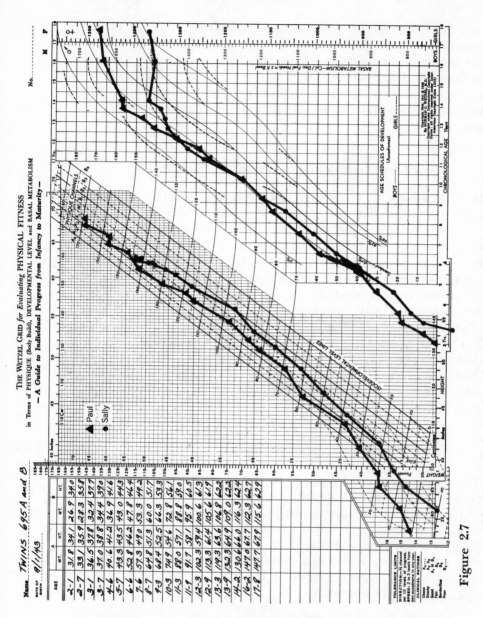

Figure 2.7   The Wetzel Grid with data plotted for Paul (A) and Sally (B) 695. Used by permission.

accounts for accidental variation which does not exceed one-half channel per 10 units of advancement. Channel-wise progress indicates development with preservation of given physique; cross-channel progress is accompanied by change in physique. The latter type, sufficiently continued, culminates in a pathologic state. An upward trend greater than that of the channel slope indicates that obesity is in the making; a downward trend less than that of the channel system suggests that "malnutrition" is not far removed. (1941, p. 1195)

The channel system of the Grid, then, portrays the child's body build and reveals the consistency with which he maintains it throughout the growth period. The child's progress up-channel can also be seen and measured from one date to another in terms of *isodevelopmental* levels. These levels are marked off by solid and broken lines that cut across the channels. The distance from one solid line to the next (10 levels) represents the growth in size that children on the average make in a period of about 10 months. Thus we can learn from the channel graph something about the child's size and his growth in size as well as his body build.

The Auxodromes

The isodevelopmental-level lines are continued across to the right portion of the Grid and thus establish the vertical-level scale for over-all body size. This scale, along with the chronological-age scale on the corresponding horizontal axis, forms the boundary of the *auxodrome field* for plotting body size against chronological age.

A set of normative growth curves are drawn in this right-hand panel. The curves are called auxodromes, or schedules of growth. They

. . . display advanced, normal and retarded patterns of developmental progress and may accordingly, be taken to show how physical development proceeds with respect to age during its channel course on the grid. These curves are, in a very real sense schedules of progress which indicate how far the advanced, regular and retarded child may be expected to have developed at a given age. . . .

The percentage figure at the lower end of each curve indicates the relative number of children who are on, or ahead of the respective schedule. Thus, only 2 per cent will have advanced in their development at successive ages to the comparatively high levels which the uppermost curve calls for; 67 per cent will have reached the levels given by the center auxodrome on or before the corresponding ages to which it refers; finally, 98 per cent of children will at least have reached the lowest curve, so that 2 per cent may be expected to remain behind this in their development. The 67 per cent curve is taken as the standard of reference by which physical advancement or retardation in a given child may be measured.

Distinction is made between boys and girls. During the earlier stages from 5 to 9 years, to which Stratz referred as "neutral childhood," boys and girls follow a common course to the lower point of bifurcation. Thenceforward girls [broken curves in Figure 2.7] tend quite characteristically to proceed ahead of boys [solid curves] toward their own upper boundaries and with earlier cessation of development. (Wetzel, 1941, p. 1191)

The Grid also provides a satisfactory means of estimating the basal metabolic rate of children, and, from that, their required daily caloric intake at the time measurements are taken. Basal heat production is estimated directly from developmental level (body size). To take proper account of sex differences the basal heat production scales for boys and girls are separately aligned with the developmental level on the right-hand edge of the grid. Furthermore,

To obtain the maximum daily caloric intake for either sex at any developmental level one has merely to multiply the corresponding basal heat value by 2. Average values, such as those given in the White House Conference Reports [1932] are, of course, somewhat lower, the factor being 1.9 for boys and 1.8 for girls. The 10, 20, 30 and 50 per cent above basal values used in calculating reducing diets are likewise easily computed. (Wetzel, 1941, p. 1193)

The Baby Grid

Later, in 1946, Wetzel published the Baby Grid, which is an application of the grid technique to the period from birth to age 3 years (see Figure 2.8). The two forms, the Big Grid and the Baby Grid, thus cover the entire preadult period of development from birth to age 18. In certain particulars, the Baby Grid differs from the child's grid. Wetzel describes an important difference:

[As in the Big Grid] the channel system provides a field or map in which the position of points plotted from the original measurements of a baby's weight and height may readily be identified by channel and by cross-graduated levels.

In the Baby Grid, however, there are two parts to the channel system; the left half, 3, 4, 5 [See Figure 2.8], represented by channels A_{12}–A_5 is required because babies do not normally travel along the main line of human development represented by the right half, 1, 2, the original A_3–M–B_3 group [in the Big Grid] of this compound system. They travel these side tracks

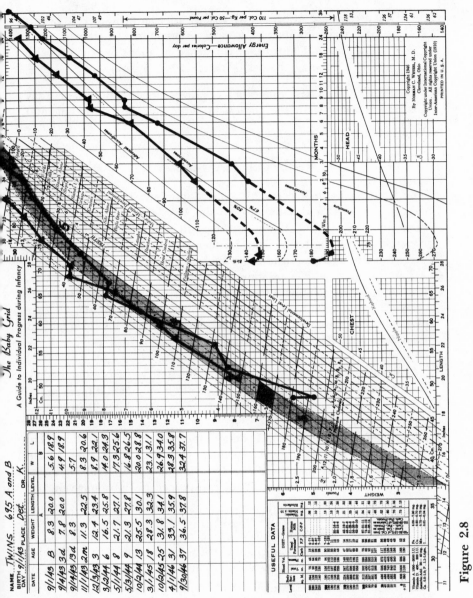

Figure 2.8 The Wetzel Baby Grid with data plotted for Paul (A) and Sally (B) 695. Used by permission.

of infancy because they are naturally more chubby than the older children on the main line or than they themselves were during intrauterine life. The direction of the course they take through the channel system is indicated by the central (pink-yellow) shaded path, 3, 4, 5. Thriving premature babies traverse the lower portion, 3, which joins the full-term strip where the weight-length points of normal newborn infants are found.

Thenceforward the path is strictly up-channel until it begins
to bear right on its way toward re-entry on the main line [in
the Big Grid]. The turn, 5, is reached in about eleven to twelve
months by average babies. (Wetzel, 1946, p. 442)

On the Baby Grid, total fuel requirements in calories per day
are read directly from the right-hand scale for each developmental
level.

The Grid Records of Twins 695

The Grid forms in Figures 2.7 and 2.8 plot the height and weight
data of Paul (A) and Sally (B). In the Baby Grid (Figure 2.8) one
notes immediately the rather striking differences at birth between
these children in both physique and developmental level. Paul, whose
weight and length placed him on the line between physique channels
A_{10} and A_{11}, is chubbier by some four channel widths than his sister,
who at this point in her development was quite slender. However,
at age 2 months, Sally had attained a physique very similar to that
of her brother, and then for a period of about 6 months their growth
lines followed very nearly the same physique channel on the Baby
Grid.

Although they soon came to be quite similar in physique, they
continued to differ significantly in terms of developmental level (size).
At birth Sally weighed only 5.6 pounds and was 18.9 inches in length.
This rather low birth weight placed her at developmental level 180,
bordering on the premature. Even at 2 months of age she had scarcely
exceeded her brother's size at birth (level 143). Although this size
difference gradually narrowed from 37 developmental levels at birth,
down to 13 at age 24 months, Paul maintained his advantage during
infancy.

There are no height and weight measurements for these babies
between ages 6 and 8 months. During this interval, however, both
children made notable cross-channel shifts in the direction of chubbiness—1 full channel width by Sally (B) and 1½ channels by Paul (A).
In view of this striking change in physique occurring in both babies
simultaneously, a careful examination of their feeding record should
be quite revealing. An account of the children's feeding record and
other factors relating to the regularity of growth are given in a later
section of this chapter, pages 59–62.

These babies made the usual switchover in growth from the "tracks
of infancy" to the "main line" of the Big Grid, and in each case
their growth proceeded fairly consistently as up-channel progress.
Although there was some slight cross-channel shifting, Paul and Sally

maintained their normal physiques fairly consistently; Paul, with his somewhat stocky build, generally held to channels A_1 and A_2, and Sally generally fluctuated about channels M and B_1. It is interesting to note that up to about age 12½ years their patterns of up-channel progress were very similar.

This similarity of pattern is seen also on the auxodrome scale of the Grid. Both children, during their first 9 or 10 years, were on growth schedules somewhat above the standard of references (67th-percentile curve), Paul following very closely the 15-percent auxodrome and Sally on a slightly later schedule. Both children followed quite closely their expected growth curves; Sally leveled off toward her adult status somewhat earlier than her brother.

By way of summary, the channel system of the Wetzel Grid has a threefold purpose: (1) it serves as a "direction finder" for ascertaining the trend of a child's growth toward chubbiness, toward slenderness, or along a channel of constant physique; (2) it identifies a child's natural physique or body build in terms of the channel along which his height-weight points tend to follow; and (3) it serves to measure body size in terms of developmental level at each height-weight measurement.

The auxodrome panel of the Wetzel Grid provides a means of plotting the child's growth in terms of age and body size (developmental level). This growth achievement curve is drawn in relation to, and for direct comparison with, five representative age schedules of development (auxodromes) which indicate the percentages of children on, or ahead of, each schedule. This five-member family of standards show how widely separated in time (age) children of the same developmental level may actually be.

The auxodrome representing the 67th percentile is taken as the standard of reference. Thus the child's developmental age at the time any particular set of height-weight measurements are made can be ascertained simply by noting the point on the chronological-age scale at which this standard of reference curve reaches his particular developmental level. For example, at age 90 months (7½ years) Paul had reached the 68th developmental level. The "standard" auxodrome reaches the 68th developmental level at chronological age 104 months (8 years 8 months).

Plotting Growth in Terms of Developmental Age

A rather meaningful method of making diverse measurements equivalent or comparable is to convert them into age equivalents and express them as developmental ages. As was pointed out in Chapter 1, the concept of the age equivalent is by no means a new one. The use of the concept as a basis for converting diverse measurement values into comparable values has had widest use in the child development laboratories of the University Elementary School, University of Michigan (Olson, 1959; Olson and Hughes, 1942). An individual measurement, or score, on any variable for which age norms have been developed can be converted into an age equivalent. A series of such measurements thus converted can then be plotted, along with other measurement series similarly treated (in terms of development ages).

A further step aimed at using one scale of measurement was the calculation of a series of "organismic ages."

To do this, growth values as of a given chronological age for each child were averaged and given the name "organismic age.". . .

Theoretically the measures taken should represent an inclusive theory of the organism. A complete account might include measures of emotionality, social adjustment, gross bodily development, circulation, efficiency of sense organs, development of

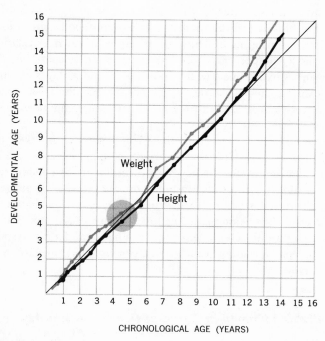

Figure 2.9

Growth progress in height and weight of Paul 695 plotted in terms of age equivalents.

educational and physical skills, and measures of metabolic function. (Olson and Hughes, 1942, pp. 525–526)

This great diversity of variables, ranging from basically organic measurements to school-achievement measurements, are all, in fact, greatly subject to variations in environmental opportunity to learn. Critics have objected to the use of the so-called organismic-age curve because, they claim, this great diversity cannot be reduced to an average.

However, for purposes of direct comparison, measurements of different aspects of development, which are all converted to developmental-age values, provides an integrated and meaningful picture of individual developmental progress.

Figure 2.9 illustrates this method of making diverse measures comparable and plotting them together. When Paul was 54 months of age, for instance, he weighed 40.6 pounds and was 41.2 inches tall. His weight of 40.6 pounds was found to be the median (Iowa) weight

Table 2.4

Growth Data (Weight and Height Measurements)
for Paul 695 Expressed in Development-Age Equivalents
Derived from Iowa Norms

CHRONOLOGICAL AGE	WEIGHT AGE	HEIGHT AGE
0-3	0-2	0-2.4
0-6	0-4.5	0-4.8
0-9	0-9	0-7.8
1-1	1-4	1-1
1-6	1-10	1-5
2-1	2-8	1-10
2-7	3-3	2-4
3-1	3-8	3-0
3-6	3-10	3-4
4-6	4-8	4-2
5-7	5-5	5-1
6-6	7-4	6-4
7-6	8-0	7-6
8-6	9-3	8-6
9-3	9-10	9-1
10-3	10-10	10-2
11-3	12-6	11-4
11-9	12-10	11-10
12-3	13-9	12-5
12-9	14-9	13-5
13-9	16-3	15-0
14-2	16-2	15-6
16-2	18-0	17-0
17-8	18-1	17-0

of boys at approximately 56 months of age, and his height of 41.2 inches was the average height of boys only 50 months of age. Thus, at age 54 months Paul's weight age-equivalent was 56 months and his height age-equivalent, was 50 months (see Figure 2.9). Paul's growth data, expressed in terms of age equivalents, are given in Table 2.4.

The developmental-age method is useful in comparing the individuals of a group with respect to a particular developmental variable. This method can also serve to provide an integrated picture of the various aspects of an individual's development (Olson, 1959, pp. 147–154).

The Standard-Score Method

Another equivalent-score method is to convert all measurements into standard scores. Standard scores are the differences between the child's measurements and the averages for his age group, as expressed in standard deviation (SD) units. Graphs of longitudinal data in this form do not depict the child's growth progress per se. They do not show, in a direct and quantitative sense, the dimensional changes that have taken place. However, standard scores plotted against chronological age do portray the child's relative status in his group at each age level, as well as changes in status from age to age. When different aspects of growth, such as stature and weight, are converted to standard scores and plotted together, the stability or change in the relationship between them as the child grows is clearly shown.

The Fels Composite Sheet

The Fels Research Institute has designed a Composite Sheet (Sontag and Reynolds, 1945) to record and interpret various kinds of developmental data in terms of standard scores. This Composite Sheet

> is designed for recording and interpreting various kinds of growth and developmental measurements. Height, weight, ossification, body measurements, age at walking, and other growth characteristics may be simultaneously recorded, in comparable units, by the composite method. . . .
>
> An interpretation of body build (height-weight relationship) may be made directly from the Composite Sheet. If a child's standard score in height is greater than the corresponding one in weight score, he tends to be relatively slender in body build. If the reverse is true, he tends toward stockiness. We have found

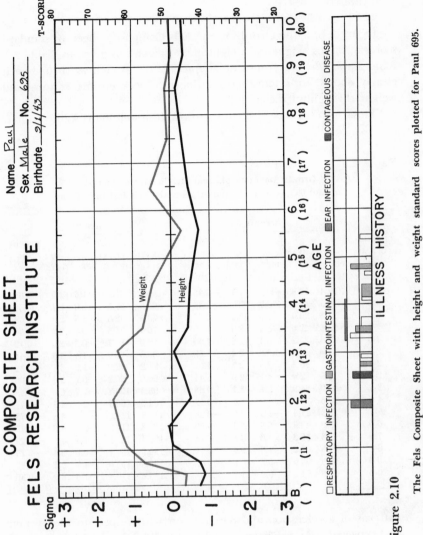

Figure 2.10 The Fels Composite Sheet with height and weight standard scores plotted for Paul 695. Used by permission.

that for practical purposes a difference of 1 standard deviation between height and weight often forms a satisfactory criterion for differentiating children into various categories of body build. Both the actual size of the child (his position with reference to the mean of zero line) and the body build (the position of height and weight with reference to each other) may be seen simultaneously on the Composite Sheet. (from a statement by the designers of the Fels Composite Sheet regarding its use and interpretation)

Figure 2.10 is the record, on the Fels Composite Sheet, of standard scores of Paul's height and weight measurements as given in Table 2.5. This graph obviously does not depict Paul's growth as such, but it clearly shows an interesting relationship between his stature and weight throughout the period.

These two aspects of Paul's growth followed remarkably similar

Table 2.5

Growth Data (Weight and Height Measurements) for Paul 695 with Means and SD from the Fels Institute Norms

CHRONO-LOGICAL AGE	WEIGHT					HEIGHT				
	MEAN POUNDS	(FELS)	DIFF.	SD (FELS)	STANDARD SCORE	CENTI-METERS	MEAN (FELS)	DIFF.	SD (FELS)	STANDARD SCORE
0-3	12.4	12.9	—0.5	1.5	—0.33	59.4	60.7	—1.3	2.0	—0.65
0-6	16.5	17.2	—0.7	2.0	—0.35	65.5	67.5	—2.0	2.4	—0.83
0-9	21.3	20.0	1.3	2.0	0.65	70.5	72.0	—1.5	2.2	—0.68
1-1	25.0	22.6	2.4	2.0	1.20	76.4	76.5	—0.1	2.3	0.00
1-6	28.3	25.2	3.1	2.2	1.40	82.0	81.7	0.3	2.5	0.12
2-1	31.8	28.0	3.8	2.4	1.58	86.6	88.0	—1.4	2.9	—0.48
2-7	33.1	30.2	2.9	2.7	1.07	91.2	92.2	—1.0	3.1	—0.32
3-1	36.5	32.4	4.1	2.9	1.41	96.0	96.2	—0.2	3.4	—0.06
3-7	37.0	34.9	2.1	3.1	0.68	98.5	100.2	—1.7	3.8	—0.45
4-6	40.6	39.0	1.6	3.7	0.52	104.6	106.7	—2.1	4.5	—0.47
5-7	43.3	44.8	—1.5	4.6	—0.33	110.5	114.0	—3.5	4.8	—0.73
6-6	52.8	49.5	3.3	5.5	0.60	117.3	119.5	—2.2	4.9	—0.45
7-6	57.3	56.3	1.0	7.3	0.14	124.4	125.8	—1.4	4.8	—0.29
8-7	64.8	63.2	1.6	9.4	0.17	130.3	131.1	—0.8	5.4	—0.15
9-3	68.4	68.6	—0.2	10.0	—0.02	133.3	135.0	—1.7	5.1	—0.33
10-3	74.9	74.0	0.9	11.2	0.08	138.8	140.4	—1.6	5.2	—0.30

patterns of acceleration and deceleration with respect to the average or "expected." As we have already seen, Paul began life somewhat smaller than the average of male babies, but even as a neonate he tended to be a bit short for his weight. After his first 3 weeks, during which he was becoming adjusted to extrauterine life, his growth, both in length and weight, began to accelerate at a remarkable rate (see Figure 2.6). At age 13 months he had gained in length from a status position of nearly 1 SD unit below average to average length. In weight the change was even more marked, from a position slightly below the mean to more than a full SD unit above the mean. At that point his weight placed him among the heaviest 16 percent of male babies according to the Fels norms.[6] This increase in weight status continued beyond age 2 years. At that age he ranked among the heaviest 6 percent of male babies of the Fels sample (1.6 SD above the mean).

Six months later, however, although he had gained more than a pound in weight, he had started on a general downward trend in weight status. This trend continued through the preschool period (to age 5½). In general, Paul's height status followed a similar pattern (Figure 2.10).

A record of growth in terms of SD values, such as that presented by the Fels Composite Sheet, has special suggestive value in relation to the factors that underlie growth. As was pointed out above, these curves do not depict the child's growth progress as such. Instead, they depict changes in his growth status in relation to the population with which he is compared. In an examination of these changes in connection with associated events—changes in feeding regime, in kind and level of daily activity, in health hazards, changes in the general developmental milieu that come naturally with increasing age —certain relationships between what is inherent in the child's nature and what the environment has contributed to the course of development do suggest themselves.

It is quite clear in Paul's record, for example, that he was inherently inclined to be somewhat stocky in build and that, even though there was a decline in growth status during his preschool years, this natural relationship between height and weight persisted. As for an explanation of the decline in status, which is largely a matter of change in relative weight, we turn to an examination of changes in the child's external conditions of living.

Factors Related to Change
in Relative Growth Status

In the first place, both Paul and his twin sister Sally were breast fed "on demand" during their first 8 months. This early period coincides with the most rapid acceleration in both height and weight status for Paul (see Figure 2.10). Day-to-day behavior charts were kept on the frequency of feedings and the times at which each was fed. Study of these charts reveals that some regularity of feeding pattern began to appear in both babies as early as the beginning of their third month when they were usually demanding four feedings per day,

---

6 In a normal distribution of measurement values, those that lie beyond +1 SD above the mean, constitute the highest 16 percent of the values. See Appendix A, Figure A.2.

with some day-to-day uniformity as to times of feeding. A month later a pattern of three feedings per day began to predominate, and by the age of 4 months this pattern had become quite well established. Apparently the twins thrived on this regime and in general gained weight in relation to their lengths as they proceeded up-channel (Figure 2.8). Between 6 and 8 months of age these fairly parallel courses changed into two isodevelopmental cross-channel shifts, as we have already noted.

At 8 months of age the babies were weaned to cup feeding, and day-to-day behavior charts were no longer kept. During the ensuing month, apparently as a result of this change in feeding, they actually lost weight while continuing to grow in length. This is seen on the Wetzel Grid (Figure 2.7) as a marked and sudden shift toward their earlier physique channels. Also associated with this change toward slimness was the fact that the twins were working through the early stages of their upright locomotor development at about this time. As the shift was made to bottle, cup, and spoon feeding, unusual care was exercised jointly by the conscientious mother and a pediatrician (who had taken the twin infants as a special project) to insure their optimal health and welfare. The "self-regulation" feeding regime was continued, although by the end of the period of breast feeding the babies had established for themselves fairly regular three-meal feeding schedules.

Normally as a child enters the so-called preschool period, certain changes are under way which may tend to altar the rate of his growth. These conditioning factors may affect some children relatively more than others and thus bring about a change in a particular child's growth status relative to his age group. In commenting on these changes which are characteristic of the preschool period, Stuart and Stitt (in Stuart and Prugh, 1960) wrote:

> After the age of 2 the child graually shifts emphasis in developmental progress from those aspects described for infancy. Growth progresses at a slower and more even year to year rate, while physical activities increase, becoming broader and more strenuous. Further mastery and coordination of functions and motor mechanisms and rapid learning now play a more obvious part.
>
> Although change in size is slight as compared with the tremendous growth rates of infancy, it must always be borne in mind that this growth takes place in an organism which is channeling its energies away from changes in size toward changes in function. Thus, even with relatively small size change, this is a costly period in energy outlay and calls for care to protect

the child from undue stress and resulting fatigue. While awake the preschool child is almost literally in perpetual motion. He is learning to coordinate motor mechanisms and functions previously developed. He has learned the elementary accomplishment of walking and talking, and is busy elaborating the more involved performances of those skills. His mind reaches with inexhaustible interest into the world about him, in pursuit of these eager explorations his body is kept in almost continuous activity. The newness and unfamiliarity of this motor performance requires an expenditure of energy with greater efficiency. (pp. 109–110)

Because of these rather radical changes in pattern of energy expenditure with the greatly increased energy requirements of activity and learning, "the preschool period, contrary to much prevailing practice, is still a period for continuation of a substantial form of closely sustained child health supervision" (p. 116).

Illness in Relation to Growth

Along with these changes in functioning and in the nurturing demands made upon the environment come a significant broadening of the child's "world" and its associated hazards to health and well-being. He is no longer confined to the protecting boundaries of his home and play yard. He ventures forth much more frequently into the larger neighborhood. He enters nursery school or a neighborhood play group, thus coming in contact with more people and increasing the chances for infection and contagion. Consequently, the preschool period generally is one in which certain communicable illnesses become somewhat more common. In summarizing the findings of the Harvard studies of child health and development regarding the relative frequence of various kinds of illnesses at different age levels, Stuart and Prugh (1960) stated that "these [communicable] diseases occurred more frequently from 0 to 6 years; they increased rapidly between 2 and 6 years, remaining high during the school age period, then rapidly declined" (p. 30).

Associated with the chronological-age scale, the Fels Composite Sheet provides a means and a system for coding and recording the illness history of the child. This illness record can be seen in association with the record of changes in the child's growth status. Figure 2.10 (the Fels Composite Sheet), presents an approximate record of Paul 695. The most frequent types of illness were respiratory infection and gastrointestinal infection. The approximate age at which the illness episode occurred is indicated by the location of the symbol on the chronological-age line. The severity of the illness, as estimated from the written record, is indicated by the height of illness symbol.

It will be noted that the age period (roughly the preschool period) during which Paul was most frequently ill is also the period during which there was a decline in his growth status. It should be emphasized once more at this point that these status curves, plotted in SD units, even though the trend is downward, do not represent a general decrease in height and weight. Paul was growing normally all the while. At only one point did he lose slightly in weight only. (He weighed 0.4 pounds lighter at age 9 months than at 8 months.) These curves, instead, show a decline in Paul's *relative* position—his growth status in relation to the total Fels sample of boys.

A Critical Comparison of Methods of Plotting Growth

As was stated earlier in this chapter, each of the methodologies for plotting individual growth has its own rationale and involves certain assumptions. Each also has its shortcomings and limitations, as well as its advantages. All have been found useful in one or another or several of the main programs of developmental research.

It is quite probable that some of the findings concerning growth in every longitudinal project have been presented in part, at least, in the form of simple growth curves. Raw, or derived, quantitative data are commonly plotted against time, as expressed in chronological age, and, in general, this method requires no special forms. Actual measurement units are easily constructed to form the ordinate and the time (age) scale is the abscissa of the graph. Plotting is simple. In this sort of plotting the curve is a real curve of growth, revealing directly and in proportion all the changes in rate of growth in its upward course. The general slant of the curve, of course, is determined by the size and spacing of the measurement units, but keeping these constant, growth curves of different children can be compared directly and meaningfully.

This simple method of plotting growth is widely used. Actually no specially prepared forms are required. However, the Iowa forms (Figures 2.4, 2.5, and 2.6) present growth data in meaningful context. The curves are plotted against the background of extensive normative data. Not only does one have the actual growth picture in both height and weight, but almost at a glance, one can place the individual within the group in terms of stature and weight. By examining the two curves (height and weight) in relation to each other, as they fit into the system of normative curves on the form, one can readily appraise body size for age at each measurement point. One can also get a picture of the child's general body type and its change or stability in form from time to time.

By use of these "Iowa curves" one can also easily derive graphically an age equivalent, in terms of the Iowa norms, for each measurement of height and weight plotted on the form.

Thus, height, weight, and age data can be exploited for their full value by use of the Iowa curves, with the limitation, of course, that the Iowa norms constitute the only standards of reference possible in their use. Furthermore, no other aspect of growth than over-all height and weight can be plotted on them, nor are the two curves, in any case, directly equivalent or comparable, since the units of measurement are quite different.

The age principle in plotting growth, as we have clearly seen, requires the conversion of raw measurements into age equivalents. By means of this conversion the developmental measurement units on the ordinate of the graph are equated with the time units (chronological age) on the abscissa. Hence the curve that results from the plotting of growth data thus converted is not a true growth curve, since it does not reflect directly the periods of positive and negative acceleration that are naturally a feature of human growth. Rather, normal growth in these "curves" generally assumes a straight-line progression upward. Deviations from the normal course of growth, however, do clearly show up as deflections up or down from the expected straight-line progression.

The conversion of raw data to age equivalents renders equivalent all series of measures so converted for a given child. This facilitated comparison is one of the great advantages of the developmental-age method of plotting. Not only are the height and the weight curves plotted together on the same scale for immediate, direct comparison, but any other aspect of development for which age norms are available can be added to give an integrated developmental picture.

Interindividual comparisons with respect to a given developmental variable, likewise, can be made with facility by use of this method of graphing. Intrafamily likenesses and differences can be portrayed when corresponding data are available (see Chapter 13).

The other comparable-score technique of portraying growth progress is the standard-score method, which has been widely used for many years. The well-known developmental studies of the University of California made extensive use of the standard score in presenting their results (H. E. Jones, 1943).

Many of the same advantages as well as certain limitations of the developmental-age method apply in standard-score plotting also. A growth curve of standard scores is not really a curve of growth, since standard scores are deviation scores and this graph depicts deviations from the normal. These deviations can be objectively evaluated. As with age-equivalent scores, height and weight (and any other developmental variable measured quantitatively and with age norms) can be plotted together for direct comparative study. From such plottings of height and weight, studied in relation to each other, appraisals of body size and body type can be made. The Fels Composite Sheet is simply a form designed to facilitate standard-score plotting. It grew out of an extensive use of the standard-score method by the Fels Research Institute.

The Wetzel Grid method of plotting and evaluating growth involves only height, weight, and age data, and is concerned only with the relationships between those three series of simultaneous observations. The Grid's advantages over other methods of plotting growth reside in the clearness with which are portrayed such growth variables as the child's natural body type, his body size at any particular point in time, unusual changes in his weight in relation to height, his "nutritional grade," his particular schedule or rate of growth in terms of size, his developmental age, and the general shape of his growth curve.

For many years the Wetzel Grids (Baby Grid and Big Grid) have been widely used by both researchers and pediatricians and have proven their usefulness in both areas. Users, however, have often been critical of certain of the assumptions underlying both the construction and the prescribed rules for the interpretation of individual Grid records. Perhaps the most basic assumption underlying the Grid system is that in the normal growth of an individual the relationship between his height and his weight remains generally constant. Studies have described many individual cases in which there appears to have been normal, healthy growth and in which this relative constancy of relationship did not hold. Some users also feel that Wetzel's criteria for judging between healthy and unhealthy "off-channel" digressions do not allow enough latitude for normal fluctuations.

Certain other aspects of the Grid have been subjected to study and testing. For example, the implicit assumption that height and weight are of equal value in relation to "Wetzel developmental age" at all levels and in all types of physique has been studied by Baer, Torgoff, and Harris (1962). One of their conclusions:

> The similarity in pattern of the curves of Wetzel developmental age and weight age was found to be significantly greater

than that between the Wetzel age curve and the height age curve. The level of analysis, based on the study of nine hypothetical height-weight relations, indicated that the Wetzel age curves maintain a close consistent relation to the weight curves and a fortuitous relation to the height curves both in distance and position. (p. 749)

As a device for the evaluation and interpretation of physical growth in children, however, the Wetzel Grid is in a class by itself.

In choosing among the various methods of plotting individual growth, the only practical criteria must arise out of consideration of the specific purpose of the experimenter.

SELECTED READING SUGGESTIONS

Jackson, R. L., and H. G. Kelly. Growth charts for use in pediatric practice. *J. Pediat.*, 1945, **27**, 215–229.

Krogman, W. M. A handbook of the measurement and interpretation of height and weight in the growing child. *Monogr. Soc. Res. Child Develpm.*, 1948, **13** (No. 3).

Krogman, W. M. The physical growth of the child. In M. Fishbein and R. J. R. Kennedy (eds.), *Modern marriage and family living*. New York: Oxford University Press, 1957.

Stuart, H. C., and Pauline G. Stitt. Physical growth and development. In H. C. Stuart and D. G. Prugh (eds.), *The healthy child: his physical, psychological and social development*. Cambridge, Mass.: Harvard University Press, 1960.

Tanner, J. M. *Education and physical growth: implications of the study of children's growth for educational theory and practice*. London: University of London Press, Ltd., 1961.

Wetzel, N. C. Assessing physical fitness in children, III: the components of physical status and physical progress and their evaluation. *J. Pediat.*, 1943, **22**, 329–361.

Wetzel, N. C. The baby grid: an application of the grid technique to growth and development in infants. *J. Pediat.*, 1946, **29**, 329–454.

CHAPTER 3

Maturation: The Qualitative Aspect of Developmental Change

During childhood we grow: that is we increase in dimensions or, less literally, we put on weight. But we also grow up. And when childhood is over and we are grown up we begin to grow older, and ultimately we grow old. This business of growing up, growing older, growing old is quite different from that of growing: it implies progressive maturity, not increased dimensions. Maturity is not experience: It is that upon which experience imprints itself and without which experience does not register. When we say that John is not yet old enough to carry that bag, does not yet take interest in girls, has not reached the marrying age, we are thinking along lines quite different from those implied by the statement that John is not tall enough to reach that shelf or not old enough to take algebra at school. If he is not tall enough his dimensions are in question: if he is not old enough for algebra the extent of his training is in doubt. But if he has not reached the stage of walking or of being interested in girls there is no implication of dimensions or of training. When we say "give him time and he will naturally walk; give him time and he will naturally marry" we imply a change or progress over which no external influence has any power: John is growing up.

Progressive maturity is something which we all share, no matter what our size, no matter what our experience.

There is, in the concept of progressive maturity, another implication not found in growth or in experience, namely, inevitability. If John has not grown so tall as his brothers or has not learned the calculus, he is not therefore handicapped for life. But suppose he should not grow up! He may be a little young for his age or a little old for his years but the possibility of a major or permanent modification in the growing up process is well-nigh unthinkable. (Todd, 1937, p. 11)

This growing-up process is what we call maturation. It is indeed "something which we all share," an aspect of development in which "there is no implication of dimensions or of training." Maturation is a biological process of change that is qualitative rather than quantitative in nature, and, therefore, it is much less open to direct observation. Sequences of intrinsic change take place in the various organs and parts of the body. New tissues and new structures emerge, differentiate, and specialize in form and function in an orderly manner. The maturing process, along with growth, prepares the different organs, organ systems, and the total organism, to begin to function in new and specific ways and to function at progressively higher levels.

Qualitative development is clearly evident from the very beginning, at conception. Not only does the tiny organism begin to grow very rapidly but it also soon changes in its shape and contours as various areas and portions differentiate, specialize, and accommodate to one another. The location or position that each cell group occupies in early embryological development seems to play a part in determining the direction and nature of its specialization.

The cells on the back or dorsal portion of the embryo form a layer called the *ectoderm*. The ventral layer of cells is referred to as *entoderm*, and the more difuse collection of cells between the ectoderm and the entoderm is termed *mesoderm*. Such structures as the outer skin and the nervous system develop from the ectoderm; the skeleton, muscles, connective tissue, heart and blood vessels are derived from mesoderm. From the entoderm come the digestive and respiratory tracts and their glandular derivatives. (Gardner, 1963, p. 55)

Thus during this early stage of prenatal development, through cell differentiation and specialization, the foundations of the grosser body parts and organ systems are laid. New forms and structures emerge which systematically are qualitative, maturational changes. Maturational development is coincidental to body growth.

Maturation is a lifelong process. The inner body structure and organization of tissues and parts continue to change throughout life. In the skeletal framework of the body, for example, qualitative change is constantly under way. At birth, even though the skeleton

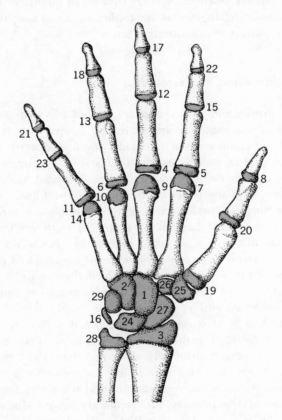

Figure 3.1

The individual centers of ossification (separate bones) numbered approximately in the order in which their ossification begins. Based on a photograph from Gruelich and Pyle (1959), p. 187, by permission.

is in an early formative stage, some twenty-one separate "bones" are already present and identifiable in the hand and wrist. By the time the child is 10 years of age, twenty-nine new bones have formed in the child's hand and wrist, making a total of fifty separate, identifiable bony structures. Ten years later certain of the bones that were apparent at age 10 are no longer present as separate entities; they have fused with each other and thus have lost their individual identity. The total number of individual bones in that region now is twenty-nine (see Figure 3.1). And all the while, throughout life, gradual changes are also taking place in the shape, the contours, and the inner structure of each of these bones as they accommodate to each other and fuse together. Fusion of separate bones in the skull, for example, along with other subtle changes in over-all shape and contour, continue into old age. Such changes are changes in quality or kind, rather than in amount, changes that no calibrated measuring device could adequately portray in quantitative terms.

Maturation and Growth

Although growth and maturation are indeed two distinct aspects of physical development, they are in reality inseparable. It is obvious that the bony framework of the body develops toward adult status through growth as well as maturation. Stature is increased through growth as well as maturation. Stature is increased mainly through the lengthening of the bones of the lower limbs. This is growth. But this lengthening is actually very largely brought about through qualitative (maturational) changes at certain "growth centers" of these bones. Qualitative changes, then, which of themselves cannot be measured in quantitative terms, often result in increased or decreased dimensions of the gross structure in which they occur.

It is evident also that the processes of maturation and growth of certain discrete systems of the body are highly related and interdependent. The most striking evidence for this fact has come from the study of cases of pathological development such as precocious puberty and hypergonadism (Greulich and Pyle, 1959, pp. 2–10). As such cases clearly show, there is a close correspondence between the maturational status of the reproductive and the skeletal systems. The development of the primary and secondary sexual characteristics is controlled by the gonadal and other related endocrine secretions. Likewise, growth of the skeleton, skeletal muscles, and other bodily features is controlled by the same system. The development of the skeleton, therefore, reflects the maturational and functional status of the reproductive system and is regarded as a reliable index of the body's general level of development. More will be said of this relationship later.

Appraising Development from Qualitative Data

In Chapter 1 the concept of the age equivalent was introduced. By converting raw-measurement values into age equivalents, developmental status in quite different and disparate aspects of development (height, motor achievement, intelligence, and so forth) are made directly comparable. In the case of growth phenomena for which the data are in the form of quantitative measurements, an age equivalent is simply the average measurement value, or average "score," of a specific age group of children. The age-level average to which an individual score corresponds is the age equivalent of that individual score. The age equivalent of a given child's measured growth status or achievement (height, weight, and so forth) is also his developmental age in that particular aspect of his growth at that particular point in time. (This method of evaluating growth status and of plotting growth progress through time was explained and illustrated in Chapter 2.)

In dealing with the qualitative aspects of development, however, the problem is somewhat more complicated. In order to assess the maturational status of the child at any point in time or to trace his development through time, qualitative information must somehow be expressed in quantitative terms.

It is obviously impossible to gain direct access to most of the maturational effects in the growing child, for they are internal and thus hidden from direct observation. The various stages of maturation in the embryo, and later in such structures as the brain, of course, have been studied and charted through the gross and microscopic examination of nonliving tissue. In that way the reality of maturational change in those parts has been established. Maturation in certain bodily structures has also been inferred on the basis of change in functional level. In most of the body systems, however, developmental status cannot be evaluated directly in the growing child with present techniques.

Expressing qualitative "events" in quantitative terms requires preliminary observational research. First, the order of occurrence of the discrete changes in the structure under consideration must be noted. Generally, in maturational development such changes occur in a fixed sequence (the concept of "stages"). Developmental change generally consists in an invariable series of stages, each in turn "growing out of" the previous one in order. The identification of such a developmental sequence is the first step in the quantification of maturational change. The next step is to observe in a large number of individual cases the age at which each stage occurs. Individual ages of occurrence, in most instances, vary over a considerable range. Individuality thus expresses itself. In a developmental process, as a rule, the *sequence*—the order of occurrence of events or of the appearance of stages—is fixed and invariable. But the *timing*—the specific ages at which they occur— is a matter of individual variation. From the distribution of individual ages at which each stage in the sequence appears, an average age and a measure of variation is obtained. These average ages (age equivalents, in each instance, of a developmental stage) can be ordered in a developmental-age scale. Thus, each qualitative event, or stage in the series, acquires a quantitative value in terms of age units.

The Concept of Maturity Indicator

In the intensive examination of many series of x-ray films of wrist and ankle bones of children, it is possible to identify series of qualitatively different stages of development. These stages (events) are fixed in order of appearance and universal in occurrence. The time intervals between these various discontinuous and qualitatively different stages, however, are highly variable from individual to individual. Since the order of their appearance is invariable, each stage in turn can be taken as an indicator of a bone developmental level that is more advanced than the one preceding. These stages are therefore called maturity indicators.

In recent years the concept of the maturity indicator has been broadened to include any clearly defined stages of development, either of a function or of a structure or body part. In 1947, for a series of discussions on the attributes of maturity indicators at Western Reserve University Medical School, Dr. Idell Pyle described maturity indicators as:

> . . . features of a body part, secretory products of the cells of a part, or specialized forms of behavior which appear in a fixed or universal order to mark the progress of a child toward young maturity, or the progress of an adult toward senescence. They are strictly ontogenetic in nature, *i.e.*, they appear in human beings around the world in an order which is universal but at a speed which is characteristic of the child or adult in question.

A maturity indicator, then, is an identifiable point or stage in the development of a structure (or function) which occupies a fixed position in a series. Series of maturity indicators fixed in order of appearance were first established in the maturation of the skeletal system. The average chronological age at which each feature made its appearance was noted. This average for each indicator was designated as its age equivalent. Thus, a series of maturity indicators, each with its age equavalent, can constitute a scale for appraising a child's maturational status in terms of developmental age for a bodily structure or its function.

Skeletal Development

In the radiographic study of the living skeleton a number of different parts of the skeleton have been intensively examined largely because of the location in them of numerous "centers" of maturational change. The hand and wrist, the foot and ankle, and the knee are among the areas given special study (Greulich and Pyle, 1959, Hoerr, Pyle, and Francis, 1962; Pyle and Hoerr, 1955). The hand of the child, of course, is easily accessible, and the procedure for taking x-ray pictures of the hand and wrist is relatively simple. Largely for these reasons most of the data accumulated are in the form of x-ray films of bones of the hand and wrist. It has been established, furthermore, that these

Figure 3.2

X-ray photographs showing stages in the development of the bones of Sally 695's hand and wrist at (left) age 3 months, (center) age 4 years 6 months, and (right) age 11 years 9 months.

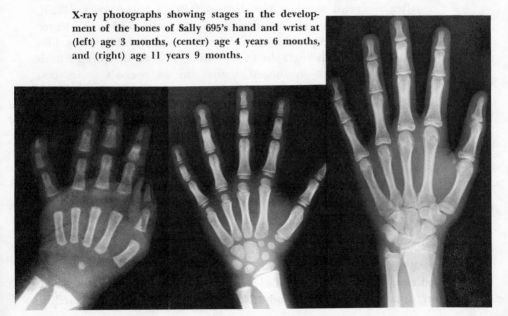

particular bones constitute a fairly representative sample of the whole skeleton and therefore that a carefully assessed skeletal age based upon that sample can be relied upon as a fair approximation of over-all developmental status of the skeleton. Figure 3.2 shows three stages of development in the bones of Sally's hand and wrist.

Assessment of Skeletal Age

The procedure for an accurate determination of skeletal age, however, is technical in nature. A reliable assessment requires knowledge of bone anatomy and understanding of the nature of the intricate processes of bone maturation as well as training and experience in the reading and interpretation of bone x-ray films. Rough estimates of skeletal age, however, can be arrived at through the use of relatively simple procedures.

At any time during childhood, for example, an estimate can be made in terms of the presence or absence of a particular maturity indicator that appears at different times in different bony centers of the child's hand. This maturity indicator is the very beginning of the process of ossification. Onset of ossification appears in a fairly regular sequence in designated bone growth centers, each of which is identified by number. The established age equivalent of onset of ossification for any particular bone growth center is then taken as an indication of the skeletal age of the child.

After a careful study of Greulich and Pyle's Hand Atlas (1959), a student can estimate skeletal developmental status with some degree of accuracy, based upon comparison of a subject-child's x-ray film with the standard photographs in the Atlas. The student simply finds the standard picture in the Atlas that, in an over-all sense, best matches the child's film. The age equivalent assigned to that particular standard in the Atlas can then be taken as the child's skeletal age at the time the film was made. An even more precise procedure, however, is matching *each* of the bony centers *separately* with a standard and assigning a developmental age to each center independently of the others. Then, an arithmetic average of all these individual estimates would provide the child's estimated skeletal age.

Determining Skeletal Developmental Progress

Bone developmental progress can be determined and plotted for an individual for whom a series of x-ray films of his hand and wrist have been made during the period of his growth. Figure 3.3, for example, is a plotting of Sally's skeletal development in terms of the ages at which onset of ossification occurred in the various bones of her hand and wrist.

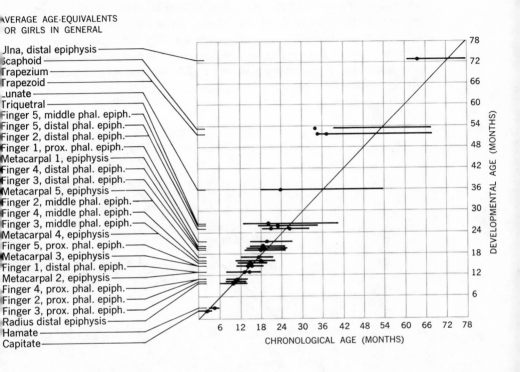

Figure 3.3

Skeletal development of Sally 695 in terms of ages of onset of ossification in twenty-eight bone growth centers of the hand and wrist. Variability equals ±1 SD. Age equivalents from Stuart et al. (1962), p. 239.

A significant difference should be noted between Figure 3.3 and Figure 2.5, which depicts progress in growth (height and weight). Both of these figures depict progress in terms of developmental age. In Figure 2.5 the developmental-age scale (on the vertical axis) is a simple age scale of years and months corresponding exactly in units, and without complications, to the chronological-age scale on the horizontal axis. The developmental-age scale is simply a scale of chronological-age equivalents for a set of *average measurements*. In Figure 3.3, by contrast, the developmental-age scale is a set of irregularly spaced average ages at which certain discrete, noncontinuous stages in a developmental sequence are reached by children. This scale is superimposed upon the age scale of years and months on the vertical axis.

Sally's progress in bone development, observed as the successive achievement of a series of stages, is thus plotted in terms of the average ages of girls in general when they reach those various stages. Since these stages are discrete and noncontinuous, the different points in the "curve" in each case are not connected with a line as was done in the case of height and weight in Figure 2.5. The curves in Figure 2.5 represent continuous increase in amount.

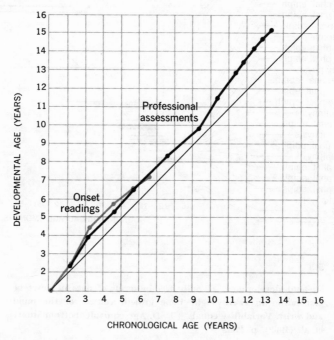

Figure 3.4

Skeletal development of Sally 695.

Figure 3.4 shows two separate evaluations of the course of Sally's skeletal development, one based upon estimates in terms of onset of ossification covering only the first 6½ years of life (see Figure 3.3), the other based upon the detailed assessments in terms of all the maturity indicators found in the films by a professional bone anatomist. It should be noted that in both instances (Figures 3.3 and 3.4) the points representing Sally's maturational levels generally are above the standard of reference (the diagonal), showing of course, that this

Table 3.1

Assessments of Skeletal Ages (Years-Months) from X-ray Series of Sally 695

	DEVELOPMENTAL AGES		
CHRONOLOGICAL AGE	STUDENT'S ESTIMATE (ONSET READINGS)	PROFESSIONAL ASSESSMENT	HEIGHT AGE
1-1	1-0	——	0-6
2-1	2-5	2-4	0-11
3-1	4-5	3-9	2-0
4-6	5-9	5-3	3-1
5-7	6-7	6-6	3-7
6-6	7-3	——	——
7-6		8-4	5-4
9-3		9-10	7-4
10-3		11-6	8-4
11-3		12-10	9-0
11-9		13-5	10-3
12-3		14-1	11-4
12-9		14-8	11-8
13-3		15-2	12-4

girl was an "early developer" in comparison with girls in general. Table 3.1 presents the data from which these figures were drawn.

SKELETAL MATURATION IN RELATION TO OTHER ASPECTS OF DEVELOPMENT   The maturation of the skeleton, more than any other single fact of development, can be taken as an index of the body's development in general. The relationship between skeletal development and the maturation of the reproductive system has already been mentioned. The girl described by Greulich and Pyle who suffered precocious puberty had her first menstruation when she was only 7 months old (1959, pp. 2–9). Other signs of sexual maturity began to appear in very early childhood. When she was only 5 years of age her skeletal age was 12 years 11 months. Along with this extreme precocity in sexual and skeletal maturation there was also acceleration of growth in stature. Growth, however, ceased very early in life, due to the early maturing of the long bones of the skeleton.

SKELETAL AND REPRODUCTIVE MATURATION IN NORMAL GIRLS   In normal girls also there is a clearly established relationship between rhythm of growth in stature, skeletal maturation, and the development of the reproductive system. Normally the menarche occurs during the period immediately following the year of maximum annual increment of growth in height. Figure 3.5 shows the annual increments

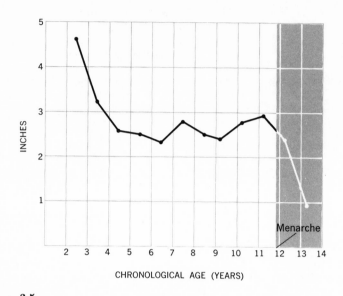

Figure 3.5

Annual increments in height of Sally 695.

in height for Sally, ages 2 years to 13 years. The period of her most consistent and rapid increase in rate of growth in stature was around 9½ to 11 years of age. Her first menstruation occurred at age 11 years 10 months.

Figure 3.6 is a plotting of Sally's height and skeletal maturation in terms of developmental ages. The corresponding developmental-age values are given in Table 3.1. It will be noted that this girl's height-age curve was considerably below the standard of reference throughout the whole period covered by the graph. The prepuberal growth spurt is clearly in evidence here, as it is in Figure 3.5. The period of most rapid growth was between ages 11 years 3 months and 11 years 9 months.

Although shorter than average in stature, Sally was somewhat advanced in her skeletal maturation. At the time her menarche occurred (11 years 10 months) her assessed skeletal age (average of the skeletal-age assessments of all the bones of the hand and wrist) was 13 years 4 months. The x-ray film taken at age 11 years 3 months matches quite well the female standard (number 21), which is the standard for skeletal age 13 in Greulich and Pyle's (1959) Atlas. This film shows the beginning of epiphysial-diaphysial fusion in the distal phalanges of the fingers. Another film, taken 6 months later at age 11 years 9 months (see Figure 3.2) shows that in the meantime fusion

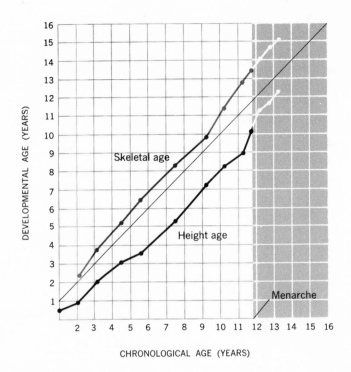

Figure 3.6

Skeletal maturation and growth in height of Sally 695 shown in relation to the time of menarche.

at those centers had been completed. This film matches the standard photo (number 22) in the Atlas that indicates a skeletal age of 13 years 6 months. According to Greulich and Pyle, this standard "illustrates the stage of skeletal development usually attained by girls at about the time of the menarche" (p. 168). Sally's menarche occurred at age 11 years 10 months, about 1 month after the latter of the two x-ray pictures was taken.

Dental Development

Dentition, as a process of development, is also manifested in a series of stages that are essentially qualitative in nature, some of which may be observed directly. For example, a child's teeth erupt above the gum in a fairly definite ordinal sequence. This sequence may be regarded as a series of maturity indicators.

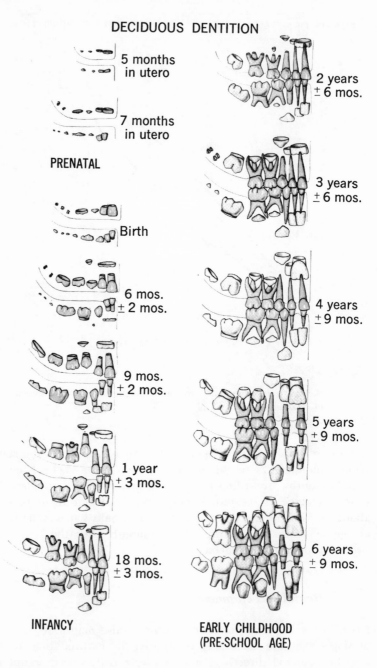

Figure 3.7

Development of the human dentition. Copyright by the

MIXED DENTITION

PERMANENT DENTITION

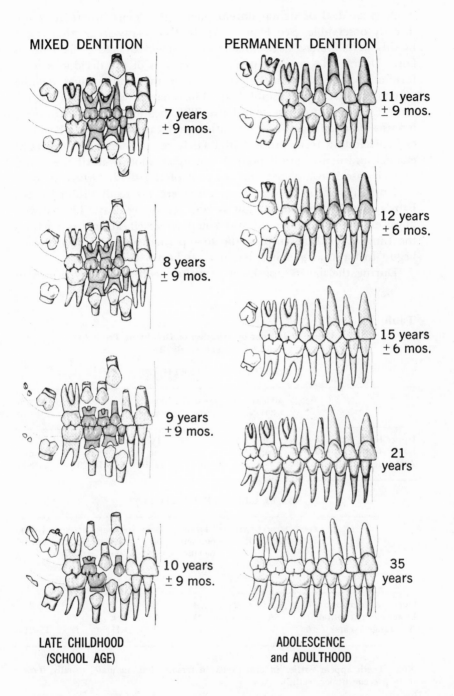

7 years
± 9 mos.

11 years
± 9 mos.

8 years
± 9 mos.

12 years
± 6 mos.

9 years
± 9 mos.

15 years
± 6 mos.

10 years
± 9 mos.

21 years

35 years

**LATE CHILDHOOD
(SCHOOL AGE)**

**ADOLESCENCE
and ADULTHOOD**

A great deal of dental development takes place where it is not directly observable (see Figure 3.7). In fact, many interesting stages in this development have already been achieved before the baby is born. During the prenatal period, the crowns of the deciduous teeth form and calcify deep in the jaws. Even in these early stages, definite sequences have been established. The enamel and dentin of the central incisors are first to calcify. This begins at about 4½ to 5 months prenatal age. The formation and calcification of the other eight deciduous teeth proceed in a fairly regular sequence. Layers of enamel and dentin are deposited one upon another until the crown in each case is completed and the root of the tooth begins to form.

Normally at birth, of course, there are no teeth visible in the baby's mouth. Root formation is not yet under way. The crowns, however, are well along toward complete calcification. As early as the time of birth, a cusp of the first permanent tooth has already begun to form, although it has not yet begun to calcify.

During the first 6 months of extrauterine life, all the permanent

Table 3.2

**Age Range and Order of Eruption of Deciduous Teeth (A)
and Permanent Teeth (B)[a]**

A. DECIDUOUS TEETH (20)

	MEDIAL INCISOR	LATERAL INCISOR	FIRST MOLAR	CUSPID OF CANINE	SECOND MOLAR
Upper teeth eruption	I	II	IV	III	V
Lower teeth eruption	a[b]	b	d	c	e
Age range (months)	6–8	8–10	12–16	16–20	20–24

B. PERMANENT TEETH (32)

	FIRST MOLAR	MEDIAL INCISOR	LATERAL INCISOR	FIRST BICUSPID OR FIRST MOLAR	CUSPID OR CANINE	SECOND BICUSPID OR SECOND PREMOLAR	SECOND MOLAR	THIRD MOLAR
Upper teeth eruption	6	1	2	4	3	5	7	8
Lower teeth eruption	F[b]	A	B	D	C	E	G	H
Age range (years)	6	7	8	10	11	11	12	15–21+

Note: Teeth appear earlier in oral cavity in female than in male, usually; Lower teeth precede upper teeth, usually.

[a] *Adapted from Schour and Massler (1941).*
[b] *These letters indicate same teeth in lower jaw.*

teeth with one exception (the upper lateral incisor) begin to grow and calcify. After the first molar, which is already beginning to form at birth, the permanent front teeth begin their formation at about 4 to 6 months of age. This occurs in a regular order. Finally, at about 10 to 11 months, the upper central incisor begins to form in the jaw.

During the second 6 months of the child's life, his deciduous teeth, whose crowns and roots by that time are formed and calcified in readiness, erupt in regular sequence through his gums. Table 3.2 shows the time range and the order of eruption of deciduous and permanent teeth. The names, and the arbitrary number and letter designations of these teeth are also given in Table 3.2. The first to appear are the four deciduous central incisors (I and a) at about age 7 months. These are soon followed by the lateral incisors (II and b). Near the end of the first year come the first deciduous molars (IV and d). The cuspids or canines (II and c) follow and are guided into position in the jaw by the teeth already there. The child is usually approaching the end of his second year when the second deciduous molars (V and e) come through. The numbers and letter designations, it must be noted, simply indicate *position* of the teeth in the jaws. In most instances these numbers do not correspond to the order of eruption.

Table 3.3 lists the deciduous and permanent teeth in the order of their expected eruption. Corresponding teeth on the two sides of the jaw are shown in the table as having the same eruption-age equivalents. Actually there are some small differences in mean age at eruption of some of these pairs, but these differences are not invariable, and for practical purposes a single age equivalent may serve for both pairs in each case.

The preschool period, ages 2 to 6 years, is characterized, so far as dentition is concerned, by a complete set of twenty deciduous teeth. During this period these temporary teeth gradually wear down from use and their roots are gradually being resorbed in preparation for their replacement by the permanent teeth.

The age period 6 to 12 years is sometimes called the period of mixed dentition. The deciduous teeth, their roots having been resorbed, are shed as the permanent replacements erupt under them.

The first permanent teeth to appear are, of course, the two pairs of first molars (6 and F in Table 3.2). These particular teeth are especially important in relation to the establishment of normal occlusion. Since they are the first permanent teeth to appear and also because they erupt in spots not previously occupied by deciduous teeth, parents sometimes mistake them for deciduous teeth and allow decay to cause their loss, thinking other teeth will replace them. In a sense they belong to the first set of teeth, but at the same time they

Table 3.3

Order of Eruption, Expected Ages of Eruption, and Variation
Ranges of Deciduous Teeth (A) and Permanent Teeth (B)[a]

A. DECIDUOUS TEETH

ORDER OF ERUPTION	AVERAGE ERUPTION AGE (MONTHS)		VARIATION RANGE (MONTHS)
	LOWER	UPPER	
Medial Incisor	6	7½	±2
Lateral Incisor	7	9	±2
First Molar	12	14	±4
Cuspid	16	18	±4
Second Molar	20	24	±4

B. PERMANENT TEETH

ORDER OF ERUPTION	ERUPTION AGE RANGE (YEARS)	
	LOWER	UPPER
First Molar	6–7	6–7
Medial Incisor	6–7	7–8
Lateral Incisor	7–8	8–9
Cuspid	9–10	11–12
First Bicuspid	10–12	10–11
Second Bicuspid	11–12	10–12
Second Molar	11–13	12–13
Third Molar	17–21	17–21

[a] *Adapted from Massler and Schour (in Nelson, 1954).*

are very important permanent ones, and they serve more or less as
guides in the location and spacing of later erupting teeth. Since the
average age at which these first molars appear is about 6 years, the
child's dental age at the time of their eruption is estimated as 6 years,
regardless of his chronological age.

The first permanent (6-year) molars are followed by the appearance of the incisors at from 6 to 8 years of age. The remaining stages
in the dental developmental sequences are shown in Table 3.3.

Appraising Status in Dentition

The validity of an appraisal of status in dentition at any particular
point in the child's life depends directly upon the degree of accuracy
with which the eruption dates are known. Owing to the relatively

wide variation in age at which the various teeth appear, the age equivalents may be taken to represent only a crude developmental scale.

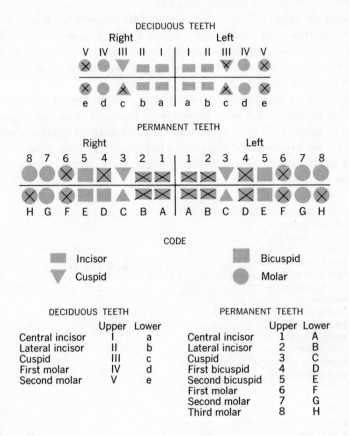

Figure 3.8

A record of dentition in Sally 695 at age 8 years 7 months.

Figure 3.8 is an adaptation of the record of Sally's dentition when she was 8 years 7 months old. She was at that time in the midst of her period of "mixed dentition." All eight of her deciduous incisors had been replaced by permanent incisors. The first (6-year) molars of course had erupted more than two years earlier. She had lost her deciduous first molars (IV and d), and the first permanent premolars (4 and D) had erupted to take their places. Sally still possessed her deciduous second molars (V and e) so that with her 6-year molars and her first premolars she still possessed a good array of back teeth. Her four deciduous canines were still present. The permanent canines, as a rule, do not appear until around age 11 years. To summarize Sally's dentition at age 8 years 7 months, she still possessed eight of her twenty deciduous teeth, and sixteen of her quota of thirty-two permanent teeth had already erupted.

A rough appraisal of Sally's dental developmental status at this particular time was made (chronological age 8 years 7 months). It was evident that Sally was somewhat advanced in dentition. Since all her first premolars were erupted, her dental age was estimated at approximately 10 years.

In order to trace dental development, examinations such as that recorded in Figure 3.8 must be made at frequent intervals beginning in early infancy. These appraisals, furthermore, must be carefully made by an experienced observer. They must be more than a casual glance in the child's mouth. Unfortunately, good dental developmental records are relatively rare.

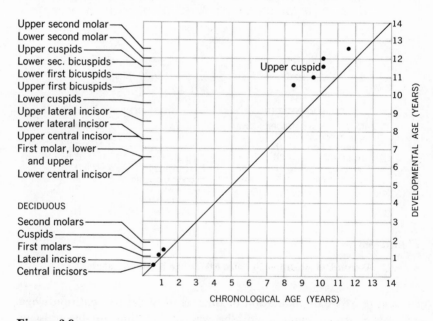

Figure 3.9

The development of dentition in Sally 695 from available records.

The dental record of Sally 695 is not entirely comprehensive. Figure 3.9 is a plotting of her record in terms of the available data in developmental-age units. It is clearly evident in this plotting that from the beginning of her second year, Sally continued to be somewhat advanced in dentition. Her dental age at 15 months to 17 months chronological age was 18 months. At 8 years 7 months, as we have seen, her dental age was 10 years, and at 10 years 4 months, the presence of her permanent second molars gave her a dental age of 12 years.

Development of the Nervous System

The processes of maturation in the nervous system are even more remarkable in their complexity and their precision than are those in other organs and systems of the body. Munn (1955) wrote of this developmental marvel:

> How is this intricate architecture of the nervous system laid down? How do the billions of embryonic nerve fibers reach their appropriate destinations in muscles, glands, receptors and central nervous nuclei and projections? They do this with precise developmental timing, in a manner characteristic of the species, and independent of activity. Indeed, until they find their destinations, no activity of the parts of the organism to which they go can normally occur. (p. 161)

Growth and Maturation of the Brain

Much of the growth in brain size occurs prenatally. In terms of weight, at birth the brain has already attained about 25 percent of its adult value. At 6 months of age it has grown to 50 percent, and by the time the child is 10 years of age his brain has gained 95 percent of its ultimate weight (Tanner, 1961).

Like physical development in general, different parts of the brain grow at different rates and reach their maximum rates of change at different times. The midbrain and the spinal cord are the most advanced-functioning parts throughout the period of growth, with the cerebrum third.

But as we have seen, growth in amount is only one aspect of development. The 10-year-old brain, although it has attained 95 percent of its ultimate weight, is far from being a mature brain. Conel (1939, 1941, 1947, 1951, 1955, 1959) has contributed greatly to our present knowledge about the early development of the human brain, particularly the cerebral cortex (Tanner, 1961).

THE EMBRYONIC STAGES   In the processes of cell differentiation and the modeling of the embryo, the nervous system develops from the ectodermal layer of cells. The first stage in this development is the thickening of a strip, or plate, of cells on the dorsal (top) side of the embryo.

> The cells at the edge of the plate grow faster than those in the middle, so that a neural groove is formed. This deepens to form a tubular structure as the cells increase in number. As the tube separates from the overlying ectoderm, the ectodermal cells at the junction become separate from both and come to lie along the dorsal side of the detached *neural tube*. The cells are known as the *neural crest* cells because of their early position over the neural tube. The entire adult nervous system, except for its blood vessels and certain neuroglial cells, is formed from the neural tube and the neural crest cells. In spite of subsequent complex morphological changes, the central nervous system remains a tube throughout the lifetime of an individual. (Gardner, 1963, p. 56)

Conel's findings concerning the prenatal development of the cerebral cortex are summarized by Tanner (1961) as follows:

> At about eight weeks of age (postmenstrual) the cortex begins to assume its typical structure of six somewhat indeterminate layers of nerve cells, the grey matter, on the outside of the cortex, with a layer of nerve fibers, the white matter, on the inside. All the nerve cells present in the adult are formed within the following two or three months, or so it is thought at present. Probably no new nerve cells appear after about six lunar months, though cells of the supporting tissue, the neuroglia, may perhaps differentiate for somewhat longer. (p. 77)

The nerve cells themselves undergo continuous change as well. At first they consist for the most part of nuclei with very little cytoplasm and with only a few small processes. As they develop they grow in size, and dendrites, axons, and smaller processes appear. Myelin sheaths form on many of the axons, particularly the larger ones. Some of the smaller axons get very little or no insulating myelin. Conel was able to formulate nine maturity indicators of the cerebrum. Presumably these maturational changes take place in a fixed and orderly sequence, but since they are not open to direct observation in the growing individual there is no direct way of assessing the development status of the brain. Detailed information about brain maturation after age 2 years is practically nonexistent.

Morphological Development

As we have noted, one of the earliest and most fundamental processes of cell specialization and organization in the embryonic development of the human organism is the formation of the three layers, *ectoderm*, *endoderm*, and *mesoderm*. This basic process of specialization and its further differential elaboration in the development of the three groups of structures and organs involved gives rise to another kind of over-all qualitative difference among individuals. Presumably, as a result of the relative predominance of one or another of these three sources of tissue origin, one or another of the corresponding structural tissue groups may tend to "dominate in the body economy," and to result in a tendency toward a particular morphological type (Sheldon, 1940).

Since the civilization of ancient Greece, students of mankind have worked to devise systems for classifying people in terms of morphological differences. This interest generally arises from the common belief that behavior is related in important ways to physical make-up.

The earliest well-known theoretical system of morphological classification was that of Hippocrates. He identified two basic physique types—the short and thick and the long and thin—and suggested that each type was especially prone to certain diseases. Associated also with these physique types, according to Hippocrates, were temperamental types, each of which was determined by the relative predominance of a particular "humor" (fluid) within the body—a suggestion not greatly different from the present-day conception of the role of the endocrine secretions in the affective life of the individual. A number of scholars after the time of Hippocrates proposed modifications of his classification scheme; others suggested systems of their own. Among the better known of these other classification schemes were the formulations of Kretschmer (1925), Rostan (1824), and Viola (1909).

Somatotypes

Perhaps the best-known modern student of morphology is W. H. Sheldon (1940, 1954), whose work was based on the fundamental belief that function is always and ever related to structure. In his search for criteria for the classification of human physiques, Sheldon studied three primary aspects of bodily constitution, selected because they appeared "to behave in bodily morphology as though each were a component of structure—something which enters in different amounts into the making of a body" (1940, p. 4). These three components of structure were briefly described by Sheldon as follows:

Endomorphy means relative predominance of soft roundness throughout the various regions of the body. When endomorphy is dominant the digestive viscera are massive and tend relatively to dominate the body economy. The digestive viscera are derived principally from the endodermal embryonic layer.

Mesomorphy means relative predominance of muscle, bone, and connective tissue. The mesomorphic physique is normally heavy, hard and rectangular in outline. Bone and muscle are prominent and the skin is made thick by a heavy underlying connective tissue. The entire bodily economy is dominated, relatively, by tissues derived from the mesodermal embryonic layer.

Ectomorphy means relative predominance of linearity and fragility. In proportion to his mass, the ectomorph has the greatest surface area and hence relatively the greatest sensory exposure to the outside world. Relative to his mass he also has the largest brain and central nervous system. In a sense therefore, his bodily economy is relatively dominated by tissues derived from the ectodermal embryonic layer. (pp. 5-6 *The Varieties of Human Physique* by W. H. Sheldon. Copyright 1940 by Harper & Row, Publishers, Inc. Reprinted by permission of the publishers.)

The particular patterning of these three morphological components in an individual determines his "somatotype." All individuals, it is assumed, possess each component to some degree. Using the method devised by Sheldon, one's somatotype is appraised from a study of nude photographs taken in three specially posed positions: front, side, and back. A recently devised refinement of Sheldon's original procedure involves the use of objective measurements taken on the photographs. Each of the three components is rated in that order, on a scale from 1 (minimum) to 7 (maximum).[1]

THE STABILITY OF THE SOMATOTYPE   One important question in relation to individual morphology is its relative stability with age. Dupertuis, a coauthor of Sheldon's, wrote as follows:

One of the tenets of the philosophy behind somatotyping is that the basic component combination of an individual remains constant throughout life. It is only recently however, that there have been objective techniques to demonstrate this thesis. The newly developed planimeter technique has shown that

---

[1] Using this scale, a rating of 7-1-1 would represent the component ratings of an extreme endomorph, ratings of 1-7-1 would describe the extreme mesomorph, and 1-1-7, the extreme ectomorph. A person with the somatotype ratings of 4-4-4 would possess a moderate, or average, amount of all three components.

certain body indices designating body proportions do remain relatively constant throughout an individual's growth period from at least a very early age to young adulthood. There are many indications also that the somatotype remains constant throughout the whole lifetime of the individual. When body indices indicating the ratio of the abdominal to the thoracic areas are calculated from planimeter or area measurements taken on serial photographs of growing children, it is found that they are remarkably constant throughout. (from personal communication)

This relative constancy of body type in children throughout the growth period has been previously expressed in the plottings of the height-weight relationship on the Wetzel Grid. (see Figure 2.7). This tendency to stability is revealed in the up-channel progression that the Wetzel curves generally assume. Walker (1962, 1963) has also demonstrated that basic differences among individuals in the relative dominance of the three morphological components can be assessed in early childhood.

Underlying the work of Sheldon and his coworkers is the assumption that individual development is largely controlled by genetic and other biological factors. Their objective, therefore, has been to discover some stable representation of this pattern of determining factors, which Sheldon refers to as the "morphogenotype," a hypothetical, biological structure that is more fundamental than the observable phenotype. The somatotype, being based directly on measurements of the physique, is regarded as an indirect approximation or representation of the morphogenotype.

SOMATOTYPES IN RELATION TO OTHER ASPECTS OF DEVELOPMENT
Even though the individual's somatotype per se does not change with age, Sheldon and his coworkers regard morphology as of fundamental importance in the development of the individual.

Researchers have revealed significant degrees of relationship between physique (and other bodily features) and aspects of development. Dupertuis and Michael (1953), for example, found that children with muscular solidarity not only tend to be shorter and heavier but also to grow at a faster rate and thus to reach the peak in their puberal growth spurt earlier than children with more linear and delicately built bodies. The California Adolescent Study (H. E. Jones, 1949) found significant differences in physical strength between Sheldon's morphological types. Glueck and Glueck (1956), in one of the best-known studies of juvenile delinquency, found that the sturdier body build was more characteristic of delinquents than of nondelinquents.

Sheldon's (1940) own research indicated rather significant relationships between morphological types and corresponding temperamental types. Walker (1962, 1963) studied this sort of relationship at the early childhood level. He obtained somatotyping photographs on a group of nursery school children and, using Sheldon's procedures, was able to rate each child in terms of the three body components. It is interesting to note that Walker also found important relationships between physique and certain behavior characteristics in the nursery school children. These relationships, furthermore, showed "considerable similarity to those described by Sheldon of college-age men" (1962, p. 79).

Other developmental studies (H. E. Jones, 1943; M. C. Jones, 1957; M. C. Jones and Bayley, 1950) leave no room for doubt that physique and other physical attributes are important in relation to different aspects of individual development. The relationship of these findings to personality development is discussed in greater detail in Chapter 12.

The Somatotyping Process

The technical procedure for determining an individual's somatotype is rather long and complicated (Sheldon, 1940, pp. 80–98). As previously stated, three standardized and carefully posed nude photographs are essential to the procedure. The first step in the actual process of somatotyping is over-all inspection of the pictures and then estimation of the approximate strength of each of the three components for the body as a whole. These estimates are recorded in terms of the scale 1 to 7. Such a tentative somatotyping was made for Paul 695, from pictures taken at age 16 years 2 months (see Figure 3.10). The three morphological components were rated 5-4-2.

In order to accomplish more than an approximation, one must have access to the *Atlas of Men* (Sheldon, Dupertius, and McDermott, 1954). Check somatotypes for whom the ratio of their heights to the cube root of their weights is the same as, or similar to, that ratio for the subject being somatotyped. (The subject's ratio can be determined from his own height and weight at the time the photographs were taken, by means of the nomograph in the Atlas on page 350.) The numbers of the identified somatotypes as pictured in the Atlas for each of the various height-over-cube-root-of-weight ratios can be found in the appropriate table, pages 340 to 344 of the *Atlas*.

With a height of 68 inches and a weight of 147 pounds, Paul's ratio as read on the nomograph was 12.9. Four somatotype numbers with this ratio are 142, 162, 453, and 533. These are among the

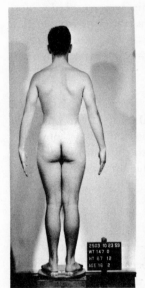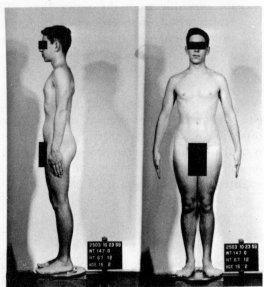

Figure 3.10

Photographs of Paul 695 in the posed positions for somato-typing. Used by permission.

hundreds of somatotype photographs included in the *Atlas of Men*. The picture of somatotype number 533 looks very similar to those of our subject. The component ratings for this somatotype are 5-3-3½ as compared with estimated ratings of Paul at 5-4-2.

A more thorough somatotype analysis may be obtained by taking a set of seventeen careful measurements from the photographs. These measurements are made on five different regions of the body—the head and neck region, the thoracic region, the arms and hands region, the lower trunk region, and the legs and feet region. Each of these measurements is divided by the individual's height and multiplied by 100 in order to express it as a percentage of height. Each of the five body regions is then somatotyped in a manner somewhat similar to the second step described above (Sheldon, 1940, pp. 82–98).

Through the cooperation of Dr. Dupertuis, we have the following somatotype appraisal of our subject Paul at age 16:

> This boy possesses one of the most displastic physiques in the entire series. He is predominantly mesomorphic above the waist and predominantly endomorphic below the waist. At the same time he shows a very high gynic (feminine) aspect of

the physique from the waist down. This boy could do most athletics but would probably be quite frustrated in competition with more mesomorphic boys. He might do very well, however, in swimming. Somatotype: 4½-4-3. (from personal communication)

This expert somatotype appraisal of 4½-4-3 may be compared with our preliminary estimate of 5-4-2 based only upon our own inspection of the photographs, and the ratings of 5-3-3½ obtained by matching the photographs of our subject with those of the standard somatotype (number 533) with the same height-over-cube-root-of-weight ratio as our subject.

Summary

This chapter has discussed the second main aspect of the development of the human organism, the aspect of change that is not measurable in quantitative units. These changes consist in the emergence of new and different stages in a sequence, new qualities, forms, features, or contours that are vital in the preparation of body parts and organs to function as they are designed to function in the integrated activity of the organism.

Change is clearly portrayed in the orderly and speedy sequence of happenings in the human embryo. The reciprocal processes of differentiation and integration during this early period are prime examples of maturational change. The course of development in the nervous and skeletal systems, both prenatally and postnatally, furnish other clear examples of maturation.

The gross morphological differences to be found among adult human beings were viewed as qualitative developments probably stemming from the relative emphasis, or "dominance," of one or another of the three specialized embryonic layers which become differentiated very early in the stages of the embryo.

SELECTED READING SUGGESTIONS

Greulich, W. W., and S. Idell Pyle. *Radiographic atlas of skeletal development of the hand and wrist.* Second ed. Stanford, Calif.: Stanford University Press, 1959. (Rationale and technique of assessing the developmental status of children from Roengenograms of the hand and wrist, pp. 1–59.)

Hall, C. S., and G. Lindzey. *Theories of personality*. New York: Wiley, 1957. (Chapter 9 covers Sheldon's constitutional psychology.)

Hamburger, Viktor. The concept of "development" in biology. In D. B. Harris, *The concept of development*. Minneapolis: University of Minnesota Press, 1957.

Schour, I., and M. Massler. The development of human dentition. *J. Amer. dent. Ass.*, 1941, **28**, 1153–1160.

Tanner, J. M. *Education and physical growth*. London: University of London Press, 1961.

PART III

Functional
Development

CHAPTER 4

The
Vital Functions

Our focus now shifts from the growth and maturation of structure—the physical body and its organ systems—to the development of the various modes of functioning and behavior of the whole individual. We must recognize first, however, that development in functional facility is contingent upon the biological development of the body structures involved. Learning in its broad sense is development made possible by the exercise of the structures made ready for functioning through maturation. This exercise, or practice of a new function, undoubtedly brings about changes in the structures involved as well as in function per se. Structural and functional development are, in a true sense, inseparable.

The evaluation of developmental status in functioning, again, presents difficult problems of measurement and quantification. The human being is characterized by a great complexity and endless variety of functions, and, thus far, appraisal of these functions is a relatively new area of study.

The development of certain specialized motor functions, for example, roller skating, high jumping, or typing, may be measured readily and directly in terms of standard units, because such development merely consists of quantitative changes, through learning, in a function the basis of which is already present or in some specific attribute of that function, such as speed. Functions of this sort are special learned skills superimposed upon basic universal human functions. They are *ontogenetic* in nature, as contrasted with the more basic *phylogenetic* functions, which are more closely tied in their development to the biological maturation of characteristically human structures.

This chapter will discuss a third class of functions which are not phylogenetic in the sense that they set the human being apart from other forms, but which are common to many, if not all, biological species because they are vital to life and well-being. The functions of this sort are eating, elimination, and sleep and rest. These functions are obviously universal and necessary to life. But they, like the other human functions, are highly modifiable through learning, and they generally bear an important relationship to the higher psychological functions.

The Eating Function

The acquisition of the ability to take and to manage foods of different qualities and consistencies and to deal with eating situations of increasing complexity is a developmental task of childhood. Eating is a vital function of the total organism and is essential to the satisfaction of a biological need. The specific nature of the need itself changes with age, as do the physiological pattern and the overt behavioral pattern of the eating function.

The Development of the Nutriture

Birth is without doubt the most severe crisis situation generally encountered by the individual in his life from conception to death. In prenatal existence the food supply to the fetus is constant and comes without effort. This food is elemental in nature, consisting of such essentials as calcium, phosphorus, and iron and entering the blood stream of the fetus directly. At birth, the way in which the infant gets his food suddenly becomes quite different; he must now take food into his own digestive system. For the first time his lungs become filled with air. The prenatal detour route of the blood for oxygen (from the fetal heart to the placenta and back to the heart) suddenly is closed and the life route for oxygen to the baby's lungs becomes functional. The necessary process of oxidation of tissue-building materials is, in turn, caused by the presence of food in the stomach. The infant's food supply must enter his mouth.

Thus, the event of birth marks the end of one stage in the development of nutriture and the beginning of another stage. The whole digestive system during the neonatal period, however, is very immature. The infant is capable of using only that food which is in a highly simplified form, and which normally continues to come to him from his mother's body. During these first days, when the transition must be made from a fetal existence to that of an independent organism, the infant is dependent upon a food substance from his mother, colostrum, which is especially adapted to his needs and his ability to take and utilize it.

Development resumes immediately, however, and continues at a rapid rate. The infant soon reaches a second developmental stage in which the products of the maternal body no longer sufficiently supply his need for nutrients. He must now utilize foods from other sources, a stage that marks a real achievement in nutritive development. The supplementary foods at this stage, however, must be in liquid form. Orange juice and other fluids furnish the infant's expanded needs for vitamins and minerals.

At this point in his development, the baby is very inept at taking in liquids by any means other than sucking. His tongue tends to push from his mouth any material that may be introduced by cup or spoon. He must be carefully helped to achieve a measure of competence in sucking into his system sufficient amounts of supplementary foods during this early period (the third developmental stage).

The introduction of semisolid foods, such as cereals and pureed vegetables and fruits, marks a fourth level in the development of the food-taking function. By this time the baby's ability to manage food in his mouth without spitting it out is improving. He is still unable to handle anything but soft and uniformly consistent foods free from chunks.

The fifth developmental stage that has been tentatively identified is characterized by the baby's ability to tolerate chopped foods. This transitional period begins with the infant's inability to deal with foods that are not at least partially liquified and ends with the more mature stage in which he can, by himself, masticate and prepare solid foods for digestion. In this period the food still must be partially broken down from the solid state because the child has an inadequate complement of teeth and has not yet learned to use them to chew. This fifth stage has been called the "premature" stage in the development of the nutriture. The ability to manage solid foods marks a sixth stage.

Rand, Sweeny, and Vincent (1953) summarize the situation with respect to this aspect of functional development:

> These six stages of maturation of the nutriture, it is believed, can be detected by observing the concurrent maturational changes of oral activities which are related to the ingestion of food. The *rooting* and *sucking* reflexes, present at birth, are the infant's mechanism for finding and taking fluids into the mouth. Some time later, a *biting reflex and salivation* appear. The infant bites and begins drooling. This behavior is an indicator for introducing pureed food. The next oral indicator includes two kinds of behavior which appear close together, namely, *the ability to swallow small lumps* and *destructive biting*. Now the infant can manage chopped foods. The final oral indicator is *chewing*, by which the infant is able to reduce food to a consistency which can be swallowed. This requires at least the first molars. By this time the child can eat solid, non-simplified adult foods. With this concept one can apply these and any other nutritive indicators to a better understanding of the reasons underlying individual differences which are not explained by age alone. It seems quite possible that a child can be five years old chronologically and yet immature nutritionally. (p. 177)

The development of the eating function, then, is a matter of maturation and learning. The nutriture, which is the changing capacity of the organism to ingest and to utilize foods of various qualitative characteristics, is tied in its development to the maturation of the bodily structures involved. But beyond the sucking and swallowing reflexes and the physiological processes of digestion, which are functional at birth, the child must *learn* to eat. He must learn to take liquids from the spoon and the cup. He must learn to manage semiliquids and lumps and later solid foods. All through the course of development from the level of simple sucking and swallowing to the ability to tolerate, then relish, the great variety of tastes, smells, and textures of adult foods and to manipulate the socially prescribed implements of eating in a manner acceptable to society, learning is an essential aspect of development.

ORAL PLEASURE   The rooting, sucking, and swallowing reflexes are built-in mechanisms for getting the life-maintaining fluid foods into the stomach of the newborn infant. In recent decades psychoanalytic theory has invested this process of food ingestion with far greater significance than the mere satisfaction of nutritional needs. Much is made of the importance of oral gratification to psychological development as well.

The psychoanalytic theory of "stages" in psychosexual development briefly stated, is that through the basic metabolic and other processes in the organism certain tensions are built up. For example, as the supply of nutrients in the body become depleted, tension increases to a point of sheer discomfort. This discomfort is experienced as hunger. The taking of food gives gratification or release from tension. The continual seeking for release from tension and for gratification of all sorts requires energy. Freud called this energy libido, or libidinal energy.

In psychoanalytic theory, the mouth is regarded as an erogenous zone—a tissue area that gives sensuous pleasure. Experimenters refer to the passionate quality of the child's thumbsucking and to the persistent continuation of sucking long after his hunger has been satisfied. In times of stress or fatigue, particularly, the child seems to find greatest relief and gratification in oral activity. The mother naturally senses the comfort and pleasure her baby derives from sucking and she is usually inclined to facilitate his indulgence and to take empathic delight in the sounds he makes and the playfulness of his oral behavior.

During early infancy, then, the taking of food through nursing at the breast and the comfort derived from this process are the totality of life. All release from tension and all gratification come from it. With gratification comes pleasure. When tension has mounted feelings of frustration are experienced and anxiety and the sense of insecurity arise.

Specialists in child care, however, long ignored the pleasure aspect of the sucking activity. Their theorizing was confined to the food-taking function of the activity. Sucking was regarded simply as a bad habit that was to be prevented or overcome, not only because of its unhygienic dangers but also because of its possible deleterious effects upon the child's dentition. Parents also tend to become concerned when their children continue to suck their fingers to an age well beyond the period of babyhood. The tendency generally has been to disregard the obviously pleasurable quality of oral activity in children and its possible influences upon their emotional and personal development.

The question as to the origin of the so-called pleasure drive in oral activity is one of considerable theoretical importance. According to Freudian theory, oral pleasure is "instinctual" in nature (that is, of phylogenetic origin). Another feasible explanation is based on the theory that the pleasure drive to oral activity is an early conditioned (learned) affective response. Since the mouth is "a utilitarian organ subordinate to the hunger drive," the gratification of the hunger drive has primacy, and, with repetition, the pleasure of relief from hunger becomes associated with (attached to) the oral reflex of sucking. This connection in the infant's experience between sucking and pleasure gets repeated reinforcement. The mouth thus becomes "a pleasure organ coordinate with other zones of libidinal satisfaction" (Munroe, 1955, p. 198).

Regardless of the origin of the pleasure aspect of sucking, eating is an important area of human experience. From early infancy oral pleasure joins forces with the hunger drive to insure adequate food intake. The alleviation of hunger through oral activity thus constitutes the main source of gratification and pleasure for the infant. The first stage in the development of the eating function, therefore, is also the first stage in affective development: the oral stage.

Furthermore, since nursing is the infant's primary pleasurable contact with the world outside himself, the experience is of great importance to his cognitive development as well. The infant naturally begins to "perceive" at the point of his greatest interest. It is through the various sense modalities that are centered in the oral region that the infant comes to be aware of and to know the world immediately around him. He sees an object; his hand comes in contact with it and he feels its shape and texture; he brings it to his mouth where he tastes it; he smells it. He gradually becomes aware of the differences between his sensory experiences of his own hands and toes and those of objects that are not a part of himself. Oral pleasure is thus an important factor in cognitive development.

Throughout the course of maturation of the nutriture, the pleasures of eating continue to spread from sheer orality and the pleasures of tactile and proprioceptive stimulation to those gustatory and olfactory in nature. Social stimuli of various sorts also combine with the rest. Sounds, colors, textures, tastes, aromas, and total Gestalts become pleasurably or unpleasurably associated with eating. Food likes and dislikes are established. The eating situation becomes an important aspect of social living.

Appraising Developmental Status of the Eating Function

Table 4.1 presents a summary of a tentative sequence of stages in the development of the eating function in children.[1] The stages appear to meet fairly well the requirements of a series of indicators of developmental progress. The table also suggests tentative age equivalents. These mean ages represent summarizations of clinical observations without benefit of actual records and should, therefore, be regarded as tentative until confirmed and until measures of variability can be established through systematic observation and recording.

Table 4.1

Tentative Progress Indicators of the Development of the Ability to Manage Increasingly Complex Foods and Feeding Situations

STAGE	BEHAVIOR	AGE EXPECTED TO BEGIN
1. Highly specialized food— colostrum, mother's milk	Sucking and swallowing	Birth–1 day
2. Liquid feeding	Sucking and swallowing supplementary liquids by spoon	4 weeks
3. Augmented liquid feeding	Able to swallow pureed foods as easily as milk	13 weeks
4. Infant solids	Capable of reducing lumps by chewing	35 weeks
5. Solids by feeding	Capable of chewing and swallowing table food	14 months
6. Self-feeding	Can feed self with spoon or fork, prefers fingers	24 months
7. Young mature eating	Can serve and feed self	36 months

To use this sequence of indicators for appraising a child's status in this area of functional development, it is necessary either to have access to records of diet and descriptions of eating behavior for the particular time in the child's life or to make first-hand observations of eating behavior and inquiries regarding the child's diet and patterns

[1] This sequence of indicators was arrived at jointly by Dr. Charles G. Jennings, Consultant in Pediatrics, and Mary E. Sweeny, former Assistant Director and Head of the Physical Growth Department, The Merrill-Palmer Institute.

of food intake. Such data may then be referred to the sequences in Table 4.1 and an appropriate age equivalent of the child's level of eating development may be made.

Plotting Developmental Progress

The process of ingesting food, then, is highly complex and involves the whole organism. The process of ingestion changes radically with the maturation of the nutriture, as well as through learning and socialization. In its learned aspects at least, this function may be regarded as a developmental task, the achievement of which, in its expected adult form, may be marked by identifiable stages.

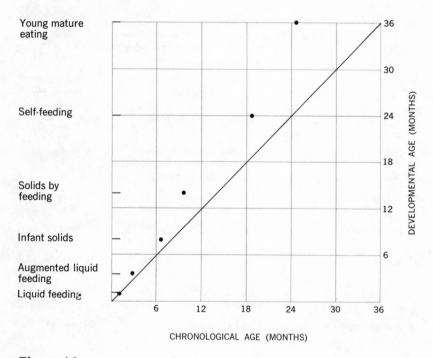

Figure 4.1

The development of the eating function in Sally 695.

Figure 4.1 represents the course of Sally's development with respect to the eating function.

A factor that may have had some bearing on Sally's eating behavior and its development is that she was fed and otherwise cared for as an infant under the self-regulation regime. Under the guidance of the pediatrician in charge, a "behavior-day-chart" (so-named by Gesell) was kept by the mother. This chart furnished a detailed record of Sally's food intake day by day as well as the exact time of day or night when each feeding occurred during the first 8 months of her life. This chart shows that by age 16 weeks the infant had established for herself a fairly regular three-feeding schedule which corresponded reasonably well with the usual morning-midday-evening eating pattern of our culture. The early stages of the development of Sally's eating function are clearly shown in her behavior-day record.

As in previous plottings of qualitative change, the developmental stages are indicated in Figure 4.1 on the developmental-age scale (vertical axis) in each case at a point representing the mean, or expected, age of its appearance. The approximate actual age at which Sally achieved each stage is plotted against the expected age.

At about 1 month of age Sally began to receive supplementary liquids such as cod liver oil and orange juice. By the time she was 3 months old she was getting cereal and pureed vegetables and fruits (augmented liquid stage). From that point on, this child's developmental progress in eating was somewhat advanced. At 10 months of age she was eating solid foods, a stage which, on the average, is not reached until approximately age 14 months. At age 19 months she was able to feed herself with a spoon like a 2-year-old child. When she was 2 years old she was almost a full year advanced in the development of her eating behavior according to the record.

Conditioning Factors in the Development of the Food-Taking Function

Although, as we have seen, there are certain more or less biologically based stages of eating development through which children generally pass, there are nevertheless certain widely varying factors, some inherent in the child, some environmental, which in interaction may profoundly affect the course of development of this particular function, and, perhaps more importantly, the total personal development of the child. Some of these factors begin to operate almost from birth and affect the direction and quality of developmental change. Perhaps the most basic factor is the inherent temperamental nature of the child. The baby with a quiet contented nature is likely from the beginning to respond differently to early food-taking experiences than the more reactive, restless, or irritable baby. A second basic factor, which can be very important in interaction with the baby's nature, is the manner in which food is presented to him, and under what conditions. I. D. Harris (1959), in discussing peculiar reactions of 8- and 9-year-old children who were "not so well adjusted," speculated that these reactions

> . . . could be indicative of a certain type of experience during the early dependency of the child, a period in which the mode of relating to the mother (the first human object) is predominantly by means of oral experience. The mother can be the source of nutriment and pleasure for the infant as he feeds, but she can also be the source of pain, tension, and frustration. (p. 25)

Thus, the early eating experiences of the infant are potentially very important in the establishment of attitudes and emotional reactions to the whole food-taking situation and in determining the direction and nature of the development which the eating function takes. It is important, therefore, that babies are fed under conditions which provide affection and security.

> In the development of hunger and feeding behavior, both of which are basic to physical survival, there grow up many conditioned feelings and emotions (closely associated with the feeding situation) which affect the vigor of the hunger drive, the willingness to try new foods, the rejection of certain once-accepted foods, and many things related to food and hunger which do not appear on the surface. As the child grows and widens his social contacts the emotional satisfactions from food or frustrations in the feeding area become extended to objects and relationships which are not always apparent to the observer. Food, generally and specifically, acquires different meanings to different people and to the same person at different times. Thus human relationships play a profound role in maintaining a sound hunger drive and thereby influence food habits. (Breckenridge and Vincent, 1965, p. 123)

Many children's appetites and their general enjoyment of eating are affected by the degree of freedom they are granted or the extent to which they are pressured into eating certain foods and certain amounts. The practice of resorting to spoon feeding the child in order to make sure that he gets the proper amounts of the proper foods long after he is capable of feeding himself makes of the eating function a passive, if not an unpleasant, unhappy process, rather than an active and enjoyable one. The development of this important function in the young child is thus hampered or facilitated by the attitudes and behavior of those who care for him.

The Eliminative Functions

The processes of living and of bodily upkeep require a constant movement of materials through the body. The eating function, including the intake of fluids, brings into the body the supply of nutritive materials. The metabolic processes within the gastrointestinal system subject these materials to complex chemical transformations in which the energy and tissue-building elements are extracted and made ready for assimilation. The remaining useless or injurious end-products must be eliminated from the body.

The processes of separating these waste products from the digestive tract and other tissues of the body and collecting them in readiness for elimination is the work of the organs of excretion—the intestinal tract and the kidneys. The main organs of elimination are the colon, the bladder, the lungs, and the skin.

The Bowel Function and Its Control

The elimination of bodily waste products obviously is necessary for health and well-being. Undigested materials, wastes from the digestive process, bacteria of the digestive tract, and waste salts are eliminated as fecal matter. The amount of fecal elimination, of course, depends upon the nature and amount of food-fluid intake. Liberal amounts of vegetables and fruits provide roughage and increase the amount of fecal elimination.

The peristaltic action of the digestive tract keeps up the movement of materials through the digestive system. The speed of the peristaltic movements is influenced mainly by the nature of the diet and occasionally by the individual's emotions.

There is no hard-and-fast rule as to when or how frequently elimination should take place. Ordinarily it occurs once a day at a regular time, but there is much variation in children. "Regularity in a child's pattern of elimination is more important than conformity of his pattern to that of others" (Breckenridge and Vincent, 1965, p. 129).

The eliminative functions in early infancy are purely passive and reflexive in nature. Voluntary control must await the maturation of the nervous and muscular structures involved. Studies indicate that it is not until near age 18 months that maturational structural readiness is reached for the achievement of voluntary sphincter control. By this time the child walks easily, is aware of, and can become interested in, the control of his eliminative functions. He also has some language facility to signal his situation and is inclined to imitate those around him. Some time is required, however, for the achievement of perfect control. There are wide individual differences in age at which readiness for eliminative learning is reached and in the length of time required for perfect control. Too frequently, parents do not recognize or understand the time factor and exert undue pressure on their child, sometimes with unfortunate results.

THE ANAL STAGE   The second stage in emotional (psychosexual) development, according to psychoanalytic theory, is the anal stage.[2] This period corresponds roughly to the second and third years of the child's life, the period when training for sphincter control is under way. The onset of this period, of course, does not mean the cessation of the activities and satisfactions of the oral period, which tend to continue through life. It means, rather, that in order to conform to social demands, the child must now be attentive to new activities. By this time the child is able to move about and explore his world. His interests in the world around him are expanding, and at the same time new demands are made upon him. For example, society's attitudes toward cleanliness require him to control his bowel and bladder functions. Since the eliminative functions pertain to and directly involve his own body and its feelings, they are "closer" to him than are any other activities in the sense that they involve tension, release from tension, frustration, and gratification. The attitudes and feelings of those about the child have much to do with the kinds of feelings, reactions, and adjustments he is able to make during this period of concentration upon eliminative activities and the anal area

The Development of Bladder Control

Urethral sphincter control and its achievement often is a problem for both the child and his parents. The wide variation in the time of readiness for learning is part of the problem. Children who are not yet ready developmentally for training are sometimes subjected to pressure or punishment. Often, too, the child, in his efforts to maintain his sense of power, resists all regulations from the outside. Munroe (1955), writing in psychoanalytic terms, clearly portrayed the parent-child interaction problem in relation to the child's personal development:

> Techniques of toilet training and, above all, the mother, are, therefore, of great moment in personality development. The

child must give up his narcissistic omnipotence. If he can identify happily with the mother and accept her requirements as his own, the emerging pride in his personal mastery of instinctual impulses can be constructively directed toward socially acceptable regulation. His own sense of achievement is enhanced by parental praise. On the other hand, if he is forced to give up his self-determination out of fear, whether of direct chastisement or severe loss of love, his inner determination tends to develop in opposition to the outside world. The upshot may be anxious effort at compliance, not from shared interest in regulation but from fear of authority. Or there may be defiance instead. Or, most common of all, a mixture of the two. (p. 197)

As a general rule, the bladder eliminative function develops gradually. Sometimes the developmental curve is quite irregular, indicating very erratic performance. This irregularity is probably due more to adult interference than to anything inherent in the process of development.

Tracing Development in Bladder Control

No maturity indicators have been suggested for evaluating status in the function of bladder control. Qualitative changes would be extremely difficult to identify. However, a tentative quantitative scale has been devised for this purpose. Table 4.2 shows the development of

Table 4.2

Average Dry Nights per Month for Boys and Girls at Different Chronological Ages

CHRONOLOGICAL AGE RANGE (MONTHS)	AVERAGE DRY NIGHTS PER MONTH	
	BOYS (N = 49)	GIRLS (N = 43)
26–28	18.2	23.2
29–31	21.0	23.5
32–34	20.6	25.7
35–37	23.9	27.8
38–40	26.5	28.6
41–43	27.5	28.9
44–46	28.5	29.2
47–49	29.2	29.3
50–52	28.6	29.9
53–55	29.1	29.6
56–58	28.4	30.0
59–61	30.0	30.0

bladder control in boys and girls in terms of the average number of "dry" nights per month for given chronological ages. These results were obtained from a short longitudinal study of the records of forty-nine boys and forty-three girls for the age range 26 months to 61 months. The figures are tentative and subject to more detailed investigation, since the records were not in every instance complete and the actual number of cases studied was so small. Moreover, the values are averages and variability within the group was wide. Note, however, that boys were, on the average, consistently behind girls in the development of overnight bladder control.

Table 4.3

Tentative Age Equivalents for Boys and Girls of Mean Number of Dry Nights per Month

DRY NIGHTS PER MONTH	AGE EQUIVALENT (MONTHS)	
	BOYS (N = 49)	GIRLS (N = 43)
18	26	21
19	28	23
20	30	24.5
21	32	26
22	34	27
23	35	28.5
24	36	30
25	37	31.5
26	38	33
27	40	35
28	44	37
29	50	42
30	66	60

Each chronological age for which an "average performance" (mean number of dry nights) was obtained may be taken as the age equivalent for that particular level of performance. A tentative developmental-age scale for bladder control in thus derived (see Table 4.3). Although these values are tentative, they may be used for an approximate assessment of a child's status in the development of this function.

Figure 4.2 depicts the course of Sally's achievement of urethral sphincter control in terms of the number of dry nights per month at different ages. The point on the chronological-age scale marked by a dot, in each case, is the midpoint of the thirty-night period. The upper curve in the figure represents the average course of achievement of the forty-three girls described in Table 4.3.

The striking feature of Figure 4.2 is the wide difference between Sally's curve of bladder-control achievement and the average curve for

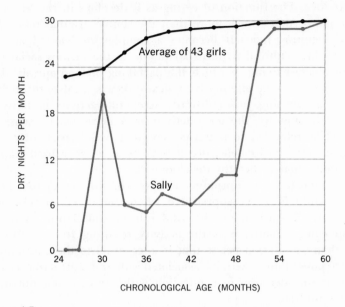

CHRONOLOGICAL AGE (MONTHS)

Figure 4.2

The development of overnight bladder control in Sally 695 as compared to the average of a tested group of forty-three girls.

the group of girls. Sally was almost 4 years old before she showed any consistent trend to remain dry through the night.

It will be recalled that Sally was reared on the self-regulation regime. The regulation of her eliminative processes as well as her feeding schedule were largely self-initiated rather than imposed upon her from without. According to the record, no "training" of any sort had been initiated at age 18 months. At age 27 months, although she still wet her bed nightly, Sally had gained good daytime control. Although she was "taken" periodically and was encouraged to indicate her need, no pressure was ever used and the only reward she received for her successful self-regulation were the words "good girl." Sally's record illustrates dramatically the wide individual variation that must be expected in the achievement of voluntary sphincter control; ultimately, when success is achieved, it may occur rapidly.

Activity, Rest, and Sleep

In this chapter we have been considering the developmental elaboration of certain specific functions of the living organism that are essential to life and to growth and maturation. These functions, to be sure, are activities. The function of eating as it develops in the life of the individual, becomes much more than the simple original reflex function of ingesting food. It becomes a complex of learned activities organized into cultural patterns adaptable to the various social situations of modern living in which the partaking of food and drink are involved. The simple eliminative reflexes likewise evolve, through the processes of learning, into culturally acceptable activity patterns.

We shall now use the term activity in a more generic sense, not with specific reference to patterns associated with a particular organ system but rather with reference to activity as a generalized function of the individual in healthy development.

The importance of optimum activity (in this sense) for the developing child is better appreciated when considered in relation to the current emphasis upon the vital role of stimulation in healthy development. Actually, it is the activity resulting from stimulation rather than stimulation per se that is so essential to the realization of inherent potentiality. Activity associated wih rest, furthermore, is an important consideration in connection with the care and nurture of growing children.

> Both activity and rest are important because of their relation to nutrition and growth. Muscular activity is important in that it improves circulation and respiration, stimulates appetite, aids digestion, improves muscle tone, thereby fostering good posture and normal elimination, lessens tensions, and increases endurance, strength, and accuracy. The amount and kind of activity satisfactory for a child depends upon his bodily strengths and weaknesses, his general physical health, and his stage of development. (Breckenridge and Vincent, 1965, p. 129)

The Importance of Proper Balance

At any age, a proper balance between activity and rest is essential to the individual's well-being. Children in their eagerness for life and experience are inclined to work their bodies constantly during their waking hours. Their need for long hours of rest, in the form of sleep, in comparison with adult need is obvious. Complete rest means complete inactivity and relaxation of the body. Since healthy children, while awake, are rarely if ever completely inactive, their rest comes largely from change in type of activity. Their relatively short span of interest and their inability, generally, to pursue a given task or maintain a particular line of activity for long are factors of advantage in their bodily economy, for their change of activity relaxes them. Children, in their early school experiences, should be helped to learn to relax and to recognize the "feel" of muscles when they are relaxed.

In the primary grades, much can be done to maintain in children an adequate balance between activity and rest through proper scheduling and management of the sequence of activities. Reading and other sedentary activities or rhythms including relaxation can be interspersed with vigorous activity such as dancing or group games. Relative proportions of time that should be spent in different kinds of activities and in activity-relaxation, of course, change with age and level of development. Furthermore, individuals differ in their need for activity and rest, as in other aspects of behavior and development. The child who has been ill or the naturally less strong and less vigorous child needs more rest and less strenuous muscular activity.

Sleep

Rest and recuperation are most complete in the condition of sleep, the natural response to fatigue. Physiologically, there is in sleep a sharp drop in body temperature and a general depression of organ activity. Blood circulation slows down. Breathing becomes more regular and its tempo is considerably reduced. Because of this general physiological slowdown, less energy is actively expended and more of it is available for growth and maturation.

Psychologically, there is in sleep a diminution or cessation of conscious activity. Munroe (1955) describes the condition as follows:

> The conscious mind is *relatively* inactive, mainly because it is released from its reality-testing functions and from immediate responsibility for the execution of its decisions. The motorium is almost entirely excluded from participation in the psychic life, the seniorium drastically limited. Thus the inward intellective and affective processes continuously operative have relatively free play without the usual corrective controls of immediate physical and social contacts. (p. 49)

Considerable learning as well as maturation are involved in the development of appropriate sleep-wakefulness patterns in children. In the neonate the pattern is subcortically controlled. Infant fatigue leads to diminution of activity and to sleep. Infant physiological needs bring about an increase in bodily activity and wakefulness. But as the cerebral cortex develops and as the experiences of living accumulate, the child's pattern begins to adapt itself to the daily periods of darkness and relative quiet followed by the light and noise of daytime. He thus gradually adjusts his schedule of sleep and wakefulness to conform to the activity timetable of society. In the words of Breckenridge and Vincent (1965):

> The process of establishing this rhythm, which is easy for some and difficult for others, will depend upon circumstances and the personality of the child. The general requirement, however, is the maintenance of regularity in the timing of the day's activities, including eating, bathing, playing, etc., initiated by the infant's physiologic clock and later tempered by reasonable adaptation of the child to his family situation and the society in which he lives. (p. 130)

This process of adaptation—of learning to regulate one's sleep and wakefulness to the social pattern—with wide individual variations, extends through the period of childhood. As Gesell and his associates point out, even during the elementary school period, bedtime is still a time when the child demands close association and confidential interaction with his parents. Such experiences apparently help the child to "release into sleep." He has not yet completely achieved for himself the ready means of going to sleep at the appropriate time, of staying asleep, and of awakening again according to the schedule of the family. Later, during the period when the child is striving to establish his sense of independence, his resistance to going to sleep is more likely to be a manifestation of his general resistance to external authority.

The amount of sleep a child needs decreases generally with age. Children of the same age have been known to vary widely in the amount of sleep they need. Such factors as health, temperament, emotional make-up, rate of growth, and the general tempo of daily activities have much to do with sleep needs.

Summary

This chapter shifted our attention from developmental change in the organism itself (structural change) to developmental change in the *functioning* of the organism. Organismic functioning is clearly a broad and inclusive topic. In fact, it relates closely to the field of psychology, since human behavior is the functioning of the human individual. Functional *development* is specifically the subject matter of developmental psychology.

SELECTED READING SUGGESTIONS

Breckenridge, Marion E., and Margaret N. Murphy. *Growth and development of the young child.* Seventh ed.; Philadelphia: Saunders, 1963. (Read Chapter 6, Physical and psychologic needs: nutrition; and Chapter 7, Eating habits; elimination.)

Breckenridge, Marion E., and E. Lee Vincent. *Child development.* Fifth ed.; Philadelphia: Saunders, 1965. (Read Chapter 4, Influences of nutrition and routines on growth.)

Harris, D. B. (ed.). *The concept of development.* Minneapolis: University of Minnesota Press, 1957. (See Part V, Nutrition.)

Munroe, Ruth L. *Schools of psychoanalytic thought.* New York: Holt, Rinehart and Winston, Inc., 1955. (Read Chapter 5, The genetic process.)

CHAPTER 5

The
Motor Functions

One of the functional areas that undergoes tremendous developmental change throughout a person's life, but particularly during infancy and early childhood, is motor, or overt, behavior. Motor behavior is primarily the functioning of the neuromuscular system. Very early in the development of the embryo, when it is less than an inch in length, complicated structural modeling is already under way. Much cell differentiation has already taken place: the brain has begun to take shape; the eye structures are emerging from the already differentiated brain and muscle tissues; the skeletal musclature is already being invaded by minute fibers from developing nerve cells, and these various differentiated structures begin to function, each according to its indigenous nature.

The very first muscular contractions arising from within the tissue itself are probably so slight as to be microscopic in extent. But soon muscle tonus and contractility come under sensory and nervous control. Muscles thus begin, almost from the beginning of their existence as such, to "practice" their contractile function. Growth and maturation of structure become interwoven with the development of function through exercise.

Involvement of the Total Person

Neuromuscular functioning does indeed involve the whole person. In the neonate, especially, the totality of his functioning, insofar as it can be observed and studied directly, is motor in nature. As the infant develops, his mental functioning cannot be distinguished as anything different from his motor behavior, if indeed it is anything different. Tests designed to appraise infant mentality are purely tests of neuromuscular functioning. They can be nothing more. Intelligence during infancy or at any other level, for that matter, can be evaluated objectively only in terms of what the individual *can do.*

Piaget (1952), in tracing the development of mentality in children, refers to the first 18 months to 24 months of life as the "sensorimotor period." During this period the child's activity becomes progressively more complicated, more controlled, and deliberate. Such behavior, of course, can be regarded in its purely motor aspects, but it can also be regarded in its mental, or cognitive, aspects. The baby's reaching for, and grasping of, an object held before him involve cognitive awareness. Such acts obviously are directed visually and with awareness and intent. The level of his mental development, however, is judged objectively in terms of the *outcome*—the quality of his motor performance.

Infant emotionality likewise can be judged only on the basis of overt behavior, and the developmental changes that occur in these areas of functioning can be inferred and traced only on the basis of what the child does.

The primary developmental task of the early months and years of a child's life is to gain control of his body and its parts. With the gradual achievement of bodily control comes control of the external environment, which means the ability to move and orient the body with reference to objects and conditions about the individual. Bodily control also makes possible the manipulation of objects—moving them about, experiencing them. The child thus perceives. He comes to know the nature of things outside himself. As control of his body is achieved, as he gains manipulative ability, he also gains a sense of adequacy and emotional control.

In later childhood and in adolescence, smoothness in bodily control and strength and skill in sports and games have far-reaching influences upon the young person's social and emotional development.

Harold Jones (1946, 1949), in studies of adolescent development, found that boys who were outstanding in strength tended also to be early maturing, taller, heavier, and of mesomorphic build. These same boys were, as a group, also high in popularity and social prestige and were rated as "well adjusted." By contrast, "the ten boys low in strength showed a pronounced tendency toward an asthenic physique, late maturing, poor health, social difficulties and lack of status, feelings of inferiority, and personal maladjustment in other areas" (1946 p. 297). Jones pointed out that relationships such as those between strength and motor ability and those between reputational and psychological variables were especially striking when extremes were compared. His earlier statistical analyses (1944) of a group of seventy-eight boys, however, portrayed the same relationship between physical ability and popularity-social esteem.

In the waning years of life, also, motor facility—habits of physical activity and manipulative skills acquired in early life—have much to do with mobility, vitality, and sense of personal adequacy (Cavan *et al.*, 1949; Lansing, 1952).

Motor Skills and Physical Fitness

The physical-fitness status of the population of the United States has become a matter of national concern. There seems to be general agreement that American children and youth do not "measure up" well on physical fitness tests, but there is lack of consensus as to how these findings are to be interpreted. McCammon and Sexton (1958) point out:

> Fitness at best is a vague concept which can only be defined in terms of the purposes for which the individual desires to be fit. . . . Fitness at the time of testing may vary markedly, dependent on the standard of measurement used. The response to conditioning programs, such as athletic participation, is a highly individual thing rather than a group or age phenomenon. . . . The expectation is unrealistic that any conditioning program applied to a general population of any age level will produce uniform response. (p. 1440)

The suggestion here is that more research, particularly of a longitudinal nature, is called for regarding the physical-fitness status of American youth. According to Govatos (1960):

It becomes evident, then, that an approach which takes cognizance of periodic measurements of a child's motor skill development in relation to size, weight, structure, speed, strength, and overall coordination is needed. . . . Furthermore, additional information in this area permits one to use the "whole child" concept and to apply it to the field of motor skill development. (p. 132)

There is no question, then, about the importance of physical fitness. Nor is there any question that the development of motor skills is still an essential aspect of development, even in a society where the trend is effortlessness and gadget living. Questions are raised only as to methods of appraising fitness level and of promoting higher levels of health and physical fitness. We shall now consider the general acquisition of motor abilities in children and the developmental factors involved.

Prenatal Beginnings of Motor Ability

Even though born with a complete lack of voluntary, consciously directed motor ability, the infant comes equipped with muscle groups that are, of themselves, strong and capable of functioning. He also possesses at birth a rather complete set of sense organs along with their essential neural connections that are structurally ready to function. This readiness is largely a product of maturation, but exercise has also been a factor. Many, perhaps all, of the muscles of the newborn infant's body have been exercised a great deal prior to birth. With this level of structural readiness and having been suddenly thrust at birth into an environment with a greatly increased range and intensity of stimulation, it is no wonder that the neonate presents a picture of mass muscular activity.

As we shall see, this congenital random activity is of real significance in relation to subsequent motor development, for it is out of the unorganized "mass" of elemental movements that the great variety of voluntary, precisely coordinated behavior patterns of later childhood and adulthood gradually are structured. It is interesting also to note that this congenital behavior, already present at birth, has a developmental history extending back to within 2 or 3 months after the time of conception. During this time, individual muscles, responding to indigenous and other sorts of stimulation, have been exercising their contractile function.

Since we tend ordinarily to think of learning that results from practice stimulated by the environment as a developmental process which begins at birth, we shall now consider in greater detail the prenatal period in relation to the development of motor behavior. What is the relative importance of learning and maturation in fetal development? What is the role of the personal environment as compared with the factor of biological inheritance?

Heredity and the Prenatal Environment

First of all, we shall reiterate the obvious fact that structure must precede the appearance of function (behavior). Sense organs and effector structures must first take form and the basic elements of the neural mechanism must establish connections between receptors and effectors before there can be any response to stimulation. The nervous system is among the first of the body tissues to begin to differentiate. (Its basic structure is already formulated before the sensory and motor organs are structured.) This qualitative development (maturation) continues, however, long after the receptors and effectors are fully functional. Progressively more intricate interconnections are established, thus providing the basis for the development of more coordinated organismic functioning.

One of the developmental mysteries not yet adequately explained is how these interconnections between receptors and effectors are made, how "the billions of embryonic nerve fibers reach their appropriate destinations in muscles, glands, receptors, and central nervous nuclei and projections" (Munn, 1955, p. 161). The important factor is that these connections *are* made, thus completing and readying the complex structures involved before motor activity can take place.

It is well known, of course, that the genes play a dominant role in not only determining but actually regulating structural development. Bits of new facts as to the exact nature and function of genes are steadily coming forth from the biochemical and genetics laboratories, but the picture, as yet, is far from complete.

From the very beginning of organismic development, the environmental factors play their part. From the very beginning, organism and environment are in interaction. In the first place, the environment must be appropriate and suitable for development or none will take place. Intercellular conditions presumably are important aspects of the early environment. Even after the first division of the fertilized ovum, each new cell in its position in relation to and its contact with the other is part of the other's environment. As further divisions occur and as the mass of cells grows, the cells in different positions in the mass become subjected to different patterns of intercellular contacts, pressures, and other influences. The regulating action of the genes in interaction with differing environmental influences causes differentiation in form and inner structure of the cells. The cells at the top of the mass give rise to the formation of the hollow ball-like structure that is the embryonic organism. Some cell masses grow more rapidly than others, and infolding and outfolding take place, giving rise to the three primary cell layers. Soon, the formation of the neural tube in the ectoderm, which will later become the central portions of the nervous system, is under way. Likewise, in the mesoderm, or middle layer, the beginnings of the skeletal and muscular structures are laid. By the end of a brief 8-week period, these structures and their interconnections have reached a stage of development where elementary functioning is possible.

ORIGINS OF MOTOR BEHAVIOR   Studies of embryos and fetuses delivered by Caesarian section have shown that by the end of the eighth week of intrauterine life the human embryo is capable of responding by muscular contraction to tactual stimuli. Histological studies also have shown that, by that time, reflex pathways between certain muscles and the fifth cranial nerve are already established. The only area responsive to light tactual stimulation at this early stage, however, is the face. These early movements have been described as "mass movements" of the trunk, arms, and legs. By the end of the third month the sensitive areas have become more extensive; tactual stimuli applied to the hands and feet bring responses that are somewhat more specific and more frequent.

During the fourth month, in addition to mass responses, a number of clear-cut reflexes can be elicited. These reflexes, according to the careful observations of Hooker (1952), "are not all in the final form they will assume, but, with the addition of a number not yet present, they lay the framework for gradual development into the reflexes of post-natal life" (p. 73). It is quite evident, then, that the neuromuscular basis for the motor behavior characteristic of the newborn is not solely a product of maturation. Much "learning" through exercise has already taken place. In a specific way, certain neuromuscular functions essential to postnatal life, such as sucking and even breathing, have actually been practiced *in utero*.

The Motor Behavior of the Newborn

Gesell and Armatruda (1941) have described the neonatal stage of development and the general character of the neonate's behavior:

> Much of the behavior of the neonate (from birth to 4 weeks) is suggestive of earlier fetal stages. The neonate is not fully

prepared for the demands of postnatal life. Hence his physiological ineptitudes. His respiration may be irregular, his temperature regulation unsteady. Peristalsis and swallowing are under precarious directional control. He startles, sneezes, or cries on slight provocation. His thresholds are low and inconstant. (p. 32)

Undifferentiated Mass Activity

The newborn infant, of course, is completely incapable of voluntarily coordinated motor responses, yet, when awake, he is the picture of muscular activity. He is active all over—kicking, wiggling, thrashing about with arms and legs—but he has no coordination or specificity of movement. This "amorphous mass of activity," because of its rapidity and nonspecificity, is difficult to observe and describe analytically. Almost any stimulus will release it, but it is largely the result of organic excitants, and, due to the immaturity of the nervous system, there is complete absence of cortical inhibition. Abrupt and intense noxious stimuli tend to produce an increase in mass activity, while mild and soothing external stimuli tend to reduce it. The important point regarding this generalized, nonreflex activity of the newborn is that the development of voluntary, coordinated motor activity common to later levels of functioning is largely an outgrowth of it.

Reflexes

In contrast to the amorphous mass activity, the newborn's reflexes are individuated and highly coordinated and specific responses. They are regulated by the spinal and subcortical nervous centers and are largely intact and functional at birth.

Of the numerous reflexes that have been observed in neonatal behavior, certain of them are vital to survival; others have protective significance. Of the former group, sucking and breathing have already been mentioned. In classifying and describing these responses, researchers have categorized them in terms of the parts of the body which produce them (Dennis, 1934). The following is a partial representative list:

1. Eyelid responses: opening and closing the eyes. Adequate stimuli for these responses, particularly for closing the eyes, are numerous—blasts of air, bright light, touching the face near the eye.

2. Pupilary responses: the size of the pupil changes in response to variations in the intensity of light to which the eyes are exposed. It has also been found that strong cutaneous stimuli also may cause widening of the pupils of the neonate's eyes.

3. Ocular reflexes: pursuit movements, coordinated compensatory eye movements. When the head is jerked quickly around, the eyes move in a compensatory direction. This has been observed in infants as early as the second day of life.

4. Facial and mouthing responses: opening and closing the mouth, sucking, grimacing, yawning, pushing objects from the mouth, frowning smiling, and so on.

5. Throat responses: crying, cooing, sobbing, sneezing, coughing, gagging, swallowing, and so on.

6. Head movements.

7. Hand and arm reflexes: closing hand, arm flexion, and so on.

8. Trunk reactions: arching the back, twisting.

9. Genital organ reflexes: cremasterec reflex (raising the testes), penis erection.

10. Foot and leg reflexes: the knee jerk and the Achilles tendon reflexes have been observed in some infants. Flexion and extension of the legs, kicking, fanning the toes in response to stroking the sole.

Numerous coordinate responses of many body parts, reflex in nature, have also been observed in very young infants. Among these are lifting the head and rear quarters, stretching, creeping, shivering and trembling, supporting body weight by grasp, and the startle response.

The Processes of Differentiation and Integration

The last category of congenital coordinate response, involving as it does many body parts and, in many instances, the total infant organism appears to constitute a class of behavior that in one respect is like mass activity in that the total organism is involved yet different in that it is coordinated. At the same time, this behavior is like the specific reflex in that it is coordinated not random; and it is unlike the simple reflex in that it is complex and widespread.

The question naturally arose among the authoritative observers as to the developmental origin of these patterns. Are they differentiations, or "individuations," from fetal mass activity or are they integrations, or coordinations, of specific reflexes that came about during fetal development? The investigators became divided on this question. Irwin (1930) took the position that since mass activity is the predominant type of prenatal behavior, coordinated patterns—simple and complex—are individuations from the matrix of primitive mass activity. Dennis (1932) and Gilmer (1933), on the other hand, maintained that the observed complex coordinated patterns are prenatal integrations of simple response units.

The truth of the matter seems to be that both differentiation and integration are involved in motor development. Some adaptive responses are differentiations from undifferentiated activity and some are integrations of simple, specific reflexes. Both of these processes, furthermore, continue throughout the developmental period. Piaget's (1952) epigenetic account of mental development emphasizes the integrative aspect of the process. He described each stage of development during the sensorimotor period as growing out of the preceding stage through a continuing process of coordination. Piaget charactized his second stage, the stage of primary circular reactions, for example, as the progressive coordination and assimilation of congenital schemata to form motor habits and perceptions. His concept of assimilation and accommodation in development implies both coordination of specifics and differentiation. During infancy, motor development can be seen as a combination of these two developmental processes. In the neonate, reflex activity has already reached the stage of almost complete individuation. We have already noted the many discrete reflexes that comprise the neonate's behavioral repertoire. As development continues, these reflexes become integrated and coordinated into effective patterns of behavior. At the same time, individuation of the nonreflex mass activity is underway. These differentiated patterns will eventually come under cortical (voluntary) control, and, as learning continues, these patterns become functionally interconnected and coordinated.

Motor Development during Infancy

The brief neonatal period is the time when the infant recovers from the effects of the sudden and radical environmental change he had to survive at birth. As these adjustments are made, developments get under way at an accelerated rate. Maturation and the exercise of neuromuscular structures, as we have already noted, give rise to more and more highly individuated and coordinated functional patterns. Although he continues to be profoundly dependent, the human infant nevertheless makes rapid progress in the development of a number of motor functions.

There are two rather complex functional areas that may be regarded as special motor "developmental tasks" of infancy. They are developmental tasks in the sense that they must be achieved by the infant if he is to live autonomously and to function as a normal human being. These are *manipulability*—the ability to reach with the hand, grasp, and manipulate objects in the external environment —and *upright locomotion*. First, let us consider the development of reaching-prehensile ability.

The Reaching-Prehensile Pattern

The prehensile function is a voluntary motor pattern quite distinct from the grasp reflex. The grasp reflex is present in the unborn fetus and is quite strong in infants during the first month or so of life. The only connection between the grasp reflex and prehension is that some of the same muscles are involved in both, and, in a sense, the muscular exercise from the grasp reflex prepares (strengthens) the structures involved in prehensile behavior. In the much more complex reaching-prehensile pattern, visual stimuli, as well as tactual, are involved. Prehensile behavior is a permanent motor function, and it soon comes under voluntary control.

As the prehensile function develops eye-hand coordinations become essential. Visually guided reaching, the portion of the total pattern preliminary to actually grasping the object, of course, becomes possible through the maturation and the exercise of the visual mechanism for space perception as well as the neuromuscular structures involved in reaching.

One of the most thorough earlier students of the reaching-prehensile function in infants was Myrtle McGraw (1943). Her insight into the nature of the prehensile pattern and of the physical structures involved is revealed in the following excerpt:

> From inception this function calls for the coordination of visual and motor mechanisms. Object vision reflects functioning of the striate area. As stated earlier there is sound reason to doubt that the newborn infant is capable of object vision. The optic nerve tracts and pathways are not myelinated at the time of birth, and Conel has pointed out that the motor area in the precentral gyrus is more advanced than is the striate area in the occipital lobe. Even during the first month of postnatal life there is not much gain in structural development of the striate area as indicated by any of the criteria for evaluating such development. Both structurally and functionally it is reasonable to assume that *object* vision is not a part of the neonate's be-

havior repertoire. Since from the onset reaching-prehensile behavior requires the collaboration of visual and motor mechanisms, the criteria used in appraising the development of this function were formulated in terms of this relationship. (p. 94)

With such criteria in mind, McGraw, in her study of the complete reaching-prehensile pattern, identified five phases in its development.

INFANT VISION   At the time McGraw made her observations, it was generally believed by students of infant vision (from the evidence at hand) that the very young infant does not yet possess the power of accommodation and convergence of the eyes, that he is unable to focus clear retinal images of objects at varying distances. Hence "object vision" would not be possible for him, even though he may appear to fixate an object held in his lines of vision. More recent studies (Fantz, 1962; Gorman *et al.*, 1957), however,

. . . give behavioral evidence that the neonatal infant in spite of being hyperopic, can focus sharply enough at a very short distance to resolve a near-threshold pattern, thus implying considerable power of accommodation. This is in agreement with anatomical and ophthalmological information [Mann, 1950; Peiper, 1949] suggesting that the optical system of the eye is functional at birth. (Fantz, 1962, p. 911)

In a later investigation Fantz (1963) studied the visual responses of eighteen neonates ranging in age from 10 hours to 5 days. These younger babies also exhibited a visual-discrimination ability in the sense that they showed a "preference" for simple, black-and-white-striped patterns over plain-colored surfaces. Fantz, however, seems to have been a bit overenthusiastic about the cognitive abilities of infants when he interpreted this simple sensory preference to indicate "an innate ability to perceive form" (p. 296).

Granting that the infant, even at birth, possesses some power of accommodation and that he is capable of a level of visual acuity sufficient to react differentially to patterns in his visual field, he may still be completely incapable of object vision, or perception, in the sense of awareness of the properties of objects and situations. There is no clear evidence that the neonate possesses this level of cognitive ability. Object vision in this sense, of course, is an essential prerequisite to the deliberate reaching-prehensile pattern with which we are here concerned.

THE EARLY DEVELOPMENT OF REACHING   Gesell and Armatruda (1941) in their study of the development of prehension emphasized the importance of another motor pattern, the congenital postural reflexes, as follows:

> Prehension emerges out of posture. It involves a focalization of posture and a coordination of eyes and hands. The tonic neck reflex (t-n-r) attitude which is one of the most conspicuous behavior patterns throughout the first 12 post-natal weeks almost literally paves the way for prehension. During much of his waking life the 4-week-old infant lies in this attitude which resembles a fencing stance—his head rotated to one side, the other tonically fixed at the shoulder. This attitude promotes and channelizes visual fixation on his extended hand. By gradual stages it leads to hand inspection, to active approach upon an object, and to manipulation of the object. (pp. 32–33)

The tonic neck reflex was also regarded as an important factor in the development of the reaching response by White *et al.* (1964). This study was concerned with the stages in reaching behavior that appear during the first 6 months of life. The subjects of the study were thirty-four infants, born and reared in an institution. All were physically normal and had acceptable medical histories. A uniform pretest and testing procedure was followed. Each infant was observed daily in an especially arranged crib, the surroundings remaining constant. First, a 10-minute observation (pretest) of spontaneous activity was made, followed by a 10-minute standardized test session. A stimulus object was especially selected to elicit attention and reaching behavior. With this procedure, these investigators "found that under our test conditions infants exhibit a relatively orderly developmental sequence which culminates in visually-directed reaching" at the end of the first 5 months of life. On the basis of frequency analysis of their data, the investigators described spontaneous behaviors exhibited during the 10-minute pretest and characteristic test responses for each half-month interval throughout the 5-month period.

During the first 2 months especially, the tonic neck reflex characterized the infants' pretest behavior. This appeared to be significant in that the infants tended to fixate and to regard the extended hand in this reflex position.

As to the question of fixation and accommodation during the early period ($1\frac{1}{2}$ to 2 months), according to these investigators:

> Retinoscopic studies indicate that infants have not yet developed flexible accommodative capacities at this age: their focal distance when attending to stimuli between 6 and 16 inches appears to be fixed at about 9 inches. Visual stimuli closer than 7 inches are rarely fixated. (White *et al.*, 1964, p. 354)

In the series of brief descriptions at half-month intervals, there was evidence of a gradual development of fixation and an emergence of hand movements in the direction of the object that gradually became more positively directed. Figure 5.1 shows the sequence of stages in the development of reaching as observed in these infants.

CHRONOLOGY OF RESPONSES

RESPONSE	OBSERVED IN[a]	N[a]	MEDIAN AND RANGE OF DATES OF FIRST OCCURRENCE

RESPONSE	OBSERVED IN[a]	N[a]
Swipes at object	13	13
Unilateral hand raising	15	15
Both hands raised	16	18
Alternating glances (hand and object)	18	19
Hands to midline and clasp	15	15
One hand raised with alternating glances, other hand to midline clutching dress	11	19
Torso oriented toward object	15	18
Hands to midline and clasp and oriented toward object	14	19
Piaget-type reach	12	18
Top level reach	14	14

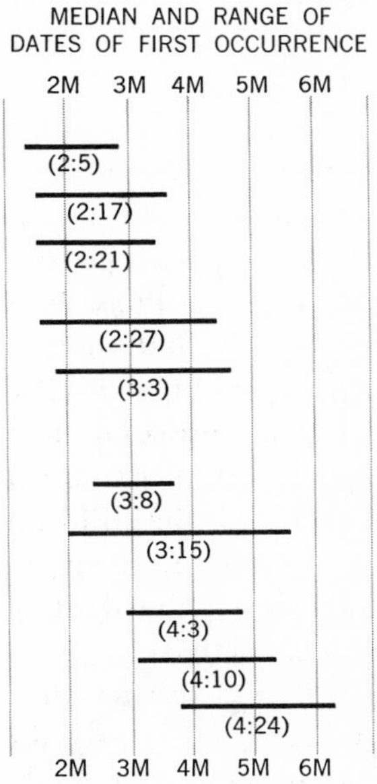

a The columns "Observed In" and "N" indicate that some of the responses were not shown by all the infants.

Figure 5.1

The chronology of ten response patterns related to the development of reaching, seen most consistently in a group of thirty-four infants during their first 6 months of life. From White et al. (1964), p. 357, by permission.

THE TOTAL REACHING-PREHENSILE-MANIPULATION PATTERN As was stated earlier, our interest is in the individual's development of the capacity to manipulate creatively with his hands the material aspects of his world. McGraw carefully observed that as the child acquires this ability he passes through five developmental phases.

The earliest of these phases (Phase A) is particularly characteristic of the neonatal period and it extends roughly through the first 4 weeks to 8 weeks of the baby's life. It is marked particularly by a lack of visual perceptual awareness of objects as such. During this period, of course, the infant will close his fingers over an object when it is brought in contact with the palm of his hand (the grasp reflex); but there is, in such grasping, no connection between seeing the object and the neuromuscular movements induced.

According to McGraw's observations, however, at about the end of the second month there is a noticeable change in the infant's visual behavior. He begins unmistakably to give attention to objects held within his near visual range. He now clearly fixes his gaze on an object. McGraw regarded this stage as the beginning of object vision. More recent work, as we have already indicated, has shown quite clearly that infants almost from birth can fixate patterns. Such "pattern vision," however, becomes progressively more acute during the first 6 months (Fantz, 1962). Also, according to these findings there is a rather marked increase in pattern-vision acuity at about the end of the second month, which corresponds roughly with the period when McGraw discerned the onset of object vision. This is the beginning of McGraw's Phase B. The infant can, without doubt, fixate and regard the object, but there is no distinct neuromuscular movement in the direction of the visual stimulus. However, McGraw did observe changes in neuromuscular activity, which characterized this onset phase of object vision. At its very beginning, diffuse movements were observed to abate as the child intently regarded the object. Later on, but before the inception of any distinct muscular movement in the direction of the object, the sight of the object would usually excite disorganized diffuse activity.

It was during the interval covered by McGraw's Phase B that White *et al.* (1964) differentiated their complete sequence of stages in the development of the infant reaching pattern. This behavior, and its changes were described by McGraw simply as random and diffuse activity, stimulated by the sight of the object but not directed specifically toward it. McGraw was looking for evidence of a functional connection between the sight of the object and specific arm movements in its direction as the indicator of the onset of a new phase.

Evidence of a new phase (Phase C) was not evident in McGraw's observations until the babies were around 7 months of age. She observed in this phase certain behavioral qualities that indicated a functional connection between the visual and the neuromuscular mechanisms involved in reaching-prehension. As the object is brought within the infant's near field of vision, approach movements of the arms and hands are evoked as he gazes at it. However, even at this stage there are no indications of any real intent on the child's part to take possession of, or to manipulate, the object. There is as yet no total, coordinated prehensile pattern. As his hand comes in contact with the object, prehension as a motor pattern is still largely undifferentiated. There is visually directed reaching, but no actual grasping or manipulation of the object.

Phase D is identified by evidence "that the child's behavior has taken on a voluntary or deliberate quality, that it has lost the compulsive quality which characterizes Phase C. It is evident that the child must give undivided attention to the performance" (McGraw, 1943, p. 97). The whole performance of reaching, grasping, and manipulating the object is given sustained concentration of attention; there is a deliberate quality about the movements involved.

With further practice and experience in grasping objects in varying sizes and shapes, the infant reaches Phase E. Now he need no longer give undivided attention to the actual reaching-grasping sequence. With one glance he may now sufficiently appraise the situation to make possible the completion of the act of taking possession of the object while glancing at other aspects of the situation. The whole performance is more precise and efficient.

In the final "mature" Phase F "both the visual and the neuromuscular aspects of the performance have been reduced to the minimum essentials required by the circumstances" (McGraw, 1943, pp. 98–99). The total operation is smooth and efficient. These phases are

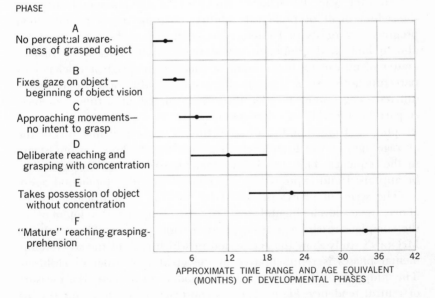

PHASE

A
No perceptual awareness of grasped object

B
Fixes gaze on object — beginning of object vision

C
Approaching movements— no intent to grasp

D
Deliberate reaching and grasping with concentration

E
Takes possession of object without concentration

F
"Mature" reaching-grasping-prehension

6   12   18   24   30   36   42
APPROXIMATE TIME RANGE AND AGE EQUIVALENT
(MONTHS) OF DEVELOPMENTAL PHASES

Figure 5.2

The chronology of phases (McGraw) in the development of the reaching-grasping-manipulative response pattern.

summarized in Figure 5.2, which represents McGraw's sequence in its time relationships.

It should be pointed out that in her full account of this developmental sequence, McGraw stressed the fact of continuity. Each phase, even though characterized by new and different qualities and features, is actually in a period of constant gradual change, merging gradually into the next phase in order. Development, in both its structural and functional aspects, is continuous and unbroken, even though qualitatively different stages or phases following each other in definite sequences may be identified.

THE ASSESSMENT OF STATUS AND PROGRESS IN PREHENSILE DEVELOPMENT   As is true of other areas of development, change that eventuates in the perfected pattern of reaching-prehension is both quantitative and qualitative in nature. For example, when true visual "following," with effective convergence and accommodation of the eyes, is established, these features continue to change in the direction of *more* precision. Eye-hand coordinations become speedier, more efficient. Such changes are quantitative in nature. Some of them, at least, are subject to standardized measurement, perhaps in units of time, and of objective efficiency.

However, when the achievement of a total developmental task, like the achievement of prehensile ability, is to be assessed, and when progress toward its perfection is to be traced, it becomes necessary also to look at development qualitatively. It becomes more than a matter of measuring the amount of increase in speed or efficiency of part functions. As is true in the case of maturation, qualitatively different stages must be identified and ordered in a time sequence. A particular child's developmental status at a particular time, and his progress from time to time, can then be appraised in terms of the average ages at which children in general reach those various stages in the sequence. Functional development, like maturation, can thus be appraised and expressed as age equivalents (developmental ages).

The series of phases described by McGraw, and briefly outlined above, is a developmental sequence covering the development of the complete reaching-grasping-manipulation pattern. The results of McGraw's study show the age period in which each of the six developmental phases is representative of the greatest number of children. The midpoint of this age period (the mode) in each case, is a measure of central tendency. Figure 5.3 was constructed as a form for tracing progress in terms of this sequence.

The appraisal of a child's developmental status in this function in terms of McGraw's criteria would of course require careful testing and observation, following the procedure used in her study (1941).

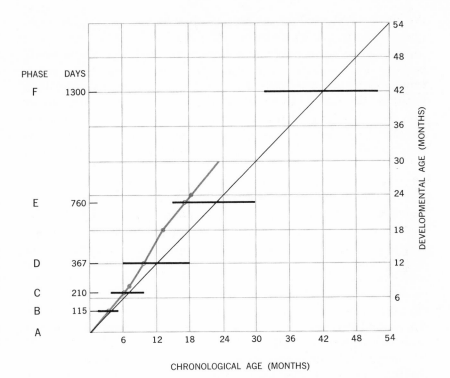

CHRONOLOGICAL AGE (MONTHS)

Figure 5.3

The course of Sally's prehensile development estimated from her performances on the relevant items of the Gesell Developmental Schedules. The dots in this curve show the developmental-age level of the child's performance at the three chronological ages indicated on the horizontal scale (7 months, 13 months, and 18 months). Horizontal lines are drawn at the mean age levels of McGraw's sequence of phases of prehensile development. The length of the line in each case represents roughly the age range during which that phase generally prevails. The point on each of these lines marked with a cross (x) indicates Sally's estimated prehensile age (McGraw) at the time the Gesell test was administered.

As was stated earlier, no such procedure was followed in the study of our subjects, Paul and Sally. The Gesell Developmental Schedules, however, were administered to them periodically. A number of items in these schedules involve eye-hand coordinated reaching, grasping, and manipulation of test materials. Each of these test items Gesell, of course, assigned to a particular age level in the Schedules.

In order to equate Sally's manipulative behavior on the Gesell Schedules roughly with McGraw's phases in prehensile development, the age equivalents of Sally's various performances on the relevant items of the Gesell Schedules are plotted in Figure 5.3. The dots on Sally's prehension-age curve in each case represent the age level of her performance at the time the Schedule was administered. The point at which her curve crosses each of the McGraw-phase developmental-age lines may be taken as an approximation of Sally's status with respect to McGraw's criteria of reaching-prehension at the chronological age indicated. For example, the Gesell Schedules were administered to Sally when she was 7 months old, and again when she was 13 months old. The average performance levels (Gesell standards) that she achieved were 8 months and 18 months, respectively. The line connecting those two points in the graph crosses the age-equivalent line for Phase D (McGraw) at a point corresponding to chronological age 9½ months. Thus Sally, at 9½ months of age, had an estimated prehension age of 367 days, or approximately 12 months according to McGraw's criteria.

Locomotor Development

The second developmental task of the human infant is the achievement of the ability to walk upright. This type of locomotor functioning, of course, facilitates visual exploration and completely frees the hands for manual exploration and manipulation, both of which are so very important in the total psychological development of the individual.

More attention has been given by parents to the achievement of erect walking in children than to any other motor activity. Learning to walk is regarded as an important milestone in the baby's development. For the child, it is a big step toward independence.

The roots of locomotor ability, in a sense, are found in the prenatal period. As we have seen, the individual muscles of the trunk and limbs, those involved in bipedal locomotion, are exercised in a random, nonspecific way even prior to birth. But the real developmental task— the individuation of specific neuromuscular units for specific functions —and the coordination of these many units into the complex, voluntary acts of balancing in the upright position, bending, turning, stooping, and of taking progressive steps are a major accomplishment of the first 12 months to 15 months of postnatal life.

Many investigators, working in their respective fields of embryology, developmental anatomy, neurology, and behavior have contributed to the understanding of this area of functional development. A number of observational studies of the activity sequence itself have been made in which stages (phases) in achievement have been identified and described.

Quadrupedal Locomotion

Various modes of infant locomotion develop in many children as intermediate means of reaching their objectives. Crawling and creeping have been analyzed by a number of careful observers with the purpose of identifying phases in the developmental sequence. Ames (1937), for example, described fourteen stages in the development of "prone progression." Her results were based on an analysis of motion pictures of this activity in twenty infants. She was able to note the time of onset of each stage and to establish a median age at which it appeared. These stages ranged from one in which the infant characteristically brought one knee and thigh forward in complete ineffectiveness (median age 28 weeks) to rather efficient quadrupedal progression, or creeping on hands and feet, the final stage (median age 49 weeks).

A few years later, McGraw (1943) published her observations of the same function in eighty-two infants. She identified nine phases. McGraw's first phase occurs some 100 days earlier than the first stage described by Ames. McGraw's observations (see **Figure 5.4**) began with the responses of the young infant placed in the prone position; both arms and legs are flexed and his face rests on the floor in complete helplessness. This phase usually subsides by about age 14 weeks and is replaced by the second phase in which the baby could hold his head off the floor for a period of time instead of simply bobbing his head up and down. This phase, McGraw felt, suggests the beginning of cortical control over posture and movement. The final phase of the sequence, begins at about 29 weeks of age, and is marked by the child's ability to creep on all fours in a rather smooth integrated fashion. According to McGraw, this series of developmental phases reflects development of control over the skeletal muscles by the cerebral cortex.

There is, of course, a lack of correspondence in the sequences described in these two studies. Other observers have presented still different formulations. Burnside (1927), for example, who also made his formulations from motion pictures a decade earlier described only three stages. These he called crawling (or prone progression with the abdomen resting on the floor), hitching, and creeping (or forward movement on hands and knees or hands and feet).

Bipedal Locomotion

The development of erect walking involves a series of qualitative changes marked by signal points along its course. The reader will recall that Chapter 3 introduced the concept of the maturity indicator,

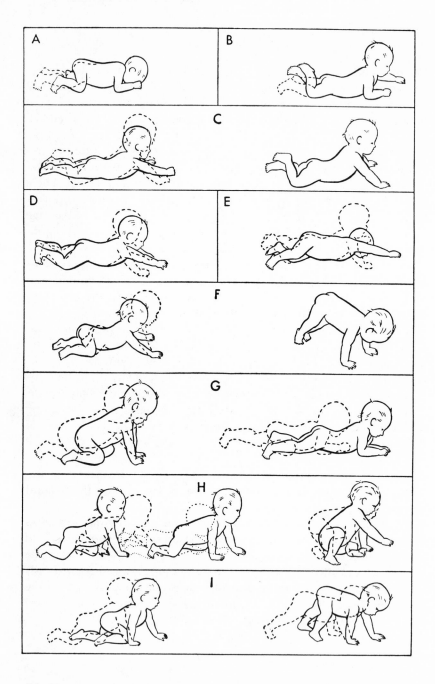

Figure 5.4

    Phases in the development of prone progression. From McGraw (1943), p. 51, by permission.

a signal point—a stage—in the sense of a new structural feature or a new pattern of performance as in the case of the development of a particular function. The development of upright walking, of course, involves the serial appearance of stages.

The sequential character of the development of walking has long been noted and described (McGraw, 1943). It is quite obvious that before a baby can get himself into a sitting position he must first achieve the ability to turn from the prone lying position to the supine position. Likewise, he must be in a standing position before he can take steps. In general, however, the findings have been that, with help from others and with the use of chairs and other pieces of furniture to pull themselves to standing positions, many babies are able to take steps alone before they can arise to their feet from the floor unaided. In other words, because of the help of others, both directly and in their encouragement of the baby's use of environmental objects, a locomotor developmental sequence that is maturationally fixed and that thus meets the criterion of universality is not to be found.

Students of locomotion, nevertheless, are generally agreed that the development of the walking function is based upon an underlying maturational sequence. McGraw, for example, relates this functional development directly to the maturation of the neuromuscular system and particularly to the progressive assumption of control by the cerebral cortex of the brain, thus emphasizing the relatively fixed sequential nature of walking development. Ames (1937), Shirley (1931), and others also have stressed the relative stability of the locomotor sequence as evidence for the idea that the *capacity* for the achievement of walking is a function of maturation.

A SEQUENCE OF PROGRESS INDICATORS Recognizing the tremendously variable effects of the environment upon the course of walking achievement, it seemed important, therefore, to look for broad functional stages that are relatively dependent upon structural maturation for their unaided performance. In that search, the lists of stages that have been described by the various investigators of the walking function were examined. The following four broad part-functions seemed, in a general way, to meet our criteria:

    I. Roll-over from supine to prone
   II. Independent sit-up
  III. Independent stand
  IV. Independent walk (on a level plane)

Babies are commonly observed quite early in infancy to perform the roll-over rather independently of help or encouragement from others. Likewise, even though they are frequently placed by others in a sitting position and are helped in their own efforts to sit up, they do gain the ability to sit up independently and later to arise unaided to their feet and to walk independently.

In order to make a preliminary test of this sequence and to identify any regular developmental phases that might appear in the course of the establishment of these stages, an investigation was conducted which involved the participation of more than a hundred mothers of young babies. These mothers were asked to keep records of the motor development of their babies on a specially prepared, illustrated record form.

An analysis of the data bearing on the four stages clearly suggested that as the child achieves and perfects each indicator stage four rather distinct phases can be noted and described in his behavior. A generalized description of these phases follows:

> **A.** Attempting: The child shows signs of readiness for the particular act (indicator) in behavior which suggests that he is *trying* to accomplish it. (For example, he appears to be trying to turn over from back to stomach.)
> **B.** Nodal phase: This phase is marked by the baby's *first observed success* in accomplishing the feat (for example, arising to stand unaided).
> **C.** Practicing phase: The feat is performed over and over. The pattern gradually takes on organization, but it is not as yet easily accomplished.
> **D.** Integrated phase: The pattern is now smoothly organized and easily performed, apparently without conscious direction. It has become automatized and *integrated to further purpose.* For example, the child sits up now, not as an end in itself, but in order to reach a desired object, or to pull himself to a stand.

The data also permitted the designation of approximate age equivalents (median ages) for each of the four main indicator stages and its four phases. Table 5.1 briefly describes each of these stages and phases and gives its approximate age equivalent in weeks. This tabulation provides a tentative scale for appraising upright locomotor developmental status of a child and a means of plotting the course of his development in this important function.

The achievement of Progress Indicator I, the roll-over, is described in considerable detail by McGraw as a separate and distinct pattern of neuromotor activity. McGraw also traces the development of this pattern through four phases (1943, pp. 43–48). In her description of Phases A and B, McGraw also begins with the newborn condition of

Table 5.1

Progress Indicators in the Development of Bipedal Locomotion

INDICATOR AND PHASE	AGE EXPECTED (MONTHS)
I. Roll-over from supine to prone	
A. While on back raises head as if trying to roll over	1.8
B. First success in rolling over	4.8
C. Roll-over not easy, practicing	5.5
D. Roll-over now easy, "automatic," apparently without conscious direction, in order to accomplish further purpose (reach toy, and so on)	5.8
II. Independent sit-up	
A. Pushes self up from stomach, apparently trying to sit up	2.5
B. First success in pushing self from stomach to sitting position	7.6
C. Practices sit-up over and over, not easily accomplished	7.8
D. Sit-up well organized and easily accomplished with attention apparently on some further purpose	8.3
III. Independent stand	
A. Tries to arise to feet by pulling on furniture	8.1
B. First success in independent stand	8.3
C. Apparently enjoys standing up and balancing without support	8.8
D. Stands apparently in order to try taking steps or to reach desired object	9.0
IV. Independent walk	
A. Tries to take independent steps, falls	8.8
B. First success with several independent steps	11.3
C. Persistently practices walking alone	12.5
D. Walks grown-up fashion, apparently without conscious direction *with purpose* of going somewhere or doing something	13.8

inert inability in which the "varying degrees of tension exhibited by different groups of muscles are often such that the baby may roll from a dorsal to a lateral position. . . . It seems clear that it is not part of the body rolling or righting mechanism" (p. 44). Only at the end of Phase B, according to McGraw's description does the baby actually achieve his first successful roll-over. McGraw's Phases C and D correspond quite closely to ours.

Our Indicator Stages II, III, and IV were also observed and described by McGraw and other investigators but they were placed in somewhat different contexts; for example, Figure 5.5 (taken from McGraw, 1935) portrays the baby's act of sitting up after he has accomplished the roll-over, (C1 and C2). But McGraw places this independent act as a phase in a developmental series beginning with the complete helplessness of the neonate.

PLOTTING LOCOMOTOR DEVELOPMENT   Obviously our progress-indicator scale (Table 5.1) has utility only during the first 2 or 3 years of the child's life. At any point during this early period, however,

Figure 5.5

Developmental phases in the assumption of an erect posture.
From McGraw (1935), p. 91, by permission.

careful observation of the child when free to play and to pursue his
interests, together, perhaps with a discussion of his locomotor behavior
with his mother, should provide sufficient data for assessing his status
in locomotor ability.

Figure 5.6 is a form designed for the purpose of plotting the development of erect locomotion in an individual child. The different
stages and phases (those listed in Table 5.1) are reordered in terms
of their age equivalents and are superimposed upon the developmental-

PROGRESS INDICATOR AND PHASE

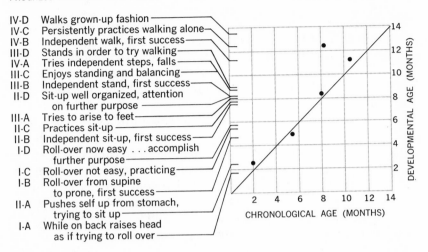

IV-D Walks grown-up fashion
IV-C Persistently practices walking alone
IV-B Independent walk, first success
III-D Stands in order to try walking
IV-A Tries independent steps, falls
III-C Enjoys standing and balancing
III-B Independent stand, first success
II-D Sit-up well organized, attention
     on further purpose
III-A Tries to arise to feet
II-C Practices sit-up
II-B Independent sit-up, first success
I-D Roll-over now easy ... accomplish
     further purpose
I-C Roll-over not easy, practicing
I-B Roll-over from supine
     to prone, first success
II-A Pushes self up from stomach,
     trying to sit up
I-A While on back raises head
     as if trying to roll over

DEVELOPMENTAL AGE (MONTHS)

CHRONOLOGICAL AGE (MONTHS)

Figure 5.6

Locomotor development of Paul 695 in terms of progress indicators outlined in Table 5.1.

age scale of the form. The five points on this scale, which we were able to identify in the record of Paul 695 are indicated in the figure. Judging from the data at hand then, locomotor development in this child was quite regular. He generally reached the various phases in the course of his development near the expected ages (median ages based on the reports of our group of mothers).

The Development of Motor Skills

As was stated early in this chapter, the two basic areas of motor development—the two major motor developmental tasks of infancy— are prehension and upright locomotion. Although these acts are commonplace and are largely taken for granted as simple accomplishments of babyhood, upon analysis each is seen as an extremely complex and variable skill. As such they represent tremendous developmental accomplishments for children so young.

These elementary patterns are, as we have seen, joint products of maturation and learning. Indigenous motivation to function is strong at each level of maturational readiness, and under ordinary environmental stimulation the various stages in the developmental sequence unfold in regular order, varying from child to child mainly in timing. Much the same over-all patterns can be followed in children generally.

Elaboration of Motor Facility

But these basic patterns constitute only the foundation for subsequent motor-skills development. Objects soon are grasped not just to be grasped but to be "handled," examined, and manipulated. New eye-hand coordinations are built upon the basic prehension pattern. Similarly, many elaborations are built upon, and into, the basic walking pattern.

At this point in development, however, greater variation among children begins to appear in the number and kinds of skills developed. Maturation now plays a less determining role. The child now learns to grasp and to manipulate the objects which his particular environment provides for him. He will soon learn to thumb through and "read" books, if they are available to him. He learns to write, to color with crayon or brush, to manipulate toys, to build with blocks, to use the typewriter or not to use it, depending upon what his environment provides and what it denies him. He learns to run, to jump, to climb, again within the limitations set by his environment and by those who care for him. A view of the activities of a nursery school play area reveals the variety of motor skills already acquired as well as wide individual differences already evident among children before elementary school age. And it is difficult to think of a single motor skill that does not bear some direct relation to either the basic prehensile function or locomotion or both.

SECONDARY SKILLS   From about 18 months of age, much of motor development consists of the acquisition of skills based upon or related to walking. Gutteridge (1939) made a rather thorough observational study of the development of these skills in children. Her purpose was "to portray the child engaged in his usual activities, under everyday conditions in school or playgrounds, without any attempt at special training or preparation, and without distracting his attention from his own pursuits" (p. 5). Her results were presented in the form of percentages of children at different ages who achieved each skill at particular defined proficiency levels.

Running, perhaps the most common of all activities developing out of walking, in the beginning "is little more than fast walking with crude, uneven steps and a general clumsiness of the entire body that leads to many falls" (Hurlock, 1964, p. 195). Like other newly acquired motor abilities, it is engaged in at first apparently because of the satisfaction the child gains from the act itself. Later it is used primarily as an instrumental activity. The child uses it to achieve some further purpose. By age 5 or 6 years, children generally can run well with relatively few falls.

Jumping also develops from exaggerated stepping into skill in propelling the body upward and forward, landing in a standing position. Gutteridge found that 42 percent of 3-year-old children jumped well and 81 percent of 5-year-olds were skillful jumpers.

Hopping on one foot is a modification of the jump. Gutteridge found that 33 percent of 4-year-olds were skillful hoppers. At age 5½ years 67 percent were rated as proficient, while 80 percent of the 6-year-olds were so rated. Again, with increasing age, hopping skill ranged from a very awkward, irregular series of jumps to a regular and precise performance.

Skipping apparently is a more difficult pattern to acquire than hopping. Only 14 percent of Gutteridge's 4-year-olds were able to skip. At age 6, however, 91 percent could skip.

Many other skills acquired during childhood, of course, involve the elaboration of basic bipedal locomotion. Riding the tricycle today is practically a universal skill among preschoolers. By age 2 years, 17 percent can ride well, and by age 4 years, 100 percent are successful according to Gutteridge's findings.

Bayley (1935) developed a scale for the measurement of motor ability in children. This scale consisted of seventy-six items arranged in order of difficulty, each with its age placement. For our particular

Table 5.2
A General Motor Developmental Sequence[a] for Paul 695, Birth to 5 Years[b]

SEQUENCE	AGE EXPECTED (MONTHS)	AGE OF ACHIEVEMENT (MONTHS)
Pulls self to feet	10	10
Stands momentarily alone	14	——
Walks alone, toddles	15	——
Walks alone well	18	17
Walks up and down stairs alone	24	18
Runs well	24	——
Walks on tiptoes	30	19
Jumps with both feet	30	31
Stands on one foot momentarily	36	19
Rides tricycle	36	——
Walks down stairs, one foot to step	48	——
Throws ball overhand	48	——
Hops on one foot	54	——
Alternate feet descending stairs	60	——

[a] *Fourteen of the seventy-six items of Bayley's scale of motor development (Bayley, 1935, p. 3).*
[b] *Paul's record did not list all of the observable items.*

purpose, we selected only those items from Bayley's scale which refer to certain of the motor skills developed by the child *after* he has achieved walking (see Table 5.2). Figure 5.7 is a form for plotting the development of these skills for an individual child (these data are for Paul 695). Bayley's age equivalents are superimposed upon the developmental-age scale of Figure 5.7.

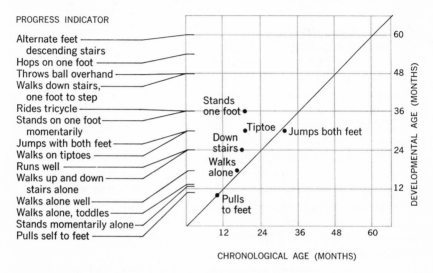

Figure 5.7

Motor development in the preschool period of Paul 695. From Bayley (1935) standards.

As might be expected, these motor progress indicators present a much more irregular pattern than do the more basic locomotor progress indicators of Figure 5.6. Secondary skills are much more closely related to experience and special environmental opportunity and encouragement than are the sequence of stages involved in upright locomotor development.

Skills of the School Years

By the time a child has reached school age, he is master of a great variety of skills, both manipulatory and locomotor. Most of the games and activities of these years involve many and various combinations, coordinations, and integrations of skills built upon the basic functions of the two pairs of limbs.

GROSS BODILY ACTIVITIES   The elementary school years are the physically active years. The child is interested in the use of his body and in the exercise of the many specific bodily coordinations and skills that he has already acquired. It is a period when toys and tools are of relatively little importance. Total bodily activities, rather than those requiring the finer muscular coordinations, are preferred. Vigorous activities are more effective in providing release of the child's abounding energy during this period: Running, jumping, climbing, swimming, bicycle riding, and "stunting" of various kinds are typical activities, varying in form and detail, of course, from culture to culture.

The element of daring is a common feature particularly in prepuberal play activities. Children during this period are concerned with little more than their status among their peers, which they enhance by achieving greater motor skills and by performing stunts and acts that require daring and courage. They challenge one another in such activities as walking high fences, climbing and swinging, performing on the high bar or the trapeze. As yet, they are not at all concerned with the general problem of achieving status as an autonomous member of adult society.

There is a steady and rapid development of the more complex gross motor skills, particularly from age 9 years to 12 years. A great variety of skills involving agility and precise, large-scale muscular coordination are features of play at these ages.

Also characteristic of the play activities of school-age children are the more formal games involving gross motor skills. Gutteridge (1939) studied the development of the skills involved in such games as baseball. She found that, although children begin practicing throwing at ages 2 or 3, it is not until they have reached 5½ or 6 years of age, that the majority (75 to 85 percent) of children can throw a ball well. Throwing a ball, of course, is a complicated act. Gesell *et al.* (1940) analyzed the process of throwing:

> Throwing involves visual localization, stance, displacement of bodily mass, reaching, release, and restoration of static equilibrium. Skill in throwing a ball requires a fine sense of static and dynamic balance, accurate timing of delivery and release, good eye-hand coordination, and appropriate functioning of the fingers, as well as the arms, trunk, head, and legs, in controlling the trajectory of the ball. (pp. 84–85)

It is during the preteen years, however, that throwing skill, along with catching, fielding, batting, and the other fine points of the game of baseball, are perfected. Team games requiring a rather high degree of motor skill constitute an important aspect of life during this period.

Girls frequently participate with the boys in certain of these games, often acquiring skills comparable to those of boys. Govatos (1959), for example, found that on the average, at 10 years of age, boys did not differ significantly from girls in such motor skills as the "jump and reach," standing broad jump, the 25-yard dash, underhand ball throw for distance, and accuracy of ball throw. Only on such tests as involved superior strength in arms and legs (soccer kick for distance, and ball throw for distance) were the boys found to be significantly superior to the girls.

It is during these preadolescent years, however, that sex cleavage generally is most pronounced. Blair and Burton (1951) describe this apparent sex antagonism:

> The apparent antagonism between boys and girls at this age is one of the most commonly observed characteristics of childhood. Parents and teachers have long recognized an inordinate amount of teasing between the sexes in the upper elementary grades as well as the almost complete exclusion of the opposite sex from the other's play groups. . . .
>
> Although this teasing and antagonism usually appears about equally reciprocal, there is some indication that it is more pronounced in boys. On the basis of her observation Zachry (1940) notes that girls of this age spend most of their time with girls of their own age. Often, however, they seem to be doing so less of choice than of necessity. If they assert that boys are horrid or nasty, their scorn does not always ring quite true. It is less convincing than the aloofness or teasing with which the young boy meets them; more often than not it is a mode of self defense or retaliation. (pp. 34–35)

Boys, nevertheless, recognize playing skill, and in spite of any tendency they may show generally to reject girls from their company, they often welcome a good girl ballplayer on their team.

FINE MOTOR COORDINATIONS   During these middle years, great strides are also made in the development of the more finely coordinated muscular skills. These middle years are the school years. The schoolroom becomes an important segment of the child's environment. It is the business of the school, among other things, to see that the child acquires some degree of proficiency in such essential skills as reading, writing, music, and the other arts.

The complicated process of learning to see objects and to discriminate fine differences, as we have seen, requires time. Reading from the printed page is a highly complex and difficult psychomotor skill which is acquired in varying degrees of proficiency during elementary school years.

The companion skill of handwriting, likewise, is acquired at many levels of proficiency. Handwriting involves a complicated pattern of learned muscular coordinations. The muscles of the shoulder and wrist develop very rapidly during the early school years, but the muscles of the fingers and hand used in writing develop more slowly. Writing is another finely coordinated skill, in which both maturational readiness and practice are important factors in its achievement. It is but one of a large repertory of finely coordinated psychomotor skills of school-age children.

Influences and Trends in Prepuberal Motor Behavior

As was stated earlier, the range of variation in the achievement of motor skills by children becomes steadily greater with age. The variable influence of the environment plays an increasingly important role in determining both the particular kinds of motor activities in which children engage and the level of proficiency that they attain.

CULTURAL DIFFERENCES The often-heard saying that children are alike the world over is true in a general sense, even with respect to the extent and nature of their motor activities. Prepubescent children, regardless of where they may be seen at play, are generally engaged in gross bodily activities—running, jumping, climbing, stunting, and the like. But the particular games they play and the specific motor behavior patterns and skills involved in their play activities may actually differ greatly from culture to culture. Skillful ice skating and the game of hockey, for example, are very common among children in certain areas of the United States, but the environment of the islands of the South Pacific does not include the essential conditions for the achievement of these specific skills. Many other common patterns of play activity in children are specific to the particular environmental conditions that surround the child's growth.

FAMILY INFLUENCES It is a common observation that children differ widely in their play interests and in the specific skills in which they become proficient, even within the environmental limitations of a particular cultural setting. Family influences, of course, are among the important factors here. To be sure, most children in an ordinary American neighborhood play ball in the vacant lot or playground or in the street, but the degree of interest in baseball and the level of baseball skill a boy develops, in many instances, depend very largely upon the father's interest and the extent of his participation in such activities as playing catch with his young children in the backyard. Skill in instrumental music most frequently develops in musical families, and mechanical skill tends to develop in families where interest and proficiency in things mechanical are aspects of the paternal model.

SEX DIFFERENCES   There is a tendency toward sex cleavage among preadolescents. During the early elementary school years, however, there is, as yet, little evidence of this antagonism. Sex differences in motor ability, in general, or interest in active muscular skills are relatively insignificant. It will be recalled that Govatos (1959), in his study of motor-skill development, observed no significant sex differences, at age 10 years, in such skills as the jump and reach, the standing broad jump, the 25-yard dash, the underhand ball throw, and accuracy of ball throw.

However, during these preadolescent years subtle changes are taking place in both boys and girls, which gradually become manifest in differences in physical strength and in motivation to excell in feats of strength and skill. In general, boys develop superiority in activities involving large muscles and those requiring strength, bodily speed, and endurance. Govatos' 12-year-old boys were significantly superior to their female counterparts in such activities. Girls, on the other hand, generally excell in the more delicate movements involving eye-hand coordination and in body balance, such as ballet dancing and fancy skating.

Associated with the development of these differences in motor skills is a gradual shift in interests common to girls in the direction of femininity and interpersonal relationships. As puberal changes take place, girls tend to lose interest in athletic activities and therefore do not practice them. It would seem to be important, from the standpoint of good health that girls be encouraged to maintain some interest in gross physical activities. Thoughtfully designed programs in physical education for adolescent girls based upon, or coordinated with, the characteristically feminine interests of that age level should have a place in the school curriculum.

The Importance of Motor Skills in Adolescence

Peer relationships during adolescence take on new significance in the life of the young person. It is very important to the boy that he be able to participate effectively in the activities of his age group. Without the appropriate motor skills for such participation the youngster may tend to withdraw and become isolated. Again, proper guidance is important. In some instances individualized help and instruction can raise a poor or mediocre performance to a level which allows the youngster to experience success and to attain social acceptance.

During the postpuberal period there is generally a marked increase in speed and accuracy of movement as well as in physical strength. Adolescence is not the "awkward age." When growth is rapid, as during the puberal growth spurt, the child might actually be unfamiliar with his own physical dimensions, and thus he may appear to be awkward as he moves about, occasionally bumping into furniture or knocking things over. Self-consciousness, which is especially characteristic of early adolescence, might also contribute to the youngster's apparent awkwardness.

In general, however, adolescence is a period of great vigor, speed, and fine muscular coordination. Agility, rather than awkwardness, generally characterizes adolescent motor behavior.

Temperament and Motor Activity

As in many other aspects of their development, Paul and Sally presented an interesting contrast in motor behavior and competence. This contrast relates back to a basic temperamental difference between them noted earlier (and examined in greater detail in Chapter 11). At various points in his developmental record, Paul is described as serious, contemplative, stable, deliberative, persistent, shy, and "a bit socially unresponsive," as compared with his vivacious, gay, friendly, charming, graceful, impulsive sister. This contrast in behavior and temperament persisted through the years of their development.

In gross bodily movements, Sally was more rapid and skillful. Paul was superior in fine muscular coordinations. As a preschooler, Paul was interested in music and liked to sing. Block building was his favorite motor activity. He designed elaborate trains and was "extremely careful in placing the blocks, being very sensitive to spacing." However, he showed interest in a wide range of play materials, particularly those that involved skillful manipulation. Although he was not as active as most 6-year-olds, he was described as "flexible" in his work with materials, showing considerable ingenuity and fine muscular control. As a school-age child in the crafts shop he "used the electric saw with confidence and accuracy far above that expected of a child of his age."

Sally, more vigorous and impulsive, delighted in the active, more social kinds of recreational activities. As a teenager she especially liked bowling, horseback riding, and swimming. Although as adolescents the twins often enjoyed some of these recreational activities together, Paul continued to spend relatively more time by himself often listening to classical music on the family record player.

As to the possible relation between Paul's constitutional nature and his preferences in motor functioning, one can only conjecture. It will be recalled, however, that his somatotype, as assessed from posed photographs by an expert, was judged to be such as not to favor Paul in competition with his peers in athletic sports. The one activity for which his particular body type was well suited was swimming. This was Paul's favorite sport.

Summary

Adequate motor performance is a tremendously important and pervasive human need. It is a source of profound satisfaction. By contrast, to be unable to *do*, or to be environmentally prevented from functioning according to the situation at hand, normally give rise to negative emotions and to ego damage. Nothing will more surely and immediately enrage a young infant, for example, than physically hampering his free bodily activity. It is the functioning process, more than the product of the activity, that is the source of human satisfaction.

Throughout the course of development beyond infancy, the child's sense of self-esteem and personal worth is largely a matter of how he views himself in terms of his motor facility and competence. And a sense of functional competence generally makes for ease and confidence in interpersonal and other social relationships.

Aside from the child's self-image his actual status in terms of others' reactions to him is largely determined by his motor competence. As we shall see in Chapter 6 the only available basis for evaluating an infant's intelligence is his motor performance. Later in his development, his motor prowess will become even more important in relation to the reactions of others toward him.

Motor functioning is completely dependent upon the maturity of the physical structures involved. Motor behavior obviously cannot appear until the structures involved have emerged within the developing organism. As a particular structure becomes established and as it reaches a point in its maturation where it is capable of performing its function, then presumably, because of its inherent nature and through stimulation mediated by neural connections, it begins to perform its function. If it is muscle tissue it begins its contractile function.

In order, then, to trace the development of motor functioning we must begin at the point where the muscle and neural tissues involved have reached the point of readiness to function, which is an early point in prenatal development. The fetus becomes "quickened." Its newly formed muscles begin to twitch. It begins to move. It is appropriate for us, therefore, to think of motor behavior as beginning its course of development through exercise months before birth.

By the time of birth two general orders of motor activity are well established: simple, specific reflexes, and uncoordinated, nonspecific mass activity. Very soon the reflexes begin to become organized and intercoordinated, and out of the mass activity are developed integrations and coordinations of muscular activity which eventually come under voluntary control.

These coordinated patterns very largely center around the functioning of the two sets of limbs, and these developments become some of the more important distinguishing characteristics of the human species. Hence, it is meaningful to identify two basic functional developmental tasks of infancy: the development of the reaching-grasping-manipulatory function of the upper limbs, and the development of erect bipedal locomotion (the basic human function of the lower limbs). From these two basic patterns of motor activity and their intercoordinations are derived the vast majority of motor activities and skills that characterize the normally functioning human being.

SELECTED READING SUGGESTIONS

Breckenridge, Marion E., and E. Lee Vincent. *Child development.* Fifth ed.; Philadelphia: Saunders, 1965. (See Chapter 8, Growth and use of motor control.)

Merry, Frieda K., and R. V. Merry. *The first two decades of life.* New York: Harper & Row, 1950. (See Chapter 5, How motor abilities develop.)

Munn, N. L. *The evolution and growth of human behavior.* Boston: Houghton Mifflin, 1955. (Read Chapter 6, Prenatal behavior; Chapter 7, Basic factors in the behavioral development of children; and Chapter 10, Motor development.)

CHAPTER 6

————————————— Cognitive
Functions: The Nature
and Development
of Intelligence

In the preceding chapter we were concerned primarily with the
development of the child's ability to function directly and overtly
in relation to his external environment. We attempted to follow the
course of this aspect of developmental change from its prenatal origins
through the relative helplessness of infancy to the smooth and efficient
performances of later adolescence. Our particular interest was in the
acquisition of the abilities to move about independently, to grasp
and manipulate manually, and to investigate and deal directly with
objects and features of the material world.

Our present concern is with a so-called higher level of functioning in relation to the environment in which the central nervous system presumably plays a more prominent role. This higher level functioning is generally referred to as cognitive activity—activity of the mind —and is in contrast to motor activity—activity of the body.

As we have noted earlier, however, this motor-mental dichotomy is rather an artificial one. Both categories involve the functioning of physical structures, but they are arbitrarily divided by the manipulative activity involved. In the one case, material objects are grasped, moved, and manipulated through the use of the physical structures of the body; in the other, symbols and ideational representations of the concrete world are centrally manipulated with relatively little involvement of gross physical structures. Thus the distinction between motor and "mental," or cognitive, is largely in the degree of overt neuromuscular activity involved. Motor activity, however, is centrally mediated and controlled, and some degree of motor functioning is usually, if not always, involved in cognitive activity.

As we have seen, the functioning of the neonate is completely neuromuscular, but with time, mental, or centrally mediated behavior, gradually emerges. Very quickly the baby begins to "know," and to cope with his environment through his motor responses to stimulation. His eyes follow a patch of color or a patterned object. He responds to the sound of another's approaching steps. He kicks and thrashes about with his arms in a random, disorganized manner thus bringing his hands in contact with objects within his reach. These he grasps, mouths, and shakes and bangs them and thus experiences them with his senses. There is no evidence, however, that in the beginning these simple sensorimotor experiences involve the awareness of the objects from which the stimulation comes.

But development is rapid. Soon, with further maturation and experience, the baby learns to differentiate objects, to respond to them *as* objects, as he sees them, grasps them, tastes them, or hears them. His motor behavior now is associated in his experience with the cognitive awareness of things and people. His behavior with respect to them becomes meaningful. All his motor manipulations become more effectively coordinated and more frequently directed toward some kind of adjustment to, or coping with, the environment. From such experiences *concepts* of objects, situations, and relationships are gradually formulated. These concepts can now be ordered and manipulated implicitly. Thus the child becomes more and more able to foresee the probable outcomes of alternate overt acts. He can try them out mentally.

The basis for differentiating between the motor activity and the cognitive activity, then, is that the latter involves, to a relatively

Figure 6.1

    An infant mentality test requiring motor performance. Courtesy
of The Merrill-Palmer Institute by Donna J. Harris.

greater degree, the functioning of the central nervous system, and so
consist, to a greater extent in the manipulation of ideational representations of objects and situations, rather than the objects and situations themselves. Implicit behavior of this sort is referred to as mental
or cognitive behavior. But the so-called motor behavior of the infant,
in a very legitimate sense, is also cognitive behavior. The infant does
reveal his mentality in a test by means of his motor performance
(see Figure 6.1).

Concepts of Intelligence

The cognitive aspect of the child's functioning continues to expand
as he develops. As he interacts with his environment, the effectiveness
of his behavior improves as central direction and control become
more and more pervasive. The term "intelligence" is generally applied
to this whole area of central functioning and its guiding and controlling influence upon behavior as the individual meets and copes
with everyday life situations.

    Because of the broadness and complexity of this aspect of the
whole of human behavior, there has always been much variation in
the usage of the term intelligence. It has been used in the very broad

sense suggested above, and it has been applied to the various narrower aspects and facets of cognitive life and activity. Historically, there are three main areas of concern about which theoretical positions have been taken and in terms of which definitions of intelligence have been formulated. These are (1) the question of the factors which determine individual differences in intelligence, (2) the question of the nature and structure of intelligence, and (3) the problem of how intelligence develops from age to age. Implicit in each of the above statements is the assumption of some sort of entity or condition that exists within the individual. Thus, intelligence is conceived of as *something* that is determined, *something* that has a nature or structure of its own, *something* that develops or changes with age.

The Determining Factors

A question that often arises is, "To what extent is intelligence genetically determined?" The answer, of course, depends upon what specifically is meant by the term intelligence.

INTELLIGENCE AS POTENTIALITY   There is, running through the text book literature on intelligence, the implication that intelligence is an inherent potentiality, a ceiling, genetically determined, above which one cannot rise developmentally. It has been referred to as "constitutional potentiality . . . and it is to be expected that this factor, popularly called general intelligence, will put a limit or ceiling upon the extent to which the other factors mentioned above can operate" (Pressey and Robinson, 1944, p. 65). In this particular sense, of course, the upper limit of possible development of intelligence is fixed by the genes at conception. This view of mentality and its development is represented in the typical mental-growth curves for individuals with different rates of increase, approaching their respective ceilings at different levels. Such individual curves are shown in Figure 6.2.

This does not mean, however, that the course of development toward that potentiality is predetermined and completely controlled genetically. Here, as in all of its other manifestations, development comes about through transaction between the organism and its environment. Should the environment be seriously lacking in proper nurturance and stimulation, development may be less than optimal. It is indeed quite probable that full potentiality for the development of mentality at any age level is rarely, if ever, reached.

INTELLIGENCE AS CAPACITY   Intelligence frequently has been defined as "the capacity to acquire and perfect new modes of adapta-

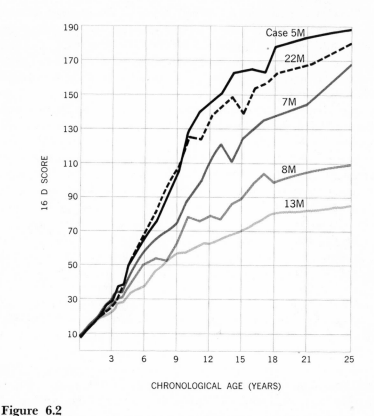

Figure 6.2

Individual curves of intelligence (16 D units) for five boys, age 1 month to 25 years. From Bayley (1955), p. 815, by permission.

tion through individual experience. . . . What makes a person intelligent is *not* what he knows or can do but is his capacity easily and quickly to acquire that knowledge or ability to do" (Dashiell, 1928, p. 306). In this sense intelligence obviously is not fixed at conception. On the contrary, it changes, increases with age as one develops within the fixed limits of inherent potential. One's mental capacity is the level of one's mental development at any particular point in his progress toward mental maturity. It is one's present aptitude for learning new patterns and modes of adjustment and functioning.

INTELLIGENCE AS ABILITY   A third common usage of the term intelligence is to refer to an individual's *present ability* to perform. Here again, the determining factors are multiple. A child's ability to perform on an intelligence test, for example, is limited by the developmental level (capacity) so far reached, but it is also limited by what he has learned. His level of performance is determined in part by past environmental opportunity, or occasion, or felt need and stimulation, to learn to perform the particular tasks and problems presented to him in the test. It is always the ability level, of course, that is observed directly in a test of intelligence. Any appraisal of mental capacity or potential, therefore, must be arrived at by inference on the basis of what the child was able (or willing) to do. Such inferences can be quite erroneous. For example, two children of the same chronological age, one growing up in a highly stimulating home environment, the other in an extremely impoverished and unstimulating home, may actually have equal endowments of intellectual potential. In terms of present mental developmental level ("capacity to acquire and perfect new modes of adaptation"), the two children could be different to some degree, depending upon the extent to which the maturational processes involved had been environmentally hampered. But the *ability* to cope with the particular tasks of the test would likely be very different in the two children due simply to unequal environmental opportunity to learn to perform such tasks. It would, however, be impossible accurately to infer equality or inequality in ultimate potentiality or even in present capacity to learn on the basis of intelligence test results alone.

All three of the above common meanings in which the word intelligence has been used represent valid views of cognitive functioning. The question, however, as to whether intelligence is fixed and determined by heredity has been, in the past, a matter of controversy (F. L. Allport, 1924; Burt *et al.*, 1934; Goodenough, 1940; Simpson, 1939; Welman, 1937, 1938). As we have seen, the answer depends upon what specific aspect of the complex area of cognitive functioning is referred to by the term. The currently prevalent view is the one so ably presented by Hunt (1961). The point of emphasis is that intellectual development, like all development, comes about through the interchange between the environment and the organism as it is at any particular point in time.

Organism-Environment Interaction

Every individual at conception, by virtue of the particular set of genes he draws, is endowed with a certain potential level, or ceiling, for the development of cognitive functioning. This potential is fixed in the same sense that his ultimate potential stature is fixed. It is obvious, furthermore, that individuals vary widely in the level of this fixed potential, from the extremely mentally deficient to the extremely richly endowed. And, even though the quality of the environment has much to do with the nearness of approach to that ceiling of development, it is unfortunate, but true, that no amount of loving nurture, no amount of pressure or coaching or environmental enrichment for those at the lower levels of potentiality can possibly close the gap between the mentally deficient and the more richly endowed. Intelligence, in the sense of original potentiality, obviously is inherited.

However, environmental accident, extreme deprivation, or other forms of interference with the developmental process might, at any point, lower an individual's potentiality for development. Brain damage at birth, for example, might bring a child's congenital mental potential to a level far below the level with which he was genetically endowed. Serious damage or interference with the development of the nervous system can also result from conditions during the prenatal period. Therapeutic irradiation of the pelvic region of expectant mothers sometimes results in microcephaly, which means serious mental retardation in the child to be born. The use of narcotics and other drugs may also have damaging effects upon the developing fetal brain. Heavy sedation during labor may profoundly affect the neonate. Excessive use of drugs "may so overload the fetal blood stream as to produce asphyxiation of the fetus at birth, with permanent brain damage of such a kind as to lead to mental impairment" (Montagu, 1963, p. 107). The postnatal potential for mental development of many children thus may be largely environmentally determined.

But the development of mentality within the limits thus determined is not a matter of heredity alone nor of environmental accident or condition alone. Mental development to whatever level it may reach in terms of capacity, or whatever level of effectiveness in functioning may be achieved at any capacity level, is a product of the interaction of the organism and its environment. This widely accepted view is well expressed by Escalona and Moriarty (1961):

> Intelligence must be viewed as an interaction phenomenon. With apologies to Piaget's and other developmental theories, we shall crudely describe intelligence as the result of a continuous stream of transactions between the organism and the surrounding field, which field is the sum total of physical and social environmental conditions. Since the organism brings to each adaptive act certain properties, both those of intrinsic biological nature and those which are the result of the impact of previous experiences upon the organism, it is correct to say that intelligence development is at all times dependent upon

what the organism is like. Yet, since it requires environmental circumstances to mobilize the organism, and since the kind of transaction which develops depends on the objective content of that to which the organism must adapt, it is equally true to say that the development of intelligence depends at all times on the experiences encountered by the growing child. (pp. 598–599)

Both the capacity level reached by the child at any particular time and the performance level (ability) are products of this interaction process. The child's cognitive facility (structure) thus expands as he meets and copes with environmental situations. But the extent and quality of that cognitive growth depends upon the nature and the content of the environmental situation with which the interchange takes place. For example, if a mother's verbal efforts to instruct or control her child are brief, perfunctory, restricted, stereotyped, and authoritarian in nature, there is little in her communication that is conducive to cognitive exercise, to reflection, to mental discrimination, or to evaluation on the child's part. He has nothing to do but to comply. The environment contributes little to his cognitive (mental) development. On the other hand, if the mother is elaborative and explanatory in her approach, if she gives reasons, suggests alternatives and their possible consequences, the interchange becomes meaningful. In the more elaborative verbal interaction, the child is stimulated to reflect, to imagine, to relate alternative behaviors to possible consequences upon others as well as himself. Clearly the "objective content to which the organism must adapt" has much to do with the quality of the individual-environment transaction that takes place, and the kind of impact it has upon the developing intelligence (Bernstein, 1961; R. D. Hess, 1964, 1965).

The "Structure" of Intellect

Theories concerning the nature, or structure, of intelligence generally have reference to mental *abilities* which are conceived of as constituting intelligence. Again, intelligence is described as if it were some sort of entity with structure and constituent parts.

The Concept of General Intelligence

The first widely accepted view among American psychologists was the concept of "general intelligence." According to this view, intelligence is unitary; all mental processes and all mentally directed activities—learning, thinking, adjusting to the environment—are functions of this single ability factor. Individual differences in the effectiveness of these various mental activities are attributed to differences in strength or amounts of general intelligence possessed.

During the thirty-five-year period when most of the currently used intelligence tests were developed, this concept of general intelligence was prevalent. William Stern (1914) formulated a definition that was representative of the thinking among psychologists of that period. "Intelligence," he wrote, "is a general capacity of an individual consciously to adjust his thinking to new requirements. It is a general mental adaptability to new problems and conditions of life" (p. 3).

Although he developed a theory known as the two-factor theory of intelligence, Charles Spearman's work (1904, 1914, 1927) did much to support the concept of general intelligence. The first and most important of his factors he called *g*. He conceived of it as a "general fund of mental energy," identified as general intelligence. In Spearman's thinking, this general factor is involved in every mental function or performance. Each specific mental function, however, also involves a second, specific factor, the individual's specific ability for that particular kind of performance.

Spearman's theory stimulated much discussion. In opposition to the idea of a general factor, a rather different view was held by an equally influential psychologist, E. L. Thorndike (1914), who saw intelligence as consisting of many specific abilities not bound together by a common factor. In his writings (Binet and Simon, 1916), Alfred Binet, the "father of intelligence testing," seemed also to share this view with Thorndike. Although Binet gave no single unified definition, he did offer a number of descriptions of the processes involved in intelligence. Intelligence, he wrote, is compounded of "judgment, common sense, initiative, the ability to adapt oneself . . . to judge well, reason well—these are essentials of intelligence" (p. 42). It would seem from these descriptions that Binet saw specific abilities in mental functioning. Nevertheless, his original test and all of its subsequent revisions clearly have been constructed on the theory that a "general fund of mental energy"—a general intelligence factor—was to be tapped into and evaluated.

Multiple Mental Abilities

As indicated above, the alternative view of the structure of intelligence was the concept of many specific abilities. Thorndike (1914), who was an outstanding early proponent of this view, wrote:

. . . the mind must be regarded not as a functional unit, nor even as a collection of a few general faculties which work irrespective of particular material, but rather as a multitude of functions each of which involves content as well as form, and so is related closely to only a few of its fellows, to the others with greater and greater degrees of remoteness. (p. 366)

It was not until some twenty years later that Thorndike's view of the nature of intelligence received substantial support from statistical research. In that interval considerable research was stimulated by Spearman's findings of the presence of a *g* factor, along with specifics (*s* factors) in mental functioning. In certain of these studies it was found that the intercorrelations between some pairs of mental tests were too high to be accounted for by their relatively low loadings of *g*. In other words, they appeared to involve a *common* factor in addition to *g*. These additional common factors came to be known as "group factors." Spearman and his coworkers came to recognize a number of group factors, such as verbal ability, numerical ability, mental speed, mechanical ability, attention, and imagination. Concurrently, other analytical (statistical) procedures designed to bring out the group factors in a battery of tests were being experimented with. As a result, some new methods of factor analysis were devised (Hotelling, 1933; Kelley, 1935; Thurstone, 1935), and the research concerning the structure of intelligence was greatly augmented.

In 1938 Thurstone reported a study in which he applied his own technique to the analysis of the relationships among fifty-seven tests that had been designed to measure general intelligence. The data for his study were the scores of 240 university students. Before the advent of the electronic computer a factor analysis involving fifty-seven variables was a tremendous task. The analysis resulted in thirteen factors. In his effort to interpret these factors, the last four of the thirteen were discarded as having no significant psychological meaning. Thurstone's tentative designations of the nine meaningful factors were spatial, perceptual, numerical, verbal relations, memory, word fluency, induction, restriction, and deduction.

In a later study Thurstone and Thurstone (1941) extended the search for "primary" mental abilities downward to younger ages. On the basis of this study the Thurstones concluded that the following six factors met their criteria of primary abilities:

V   verbal comprehension
W   word fluency
S   space

N   number relations
M   memory
I   induction

Thus, "general intelligence" was found to consist of at least six mental abilities. However, in an evaluation of these findings, Stoddard (1943) stated:

> None of these factors is considered as fixed, indivisible, or non-combining; each one is dependent for its validity on the nature of the tests and the population examined. But each primary ability behaves as a functional unit that is strongly present in some tests and almost completely absent in many others. (p. 165)

A Three-Dimensional Model of Mentality

Among other investigators using the multiple-factor-analysis approach to the problem of discovering and identifying the components of intelligence are R. B. Cattell (1957) and Guilford (1956, 1957, 1958b, 1959). Guilford and his coworkers, especially in connection with their aptitudes project, have concentrated particularly on the study of cognitive and thinking abilities. According to Guilford, "the most significant outcome (of the project) has been the development of a unified theory of human intellect, which organizes the known, unique or primary intellectual abilities into a single system called the 'structure of intellect' " (1959, p. 469).

This system (the three-dimensional model is shown in Figure 6.3) makes room for a large number of factors, each representing a distinct ability. These various ability factors are identified and ordered in terms of three sets of classification categories. One of these bases of classification is a set of categories of mental operations. These categories are *cognition, memory, divergent thinking, convergent thinking,* and *evaluation.* In Guilford's conceptualization, these categories constitute the basic kinds of mental processes, or *operations,* of the intellect.

The second set of classification categories is concerned with the kinds of content involved in the intellectual operations. In terms of an intelligence test, the actual material—the objects, the tasks, and problems which compose the test—would be *content.* Mental tests ordinarily contain four kinds of content as follows: *figural content,* concrete objects actually set before the child; *symbolic content,* com-

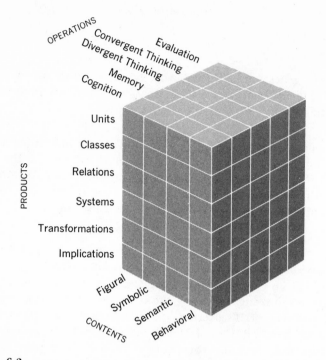

Figure 6.3

Guilford's theoretical model for the complete structure of intellect.

posed of letters, digits, and other conventional signs which are usually organized into systems, such as the alphabet or the number system; *semantic content,* in the form of verbal meaning—ideas and concepts; and *behavioral content,* representing the area of interpersonal relationships sometimes called social intelligence.

The third classification is in terms of the outcomes, or *products,* of the various operations as they are applied to any of the four kinds of content. Again, in terms of the test situation, the products are what the child "makes of," or does with, the material with which he is confronted. Guilford's words may be helpful here:

> When a certain operation is applied to a certain kind of content, as many as six general kinds of products may be involved. There is enough evidence available to suggest that, regardless of the combinations of operations and content the same six kinds of products are: units, classes, relations, systems, transformations and implications. So far as we have determined from factor

analysis, these are the only kinds of products that we can know. As such, they may serve as basic classes into which one might fit all kinds of information psychologically. (1959, p. 470)

In the simplest possible test situation, a set of small wooden cubes (figural content) is placed before the baby. He looks at and grasps one of the cubes, thus becoming aware of it (cognitive operation) as a single, unitary object (a unit). Or, he may become aware of it as one of a group of similar objects and begin to manipulate others with it in the same way. In this case the product of his cognitive operation in relation to simple figural content would be a *class*. An example at the other end of the complexity continuum in mental functioning in terms of operation, content, and product would be the *evaluation of behavioral implications*.

To summarize Guilford's view, the structure of the adult intellect is represented as a solid, three-dimensional figure (see Figure 6.3), the dimensions of which are the three sets of classification categories —the operations, the content, and the products. This conceptualization makes room for 120 separate factors of intelligence, many of which have already been identified and measured. By slicing the model into vertical layers in terms of the five categories of operations, we have five sets of twenty-four small cubes each. Each of these five sets, then, would represent a particular type of mental ability. Thus, there are cognitive abilities, memory abilities, convergent thinking abilities, divergent (creative) thinking abilities, and evaluative, or judgmental, abilities. According to the model, each of the twenty-four cognitive abilities, for example, is an ability to be aware of and deal with a particular kind of material, such as symbolic content. The outcome or product of that particular mental operation would then be the cognition of a symbolic unit or class or system, and so forth.

Since the early days of intelligence testing, then, we have seen an interesting shift in the nature of the prevailing notions about the structure of intelligence. As techniques of data analysis have been developed, many researchers have rejected the original view of intelligence as a unitary general ability that accounts for individual differences in any and all sorts of mental functioning in favor of a concept of greater and greater complexity. First, in addition to the *g* factor, certain specific, or group, factors were postulated to account for the observed relationships among test variables. More refined analysis, however, soon led to the notion of multiple factors, as *g* became broken down into a relatively small number of primary mental abilities. The advent of the electronic computer, of course, led to a tremendous increase in factor analytic capacity and efficiency. The current concept is of a great variety of relatively independent mental abilities. The enormous job of extracting these factors, identifying them, and testing them is under way.

The Nature of Cognitive Development

As we shall see, the nature of the constant change that takes place in cognitive functioning between birth and maturity is a problem of considerable practical import as well as intriguing theory. This is one of the areas of concern referred to early in this chapter about which there has been considerable discussion in the literature on intelligence.

The Lack of Predictive Value in Infant Tests

Many studies have been made of the relationship between the scores and ratings babies get on infant intelligence tests administered during their first year of life and the intelligence scores they obtain later as school-age children. Nancy Bayley (1933, 1940a, 1940b, 1955), an outstanding student of this problem, has been involved in the Berkeley Growth Study since its inception in 1928 and has made numerous studies of the cognitive test data of the project. She has been especially concerned with problems of testing intelligence in infancy and the early preschool period and the relation between these early test performances and scores made at later ages.

In one of her studies Bayley (1955) compared scores made by forty-five infants at ages 6, 9, and 12 months on a test consisting of thirty-one items selected from her California First-Year Scale, with mental test scores made by these same individuals at ages 16, 17, and 18 years. The thirty-one test items of the infant scale were selected for this purpose because in previous studies they had shown the highest statistical association with later test scores. However, Bayley's correlations between these two sets of scores again showed the usual lack of significant relationship. They were +.09 for the 6-months test, +.32 for the 9-months test, and +.30 at 12 months.

These findings agree essentially with other studies of this problem. The general conclusion is that it is impossible to predict from an infant's performance on a mental test what his mental functioning is likely to be when he reaches 5 or 8 or 10 years of age.

REASONS FOR LACK OF PREDICTABILITY   There are, of course, many possible reasons for this lack of predictability in infant tests. Actually, findings such as Bayley's are just what is to be expected when mental development is regarded as a process of transaction between organism and environment. When the interval between tests is short, performance on the second test depends upon interchange that was perhaps actually under way at the time of the first test. When the interval is long, however (6 months to 16 years), a great variety of transactions have taken place, bringing about changes that bear little relationship with performance on the early test. In Bayley's words, "scores may be altered by such conditions as emotional climate, cultural milieu, and environmental deprivation, on the one hand, and by developmental changes on the other" (1955, p. 806).

INDIVIDUAL IQ CHANGES AND INTERAGE CORRELATIONS   Recently, Bloom (1964) analyzed and reworked some of the results of the major longitudinal studies that have been conducted during the past two or three decades, hoping to advance the general problem of stability and change in human characteristics. His work, in part, was concerned with the lack of predictability of infant mental tests. His graphs show quite clearly that developmental changes in mentality between birth and maturity are reflected in changes in the magnitude of the correlations between IQ's at the various intervening age levels. Bloom stated that "the magnitude of the correlation between two sets of measurements is determined by the change or lack of change in the measurements of the individuals in the sample" (1964, p. 1). During the long stretch between infancy and age 18 years, for example, individual differences in measured IQ in a group of children become greatly magnified. Some of the changes would be increases, some would be decreases. Hence the expectation would be that the correlation .between the two sets of IQ's would approach zero.

A reliable means of appraising cognitive developmental potential and thus predicting future mental capacity would be of considerable practical value, for instance to adoption agencies and prospective adoptive parents. The lack of such predictive value in the available infant tests, as we have already suggested, brings into question the nature of infant mentality and of developmental change in intelligence with age.

Mental Development as Quantitative Change

That mentality grows in amount is obvious. The school child has more mental ability than he had as an infant. But to assume that this difference is nothing more than a quantitative one is quite another matter.

This assumption, which from the beginning of testing was implicit in the literature dealing with intelligence, is quite consistent with the concurrently held view of its nature and structure: intelligence is a unitary, general ability. This general ability was thought to develop according to a genetically fixed pattern, simply as a gradual increase in amount.

That the theory of quantitative mental change was more in the nature of an assumption taken for granted than a logically developed conceptualization is suggested by the fact that it is difficult to find definite statements in the writings of psychologists during the period of the early 1930s regarding the nature of infant mentality or the nature of developmental change in intelligence. The quantitative growth of intelligence was generally assumed with relatively little discussion of other possible aspects of change.

The whole intelligence testing movement, of course, was based upon the assumption of a single universal factor in which individuals differ only in the amount possessed at a particular age level and of gain in *amount* as they grow older. This theory of gradual increase implies that a *quantitative* scale, or system of quantitative units, must be available to measure intelligence.

As stated above, it is obvious that intelligence "grows" in a quantitative sense when reference is made to the child's present abilities or to his capacity to acquire new abilities, to learn, or to make new adaptations to his environment. Increase in capacity certainly is one aspect of mental development. The 10-year-old child can learn to solve more difficult problems than he could when he was 5.

But this increase in capacity, in a sense, is of a different order than other kinds of quantitative change, such as increase in physical size. There is no readily available device for directly measuring mental capacity. It is not possible, therefore, to construct a precise mental growth curve for an individual child in terms of standard measuring units comparable to the growth curves shown in Chapter 2 (Figures 2.2, 2.3, and 2.4), which traced growth in stature as increase in inches from time to time.

THE GENERAL COURSE OF MENTAL GROWTH   Investigators of mental development, however, have given the problem of measuring units considerable attention. A number of methods for providing standardized units have been proposed. The best known and most widely used method is to express the different levels of test performance in terms of age equivalents, or mental ages. A mental age, it will be recalled, is a developmental age. A developmental age in quantitative measurement is simply the specific chronological age of a child whose average developmental status (height, weight, performance on a test) is at a certain level. For example, a child whose tested mental age is 10 years has performed on the test at the *average* level of performance of 10-year-old children. Mental-age units thus are equated to time units.

As we have seen, developmental-age units are very useful in that progress in diverse aspects of development can be rendered comparable. But when the purpose is to study the actual course of development in a particular structure or function, such as intelligence— in which there are periods of rapid *and* relatively slow change and with gradual leveling off as adulthood is approached—then the need is for equal or absolute units of amount not equated with the passage of time.

There has been much interest in the shape of the mental-growth curve and in differences in these curves of individuals with differing mental endowment. Opinions differ as to the ages at which test performance of children with different degrees of endowment reaches its upper limit. As was pointed out by Thurstone (1925) in order to solve such problems, units for the measurement of mental growth must be devised in which equal increments of growth are represented equally in all parts of the curve. Thurstone devised a method for determining such measurement units using the statistical determination of an "absolute zero" as a starting point from which theoretically equal scale points are determined. Using this method, Thurstone plotted average mental-growth curves based upon data from various individual tests.

More recently, Bayley (1949, 1955) devised a method for transposing scores from different tests administered at different age levels into comparable units. In the use of this method each individual's scores "at all ages are expressed in terms of the 16-year standard deviations from the mean score at 16 years" (1955, p. 811). This procedure was applied to the test data of the Berkeley Growth Study. The resulting curve is shown in Figure 6.4.

It will be noted that, according to Figure 6.4, mental growth on the average is positively accelerated up to about 9 years of age at which point it begins its negative acceleration, leveling off somewhere beyond 20 years of age. This generalized curve may be taken tentatively to represent the *average* development of mental capacity.

INDIVIDUAL VARIATION   A general curve of mental growth does not tell the whole story. As in every other aspect of development every individual follows his own pattern, which differs in its details from those of others. Bayley (1949) clearly demonstrated this fact in a longitudinal study of five boys from 1 month to 25 years of age. She derived equalized units of measurement throughout by expressing

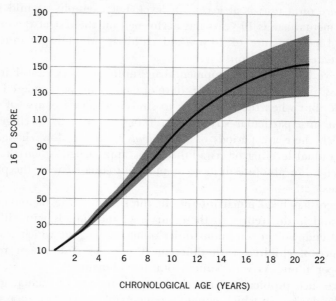

CHRONOLOGICAL AGE (YEARS)

Figure 6.4

Curves of means and SD's of intelligence by 16 D units from birth to age 21 years. From Bayley (1955), p. 811, by permission.

each test score in terms of SD units from the 16-year-old mean. Figure 6.2 shows five individual curves of mental growth (Bayley, 1955, p. 814). Note that each of these curves has something of the character of the general curve (see Figure 6.4), yet each has its unique characteristics.

INTERAGE LEVEL CORRELATIONS AND MENTAL GROWTH Bloom (1964), in studies of longitudinal data, plotted mental-growth curves in terms of increases in correlation between IQ's derived at increasing age levels below the terminal age of 17 years and the IQ's obtained at that terminal age. He assumed that individual differences in amount and direction of IQ changes in a group of children which take place between test periods become progressively smaller as the interval between becomes shorter and that the shorter the interval the more progressively increasing the correlations.

In terms of the quantitative aspect of mental development this increase in interage correlation can be viewed as an increase in closeness of relationship between a part and a whole which includes the part. The mental capacity of a child at at age 15, for example, is

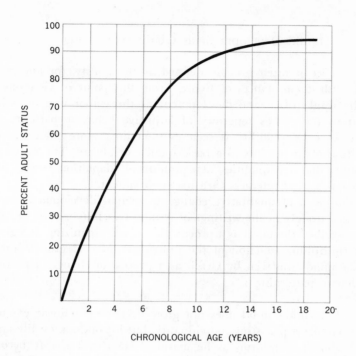

CHRONOLOGICAL AGE (YEARS)

Figure 6.5

A general curve of mental growth as suggested by Bloom (1964) and plotted in terms of percentage of adult status achieved at different ages.

greater than, but includes (overlaps with), his capacity when he was 10. The greater the overlap the higher the correlation between the two sets of measurements.

One outcome of Bloom's work was a suggested general mental-growth curve (1964, p. 68) plotted in terms of percentages of adult status achieved, on the average, by children at various age levels. Figure 6.5 shows Bloom's suggested mental-growth curve. This curve is interesting in that it can be compared directly or plotted with the well-known Scammon (1930) curves of the growth of the various types of body tissue. It is interesting to compare the mental curve to the curve of growth in neural tissue—a direct confrontation of structural and functional development.

Thus far we have been concerned primarily with quantitative change in mentality with increasing age. But there is more involved in the problem of mental development than simply tracing quantitative growth.

Mental Development as Qualitative Change

Intelligence is often broadly defined as the ability (or abilities) to cope with circumstances of living. From this point of view one naturally thinks of mental development as the elaboration or enlargement of the child's repertory of adjustive behavior patterns. This increase in adaptability is seen as something more than the mere addition of increments to a basic quality or ability. The implication is rather that *new* qualities, new patterns of adaptation, emerge as the child grows and interacts with his environment.

This idea of qualitative change in mental development was expressed strongly in the writings of Arnold Gesell (Gesell *et al.*, 1940). He described the mind as a process that is the organizing, integrating, and controlling function of the individual. Mental growth (growth of the mind) was seen by Gesell as a process of change, a process of "behavior patterning":

> The child's mind does not grow by a simple linear extension. He has a persisting individuality, but his outlook on life and on himself transforms as he matures. He is not *simply* becoming *more* "intelligent" in a narrow sense of this misused term. He alters as he grows. (Gesell *et al.*, 1940, p. 15, italics added)

Gesell identified "mind" with the functioning of the neuromuscular system and the other involved physical structures and "mental growth" with the maturation of these structures. In other words, mental development is the functional aspect of biological maturation—a process which is qualitative, as well as quantitative, in nature. A further implication to Gesell was that this process, in which environment plays only an "inflecting" and "specifying," rather than an "engendering" role, takes place under the control and within the limits of a genetically determined developmental pattern.

Piaget's Epigenetic Theory of Mental Development

Piaget's views regarding mental development were referred to in the discussion of motor development in Chapter 5. He and his associates were the first actually to formulate a theory of intellectual development in which the nature of developmental change as such was a primary concern (Piaget, 1952). Piaget views intelligence in very dynamic terms. He defines it as a process of organization, "an assimilatory activity whose functional laws are laid down as early as organic life and whose successive structures serving it as organs are elaborated by interaction between itself and the external environment" (1952, p. 359). Three essential elements in his theory are referred to in this definition. First is the idea that intelligence is not an entity, not a quantity, not a latent potentiality, but a dynamic process, an activity. Second, he indicates the nature of that process—organization and adaptation. The third point is that the process (the operation of certain invariant functional laws, assimilation and accommodation) results in many variable structures (schemata or behavior patterns) which in turn become the tools, or means, for further interaction with the environment through assimilation and accommodation.

Piaget's concept of invariant functional laws is central and essential to his theory. The functioning of *assimilation* and *accommodation* "extends that of the biological organization." These processes, in other words, are fundamental to all aspects of mental development and at all levels. In discussing these principles in their broader application, Piaget wrote:

> . . . it can be said that the living being *assimilates* to himself the whole universe, at the same time that he accommodates himself to it. . . . It is therefore permissible to conceive assimilation in a general sense as being the incorporation of any external reality whatever to one part or another, of the cycle of organization. In other words, everything that answers a need of the organism is material for assimilation, the need even being the expression of assimilatory activity as such. (pp. 407–408, italics added)

It is clear that in Piaget's thinking developmental changes in mentality from birth to maturity constitute a fixed sequence of stages, each characterized by its particular organization of structures (schemata) and thus being qualitatively different from the one from which it emerges. At the same time, there is complete continuity in the course of this development. The same invariant processes are at work from the beginning in the organization of new schemata on the basis of the older, more simple ones. He states that new schemata "whose appearance marks each stage, are always revealed as developing those of the preceding stage" (p. 384).

Both Piaget and Gesell see mental development as qualitative change, but there was considerable difference in their thinking as to the basis or explanation of that change. Gesell placed great emphasis upon the importance of the "mechanism of maturation" which brings about these qualitative changes through the natural unfoldment of a predetermined developmental design. Piaget, on the other hand, recognized the important role of the environment. Mental development for him, is not predetermined, is not solely a product of biological maturation, but is rather a result of continuous interaction (accommodation and assimilation) between the individual and his environment.

PERIODS AND STAGES IN MENTAL DEVELOPMENT   From Piaget's point of view the character and variety of environmental stimulation looms as a matter of prime importance. In the very early weeks of life the infant is incapable of direct, voluntary action on his own initiative. He can simply respond to changes and variations in his immediate environment and internal condition. Therefore, if he is to develop functionally to an optimal degree, his environment must provide changes and variation in conditions for him to cope with. As Hunt (1961) wrote:

> The more new things an infant has seen, and the more new things he has heard, the more new things he is interested in seeing and hearing; and the more variation in reality he has coped with, the greater is his capacity for coping. Such relationships derive from the conception that change in circumstances is required during the early sensorimotor stages to force the accommodative modifications in schemata and the assimilations that, in combination, constitute development. (p. 262)

Piaget (1952, 1960) traced the development of intelligence through five major periods, maintaining throughout, of course, that development is continuous and that each stage grows out of (or develops from) the preceeding one.

THE SENSORIMOTOR PERIOD   Piaget elaborated in considerable detail the earliest period, the sensorimotor period, tracing development through six stages. His description of these early stages were derived mainly from carefully recorded observations of his own three children.

This series of "organizations," which are the products as well as the tools of assimilation and accommodation, begins at birth. But at birth the organizations consist only of congenital sensorimotor schemata, and these, as they are further coordinated and elaborated, continue to characterize intelligence throughout the first 18 months or 2 years of the child's life.

The first stage of the sensorimotor period extends roughly through the first month of life. It is characterized by the exercise of the ready-made congenital schemata such as sucking, vocalizing, listening, looking, and so forth. In the very beginning, there is simply passive release of these patterns by stimulation. There is, however, during this stage, a gradual shift to an active "groping." "The subject does not remain passive but, on the contrary, manifests the behavior pattern emphasized by Jennings: He gropes and abandons himself to a series of 'trials and errors.' That is . . . the origin of intelligence" (Piaget, 1952, p. 396). The reflex thus becomes "consolidated and strengthened by virtue of its own functioning" (p. 32). It is assimilated to the child's needs and functioning. At the same time it becomes adapted (accommodated) to the realities of the situation through the groping trial-and-error process.

The second stage is characterized by the progressive coordination and assimilation of the ready-made schemata to form motor habits and perceptions. "The reflex processes are progressively integrated into cortical activity." Three main developments are recognized during this stage. (1) Variations in schemata appear as a variety of stimuli become assimilated to them. (2) A reciprocal coordination among schemata takes place, for example, hand movements, to a degree, become coordinated with sucking, and things looked at become something to be reached for and grasped. (3) Although the child is unable to respond to a "vanished object," repeated stimulation by objects leads to perceptual recognition of them. This second stage, according to Piaget's observations, extends from about the end of the first month to about age 5 months.

Stage three extends to about 8 or 9 months of age. Here again there is functional continuity between the earlier stage and the increasingly complex structures. As contrasted with the earlier stage when the baby's actions are "centered on themselves" (when he grasps for the sake of grasping), his actions in this third stage become:

> . . . centered on a result produced in the external environment, and the sole aim of the action is to maintain this result; furthermore, it is more complex, the means beginning to be differentiated from the ends, at least after the event. (Piaget, 1952, p. 157)

The child now begins to show some anticipation of the consequences of his own acts—the beginning of intentionality.

The fourth stage of the sensorimotor period is characterized by the "coordination of the secondary schemata and their application to new situations." It is during this stage (8 or 9 months to 11 or 12 months of age) that "the first actually intelligent behavior patterns" appear (p 210). Behavior patterns which heretofore were detached now become coordinated into a single, more complex act with the aim of attaining an end which is not immediately attainable or within reach. He thus put to work, *by intention*, series of single schemata now coordinated for a new purpose. In this way the child begins to exhibit behavior in which means are clearly differentiated from ends. In his new relationships with his environment the accommodation aspect of his adaptations is especially apparent as he begins to differentiate self from not-self and is able to search, to a limited degree, for the "vanished object." He also shows evidence of an implicit conception of causality, and he appears to foresee events that are independent of his own acts.

This stage four, although it evolves from and is a further development of the earlier stage, is clearly marked by features that are qualitatively different. However, as Piaget pointed out, the child is still quite limited in the effectiveness of his coping by two related conditions. First, he is limited in his ability to reach his goal through the removal of obstacles or the taking an essential intermediate step by the fact that, so far, he is able to intercoordinate and thus to utilize only *familiar* schemata. Second, and because of the first condition, he can see relationships between things in his environment only in terms of his own familiar acts in relation to them. Only the coordinations, not the acts themselves, are new, and these "do not lead to the elaboration of objects entirely independent of the actions."

The fifth stage, approximately coincidental in its beginning with the beginning of he second year of life, by contrast, "is primarily the stage of the elaboration of the object." The limitations of the previous stages now are being overcome. *New* schemata are established through a sort of experimentation involving an apparent search for new behavioral facilities. These new facilities (schemata) come about, in other words, through efforts directed with more of a purpose to seek novelty for its own sake rather than simply to practice familiar acts which produce desired results by chance, as in the earlier stage.

New relationships, new meanings in environmental objects and situations, thus become established through simple experimentation. The child lets an object, which he is holding, fall to the floor, watching intently what happens to it. He shakes objects, knocks them, listens to the sounds they make, throws them, and watches them bounce and roll. He is constantly "experimenting in order to see." In the process of experimentation there is a constant accommodation of patterns (schemata) to the situation and the assimilation of new schemata. This naturally leads to "the discovery of new means" based on the apprehension of new relationships.

Piaget refers to this type of mental activity as "inventive intelligence." In his observations, one of its earliest manifestations was what he called the "behavior pattern of the support." The pattern, based upon perceiving the relation between an object and whatever is supporting it, consists of grasping the underlying support of the object in order to draw it within reach. For example, the child grasps a cushion and draws it toward him in order to obtain a box placed upon it. A new means of obtaining a desired object is thus discovered and utilized. In the opinion of Piaget, such new means can be discovered only through this experimenting-in-order-to-see activity which is characteristic of stage five.

Much groping, trial-and-error behavior is manifest in the child's experimental attempt to obtain desired objects during this stage. Such behavior leads gradually to an appreciation in him of spacial relations and of causal and temporal sequences. This drive to active exploration and manipulation of objects makes evident the great importance during this stage of an environment rich in appropriate stimulation.

The sixth and last stage of sensorimotor, or "practical," intelligence characterizes generally the latter portion of the child's second year as the deductive or reflective level of intelligence. In discussing this stage, Piaget took pains once more to emphasize the fact that the beginning of a new stage "does not abolish in any way the behavior patterns of the preceding stages and that new behavior patterns are simply superimposed on the old ones" (1952, p. 331).

This transitional stage of mental functioning (the sixth stage), in other words, is new not in the sense that the earlier patterns disappear but rather that "they will henceforth be *completed* by behavior patterns of a new type: invention through deduction or mental combination." There is at this point an emerging awareness of relationships, and the child's mental functioning, which formerly was characterized by empirical groping, now is controlled to a greater extent by this new awareness. Awareness of relationships allows for simple mental combinations and deductions, and new means may now be "invented." This, of course, implies a rudimentary kind of representation. The child now begins to foresee which acts are likely to succeed or fail without empirically testing them.

Thus, sensorimotor intelligence lies at the source of thought. "But there is still a very long way to go from preverbal intelligence to operational thought." Sensorimotor intelligence, as we have seen, consists in coordinating successive perceptions and successive overt movements. Mental functioning is thus limited at those levels to a "succession of states. . . . but never arriving at an all-embracing representation" (Piaget, 1960, p. 120). This is one point of contrast between sensorimotor and conceptual intelligence. Ability to conceptualize frees the mental processes from the bonds of time and space which characterize perception and overt action. "Thought alone breaks away from these short distances and physical pathways. . . . This infinite expansion of spacio-temporal distance between subject and object comprises the principle innovation of conceptual intelligence" (Piaget, 1960, p. 121).

The awareness of relationships and invention through deduction or mental combination become evident. But these are mere rudiments. Generally the child must still try things out in a concrete, motor way.

PERIODS IN THE DEVELOPMENT OF MENTAL OPERATIONS   In the further development of conceptual intelligence Piaget (1960) described four additional periods. During the first of these periods the child acquires the symbolic function that makes possible the acquisition of language. This is the period of symbolic and preconceptual thought, and it grows out of the sixth stage of the sensorimotor period. Its age boundaries are roughly 1½ years to 4 years. At the beginning of this period the child can imitate certain words, and there is evidence that he attaches some meaning to them. It is usually not until the end of the second year that language development is fully under way. The child, as a rule, is already using symbols of his own in his play to represent objects while he is in the process of acquiring the use of the system of conventional signs that constitute language. The relationship between this aspect of the preconceptual period and sensorimotor intelligence is explained by Piaget (1960).

> . . . it should be noted that the acquisition of language, i.e. the system of collective signs, in the child coincides with the formation of the symbol, i.e. the systems of individual significants. In fact, we cannot properly speak of symbolic play during the sensorimotor period. . . . the true symbol appears only when an object or a gesture represents to the perceptible data. Accordingly we note the appearance, at the sixth of the stages of sensorimotor intelligence, of "symbolic schemata," i.e. schemata of action removed from their context and evoking an absent situation (e.g. pretending to sleep). But the symbol itself appears only when we have representation dissociated from subject's own action: e.g. putting a doll or a teddy-bear to bed. Now precisely at the stage at which the symbol in the strict sense appears in play, speech brings about in addition the understanding of signs. (p. 125)

This period, then, marks the beginnings of thought, the beginnings of the development of representational intelligence.

The second period in the development of conceptual intelligence (ages 4 years to 7 or 8 years) Piaget called the period of intuitive thought. The child's thinking during this period is still lacking in logical analysis. It is intuitive in the sense that it is based upon immediate, unanalyzed impressions of the objective situation. It is dominated by subjective perceptual judgments. For example, when confronted with two like glasses filled to the same level with water he will correctly observe that each contains the same amount of water. But after he has observed one of the glasses being emptied into a taller, slenderer glass, he will now say that the tall, slender glass contains more water than the other. His judgment is not a logical one based upon observed relationships and related events. It is a prelogical schematization of perceptual data, an incomplete intellectual construction. The child at this level is not aware of his own mental processes. He does not think about his own thoughts. He "acts *only* with a view toward achieving the goal; he does not ask himself why he succeeds" (Inhelder and Piaget, 1958, p. 6). Development through this intuitive period, however, leads to the threshold of operational functioning.

The third period is the period of concrete operations (7 years to 11 years). An operation in Piaget's sense, is a mental or representational process. Concrete operations are those that are concerned with "objects that can be manipulated or known through the senses." At this time the child begins to exhibit logic in his reasoning and his conclusions. For example, the child reaches a point in his development where he no longer illogically equates the amount of water in the glass with the height of the column regardless of other known relationships and observed events. He decides immediately that the amount has not changed because of the shape of the container; he is now sure that nothing has been added. He immediately infers identity. He recognizes that certain properties of objects are invariant in the face of changes in circumstances. This awareness is called "conservation."

Other concrete operations, for example, are those involved in simple arithmetic. With the acquisition of these operations the child shows an increased ability to handle number concepts. He now is able to think about parts and wholes independently of each other. He can place objects in various serial orders, and he internalizes and integrates his actions as operations.

During the final period (11 or 12 years through adolescence), reflective intelligence becomes established and perfected. The "level of formal operations marks a final differentiation between operations tied to real action and hypothetico-deductive operations concerning pure implications from propositions stated as postulates" (Piaget, 1950, p. 153). It is now that the person makes the final advance to true abstract conceptual thinking. He can create hypotheses and deduce logical conclusions.

Piaget thus portrays the development of mentality as a continuous process from birth to its final stage of adultlike functioning, identifying throughout its course a series of periods and stages that are qualitatively different each from all the others. At the same time, it being a process of continuous change, each period and each stage in the series grows out of (continues the further development of) the preceding one. In this series of qualitatively different levels (stages) is suggested a *developmental sequence* in terms of which an effective intelligence testing program might be developed.

The Assessment of Mental Status in Infants

Whether such a developmental-sequence approach would result in an infant testing procedure with *predictive* validity, of course, is a matter of conjecture. As mentioned earlier, however, many users of the infant mental scales presently available find them valuable tools, in spite of their lack of predictive power, in evaluating infant developmental status. According to a recent survey (Stott and Ball, 1965) the two of these tests most frequently used are the Cattell Infant Intelligence Test (Psyche Cattell, 1940) and the Gesell Developmental Schedules (Gesell, 1925). The latter particularly was designed to appraise the level of total functioning of the infant.

The Gesell Developmental Schedules

Over a long period of careful observation involving many infants, Gesell and his coworkers were able to assemble lists of behavior items which normally appear at different age levels from 4 months to 5 years. These items at all levels are grouped into four behavior categories: motor behavior, language behavior, adaptive behavior, and personal-social behavior. For example, the 6-months "schedule" is listed in abbreviated form by Gesell as follows (1925, p. 379):

Motor characteristics
Prefers to sit up with support
Can roll from back to stomach (or stomach to back)
Uses hands to reach, grasp, crumple, bank and splash
Opposes thumb in grasping cube

Language
Coos to music
Articulates many syllables in spontaneous vocalization
Frequently laughs at sights and sounds
Is responsive to animated facial expression

Adaptive behavior
Notices small objects like a cube on table
Picks up objects from table

Bangs spoon
Grasps dangling ring
Shows varied selective attention to environment

Personal-Social behavior
Plays actively with rattle
Expresses recognition of familiar persons
May show consciousness of strangers
Enjoys presence and playfulness of persons

Various objects—a small wooden cube, a spoon, a brightly colored plastic ring, a small pellet—are placed before the child one at a time, or in combination and according to a prescribed procedure, and his responses to these objects are carefully observed and recorded. His behavior in general—his vocalizations, smiles, startles, withdrawals—are incorporated in the record. This record, along with the mother's report of her own observations, is then evaluated in terms of established criteria and standards, and the child is given a rating on each of the four behavior categories.

Gesell took care to make clear that he did not regard his Schedules as tests of intelligence. "It is not presumed that these normative items always bear a significant relation to so-called general intelligence. They, however, always have some significance with respect to developmental status" (1925, p. 44). The extent to which they involve true mental ability, as we have seen, depends upon just what is meant by the terms "mental" and "intelligence." The level of the child's performance on these Schedules is rated separately for each of the four behavior categories. The final step in the evaluation is the assignment of a generalized developmental quotient (DQ) rather than the usual intelligence quotient (IQ).

Gesell's Schedules, even though they were never claimed by their authors to be tests of intelligence, nevertheless, are probably as valid as a measure of infant mental functioning as any other infant scale presently available.

Tracing the Course of Individual Mental Development

As stated above, the functional status ratings based upon the results of the Gesell Schedules are expressed in terms of developmental ages, and the indexes of relative rates of development are expressed as DQ's rather than IQ's. In other connections we have reviewed the nature of the developmental-age unit in graphic representations of progress. Such graphs are not true growth curves since this unit of progress does not equally represent equal increments of change in different segments of the age period covered. This method of graphing is useful, however, in making comparisons. It will serve our present purpose.

Plotting in Terms of Quantitative Measurements

Paul and Sally 695 were tested periodically during their first 2 years of life by means of the Gesell Schedules. The developmental progress of each child during that period is shown in Figure 6.6. The diagonal line in the figure, of course, represents the average or expected one-to-one relationship between chronological age and developmental age. At all ages at which these children were tested they performed at an above-average level. As is generally true with curves based upon developmental-age units, the divergence between the average, or standard-

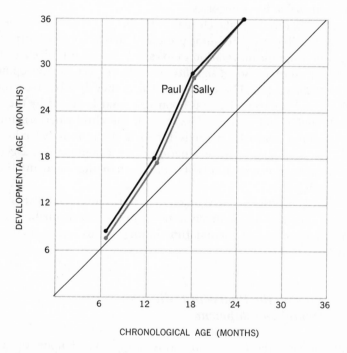

Figure 6.6

Progress in mental development of Paul and Sally 695 during their first 2 years of life.

of-reference, line and the developmental curves become greater with increase in age. This is always, in part at least, a function of the fact that the developmental-age unit registers the increment of progress in relative rather than in absolute terms.

An interesting feature of Figure 6.6 is the very close correspondence between the two curves. At each administration of the Schedule, the ratings for the two children were very similar. The extent to which this close similarity was a function of the feelings of the examiner and her need to be "impartial" in her judgments is not known.

Figure 6.7 is an extension of the curves of Figure 6.6 into early adolescence. The data for both figures are presented in Table 6.1. The developmental (mental) ages of the two children continue to be very similar at each testing. It should be pointed out that beginning with the test administered at the chronological age 3 years 2 months the Stanford-Binet scale was used. It is interesting to note the smoothness with which the curves connect at that point and continue without change in their course.

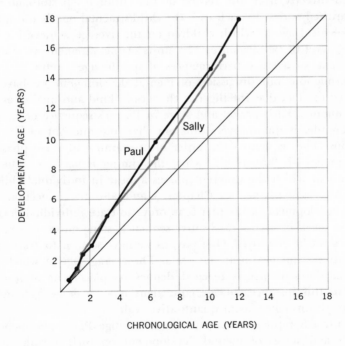

CHRONOLOGICAL AGE (YEARS)

Figure 6.7

Progress in mental development of Paul and Sally 695 from babyhood to age 12 years.

Table 6.1

Mental Test Data for Paul and Sally 695

	PAUL		SALLY	
CA	DA OR MA	DQ OR IQ	DA OR MA	DQ OR IQ
0-6.5	0–8	125	0–7.5	116
1-1	1–6	140	1–5	128
1-6	2–4	155	2–5	160
2-1	3–0	144	3–0	144
3-2	4–10	153	4–11	155
6-6	9–10	151	8–8	133
10-3	14–7	142	——	——
11-2	——	——	15–4	130
12-3	17–10	146	——	——

These curves are examples of plotting developmental change in terms of quantitative measurements. The developmental ages were derived directly from the record of the children's performances on standardized scales. In each case the child's mental age is the specific chronological age at which children on the average achieve his (our child's) level of performance. The units of measurement are the age equivalents of average performances of specific age groups.

Throughout our discussion of mental development we have emphasized the fact that intelligence changes in kind and quality as well as in amount. Each period and stage in Piaget's sequence of changes, for example, is qualitatively different than the one out of which it develops. The sequence—the order of appearance of these phases of development—is "invariant," while the timing is variable. The specific ages at which the different phases appear in individual children vary. As was explained in Chapter 3 and also in connection with motor development in Chapter 5, in order to trace individual development in terms of such a qualitative sequence, some means of quantification must be employed. One way, as we have seen, is to arrange the qualitative sequence on an age scale. The average age at which each stage in the sequence is reached defines its placement on the age scale. In this instance, an age equivalent is an average age, not an average performance, as in quantitative scales.

Figure 6.8 represents an attempt to arrange Piaget's sequence of periods and stages of mental development on such a scale of age equivalents. The lower portion of the figure covers only the first (sensorimotor) period with its six stages. Since Piaget designates in each case a period, or range of time, rather than a specific average age of appearance, these time periods are indicated on the developmental-age

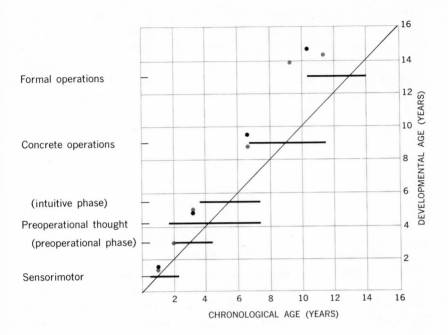

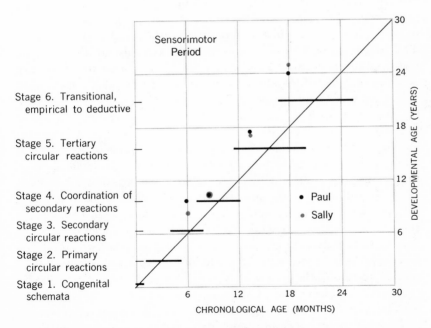

Figure 6.8

  Mental development of Paul and Sally 695 portrayed in terms
of Piaget's sequence of periods and stages.

scale, with a suggested median (average) point for each. The upper portion of the figure covers in like manner the whole course of the development of intelligence in children as conceived by Piaget.

An attempt was then made to identify in the test protocols of our subjects, Paul and Sally, signs for approximating, in each instance the achieved stage or period in Piaget's sequence. Only rough approximations were possible, since the test scales and their items were not conceived in terms of this sequence and the behavioral descriptions and comments of the testers were not made with Piaget's descriptions in mind. These approximations, however, are entered as points in Figure 6.8.

Summary

Three quite different concepts of intelligence were discussed. These were the concepts of potentiality, capacity, and ability. Conceived as "potentiality"—as the possible upper limit for mental development—intelligence generally *is* genetically determined at conception. As "capacity," one's intelligence changes constantly as mental development progresses within the limits of one's potentiality, through the interaction of organism and environment. Intelligence as "ability," of course, should refer to what one is able to do at a particular time. This ability to perform—to cope with the circumstances of the moment—also changes with further increase in capacity, with experience and exercise, with functioning. Intelligence, in this last sense, might differ significantly in two individuals with equal inherent potentialities, and even with the same level of capacity, depending upon past experience and opportunities to learn.

Obviously, it is the child's ability that is appraised by means of a test, and it is in connection with testing that the problem of structure looms important. Intelligence tests, from the beginning, have been designed and constructed in terms of the prevailing conception of the structural nature of intelligence. Tests were first designed to appraise a unitary "general ability." Then came the concept of "primary mental abilities" and the need for specific tests for those specific abilities. Now, with the model of an extremely complex structure of mental abilities before us, new and different approaches to mental measurement must be developed.

The third general area of concern, which further complicates the problem of mental measurement, involves the nature of mental development. If intelligence were a single unitary factor, then development would be a matter of simple accretion and construction of tests for its measurement would be relatively simple. If, on the other hand, the adult mental structure is complex and multifactored, then by contrast the infant structure is presumed to be quite simple. From this point of view, adult intelligence is more than a blown-up version of native intelligence. Different levels of mentality are different in qualitative make-up. The developmental process, therefore, involves the continuous emergence of new abilities. It would follow, furthermore, that series of mental tests must be designed in terms of such qualitatively different stages and levels of complexity, if mental status is to be appraised more accurately and if progress in mental development is to be effectively predicted and traced.

Clearly one of our main concerns in the study of individual functional development is the valid appraisal of cognitive functioning. This appraisal is the purpose of intelligence testing. When a child performs effectively in the test situation he is judged to have acted intelligently and with effectiveness. Similarly, when in daily life we see an individual meet a particularly difficult situation in an adequate and effective manner we regard him as a capable, clever, intelligent person. Intelligence is manifest in the level of functional adequacy.

There are, of course, many factors which presumably might affect the development of one's general functional level. Certainly one's inherent potentiality for cognitive development is a basic factor. The pattern of already acquired abilities—skills, manual and social, as well as cognitive—can also condition, in important ways, one's future functional development.

SELECTED READING SUGGESTIONS

Bayley, Nancy. On the growth of intelligence. *Amer. Psychologist*, 1955, **10,** 805–818.

Hunt, J. McV. *Intelligence and experience.* New York: Ronald, 1961.

Murphy, G. *Human potentialities.* New York: Basic Books, 1958. (Read Chapter 7, The freeing of intelligence; Chapter 8, Individual creativeness.

Piaget, J. *The psychology of intelligence.* Paterson, N.J.: Littlefield, Adams 1960.

Sigel, I. E. The attainment of concepts. In M. L. Hoffman and Lois W. Hoffman, *Review of child development research.* New York: Russell Sage Foundation, 1964.

Stoddard, G. D. *The meaning of intelligence.* New York: Macmillan, 1943. (Read Part I, The nature of intelligence.)

CHAPTER 7

———————————— *Factors*
in the *Achievement* of
General Functional
Effectiveness

This chapter shall attempt to detail the factors involved in personal
effectiveness. We shall examine and attempt to evaluate some of the
factors, both intraindividual and environmental, which in their various combinations and patterns of interaction are presumed to affect
the cognitive and behavioral aspects of personal effectiveness. It will
also be our purpose, wherever possible, to appraise the relative valence
of those determinants at different levels of maturity and to relate
them to developmental change in our subjects Paul and Sally 695.
    Among the determining factors of personal adequacy in general

functioning are (1) cognitive potentiality and its development in terms of levels of capacity to learn and to adapt, (2) temperamental nature and its modifications, (3) level of attainment of personal integrity, (4) habitual attitudinal approach to task or problem situations, (5) repertory of habits and skills, (6) social behavior dispositions and other facilities, including communication, and (7) nature, quality, and general level of emotional development. Almost all of these factors receive attention in this chapter. The remaining ones are considered in detail in other chapters. These seven factors, it will be noted, are developed mostly through individual experience and are, therefore, likely to change in their relation to personal effectiveness as the individual develops.

The first factor—the level of potentiality for cognitive development —is, of course, most basic and it is always within the limits of this potentiality that the various habits, skills, and facilities for functioning (abilities) are acquired. This factor was the major concern of the preceding chapter and needs no further discussion here.

Temperamental Nature

Every individual possesses a "constitution" which in its total design and make-up, is peculiarly his own. His sensorium has a unique patterning of relative sensitivities to stimulation, his nervous system a particular level of plasticity, conductivity, and retentivity. The total combination and its interrelatedness constitute what we refer to as an individual's constitutional nature. His "temperatmental nature" is the functional aspect of his constitutional nature, which consists of the peculiar combination of behavioral and affective predispositions mediated by his constitutional, or structural, make-up. Individual differences in constitutional make-up and the temperamental predispositions deriving therefrom are presumed to be due largely to genetic differences. Predispositions are, for the most part, discernible from birth and as such are important factors that interact with the child's early environment to determine the nature of functional development and facility throughout his life.

Students of infant behavior have described a number of differing behavior characteristics in newborn babies. These behaviors are presumed to be expressions of temperamental predispositions. Two young children who differ in the strength of a given predisposition may respond quite individually to the same set of environmental circumstances. Their behaviors show important differences between them in the effectiveness with which they characteristically meet and cope with problems.

Some Behavioral Predispositions

Original temperamental tendencies in children can be differentiated only through careful and systematic observation. In the early days of child development relatively little attention was given to this important area of behavior and development.

ACTIVITY TYPES Some of the earlier observations of temperament in children were made by Margaret Fries (Fries and Lewi, 1938; Fries, 1941, 1944; Fries and Woolf, 1953). Fries carefully observed the amount and vigor of bodily activity in infants from birth to 10 days of age under controlled conditions of stimulation and motivation. She differentiated three *activity types* of infants in terms of amount of activity, differences in characteristic muscle tonus, and crying within the "normal" range. She labeled these types the *active*, the *moderately active*, and the *quiet*. Extremes beyond either end of the normal range were considered pathological. Fries regarded this variable as biological (constitutional) in basic nature but congenital rather than hereditary in that it is a joint product of the action of genes, intrauterine influences, and birth experiences.

Fries and her associates devised some rather interesting experimental methods of eliciting bodily activity in the infant and of rating the resultant behavior. The methods included the startle-response test and the oral test. In the former test situation, an object of standard weight was dropped from a given height striking the table surface near the infant's head. The infant's responses were observed and recorded as to the "number, extent, tempo and duration of movements, and crying." In the oral test, "the breast or bottle was presented to the infant. After he had been sucking well for one minute (no longer, as satiation might occur), the nipple was removed. After one minute, it was restored to him" (1944, p. 160). On the basis of these infant reactions, she classified individuals in terms of the three normal and two pathological congenital activity types.

In elaborating on the probable developmental trends and relationships with the environment deriving from such congenital predispositions, Fries and Woolf (1953) suggested those trends appearing in the following list.

1. Parents with different temperaments differ in their conscious or unconscious preferences for types of children. To the extent to which this is true, the child's activity type may significantly influence the quality of the parent-child relationship and the consequent trend in the child's personal

development. The quiet child, for example, in interacting with certain temperamental tendencies in the parent, may predispose toward the establishment of a strongly dependent relationship. With a different parental temperament pattern the outcome might be quite different.

2. Because of cultural mores, a girl of a quiet type and a boy of an active type tend in general to have an easier adjustment respectively to their sex roles. Hence, the functional effectiveness of the child in terms of sex-role expectations could be conditioned significantly by his own activity type.

3. The form that the child's reality testing and mastery behavior take may be, in part at least, a function of his activity type. As was suggested in Fries' (1944) discussion, the highly active child is prone to test reality, and to master the situation through his own efforts, whereas the quiet child would be more likely to appeal to and depend upon the adult for help in meeting a situation. The implications for relative adequacy of functioning are apparent here.

4. To the extent to which these early activity patterns are biological forerunners of later reactions to difficulties, a child's congenital activity type might predispose him to adopt certain defense and escape mechanisms. The quiet type, for example, may be more predisposed to adopt the defenses of withdrawal and fantasy—generally very inadequate modes of functioning as judged externally.

5. The activity type may, to some degree, predispose the child in the direction of a particular neurosis or symptom formation. Fries points out that all types seem to be capable of developing any character trait or neurosis, but individuals also seem to have predispositions to one or another. For example, the two extreme types—the excessively quiet and the excessively active—seem to be more vulnerable to psychological illness. The autistic child described by Kanner (1944) appears to be developmentally related to the pathologically quiet type.

Stability of congenital activity characteristics   In distinguishing between activity types, Fries considered a number of behavioral attributes such as muscle tonus, crying or the lack of crying, and amount and vigor of activity. A child's activity type as judged in terms of these criteria in combination is generally assumed to be rather stable temperamentally.

A prediction study by Escalona and Heider (1959) proposed to identify those personal and behavioral traits observable in young infants which do persist over a period of years. This study observed differences in motor activity among infants, particularly in characteristic level of activity, which was one of the traits tested for stability (due to the level of its vigor and intensity). *Level of activity*, it will be noted, was one of the attributes of behavior used by Fries in differentiating activity "types."

It is interesting to note that out of twenty-seven individual predictions of later activity level made by Escalona and Heider, only eighteen, or 67 percent, were confirmed. "Amount and vigor of activity as assessed by two ratings made several years apart, varies more than is compatible with the view that this is ordinarily a highly stable trait" (1959, p. 70). These investigators further concluded that *"variability* and *range* in bodily activity, and such characteristics as restlessness or the capacity to remain quiet, are relatively more stable traits than is activity level as such" (p. 73, italics added).

From the point of view of the interaction hypothesis with respect to development, low predictive correlations between ratings of infant activity characteristics and ratings of the same traits made later in childhood are just what might be expected. Congenital predispositions to activity, strong as they may be, are only predispositions. And, as Fries suggested, the kind of parental handling and the various other environmental situations with which the child must cope during his early years also constitute an important factor influencing the direction of developmental change.

INFLUENCES UPON INTERACTIONS WITH OTHERS   Congenital predispositions to different levels of tempo and vigor of activity in the baby are likely to influence other developments as well. They undoubtedly influence the reactions of others toward him, which in turn could be important factors in relation to other aspects of his temperamental development. Cameron and Magaret (1951) suggested some possible developments:

> An active, irritable infant participates in a wider environment than does a quiet, phlegmatic one, and he invites different reactions from those who share the environment with him. The baby who turns, reaches, and kicks restlessly in his crib; who cries, smiles, or coos a great deal; or who nurses actively and long, inevitably exposes himself to situations which differ from those which the placid, unreactive child encounters. What these differences in reactivity may mean for the infant's behavior organization is also importantly determined, of course, by the needs and attitudes of his parents and of the others who respond

to him. An exuberant, accepting family may welcome noisy activity in its newest member which quieter more restrictive parents would consider irritating, frightening, or bad. (p. 52, by permission)

Congenital Characteristics of Reactivity

Currently, the matter of original individual differences in the characteristic nature of behavior with respect to congenital differences is the concern of a longitudinal study by Thomas, Chess, Birch, Hertzig, and Korn (1963).[1] These investigators clearly recognized the importance of congenital predispositions in relations to later behavioral development and personal effectiveness. They introduced their initial report (1963) with this statement:

> . . . temperamental characteristics of the infant make a fundamental contribution to psychological individuality. It is our view that personality development is the result of the interaction of a baby endowed with definable characteristics of initial reactivity, and an environmental complex including familial and extrafamilial factors. (p. ix)

In order to obtain adequate data on "initial reactivity" and changes with respect to it, continuous observations of many children would be necessary during their natural course of development. Since parents are in constant observational contact and in virtually continuous interaction with their babies, Thomas and his coworkers decided that carefully conducted interviews with parents was the most feasible approach to collecting the necessary observational data. A carefully formulated interview procedure was devised so as "to satisfy the criteria of concreteness and closeness in time to the behavior to be described." The method proved to be both reliable and valid in terms of their statistical tests.

Many areas of background, parental care, and handling, and particularly characteristics of reactivity as they appeared in the baby were covered in these structured but flexible interviews. They were conducted generally every three months during the child's first two years. Data on eighty children are included in the 1963 report.

On the basis of a content analysis of the interview protocols of the first twenty-two children, the following nine "categories for the assessment of individuality in behavioral functioning" were adopted:

---

[1] Preliminary published papers connected with this project are: Thomas and Chess, 1957; Chess, Thomas, and Birch, 1958; Thomas, Chess, Birch, and Hertzig, 1960; Thomas, Birch, Chess, and Robins, 1961.

1. Activity level: the extent to which the motor component characterized the baby's functioning.
2. Rhythmicity: the degree of regularity of repetitive functions, such as sleeping and waking, eating and appetite, and bowel and bladder functions.
3. Approach or withdrawal: a description of the child's characteristic initial reaction to any new stimulus pattern, "be it food, people, places, toys, or procedures."
4. Adaptability: "the sequential course of responses that are made to new or altered situations."
5. Intensity of reaction: the "energy content of the reaction irrespective of its direction" (negative or positive).
6. Threshold of responsiveness: "the intensity level of stimulation that is necessary to evoke a discernible response," the explicit form of the response, in this instance, being irrelevant.
7. Quality of mood: "the amount of pleasant, joyful, friendly behavior as contrasted with unpleasant, crying, unfriendly behavior."
8. Distractibility: "the effectiveness of extraneous environmental stimuli in interfering with, or in altering the direction of, ongoing behavior."
9. Attention span and persistence: "this category refers to the definition of a direction of functioning and to the difficulty with which such an established direction of functioning can be altered."

The data relevant to each of these nine behavior characteristics for the eighty children during their first two years of life were analyzed with two objectives in mind: "to determine whether children are discriminably different in the patterning of behavioral reactivity in early infancy; to analyze the degree to which features of behavioral reactivity identifiable in early infancy continue to characterize the child during his first two years" (p. 56).

In brief, the conclusions were as follows: (1) "Individual differences among children are demonstrable, particularly for such characteristics as *activity level, threshold, intensity of reaction, mood,* and *distractibility*" (p. 57); in terms of the total pattern of reactivity ratings, each baby was unique. (2) Statistical analysis of the data "has contributed evidence that identifiable characteristics of reactivity are persistent features of the child's behavior throughout the first two years of life" (p. 71).

Such characteristics of early behavior, when patterned with other temperamental variables, undoubtedly play an important part in the development of psychological individuality and may thus influence

significantly the individual's general functional effectiveness throughout life.

The Predicament of Early Infancy

Some of the aspects of infant existence have been mentioned in other
connections. We have noted the very limited motor capacities of the
young infant and also the fact that his mental capacity can be appraised only in terms of his motor activity. We have reviewed some
of the temperamental predispositions that underlie individual differences in activity level and tempo. Behavioral predispositions appear
to portend the development of the emotions and thus to further
accent the "predicament" aspects of being a human infant.

SENSITIVITY TO FEAR-ANXIETY STIMULI   Babies are observed to
differ rather widely in the strength of their tendency to startle and
generally to show avoidance reactions to strong and noxious stimuli.
This predisposition is particularly in evidence during the earliest
weeks of the child's life when his extremely immature brain has not
yet acquired an inhibitory control over visceral change and upset.
Even though normal infants differ widely in sensitivity and ease of
arousal, as well as in intensity of reaction, this tendency nevertheless
is present to some degree in all, and, as Diamond (1957) suggests,
"this normal emotional instability of the infant constitutes a predisposition to anxiety, or generalized fearfulness, which is likely to be
established as a lasting disposition if it is given frequent exercise in
this period" (p. 106).

Many clinicians and keen observers of the plight and of the reactions of newborn infants have stressed the significance of this period
of instability. They have described it in its various aspects, and, in
some instances, they undoubtedly have overemphasized the hazards
to the neonate's survival as well as to his healthy emotional development when adequate understanding care and nurturance are not
provided (Ribble, 1943). The early fear pattern associated with this
period is regarded as the organism's natural response to threatened
denial of its basic needs, as, for example, the need for oxygen during
the period immediately following birth when independent respiration
must be established. Another vital need is believed to be the need
for the security and comfort of warm, relaxed "mothering."

INFANT ANXIETY   Harry Stack Sullivan, who wielded a great
influence upon modern psychiatric thinking, has made much of the
concept of anxiety in early infancy in relation to emotional develop-

ment. It is quite apparent that in his discussions of the early infant-mother relationship Sullivan used the term anxiety to refer to the characteristic physiological instability and sensitivity and the startle-fear-withdrawal pattern with which we are here concerned. Sullivan (1953) wrote:

> I cannot tell you what anxiety feels like to the infant, but I can make an inference which I believe has very high probability of accuracy—that there is no difference between anxiety and fear so far as the vague mental state of the infant is concerned. . . . I would like to point out that if an infant is exposed to a sudden loud noise, he is pretty much upset; certain other experiences of that kind which impinge on his zones of connection with the outside world cause the same kind of upset. Almost anybody watching the infant during these upsets would agree that it didn't seem to be fun; the infant didn't enjoy it. . . . I have reason to suppose then, that a fearlike state can be induced in an infant under two circumstances: one is by the rather violent disturbance of his zones of contact with circum-ambient reality; and the other is by certain types of emotional disturbance within the mothering one. From the latter grows the whole exceedingly important structure of anxiety, and performances that can be understood only by reference to the concept of anxiety. (p. 9, by permission)

Later in his discussion, Sullivan is more specific as to the nature of the emotional disturbance within the mothering one which leads to "upset" and the "fearlike state" in the infant:

> *The tension of anxiety, when present in the mothering one, induces anxiety in the infant.* The rationale of this induction —that is, *how* anxiety in the mother induces anxiety in the infant—is thoroughly obscure. This gap, this failure of our grasp on reality has given rise to some beautifully plausible and perhaps correct explanations of how the anxiety in the mother causes anxiety in the infant. I bridge the gap simply by referring to it as a manifestation of an indefinite—that is, not yet defined —interpersonal process to which I apply the term *empathy.* (p. 41, by permission)

As stated earlier, the infant's recurrent organic need and the physiological disequilibrium resulting from them when not immediately satisfied is also a source of the fear-anxiety state. Thus, the importance of the care of a "mothering one" is obvious. Sullivan describes the significance of this factor in the interpersonal relationship of infant and mother. As the baby's need for food or water or for comfortable body temperature increases, thus disturbing the equilibrium of his being, a "tension of needs" mounts in him. This tension is made manifest to the mother in terms of the changed level or character of the baby's activity. Continuing, in Sullivan's words:

> . . . however manifest the increasing tension of needs in an infant may be . . . the observation of these tensions or of the activity which manifests their presence calls out, in the mothering one, a certain tension which may be described as that of tenderness, which is a potentiality for or an impulsion to activities suited to—or more or less suited to—the relief of the infant's needs. This in its way, is a definition of tenderness—a very important conception, very different indeed from the miscellaneous and in general, meaningless term "love." (p. 40, by permission)

Sullivan thus stresses the crucial importance of the quality of the mother's emotional reactions in relation to her baby. The particular emotional reactions in her to which the baby is sensitive as stimuli to the fear-anxiety pattern could influence profoundly his emotional development and later self-realization.

In this connection individual differences among infants must again be emphasized. Infants undoubtedly differ rather widely in level of senstivity not only to particular organic needs and other noxious conditions but to the mother's affective reactions to the child's needs and behavior. Hence, the quality and intensity of the tension experience resulting from objectively the same environmental or interpersonal situation would vary according to the infant's basic sensitivity. The mother's empathic understanding of these differences is presumed to be an important factor to the child's further affective development.

Appraisal of Temperamental Variables

The meaningful appraisal in an infant of the various temperamental predispositions requires careful observation under appropriate conditions by one who is especially alerted to see the relevant behavior. No such specifically oriented observations were made of Paul and Sally. However, their records contain many comments descriptive of their behavior, particularly statements comparing their reactions to people and to various environmental situations that have relevance to their respective temperamental natures. A careful perusal of these records was made, and on the basis of general impressions thus gained

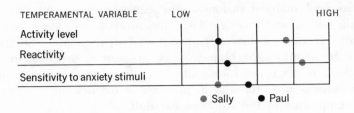

Figure 7.1

Rating profiles of Paul and Sally 695 as infants in three temperamental variables. Based upon data in their developmental records.

ratings of two types were attempted. Each child was thought of in comparison with infants in general and a tentative placement on a subjective continuum of the variable in question was made. Then, the two "pictures" were compared and adjustments were made in the ratings on the basis of this infant-to-infant comparison. Their rating profiles are shown in Figure 7.1.

There was clearly a contrast between the two babies in temperamental reactivity as well as in activity tempo. Sally was rather quick in her responsiveness, while Paul was slow in the sense of being deliberative. Paul, from the beginning, was inclined to look the situation over and appear to evaluate it before reacting. This continued to be one of his outstanding characteristics.[2] Reference might be made here to the earlier discussion of differences between these children in motor behavior (Chapter 5).

As for the fear-avoidance tendency, both Paul and Sally seemed to show somewhat less than average sensitivity to anxiety-provoking stimuli. Paul was perhaps a bit more guarded and more reluctant to accept a stranger or react to a new situation than was Sally.

Achievement of a Sense of Personal Identity and Integrity

The developmental metamorphosis that takes place in the human individual between birth and adulthood continues to be a fascinating phenomenon for analysis. It has been viewed from different points

[2] As an adolescent when for the first time he was asked to "rate" himself by sorting a collection of "self" descriptions (to be referred to later), Paul was unable to complete the task in the time available because he critically examined and deliberated upon each item, analyzing it in terms of its various possible implications. He did not provide for us a self-rating of his "self-concept" but he did offer some helpful suggestions for eliminating ambiguities and otherwise revising many of the "Q-sort" items.

of view and analyzed variously into sequences of periods and stages within which, and among which, the processes of change are continuous. In each of these attempts at analysis the major concern has been the identification of milestones, or signs of progress, in terms of which to trace the course of change from the complete unselfconsciousness and profound helplessness of the newborn to the relative competence of the autonomous adult.

Emergence of Social Responsiveness

Without cognitive awareness of his own helplessness, the neonate's first developmental task is the organismic one of recovering from the crisis of birth and of adapting to extrauterine conditions of living. But development is exceedingly rapid during infancy. The baby soon begins to react to visual and auditory stimulation. By the middle of his first year he is much aware of objects and events external to himself. He is beginning to differentiate between his mother and other moving objects (people) before him. The presence of his mother now becomes an essential factor in his life, and in his reactions to her care and ministrations he demonstrates his *affiliative need*—the tendency and the need to relate affectionately to another.

It is important at this stage, particularly, that the mothering one be warmly dependable (I. D. Harris, 1959). The baby is emerging from his earlier predicament of infancy into a period where he can make differential responses to certain stable aspects of his environment. It is the beginning of what Erikson (1950) calls the stage of trust:

> The first demonstration of social trust in the baby is the ease of his feeding, the depth of his sleep, the relaxation of his bowels. The experience of a mutual regulation of his increasingly receptive capacities with the maternal techniques of provision gradually helps him to balance the discomfort caused by the immaturity of homeostasis with which he was born. In his gradually increasing waking hours he finds that more and more adventures of the senses arouse a feeling of familiarity, of having coincided with a feeling of inner goodness. (p. 219, by permission)

As this trusting affiliativeness develops, the baby also learns something in the way of control techniques. He readily learns that his crying will bring immediate relief from discomfort and immediate gratification of his needs. This, then, is also the period of the *sense of omnipotence* and *volitional independence* (Ausubel, 1958). His trust is reinforced by the fact that what he "wills" happens.

The strength of this tendency to relate with trust to others, as expressed particularly in the infant's attachment to his mother, apparently continues to increase during the latter half of the first year of life. Its early development appears to be dependent upon the constancy and the quality of maternal care the baby receives. "But let it be said here," wrote Erikson (1950), "that the amount of trust derived from earliest infantile experiences does not seem to depend on absolute quantities of food or demonstrations of love, but rather on the quality of the maternal relationship" (p. 221).

This early capacity for trustful affiliation and its nurturance (or lack of nurturance) are presumed to be the basis of individual differences in the adult ability to interact with others in affectionate and love relationships and to respond generally to social stimuli. To the extent to which this is true, this variable of temperament constitutes an important conditioning factor to personal effectiveness in the area of interpersonal and social relationships.

Actually there is relatively little research evidence as to the relation between the kind of mothering young infants receive and their social development (Yarrow, 1961, 1964). Preliminary findings in a longitudinal study of mother-infant interaction indicate, however, that 1-year-old infants who had been cared for by their own mothers only were more active, more emotionally dependent on their mothers, and more emotional in their interactions with their mothers than were infants of the same age who had experienced "polymatric" care (Caldwell *et al.*, 1963). These differences, which were statistically significant, supported the hypothesis that infants reared in monomatric families become more affiliative and more emotionally responsive than those who do not experience single-mother nurturance.

Beginnings of Functional Independence

As the child's manipulative and locomotor capacities develop, his drive to explore and perceive more and more of his environment becomes a dominant factor in his behavioral and emotional development. As he moves about among the objects of his environment, grasping and manipulating them in space, he makes real gains in self-identification and in his awareness of the relation of his own acts to the objects about him.

At about the same time in the infant's life, those significant persons in his environment begin to relate to him in a new way. With his achievement of a measure of independence (and competence) the dependable ones about him are no longer completely subservient to his demands. They begin now to be more restrictive and even punitive. He may not now be permitted to grasp and to experiment with many of the attractive objects about him.

A further complication of the child's life is the pressure being put upon him to learn to control his eliminative functions as he moves about the house. This concern of others and their interference with his freedom makes him more aware of these functions and the frustrations and gratifications associated with them. He thus becomes more preoccupied with them in relation to his growing sense of autonomy. In Erikson's (1950) words, "anal-muscular maturation sets the stage for experimentation with two simultaneous sets of social modalities: holding on and letting go. . . . basic conflicts (between these two modalities) can lead in the end to either hostile or benign expectations and attitudes" (p. 222). The child is now in the midst of the anal stage of his personal development, the stage that Erikson characterizes as "autonomy vs shame and doubt." The outcome in terms of personal functioning depends largely upon the wisdom of parental care and handling. According to Erikson (1950):

> Outer control at this stage, therefore, must be firmly reassuring. The infant must come to feel that the basic faith in existence which is the lasting treasure saved from the rages of the oral stage, will not be jeopardized by this about-face of his, this sudden violent wish to have a choice, to appropriate demandingly, and to eliminate stubbornly. Firmness must protect him against the potential anarchy of his as yet untrained sense of discrimination, his inability to hold on and to let go with discretion. (p. 223, by permission)

The inner conflicting tendencies interacting with parental efforts at outer control render this period of growing autonomy a crucial one in relation to further development of self-realization and functional adequacy. Perhaps partly in reaction to the restrictive socializing efforts of others, but also because the child's own pattern of interests and drives is changing, he begins now to be even more aggressive and resistant to outer control.

The Period of Aggressivity

The negativistic period of infant aggressivity is a time in the life of the young child when he is presumed to be meeting a developmental crisis: He is more keenly sensing the loss of the sense of status that he enjoyed during the dependency of earlier babyhood. He seems to be reacting to that vague sense of loss with resistance and with efforts to dominate others. He now says "no" or "I won't" in response to efforts of others to direct or control his behavior. The age at which this period occurs is 2 to 3 years.

The young child not only resists the control of others but he now tries to exercise control over and manipulate others. It is a period of "initiative and guilt" (Erikson, 1950). The child has gained in his ability to observe and to experience interpersonal relationships. He normally develops an intense identification with his same-sexed parent. According to psychoanalytic theory this identification is carried to the point of becoming that parent's rival for the love of the opposite-sexed parent. Quoting from Erikson (1950):

> The danger of this stage is a sense of guilt over the goals contemplated and the acts initiated in one's exuberant enjoyment of new locomotor and mental power: acts of aggressive manipulation and coercion which go far beyond the executive capacity of organism and mind and therefore call for an energetic halt on one's contemplated initiative. (p. 224, by permission)

This presumably is a stressful period for the child and a difficult one for the parent. It is also a significant period in the development of the child's self concept. Its successful resolution can also provide a basis for later, more mature affectional and other interpersonal relationships.

The Period of Motor-Skills Acquisition

By the end of the preschool period the child normally has met and coped with the crisis of his loss of infant status. Although he does not yet possess the executive competence necessary for functioning as an independent member of society, he, nevertheless, is now free to enjoy a sense secondary status in a satellite relationship with his parents (Ausubel, 1958).

With the beginning of school attendance, of course, his horizons greatly broaden. He forms constructive relationships with teachers and other adults. His peer relationships now become especially important too. It is in association with his peers and in friendly competition with them that he learns many skills. He learns to handle with skill play and recreational equipment. He learns to work with tools and to carry a production task through to completion.

Of course, here, as in all activities and at all levels, wide individual differences are apparent. The individual hazard during this period of acquisition is that of developing a sense of inadequacy and inferiority because of the inability to measure up or to compete successfully with peers.

In anticipation of later developmental problems, the stage of motor-skills acquisition becomes especially important. Through the achievement of these many skills the youngster makes measurable progress toward that level of competence necessary for autonomous functioning and the sense of primary status.

Transition

At a particular time and stage of individual development and through some genetically controlled mechanisms within the organism not yet well understood, a tiny organ—the pituitary gland—is geared into greater activity. The stimulating influences of the increased secretions of that gland activate the beginning of a complex series of change processes which we refer to as the onset of puberty. The immature reproductive system is stimulated to develop and to begin to secrete its hormone (androgen in the male and estrogen in the female). The sex hormone, in turn, initiates and guides the development of those body characteristics which differentiate the sexes. Other glands also act in coordination with the pituitary to perform an appropriately balanced function. The whole organism is stimulated to begin its growth spurt and rapid growth and change, physically and physiologically, result.

Structural changes must bring changes in functioning. Such profound body changes as those beginning at puberty have important psychological accompaniments. The child's rapidly growing body is likely to seem a bit strange to him and he may misjudge its unfamiliar dimensions. His changing physiology gives rise to feelings and interests that are new and strange to him. Being keenly aware of the outward changes in his body and experiencing the effects of the physiological revolution going on within him, the child may wonder how he is being seen by others. The regard of others is likely to become very important to him because he is unsure as to how to regard and evaluate himself. He is "concerned with the question of how to connect the roles and skills cultivated earlier with the occupational prototypes of the day" (Erikson, 1950, p. 228). In the confusion and uncertainty of change he is "searching for a new sense of continuity and sameness." A developmental task of importance to him is the achievement of a sense of ego identity—"the accrued confidence that the inner sameness and continuity are matched by the sameness and continuity of one's meaning for others" (p. 228). This period of transition from childhood to young adulthood is a crucial stage in the development of dominant feelings and attitudes toward self.

One's attitudes and feelings toward one's self and others, attitudes and approaches to life and to the challenges it presents and the tasks it imposes all may have some foundation in one's temperamental nature. For the most part, attitudes and feelings are acquired through contacts and associations with others.

The Self Concept

A great deal has been written about the self, about perceptions of one's self, and about the various attitudes and feelings toward self. Some of these writings are theoretical, often based upon general observation and generalized clinical experience (Erikson, 1950; Jourard, 1964; Moustakas, 1956; Snygg and Combs, 1949; Sullivan, 1947). Others are reports of research studies that involved measurement or evaluation of the self concept, usually with the assessment of its developmental aspects (Ames, 1952; Dixon, 1957; Jersild, 1952; Rogers and Dymond, 1954; Stephenson, 1953; Wylie, 1961).

Jersild (1960) has studied the development of the attitude toward self in children. One of his approaches was to ask children at different grade levels in school to prepare written descriptions of qualities in themselves that they admired and others that they disliked. The general finding was that "many of the criteria young people use in judging themselves at any level tend to stand out prominently at all levels" (p. 449). The standards used by the children appeared not to be related to age or developmental status. Experiences at school and their attitudes toward school, however, were significantly related to their self attitudes. In an earlier study (Jersild *et al.*, 1941), results indicated that children "worried" more about school than they did about out-of-school matters. Jersild offered this conclusion:

> Self-acceptance and understanding of self are closely associated. To accept himself, the growing person must be aware of himself. To accept his limitations he must be able to recognize them. Self-acceptance, in other words, requires awareness and perception. But the child's ability to become aware of himself will be influenced by the way he feels about himself, and the way he feels about himself will depend, in part, on the way others feel about him and encourage him in the process of self-discovery. (1960, p. 457)

There are, of course, a number of aspects of the self about which people, especially adolescents may have strong and sometimes very disturbing feelings. Among these areas of concern are one's physical body—its size, proportions and other characteristics—one's capabilities and competences, and one's personal worth.

Youngsters are often quite unhappy with their bodies. They would like to be taller or not so tall, to be heavier and stronger looking or not so heavy, or to possess facial and other bodily features that conform more nearly to some idealized stereoytpe. Slow-growing boys who fall behind their age mates at the time of the so-called physical growth spurt often become anxious and fearful about their prospects of attaining adult status.

Some youngsters also have unfounded misgivings about their intellectual capabilities. These feelings are often combined with the tendency to be "shy" and to feel incompetent in, and to withdraw from, social situations.

Other children, who may or may not have disturbing feelings about their physical selves or their competence, have acquired feelings of unworthiness. Perhaps too frequently the little boy has been told that he is a "naughty" or a "nasty" boy, and he comes to believe that he is. At any rate, some children develop the conviction that they do not deserve the regard and affection others demonstrate toward them. They are inclined to feel that others overvalue them because they themselves give others a dishonest impression of their value and worth; consequently, these children feel guilty and even less worthy. Such disturbed feelings and preoccupations often interfere with effective functioning at the time. For optimal functional development, being free to learn, in the sense of being free from disturbing thoughts and worries, is an important asset.

THE "Q-SORT" STUDY OF THE SELF CONCEPT   Various techniques and devices have been tried in the general study of the self concept and for its assessment in the individual child. One such technique, which has much to recommend it, is the Q-technique, a self-rating method devised and described by Stephenson (1953). This methodology makes possible the statistical study, in a single individual, of any psychological variable that can be defined and described by means of methods of variance and factor analysis.

In the application of Q-technique to the study of an individual's self concept, the first step is to formulate a theory as to the nature or structure of the self concept. One such structure often suggested consists of three main components (or independencies): the body image (feelings of satisfaction or dissatisfaction about one's body); feelings about one's competence; and one's sense of worthiness or unworthiness.

The Q-technique involves the formation of a list of statements describing the various feelings about self, which is constructed in terms of a balanced block design where the positive and the negative feelings about each of the three independencies are equally expressed. This list thus constitutes a balanced sample of the population of attitudes about self.

The subject's self-rating task is to sort these statements (each typed on a separate card), each in terms of its relevance to his own feelings about himself. He is instructed to sort them into an arbitrary number of piles (say, nine piles) containing statements ranging from those judged to be "most *like* the way I feel" to those judged to be "most *unlike* the way I feel." The numbers of statements in the piles form a bilaterally symmetrical distribution approximating a normal probability distribution. These sorting categories (piles) are assigned scoring values ranging from 1, for the pile selected as "most unlike," to 9, for the one selected as "most like." The scores for the "most unlike" statements can then be compared with those of the "most like" statements. Statistical analyses of the whole distribution can also be performed showing relative strength of negative and positive feelings in each of the three components of the self concept.

Such a Q-sort study was made of the self concept of each of twenty-two adolescent-age members of The Merrill-Palmer Institute's Longitudinal Research Series. This group included the twin subjects Paul and Sally 695. Each subject's sorting was subjected to variance analysis. The analysis of Paul's sorting indicated that he felt "very significantly" more satisfied with himself physically than unsatisfied, more capable than incapable, and more worthy than unworthy. In other

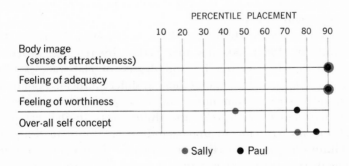

Figure 7.2

Q-sort self-ratings of Paul and Sally 695 at age 15 years expressed as percentile scores based on self-ratings of twenty-two adolescents.

words, his self attitudes were very definitely on the positive side. The same pattern held for Sally also, except for the worthiness component, in which the favorable and unfavorable statements were about equal in frequency.

In addition to the individual analysis, total favorableness-of-attitude scores on each of the three components were computed for the twenty-two subjects. These raw scores were converted into percentile scores. Figure 7.2 is a profile representation of the twins' percentile ratings. The only exception to extremely positive ratings in relation to the group was Sally's rating in feeling of worthiness. Her self-rating placed her very near the median of the group.

Learned Patterns of Adaptation

As the child develops he is constantly forming and refining behavior patterns. At any particular point in his life, the level of effectiveness with which he meets and deals with life situations, generally, is clearly dependent upon what he has learned up to that point.

Basic Orientation to the World

One of the most basically important patterns of adaptation is one's general orientation to the world in which he lives and to which he must relate—the world of people, social inventions, institutions, and relationships. The child gets, or fails to get, this vital orientation very early in life, mainly from the person-to-person (largely verbal) interaction with his mother.

Ongoing research (Bernstein, 1961; R. D. Hess, 1964; R. D. Hess and Shipman, 1965) indicates that verbal interchange varies rather widely in "mode"—in quality and degree of elaborateness—among families and particularly among those at different socioeconomic levels. At the one extreme, communication is so perfunctory, so restricted, so "status-oriented" as to offer the child a very limited grasp of the world and no basis for an understanding or ability to deal with it. Communication is "restrictive, stereotyped, limited, and condensed, lacking in specificity and exactness needed for precise conceptualization and differentiation" (R. D. Hess, 1964, p. 424).

The other end of the continuum offers much more cognitive stimulation in verbal interchange. The parent is more specific and informative. Of the mother's communication, Hess said it is

. . . individualized and the message is specific to a particular situation, topic, or person. It is more particular, more differentiated, and more precise. It permits expression of a wider and more complex range of thought, tending toward discrimination among cognitive and affective content. (1964, p. 424)

The difference in outcome between these two modes of verbal interaction, along with other associated variables, is presumed to be one of educability. It is a difference in cognitive development, and, since learning is a matter of "subsuming" the new into the already existing cognitive structure, the difference becomes one of learning acquisition (the acquired level of orientation to the world and the problems of living).

Early verbal interchange viewed as an important home-environmental factor is discussed further in Chapter 13.

Habitual Approach to Tasks and Problems

A product of learning that is also related to competence is one's habitual approach to a task or a problem situation. After an appraisal of the situation, whether one is able to come immediately and vigorously to grips with it or evades and stalls at making a decision often makes the difference between competence and ineffectiveness (Pressey and Robinson, 1944).

Although the approach to tasks and problems is in the nature of an habituated pattern, it is nevertheless related to temperamental nature. The individual who is, by nature, very active and restless is more likely to be unmethodical and haphazard rather than planful and systematic in his approach. The naturally withdrawing child is likely to approach a new problem with tentativeness and a lack of vigor and perhaps without much careful detailed planning. One's characteristic mode of approach in any case, however, is learned— a product of the interaction of environmental stimulation and original temperament.

One's habitual emotional patterns may also constitute an important conditioning factor. Emotionality can be either an impeding or a facilitating factor in relation to personal adequacy. One of the lessons from common experience is that thought and rational behavior are incompatible with "emotional upset." On the other hand, the physiological aspect of an emotional episode makes readily available extra amounts of physical energy that can be mobilized for more effective attack upon certain kinds of problem situations.

Skills and Information

Apart from one's mode of approach to a particular life situation, perhaps even more important is his fund of readily available information or his repertory of skills ("know-how") applicable to the situation. The technology that characterizes the world today makes increasingly greater demands upon individuals in terms of training and specialized skills. The place of an unskilled person in the present world economy is practically nonexistent. A disturbing but true fact of economics is that today's useful skill may not long continue to be useful. Flexibility, and a general "learning set" for continued new acquisitions and new adjustments are great assets to individuals facing the present world, economically, intellectually, and socially as well.

TRACING THE DEVELOPMENT OF SKILLS AND INFORMATION   The best source of data concerning the development of skills and informa-

Table 7.1

Achievement of Skills and Information
for Paul (A) and Sally (B) in Terms of Age Equivalents

A. PAUL 695

CHRONOLOGICAL AGE	DEVELOPMENTAL AGES			
	MANIPULATION	LANGUAGE	SOCIAL	INTELLECTUAL
0-6.5	0-9	0-7	0-9	0-9
1-1	1-6	1-6	1-6	1-8
1-6	2-2	2-5	2-4	2-4
2-1	2-6	2-9	2-6	3-4
3-2	4-0	5-0	4-0	4-8
6-6	7-6	10-0	7-0	10-6
10-4	12-0	15-0	10-0	15-0
12-3	17-0	17-6	12-0	18-0

B. SALLY 695

CHRONOLOGICAL AGE	DEVELOPMENTAL AGES			
	MANIPULATION	LANGUAGE	SOCIAL	INTELLECTUAL
0-6.5	0-7	0-7.5	0-8	0-7.5
1-1	1-6	1-3.5	1-5	1-3.5
1-6	2-8	2-3	2-4	2-4
2-1	2-8	3-0	3-0	3-0
3-2	3-6	4-6	4-0	4-8
6-6	7-0	8-0	7-0	8-6
11-3	12-2	15-6	13-0	15-5

tion in Paul and Sally 695 is the series of developmental and intelligence tests that were administered to them during the period of their growth. The content of the Gesell Developmental Schedules suggested a set of useful categories for the classification of this material: motor or manipulative skills; language skills; social skills; and intellectual facilities, actually measured largely in terms of already acquired information.

Table 7.1 (A and B) presents the results of the tests administered to Paul and Sally between the ages of 6 months and 11 to 12 years in terms of age equivalents (developmental ages). These values are shown graphically in Figures 7.3 and 7.4. These figures represent a qualitative analysis of the relative importance of the different areas

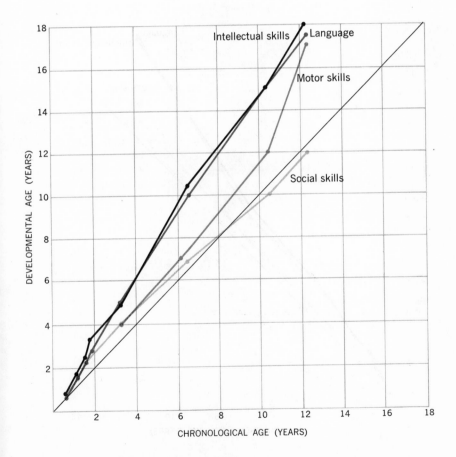

Figure 7.3

Development of skills in Paul 695.

of skills and information that largely determined the level of functioning at the various age levels at which appraisals were made. In combination of course, the over-all skill level was taken as a measure of general functional adequacy at each age level represented.

Figures 7.3 and 7.4 clearly show that both of these children were well above average in all four skill areas and at practically all levels of development. It is equally clear, however, that the main areas of their functional superiority were in the language and intellectual areas. As a matter of fact, these two areas have much the same meaning, particularly beyond the preschool period, since information is largely gained through the use of language. Tests of school-age mental functioning, furthermore, consist largely of verbal items. Perhaps the

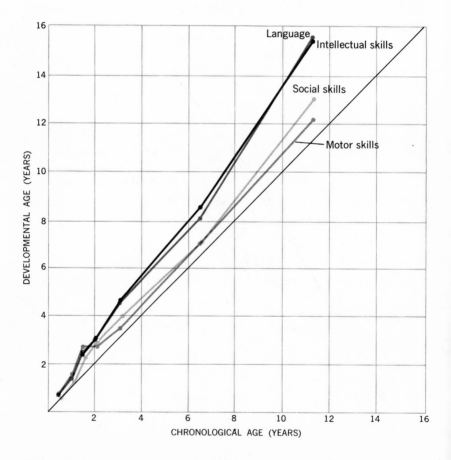

Figure 7.4

Development of skills in Sally 695.

most outstanding difference between the functional patterns of Paul and Sally is in social skills. Paul, from the beginning, as we have seen in other connections, was less immediately responsive to others, more individualistic, and more deliberative than his sister.

People obviously vary widely in pattern of basic personality structure, and these differences appear very early in the life of the child (as we shall see in Chapter 10). Each of the various behavior dispositions that, in combination, constitute personality structure in any given individual child or adult can be an important factor in his over-all functional adequacy. One's convictions, attitudes, prejudices, and the like may also be factors of importance. The extent to which one's emotions either interfere with or facilitate effective functioning is another important area for consideration. Chapter 11 will deal with the emotions, their development, and the important bearing they have upon personal effectiveness in life.

SELECTED READING SUGGESTIONS

Association for Supervision and Curriculum Development. *Perceiving, behaving, becoming: a new focus for education.* Washington, D.C.: National Education Association, 1962. (Read Chapter 2, The fully functioning self; Chapter 3, Toward becoming a fully functioning person; Chapter 4, Some basic propositions of a growth and self-actualization psychology; Chapter 5, A perceptual view of the adequate personality.)

Hess, R. D., and Virginia C. Shipman. Early experience and the socialization of cognitive modes in children. *Child Develpm.,* 1965, **36,** 869–886.

Murphy, G. *Human potentialities.* New York: Basic Books, 1958. (See Chapter 2, Three kinds of human nature.)

Pressey, S. L., and F. P. Robinson. *Psychology and the new education.* New York: Harper & Row, 1944.

CHAPTER 8

Learning

As has been stated earlier and in other connections, behavioral development is largely a product of learning (in the broad sense of the term). Even though one's intellectual potentiality is genetically determined, one's mental abilities, which develop within the limits of that potentiality, are acquired as one copes with, gains control over, or accommodates to his environment. An individual's temperamental predispositions, constitutionally based as they are, also undergo change through learning from the beginning of one's life. The direction and extent of learning is of great significance in the individual's life. Total adequacy of functioning, even insofar as organically based factors are involved, is very largely a matter of learning.

The very processes of living are processes of change. Living itself thus constitutes a continuous progression of changes in the way the individual (and his behavior) interacts with his environment. These are changes in functional facility due to the exercise of function. This is learning.

Learning as a Process of Developmental Change

Learning is regarded as a process of change in functioning, just as maturation is a process of change in a bodily structure. But this change in functioning results from functioning itself, from something the learner does.

Functioning, as we have been using the term, is simply *doing something*. It is behavior that involves, in a sense, the whole individual but it is performed by a particular bodily structure. The pattern of behavior, of course, may be simple or it may be very complex; it may be overt, it may be covert, or "central." Behavior is always the functioning of segments of three complex structural systems: the sensorium, the nervous system, and the effector system.

Behavioral functioning must always leave something in the nature of "traces" in the physical structures involved. As functional patterns are repeated and as new related acts or functions are performed, portions of already present traces become augmented and new traces are left. Complex systems of interrelated and interconnected traces are thus established.

The psychological counterpart of this organization of structural modifications is the cognitive structure. In terms of cognitive theory, new learnings (new "knowledge," new patterns of functioning) are acquired as they become incorporated or assimilated into this hierarchically organized cognitive system. In other words, we learn new things in terms of what we already know.

Obviously, there are various specific ways in which functional patterns become changed with experience. There may be an increase in the strength or the precision of the behavior pattern itself. The golf player, for example, learns to combine an appropriate measure of strength with the accuracy of his stroke for each situation in which he finds himself. Or, the change may be a matter of replacing a customary, or "natural," response with a different, perhaps more appropriate or effective, one. It may also be a matter of becoming responsive to new and different stimuli in the situation. As we have seen, temperamental predispositions may be modified, strengthened, or directed into different behavioral channels. Attitudes, values, and interests change through experience and through the interests of others.

In any event, *what* the child has learned and *how well* he has learned to perform in relation to life's requirements and the expectations of the environment at any particular point in his course toward adulthood determine his level of "ability" (see Chapter 6). Ability means functional effectiveness without interference from other factors.

Ability, in the sense of one's repertory of available learned reactions to the environment and the tasks it presents, is what tests of so-called intelligence purport to sample and thus measure directly. This repertory of acquired responses, of course, depends upon one's capacity to acquire progressively more adequate behavior patterns, but it also depends upon the richness of the environment in terms of stimulation and opportunity to learn.

Subjective Conditions of Learning

Since the child is constantly doing something, he is constantly learning something. The conditions about him, the events that happen to him or about him, the attitudes and behaviors of others toward him, and the many aspects of his daily milieu all conspire to determine what he learns. But subjective ("inner") factors also play a vital role as conditions of learning.

A number of subjective factors affecting learning have been discussed in other connections (mental capacity, for instance, was described in Chapter 6 as a most fundamental condition of learning). The child's capacity to acquire new levels of functioning controls his learning at any particular point in his development. In other words, an individual must be ready to learn. This readiness level, as we have seen, is largely a matter of structural maturation.

Previous Learning

Another important subjective condition of learning that determines not only what but how well or how rapidly the child learns in a given situation, is "what he already knows." In the words of Gagné (1965):

> The child who is learning to tie his shoelaces does not begin this learning "from scratch"; he already knows how to hold the laces, how to loop one over the other, how to tighten a loop and so on. The child who learns to call the mailman "Mr. Wells" also does not begin without some prior capabilities: he already knows how to imitate the words "Mister" and "Wells," among other things. The theme is the same with more complex learning. The student who learns to multiply natural numbers has already acquired many capabilities, including adding and counting and recognizing numerals and drawing them with a pencil. The student who

is learning how to write clear descriptive paragraphs already knows how to write sentences and to choose words. (p. 21, by permission)

The parent or the teacher who is concerned with providing a child with optimal conditions for further learning must obviously use as his guide the child's already acquired capabilities. The child can learn only what he is "ready" (able) to learn in terms of his level of maturation *and* what he already knows or has learned to do. He is not "ready" to learn trigonometry if he has not yet mastered the operations of simple arithmetic.

Motivation

The problem of motivation is an extremely complex and involved subject, far too complicated for adequate treatment here. Our purpose therefore is simply to touch upon a few broad aspects of motivation that seem particularly pertinent to the matter of increasing individual functional effectiveness.

In connection with the discussion of the relation between the learner's present capabilities and new learnings, the factors of interest and challenge are of crucial importance. Clearly, there must be a "felt need," a desire on the child's part to learn the new material or to acquire a new level of ability. If the new learning task does not have a basis for its achievement in the child's present capabilities, he will be perplexed, frustrated, and discouraged, rather than motivated with a desire to achieve the new learning. On the other hand, new material must be new enough to be challenging, not boring.

SELF-CONSISTENCY   A somewhat related motivational factor is that if the material to be learned or the tasks to be engaged in are to have value in promoting personal effectiveness, they must have real relevance to and be consistent with the child's cognitive-emotional structure, including his self image. Lecky (1951) discussed the principle of self-consistency in the following words:

According to self-consistency, the mind is a unit, an organized system of ideas. All of the ideas which belong to the system must seem to be consistent with one another. The center or nucleus of the mind is the individual's idea or conception of himself. If a new idea seems to be consistent with the ideas already present in the system, and particularly with the individual's conception of himself, it is accepted and assimilated easily. If it seems to be inconsistent, however, it meets with resistance and is likely to be rejected. This resistance is a natural phenomenon, it is essential for the maintenance of individuality. (p. 246)

The nature of the child's "mind," in the sense in which it was used in the above quotation, of course, varies greatly among children. It is true that preadolescent boys generally have a strong need to regard themselves and to be regarded by others as "manly." Sex typing, by the time children reach the age of 8 or 9 years, has been very effective in establishing an image of manliness in the minds of boys (as well as a general idealized cultural stereotype of the attractive female in the minds of girls). But self images vary widely from one subculture to another, from one occupational group to another, and from one social class to another. A boy in a lower-class family, whose father and perhaps other adult males who play prominent roles in his life are engaged in work requiring physical strength, courage, and skill (for example, in the operation of machines and massive equipment), gets a very different view of what is manly than does a boy in a middle- or upper-class home, whose father is engaged in a high-prestige profession or business. Likewise what a girl develops as her image of the appropriate or desirable feminine role is determined very largely by the models she lives with and associates with but modified in various ways by what she sees on television or the motion picture screen or what she reads.

With such wide differences in experimental background, what is self-consistent for one child in the way of subject matter to be learned or school activities and interests might be anything but self-consistent for another. What is regarded as "sissy" by one boy might be quite consistent with another boy's conception of manliness.

Environmental Conditions of Living and Learning

Motivating conditions are often stimulated externally. Interest, for example, a subjective process so vital to school learning, also depends to a large extent upon the nature of the material to be learned, the objects to be examined and manipulated, and other physical facilities and surroundings provided by the school. Certainly the little boy's concept of manliness has its origin in the models of manhood about him and the portrayals of manly acts he is exposed to via the mass media. Our present purpose, however, is to center attention more directly and specifically upon the external, or environmental, conditions of learning.

Early Stimulation

Our basic assumption has been that all development comes about through the interaction of organism and environment. Activity in response to environmental stimulation is an outcome of such interaction. Since changes in the level of one's functioning result directly from functioning and since functioning (activity) is basically a matter of responding to the stimuli, internal and external, that impinge upon one's sense receptors, the vital importance of stimulation—its quality and appropriateness as well as its adequacy—becomes clearly apparent.

Only in recent years has the importance of stimulation to development in general become an area of special concern and active research by psychologists. The earlier assumption was that the development of mentality, during infancy and early childhood particularly, along with the development of the organism in general, was a function of maturation. This assumption was especially apparent in the prevailing theories of mental development during the first quarter of the present century. Chapter 6 pointed out that intelligence had been generally thought of as a single, general ability factor that was fixed by heredity and impervious to environmental influences.

The first real challenge to this point of view came during the 1930s with the publication of the research findings of the Iowa Child Welfare Station concerning the influence of nursery school attendance upon children's tested IQ's (Welman, 1934, 1937, 1938; Welman and Coffey, 1936). The main implication of these and other related studies (Skeels and Filmore, 1937; Skeel's *et al.*, 1938; Skodak, 1939) was the importance of the factor of variable environmental stimulation in mental development. The controversy among students of intelligence provoked by the Iowa findings finally led to the only tenable position regarding the factors of mental development, namely, the interaction point of view (see Chapter 6). Mental development, in the sense of the acquisition of new functional capabilities, results from the interaction between organism and environment. Thus, optimal learning, from the beginning, requires optimal stimulation. (Hunt, 1961, p. 263).

EVIDENCE FROM STUDIES OF INSTITUTION-REARED CHILDREN   Certain of the earlier studies of the effects of institution care during infancy upon functional development in children provided what appeared to be rather substantial evidence of its retarding effects

(Bowlby, 1940; Brodbeck and Irwin, 1946; Goldfarb, 1943, 1944, 1945; Spitz, 1945, 1946; Spitz and Wolf, 1946). Spitz (1945), for example, found that the measured developmental quotients (DQ's) of an orphanage group dropped from between 130 and 140 at 2 months of age, to an average of 76 after 4 months in the institution, while a control group of home-reared infants with the same range of initial DQ's maintained that level through the 4-month period.

Spitz's studies (along with the other contemporary studies of the effects of institution care) have been severely criticized on various counts, including the lack of rigorous control of variables (Casler, 1961; Orlansky, 1949; Pinneau, 1955). Pinneau (1955), for example, noted specifically that Spitz's data did not support the conclusions and interpretations he placed upon them.

Dennis and Najarian (1957) conducted a study in Lebanon which in certain respects was comparable to the Spitz (1945) study. These experimenters concluded that their data with respect to behavioral development in the institution environment showed no effect during the first 2 months of life, but there was marked retardation during the age period of 3 to 12 months.

We have already noted that the neonate has very limited (if existing) visual ability to perceive objects and persons *as such* (see Chapter 5). He also almost completely lacks responsiveness to social stimuli (see Chapter 7). These observations are pertinent in relation to the the Spitz and the Dennis and Najarian studies. On the basis of such observations it seems reasonable to conclude that with normal infant handling and adequate physical care (apart from the tactual and kinesthetic stimulation) visual and other kinds of stimuli from the external environment are relatively unimportant to functional development during these early weeks of life.

But developmental change in infancy is very rapid. As the baby's sensorimotor and perceptual abilities emerge and develop and as his affiliative need arises, the external environment—particularly its social aspects—becomes increasingly important to his continued cognitive and affective development. Dennis concluded that the relatively unstimulating environment of the foundling home, or the *Creche* of Lebanon, provided no opportunity for the infants to learn to perform the tasks or react effectively to the situations presented to them in the developmental test. Hence, their poor showing and low DQ's during infancy beyond age 3 months.

Adequate and appropriate stimulation is essential to optimal development from the very beginning. Many of the more recent observers of infant behavior have stressed the importance to the newborn, especially, of the stimulation he gets from maternal handling and holding, particularly from close skin-to-skin contact (Brody, 1956; Escalona, 1953; Frank, 1957; Montagu, 1953; Wolff, 1959). Mirsky (in Escalona, 1953), for example, wrote, "In the earliest stages, an infant's security is a matter of skin contact and of the kinesthetic sensations of being held and supported" (p. 29). Frank (1957), views the "tactile-cutaneous processes" as an extremely important communication facility particularly for the young infant. "The skin is the outer boundary, the envelope which contains the human organism and provides its earliest and most elemental mode of communication" (p. 211). Frank further stated:

> . . . babies and children especially require these [tactual] contacts to recover from acute disturbances. Prolonged deprivation of such tactual contacts and soothings may establish in the baby persistent emotional or affective responses to the world, since his initial biological reactions to threat have not been allayed and hence may become chronic. (p. 220)

In discussions of the importance of tactile and kinesthetic stimulation during infancy, little mention is made of their specific relationships to learning or cognitive development. Instead, most of us have generally assumed that emotional and general adjustment encompasses cognitive development. However, the theoretical question remains of whether or to what extent stimulation during childhood is a factor affecting the maturation of the bodily structure underlying functional capacity or whether the factor is merely a matter of the relative abundance of learning opportunities (as Dennis prefers to believe). The bulk of the evidence suggests that under conditions of extreme stimulus deprivation some irreversible retardation in development may result, but there is no doubt that, in a general sense, stimulation is a prime condition for learning as well as for other aspects of development.

There has also been some discussion in the psychological literature as to whether extensive intellectual stimulation during the early years of childhood might have deleterious effects, such as frustration resulting in negative attitudes, learning inhibitions, and over-all psychosocial maladjustment. Fowler (1962a) summarized the literature concerned with this question. He found much expression of opinion on the matter but little research evidence. On the basis of available evidence and in terms of his own experience in teaching a 2-year-old to read, however, Fowler (1962b) came to the conclusion that the risk is minimal and that there is "promise of considerable success with other young children, given further refinement of techniques and method" (p. 277).

The Nature of the Learning Processes

"Not only has man wanted to learn, but often his curiosity has impelled him to try to learn *how* he learns" (Bigge, 1964, p. 3). To learn the "how" of learning is a difficult and involved problem. Human functioning is multifaceted, and since learning is functional change resulting from functioning, there are, in a sense, as many kinds of learning as there are kinds of activities in which human beings engage. Nevertheless, because of man's curiosity about the fundamental nature of learning, certain individuals through the ages have speculated and experimented and thus developed explanatory ideas. During the past three hundred years many of these speculations have been formulated into theoretical proposals designed to account for at least some of the facts of learning. Because of the extreme complexity of the problem, however, these theories generally leave much yet to be explained.

General Theories of Learning

The various currently held learning theories can be grouped very roughly into two main categories, each representing a fundamentally different point of view in psychology. One of these is the so-called objective, or behavioristic, the other, the relativistic, mentalistic, or cognitive point of view.

From the first point of view, the phenomena to be observed and measured are behavior patterns, functions of the organism in response to stimuli of external or internal origin. This basic concept, the *stimulus-response relationship*, is symbolized by the simple formula $S \rightarrow R$. From the mentalistic point of view, the basic phenomena of psychology are of quite a different order. They are conscious experiences, rather than objectively observable acts or responses to stimuli. Ausubel (Anderson and Ausubel, 1965) draws a sharp contrast between these two viewpoints:

> Like the behavioristic position from which it was derived, the neobehavioristic view focuses on publicly observable responses and their environmental instigators and reinforcers as the proper objects of investigation in psychology. Consciousness is regarded as a "mentalistic" concept that is both highly resistive to scientific inquiry and not very pertinent to the real purposes of psychology as a science; it is considered an epiphenomenon that is important neither in its own right nor as a

determinant of behavior. Furthermore, say the neobehaviorists, it cannot be reliably (objectively) observed and is so extremely idiosyncratic as to render virtually impossible the kinds of categorization necessary for making scientific generalizations.

Exponents of the cognitive viewpoint, on the other hand, take precisely the opposite theoretical stance. Using perception as their model they regard differentiated and clearly articulated conscious experience (for example, knowing, meaning, understanding) as providing the most significant data for a science of psychology. (pp. 3–4)

It should be emphasized that we are here comparing two very general *classes* of approaches and points of view about learning, and that within each of these classes are different specific conceptions of the nature of the learning process. Hence the specific terms used by different theorists here roughly classed together are, only in a very broad sense, equivalent in meaning. Terms such as *behavioristic, neobehavioristic, objective, associationistic,* and *stimulus-response* characterize in a very general way a number of different specific points of view, but they have in common, however, a more empirical, mechanistic, and absolutistic way of viewing human behavior. On the other hand, the second group tends to be more pragmatic and relativistic, being labeled by terms such as *mentalistic, cognitive,* and *Gestalt-field* which are not univocal but are used by different students of learning with different shades of meaning. The term mentalistic, for example, is more frequently used by adherents of the so-called objective school in referring to the contrasting theoretical position, whereas the term cognitive is most frequently used by the adherents of that position themselves in referring to their own viewpoint.

As a general rule, neither the neobehaviorists nor the cognitive psychologists are particularly concerned with the structure-function relationship, which is an integrating concept throughout this book. The adherents of the objective school are intent rather upon establishing cause-and-effect relationships between objective happenings as symbolized by the $S \rightarrow R$ formula, whereas the cognitive people are concerned with the structure of consciousness and with the activities and manipulations within the cognitive field itself, that constitute meaning and "coming to know."

Each in his own way, however, both the neobehaviorist and the mentalist, of necessity, deal with the individual-environment relationship. As Bigge (1964) points out:

The term *interaction* is commonly used in describing the person-environment process through which reality is perceived.

Both families of psychology use the term but define it in sharply different ways. Whereas S → R association theorists mean the *alternating reaction* of organism, then of environment, Gestalt-field psychologists always imply that the interaction of a person and his environment are *simultaneous* and *mutual*—both mutually participate at the same time. (pp. 74–75)

The objectivist is much more specific and atomistic in his references to the environment. He speaks of stimuli, and his objective is to identify direct connections between specific stimuli (forms of energy) and discrete reactions. However, the present tendency is somewhat more often to use "stimulus situation" and "moral behavior," thus recognizing the complexity of the behavior interaction process (Bigge, 1964, p. 60).

The cognitive-field psychologist, on the other hand, is more likely to see the environment in less specific and more relativistic terms. The cognitive field varies from moment to moment. It includes every aspect of the momentary situation—even the behaving individual himself—which, at the moment, plays a part in influencing behavior. The individual, from this point of view, is not seen simply as one end of an acting and reacting bipolar system (S → R relationship) but rather as an integral aspect of the cognitive field.

Objective Theories

The problem in connection with learning theory is that of conceptualizing the essential nature of the changes—that is, the variations, the complications, the elaborations that take place in the functioning person—largely as a consequence of his own activity. We shall first examine some of the more prominent theories of the objective school of thought.

The Substitute Response

E. L. Thorndike, one of the earliest American learning theorists, began publishing his work on learning (the associative processes) in animals in 1898. In Thorndike's thinking, learning is a matter of substituting effective or satisfying responses to stimulating situations, for responses that do not produce satisfying results. For example, a hungry animal in a new situation will perform many ineffective acts in response to the total stimulating situation. Eventually it will, by chance, hit upon the act that will make food available to it. According to

Thorndike's theory, the "bond" between the response that brought relief from hunger and the stimulus is strengthened. Learning has taken place. A "connection" is established between the situation and the response. The effective response from that time on, in that and similar situations, will tend to be substituted for the ineffective ones. This is trial-and-error learning, and Thorndike believed it to be the basic process in all learning (see Figure 8.1).

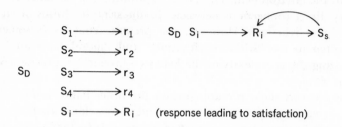

Figure 8.1

> Trial-and-error learning. S_D represents the motivating stimulus, hunger. S_1 to S_4 represent stimuli arising from the various features of the situation to which the learner responds in a random way (trial-and-error behavior). S_i is the specific stimulus that elicits R_i, the response which is instrumental in leading to food and thus bringing about a satisfying state of affairs S_s. The "bond" between S_i and the effective response R_i becomes "stamped in."

It will be noted in Figure 8.1 that two sorts of stimuli are involved in trial-and-error learning: the internal stimulus (the hunger); and the stimuli, mainly visual, which arise from the various objective features of the situation and to which the animal has been responding differentially. The former, the internal stimulus of hunger, is referred to as the *drive*, the motivating factor that keeps the animal active until he chances to make the response that is instrumental in bringing satisfaction. Motivation brings about activity, which consists of random "seeking" responses to the various aspects of the situation, and which is necessary if learning is to take place. Learning thus consists of forming connections (bonds) between specific stimuli and specific responses.

THORNDIKE'S LAWS OF LEARNING　As an elaboration of his theory and based upon his observations and experimentation, Thorndike formulated his well known laws of learning. Among his primary laws are the following:

1. The law of exercise. "Other things being equal, exercise, strengthens the bond between stimulus and response" (Thorndike, 1912, p. 95). By the same principle, the lack of exercise of a connection tends to weaken it. This law, of course, is universally taken for granted and is implicit in all efforts of rote memorization.

2. The law of effect. Again, in Thorndike's words, when a "modifiable" connection is being made "between an S and an R and being accompanied or followed by a satisfying state of affairs man responds, other things being equal, by an increase in the strength of that connection. To a connection similar, save that an *annoying* state of affairs goes with or follows it, man responds, other things being equal, by a decrease in the strength of the connection" (p. 172). This law has special significance in connection with current theoretical developments discussed later in this chapter.

3. The law of readiness. This law is concerned with the physiological functioning of the nervous system and its conductive units. Thorndike assumed that when an S → R connection is formed, a conduction unit, consisting of a specific set of neurones and their synapses, is established. These conduction units vary in degree of readiness to function according to the particular situation" . . . *for a conduction unit ready to conduct, to do so is satisfying,* and *for it not to do so is annoying"* (p. 127).

Thorndike and his followers in theory regarded this conceptualized process of establishing S → R bonds through the stamping-in effects of "drive reduction" and the stamping-out effects of unsatisfying or painful responses as the prototype of all learning.

The Conditioned Response

From the work of Pavlov (1927), the famous Russian physiologist, came the concept of the conditioned reflex. A conditioned reflex is a unit of behavior which can be elicited by a previously inadequate (neutral) stimulus. The learning process in which the substitute stimulus becomes "connected" to the response is called conditioning. This process is as follows: the neutral stimulus is paired with an adequate stimulus—one that already has the capacity to elicit a particular response. In a series of joint occurrence of these two stimuli (the originally inadequate one slightly preceding in time the adequate one), the inadequate stimulus becomes functionally connected with (conditioned to) the response. The learning, in this case, is the acquisition of a substitute stimulus, rather than a substitute response as in Thorndike's formulation. Conditioned-response learning is diagrammed in Figure 8.2.

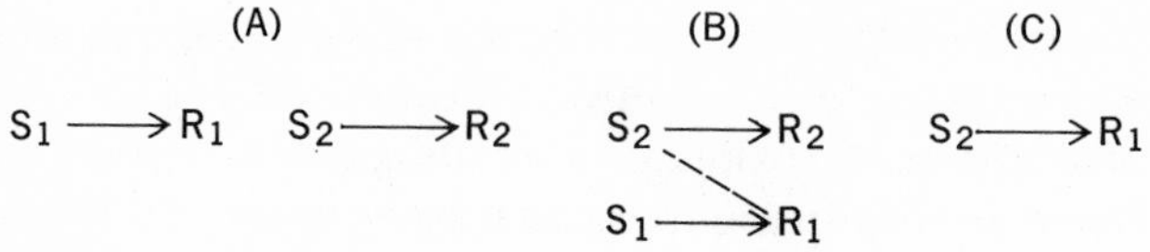

(A)   (B)   (C)

$S_1 \longrightarrow R_1$ $S_2 \longrightarrow R_2$ $S_2 \longrightarrow R_2$ $S_2 \longrightarrow R_1$

$S_1 \longrightarrow R_1$

Figure 8.2

The conditioned response. (A) S_1 is the originally adequate stimulus (nipple in baby's mouth) to R_1, the "natural" (unconditioned) response of sucking. S_2 is the "neutral" stimulus (sight of the nursing bottle), R_2 is, perhaps the visual fixation of the bottle. The sight of the bottle (S_2) always precedes its being placed in baby's mouth (S_1 stage B) and in a sense, becomes a sign that it will be placed in his mouth and sucking will begin. S_2 thus becomes "connected" to R_1. (C) Sucking thereafter begins at sight of bottle.

Many experiments in conditioning have been conducted with both human and animal subjects, thus establishing it as an important learning process. Attempts have been made to expand the concept to explain all learning. Conditioned-response theory quite soon became a rival to the trial-and-error, or connectionist, point of view that Thorndike developed.

Modifications and Extensions of Basic Concepts

Clearly, both trial-and-error learning and conditioning are importantly involved in functional change. Neither theory by itself, however, has been found adequate to account for all forms of learning. Each of them specified conditions essential to certain forms of learning but neither accounted for, or explained, the basic nature of the process of learning. The quest continued, therefore, for more adequate theoretical models.

All of the so-called associationistic, or connectionistic, theories and viewpoints that have been developed since the time of Thorndike and of Pavlov have taken as their starting point the concept of the stimulus-response relationship. They differ mainly as to the specific aspect of the process that is regarded as crucial in establishing the connection between the stimulus and the response. Some theorists have found it necessary to postulate certain conditions, or intervening variables, within the S → R sequence to account for the fixation of the bond; others have seen no such need.

BEHAVIORISM   John B. Watson "the behaviorist" (1928) regarded Pavlov's simple formulation of the conditioned reflex as a sufficient basis for explaining all learning. He simply generalized and expanded the concept by adopting Thorndike's law of associative shifting, which states that it is possible to *"get any response of which a learner is capable* associated with *any situation to which he is sensitive"* (Thorndike, 1913, p. 15).

CONTIGUOUS CONDITIONING   Edwin R. Guthrie (1952) is strictly an S → R learning theorist, but he views the S → R situation in quite a different way than do other students of conditioning. In his thinking, the objective, measurable stimulus and the outcome (the conditioned response or act that follows) are not the crucial elements in the associative, or learning, process. Rather, the elemental movements that *constitute* the response in the usual sense and the stimuli produced by, or inherent in, those movements, become connected by association. This simultaneous contiguity between movement and movement-produced stimuli in a single occurrence, according to Guthrie, results in a conditioned response. Guthrie's one law of learning is, "A combination of stimuli which has *accompanied* a movement will on its recurrence tend to be followed by that movement" (1952, p. 23). In an earlier paper he also stated that "a stimulus pattern gains its full associative strength on the occasion of its first pairing with a response" (1942, p. 30). Guthrie thus saw no need for such concepts as reinforcement or drive reduction to explain learning.

THE BIOLOGICAL ADAPTATION THEORY   One of the most influential theorists particularly during the 1930s was Clark L. Hull. More than any of his predecessors, Hull worked consistently toward a completely comprehensive formulation of the learning process. His theory is basically S → R conditioning. In contrast to Guthrie's principle of simultaneous contiguity, Hull assigned great importance to what happens during the brief interval between stimulus and response. He spelled out in considerable detail these happenings and the integrating elements involved, as he envisaged them, as "intervening variables," and he postulated a series of laws that defined the roles of these variables in the learning process.

Hull's (1943) formulation, however, is characterized particularly by his concept of reinforcement. He viewed a drive arising from a state of organic need as an indication that the conditions of survival for the organism are not being adequately met. When such a need, with its drive stimuli, develops, the organism becomes active, and when a particular act alleviates the need, that act tends to be stamped in as a biological adaptation of the organism. Thus, Hull theorized that all learning, whether of the conditioned-response order or the Thorndikian trial-and-error habit formation, might be explained in terms of a process of reinforcement from biological adaptation.

Operant Conditioning

Under the leadership of B. F. Skinner, a vigorous movement is currently under way among "objective" psychologists in the experimental study of learning. The underlying theory in this work is known as operant conditioning (Skinner, 1938, 1953, 1957, 1958, 1959; Staats, 1957, 1961, 1964; Staats and Staats, 1959, 1962). Reinforcement is also fundamental to this point of view. The unique feature of the operant conditioning theory, however, is that reinforcement comes not between the stimulus and response and *not* simultaneously with the response as in the case of Guthrie's theory of contiguity but *following* the response. Staats and Staats (1963) state this concept of reinforcement as follows:

> When certain stimuli closely follow a certain behavior they increase the probability of that behavior occurring again in the future. Stimuli that serve this function are called positive reinforcers, S_r. Other stimuli increase the probability of behavior occurring again when their *removal* closely follows that behavior. These stimuli are called negative reinforcers, S_p. (pp. 47–48, italics added)

The idea of the reinforcement following the response was first enunciated and studied by Thorndike (1913). This idea has been elaborated and refined, however, by Skinner and his collaborators. The concept of the "feedback" is used to explain the operation of the reinforcer.

A common example of operant learning is seen in the behavior of a young infant who awakens hungry from his nap. The condition of hunger motivates much overt activity. He kicks, squirms, thrashes about with his arms, sucks his fist (which finds it way into his mouth), and begins to cry lustily. As a result of his crying he is immediately fed. Crying, then, is the successful (instrumental) response bringing relief from hunger, which relief is a satisfying stimulus closely follow-

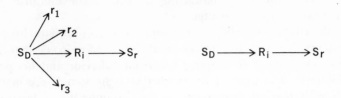

Figure 8.3

> The process of operant conditioning. S_D represents the hunger "drive" in the infant. r_1 r_2, R_i, and r_3 represent the random activity set off by the hunger stimulus. R_i, one of these acts, is crying which turns out to be instrumental in bringing relief. The response of crying thus is followed immediately by comfort and satisfaction, the reinforcing stimulus S_r. The baby thus learns to cry immediately to bring relief.

ing his crying response. Crying when hungry is thus reinforced, and the probabilities of his crying when hungry thereafter are increased. He has learned a *habit*. Figure 8.3 is a schematic representation of the operant-conditioning process.

The reinforcing stimulus in the foregoing example was *intrinsic* in the situation. The natural outcome of drive reduction was the satisfaction of hunger. This was the primary reinforcer. There are, of course, other sorts of reinforcers, both positive and negative. In experimental work in learning, the experimentor can arbitrarily introduce various rewards for a correct response. Punishments which can be avoided only by the correct response are also in the nature of primary reinforcers because the rewards are made direct consequences of the instrumental act. By their nature rewards are either pleasant and satisfying or unpleasant. An electric shock, for example, is naturally painful to the animal; a piece of candy or a colorful trinket is immediately pleasant to the child.

SECONDARY REINFORCEMENT *in contact* Other stimuli, which are associated in time and are contiguous with the performance of the correct (instrumental) response and its primary reinforcement, may quickly become conditioned (secondary) reinforcers. Such acquired reinforcers have become very important in learning theory as intervening variables. There are, of course, inherent in any learning situation, extraneous stimuli that are potential conditioned reinforcers. Noises connected with the training box in animal experimentation may quickly acquire reinforcing value with respect to the instrumental response and thus become crucial factors in the acquisition and "shaping" of behavior. Skinner (1959) found that conditioned reinforcers were important facilitating factors in the establishment of new behavior patterns in pigeons.

In the course of a child's experience (interaction with his parents and others), he acquires many conditioned reinforcers that are of extreme importance in shaping his social behavior and his personal development. The sight of his mother and the sounds she makes are paired with natural reinforcers to the responses he is learning. As a young infant he clings close to his mother as part of the total pattern of nursing behavior which is instrumental to his experience of satisfaction and comfort (primary reinforcer). As he nurses he gazes into his mother's face and hears her voice. He also experiences olfactory, tactile, and kinesthetic stimulation, all of which become part and parcel of his experience of comfort and satisfaction. They thus become conditioned reinforcers to his clinging "attachment" to his mother. During the first 12 to 15 months of the child's life this attachment to his mother is an important factor in his emotional development.

RESEARCH IN OPERANT CONDITIONING   Operant conditioning concepts and procedures lend themselves readily to precise mechanical regulation. Through early experimentation, largely with animal subjects, the basic principles of operant conditioning as formulated by Skinner in 1938 and others have been established. As a consequence much interest has been generated in this approach to the study of learning. Recent work has more frequently involved human subjects. Many neobehavioristically inclined students of psychology have been attracted by the apparent ease with which the experimental variables and procedures involved in operant work can be placed under rigid mechanical control.

Currently the operant-conditioning approach is being used in the experimental modification of behavior in a wide variety of human subjects. It is particularly adaptable to learning experiments with infants and young children because with them stimulus controls and procedures other than those built into the experimental apparatus are very difficult to impose. Hence, a greatly increased interest in the learning capabilities of infants and very young children has recently developed (Bijou, 1957; Brackbill, 1958; Rheingold, Gewirtz, and Ross, 1959; Simmons and Lipsitt, 1961).

Exceptional children are also being studied by use of operant-learning techniques. Some of these studies have been concerned with the experimental evaluation of variations in stimulus controls (Bijou and Orlando, 1965; Ellis, Barnett, and Pryer, 1960). D. M. Baer (1962a and b) and others have applied these approaches to the treatment of child problems such as thumbsucking.

In general, wide interest has developed in the operant conditioning point of view, particularly in its potential application to practical problems. Skinner (1938, 1953, 1957, 1958, 1959) has led out in demonstrating as well as proposing practical applications of his procedures. He believes that "programmed" instruction with reinforcements spaced properly to make them contingent upon the desired behavior in the schoolroom setting, could result in greatly increased effectiveness in teaching.

D. M. Baer (1962b) and Bijou and Baer (1963) particularly have applied operant principles to problems of social learning and the modification of social behavior patterns in children. They have developed both laboratory (experimental) techniques and field-experimental methods of behavior modification through the control of stimulus consequences. Baer (1962b), by means of a mechanized, talking puppet, demonstrated the use of attention and approval as social reinforcers. He also found wide individual differences in the effectiveness of these two classes of social stimuli as reinforcers.

Bijou and Baer (1963) even more strongly emphasized the importance of individuality among children at the preschool level and the different kinds of social reinforcements which have, in the children's past, operated in the development of their social behavior patterns and problems. These authors point out that through the careful and continuous observation of a child with a particular behavior problem it is possible to note the various stimulus situations in which the objectionable behavior occurs, and particularly its *stimulus consequence* in each instance. Then by controlling and modifying the consequences (reinforcements) of the behavior, the behavior itself is controlled and modified. The most effective consequences which reinforced these undesirable patterns, they found, were the reactions of others, such as their attention, their approval or disapproval, their support and affection. Bijou and Baer briefly describe an example:

> This program has been applied to a case in which the child crawled rather than walked almost all of every morning. It was observed that the teachers responded to crawling with a great deal of attention and support, with a view toward improving the child's "security." When this was stopped, and the reinforcement shifted to the child's "upright" behavior, the crawling weakened greatly within a few days and was largely replaced by upright behaviors of standing, walking, running, etc. Reversal of the contingencies to the old pattern reverse this outcome; reinstatement of the new contingencies again produced the new, desirable pattern. The result generalized well to the child's

home environment, where the parents used similar contingencies (demonstrated for them in the nursery school) to maintain the upright behavior. (1963, pp. 227–228)

Bijou and Baer also found that other behavior problems such as excessive crying, overdependence, aggression, and inattention could be successfully treated through this method of social reinforcement control.

A lively interest is also developing in verbal behavior as an area of operant-learning research. (Rheingold, Gewirtz, and Ross, 1959; Skinner, 1957; Staats, 1961; Staats and Staats, 1959, 1962). This research area gives promise of considerable practical significance. (This topic is further dealt with in Chapter 9.)

Neobehaviorism and the Problem of Meaning

One of the most intriguing problems connected with human learning is the problem of meaning. That one thing comes to mean (represent) another in human experience is a matter of common experience and observation. This process of signification is involved in functional modification at all levels. Even in the simplest forms of learning such as the conditioned reflex, one stimulus, or sign, comes to mean (represent, or become a substitute for) another. In perceptual learning, which is more fully dealt with in a later section, the mere smell of an orange, for example, becomes a sign which represents the complete pattern of sense experiences that have become associated with the object (orange). The smell (or the sight or the feel) of the object alone becomes sufficient as a basis for the act of categorization. The object is immediately placed in the category (orange).

In other aspects of human learning, however, the signification process is not so readily understood or so easily described. In the psychology of language, for example, the phenomenon of meaning involves learned reactions more complex than any we have so far discussed. In our study of these more complex learning processes the concept of mediation (the role of intervening variables) becomes especially important.

As we have seen, the problem of mediation has long been a central one in learning theory. Hull (1943), in the elaboration of his point of view, postulated a set of laws in which he defined the intervening variables essential to learning. In the more recent operant-conditioning formulations, secondary reinforcement and the concept of feedback are regarded as important mediating factors.

On the basis of a great deal of animal experimentation, the fact of a mediating process in learning is rather generally accepted. As to the nature of this process—the mechanism per se—there is considerable disagreement. Mowrer (1960a and b), Staats and Staats (1959), and others hold that meaning and representational reactions constitute the mediating factor. Skinner and others of his school, on the other hand, rather generally reject the concept of meaning, or understanding, insisting that mediation involves nothing more than vocal or subvocal responses of an associative nature, and that ultimately what is involved is simple shaping of behavior through the mediation of conditioned reinforcers.

THE NATURE AND ROLE OF PUNISHMENT The explanation of the role of punishment (negative reinforcement) in learning in terms of a mediating process has been particularly difficult. Thorndike in his original formulation stated the matter simply and in terms of human experience: "When a modifiable connection between a situation and a response . . . is made and is accompanied or followed by an annoying state of affairs, its [the connection's] strength is decreased" (1913, p. 4).

In his discussion of the punishment aspect of Thorndike's original theory, Mowrer (1960a) wrote as follows:

> For at least two decades now, it has been clear that the "negative" half of the law (Law of Effect), in its more molecular aspects, was miscast. . . .
> Whatever learning may be in its "forward," position phase, it became increasingly clear that unlearning, or *"punishment,"* is *not* a simple matter of obliterating, stamping out stimulus-response "bonds." But a more declarative approach to the negative side of learning could not occur until at least certain forms of that type of learning known as conditioning were taken into account. (pp. 23–24)

As Mowrer pointed out, Thorndike himself came seriously to question the punishment side of his theory. He came to the conclusion, after a long series of learning experiments, that punishment was *not* instrumental in eliminating wrong responses. This reversal of his position, in the face of much accumulated evidence that punishment was indeed an effective factor in learning, clearly suggested a need for a more adequate account of the operation of mediating variables in "negative" learning. Most writers in discussing the role of punishment in learning have little to say regarding the mediation process involved. Conditioned aversive stimuli (negative reinforcers), however, are mentioned in explanations of the effects of punishment. Staats and Staats (1963), for example, explain that the stimuli produced by the punished act "acquire negative reinforcing properties, that is, elicit conditioned aversive, or *anxiety* responses (p. 98, italics added). In effect, the punished act produces its own negative conditioned reinforcers (anxiety). Thus, "stopping the response, or responding in another manner is strengthened" (p. 98).

The rather common spanking-the-hand training procedure used by parents with their toddler-age children exemplifies the indirect effects of punishment. The child reaches for a breakable object on the shelf. As he reaches, the parent says "No, no" and then spanks the reaching hand. The natural response to the pain from the spanking is the fear-withdrawal reaction. The proprioceptive stimuli inherent in (produced by) the act of reaching, *and* the "No, no"—both of which slightly precede the pain—immediately become conditioned stimuli to the fear naturally elicited by the pain stimulus. On future occasions, as soon as the child begins to reach for the forbidden object or hears the command "No, no," he becomes afraid or anxious and inhibits the act which gives rise to the fear. "This notion of punish-

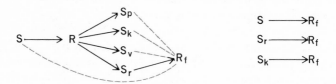

Figure 8.4

Avoidance learning. S represents the situation: vase on shelf within baby's reach. R is the natural response of reaching and grasping vase. S_k represents kinaesthetic, tactile and other response-produced stimuli. S_v represents the word stimulus "No, No!" and S_p the pain from "spanked" hand, both of which are also response produced. The various other features of the whole situation, (S_k, S_r, and so forth) thus become conditioned stimuli to fear and the avoidance reaction. Adapted from Mowrer (1960a), p. 26.

ment is obviously and importantly different from Thorndike's conception of bond erasure; and it is now generally conceded that punishment achieves its inhibitory effect, not by the direct stamping out of S-R bonds, but by the intermediation of fear" (Mowrer, 1960a, p. 25). Figure 8.4 is a representation of this view of the role of punishment in learning.

RESPONSE-PRODUCED STIMULI AND THE FEEDBACK   The inadequacy of earlier learning theory in explaining the "how" of reinforcement effects has been pointed out by Mowrer. In rather close agreement with the view of Staats and Staats mentioned above, Mowrer (1960a) postulated an intermediary emotional variable in the learning process which constitutes a modification of the concept of secondary reinforcement, and which, he feels, more adequately deals with this problem. In Mowrer's thinking, the effective conditioned reinforcers are the *response-produced stimuli*—proprioceptive, tactile, and other—that are inherent in the instrumental response itself. As we saw in the case of punishment, these stimuli (since they occur *with* the act) precede the reward, the satisfying (or dissatisfying) state of affairs which that instrumental act brings about. Through the repeated pairing of these response-produced stimuli with the reward, the former become conditioned to the affective component of the outcome. In the case of positive reinforcement, the emotional component is hope; in the case of negative reinforcement it is fear. Mowrer's contention is that these emotions of hope and fear, which become connected through the process of conditioning to response-produced stimuli (stimuli inherent in the response itself), are the effective conditioned reinforcers. In effect, the response itself acquires the function of signaling, through hope or fear, its own outcome. Figure 8.5 is designed to represent the establishment and operation of secondary reinforcement in terms of Mowrer's theory. An important point which Mowrer emphasizes is that only the involuntary, autonomically controlled reflexive responses involved in emotion, such as changes in heartbeat rate, constriction of the blood vessels, endocrine secretions, and so forth, rather than voluntary acts, are subject to conditioning in the classical sense.

To further illustrate Mowrer's formulation in terms of functional development in children we shall reillustrate the infant in the process of acquiring an emotional attachment to his mother. As the infant nurses at his mother's breast he clings close to her as part of the total pattern of nursing behavior. This pattern of behavior (R_i in Figure 8.5) is accompanied by and gives rise to a great deal of sensory stimulation, much of which is response-produced. The infant's muscles involved in clinging, grasping, and so forth, and in sucking and other motor components of the total pattern, produce proprioceptive stimuli (s, s, s,). These stimuli begin slightly in advance of the pleasure-producing reward, gratification (S_r). "It is assumed that a part of the total response, R_r, which is produced by S_r, will become conditioned to the stimuli (s, s, s), inherently connected with R_i" (Mowrer 1960b, p. 14). This component of R_r Mowrer calls hope (r_h). The connection between the response-produced stimuli (s, s, s) and the

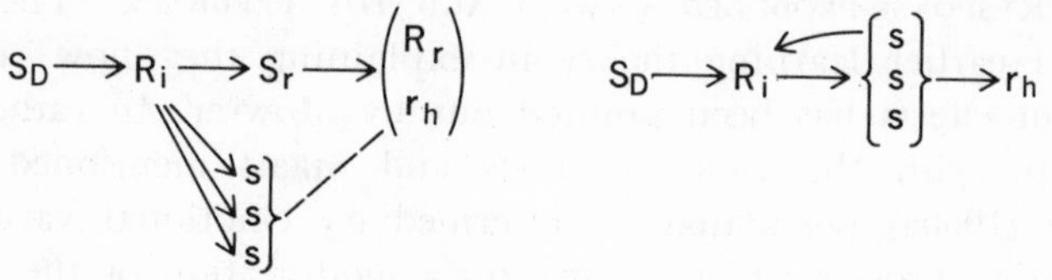

Figure 8.5

Positive secondary (conditioned) reinforcement in the establishment of a "habit". The hungry (S_D) infant nurses at his mother's breast, R_1. R_1 is a complex pattern including clinging grasping behavior. Hence there are many response-produced stimuli, s, s, s. These precede slightly the primary reinforcer, gratification (S_r). S_r, in turn, elicits R_r, of which r_h, the affective reaction of "hope" is a component. In association with S_r, stimuli s, s, s also become functionally connected with r_h. They can now "signal" hope, and thus have become secondary reinforcers to the response (R_1) which produces them. Adapted from Mowrer (1960b), p. 14.

positive *emotion* (hope) thus becomes established. These stimuli come to mean (signal) hope. The baby's clinging-nursing activity has its built-in reinforcers. The stimuli that are inherently a part of the response pattern itself quickly become conditioned stimuli that elicit the same positive, hopeful reaction that gratification (S_r) originally elicited. These conditioned, response-produced stimuli are the effective secondary reinforcers.

The Mentalistic or Cognitive Viewpoint

During the first quarter of the present century, the thinking of American psychologists about learning was predominantly associationistic (behavioristic) in character. As we have seen, a number of competing theoretical positions were developed, but they were all primarily concerned with the problem of explaining the nature of the process by which stimuli become connected with responses. It was in 1924 when Kurt Koffka's book *Growth of the Mind* was published in English and was introduced to American psychologists. A year later Kohler's book *Mentality of Apes* appeared. These two books introduced into the United States for the first time a view of learning that was in direct contrast to the theories current at the time.

From this "new" point of view, learning (that is, change in functional adequacy) occurred as a result of *insight*—seeing into the total complex and integrated situation by the learner—rather than one's going "through the laborious processes of stamping out incorrect responses and stamping in correct ones" (Hilgard, 1956, p. 222). The principle of insightful learning was demonstrated in the learning behavior of Kohler's chimpanzees. Kohler's and Koffka's attacks were specifically leveled at Thorndike's view of learning. As Hilgard pointed out, the idea of insight was not a new idea. "It was a return to a conception laymen had never abandoned" (p. 224). The influence of the Gestalt viewpoint in psychology was a timely and useful one.

A central concept in the Gestalt point of view concerns the essential nature of the situation in which the individual acts and learns. Insightful perception in relation to the total situation was an area of great emphasis. We shall return to the topic of perception in a later section.

The "Cognitive-Field" View of Learning

The name of Kurt Lewin is inseparably connected with the "field" theory of learning in the United States. Lewin was a German and a member of the Gestalt group. His thinking concerning learning, therefore, grew out of the Gestalt tradition. His theoretical position is usually referred to as the field-theoretical position.

A basic feature of field theory is its relativistic emphasis, as contrasted with the absolutistic and mechanistic view of behavior and its changes held by the objectivists. "The basic principle of relativism is that nothing is perceivable or conceivable as a thing-in-itself. Rather, everything is perceived or conceived in relation to other things" (Bigge, 1964, p. 176). Learning is regarded as a process by which the learner gains insights into a situation in terms of the relationships among its various aspects and component parts. Lewin conceptualized the psychological field as a space in which the individual moves or lives psychologically. It is one's "life space" at the moment and it includes everything in one's life with which one has anything to do —people, objects, ideas, memories. The life space is influenced and conditioned by what is ordinarily referred to as the environment— physical, social, and so on—but life space and environment are not identical. Life space can change independently of environment. It is conceived, in a sense, to account for the psychological situation from moment to moment (Hilgard, 1956).

COGNITIVE STRUCTURE The life space is structured in varying degrees. An unstructured region represents an unresolved problem situation or a lack of understanding. As learning progresses, the total space becomes more and more structured in the sense of being more highly differentiated, and paths connect the various subregions. This means, simply, that increased learning enables us to see facts more clearly in their interrelationships. Facility in problem solving increases as structuring progresses. One learns only in relation to his cognitive structure: New facts are related to and integrated with already understood and interrelated facts; they are integrated into the cognitive structure.

As activities are repeated, they are learned. The cognitive structure is thus changed. The need-tension system is also changed as goals are attained. The relative attractiveness (valence) of goals and values also change with attainment.

THE PROBLEM OF MEANING   The difficulty of dealing with the problem of meaning in behavioristic terms was previously noted. Since the concept of meaning is basically mentalistic in nature it presents no special problem for the cognitive-field theorist. In his discussion of the concept, Ausubel explained the acquisition of meaning.

> According to the cognitive structure view, meaning is an idiosyncratic phenomenological product of a meaningful learning process in which the potential meaning inherent in symbols and sets of symbols become converted into differentiated cognitive content within a given individual. Potential meaning thus becomes converted into phenomenological meaning when a particular individual, employing a meaningful learning set, incorporates a *potentially* meaningful sign or proposition within his cognitive structure.
>
> New meanings are therefore acquired when potentially meaningful symbols, concepts and propositions are related to and incorporated within the cognitive structure on a nonarbitrary, substantive basis. (Anderson and Ausubel, 1965, pp. 67–68)

Ausubel has been particularly concerned with the kind of learning that hopefully takes place in the schoolroom, namely reception learning—the learning and retention of new subject matter—and with the problem of how such learning and retention can be facilitated. His research has been based

> . . . on the premise that existing cognitive structure, that is, an individual's organization, stability, and clarity of knowledge in a particular subject matter field at any given time, is the principal factor influencing the learning and retention of meaningful new material. If existing cognitive structure is clear,

stable, and suitably organized, it facilitates the learning and retention of new subject matter. If it is unstable, ambiguous, disorganized, or chaotically organized, it inhibits learning and retention. Hence it is largely by strengthening relevant aspects of cognitive structure that new learning and retention can be facilitated. When we deliberately attempt to influence cognitive structure so as to maximize meaningful learning and retention, we come to the heart of the educative process. (Ausubel, 1963, p. 217)

The concern of the cognitive-field theorists is with what transpires psychologically. Overt behavior to them is significant insofar as it provides clues to what is being incorporated psychologically. Cognitive-field theory has real relevance and significance, therefore, in relation to the problem of understanding the nature of developmental change in mental functioning. Functional adequacy generally is very largely a result of learning. One's level of functional effectiveness is raised as one gradually subsumes new facts, new ideas, and new abilities to the stable, organized elements of one's cognitive structure.

Perceptual Learning

The function of perceiving—the process of coming to know of conditions external to as well as within the organism by means of the sense organs—is the primary cognitive (mental) process. It is important at the outset to point out that perceptual knowledge is a highly personal matter; there is considerable variaion in perceived reality among individuals and from time to time in the same individual (Berlyne, 1957). Many studies have shown that perceiving is influenced to a remarkable degree by motivational factors, personal experiences, and the over-all psychological organization (personality) of the perceiver (Henle, 1955; Prentice, 1961; Witkin *et al.*, 1954).

Individual variation in perception is not surprising, however, with the realization that perceptual ability, like human abilities generally, is not innate but is developed through living experience. The newborn infant possesses a full complement of sense organs which for the most part are ready to function, but there is no real evidence for actual perception on the part of the neonate. Ausubel (1958) draws the distinction between preperceptual behavior and perception:

Since all perceptual and cognitive phenomena deal by definition with the *contents of processes of awareness*, they cannot always be inferred from overt behavior. Behavior, for example, frequently reflects the organism's capacity for experiencing differentially the differential properties of stimuli. Nevertheless, since all differential psychological experience preceding or accompanying behavior does *not* necessarily involve a content or process of awareness, we cannot always consider it perceptual or cognitive in nature. Several examples may help to elucidate this distinction.

We have previously shown that a young infant will follow a patch of color moving across a multi-colored background, will cease crying when he hears his mother's footsteps, and will respond differentially to various verbal commands. Conditioning experiments during infancy also show that the child is able to "discriminate" between different sizes, colors, and shapes of objects and between pitches of sound. Does this constitute evidence of genuine perception, memory, discrimination, and understanding of representational symbols?

. . . it is reasonable to suppose that much of the sensory experience impinging on the infant is too diffuse, disorganized, and uninterpretable to constitute the raw material of perception and cognition, despite evidence of differential response to stimulation. Clear and meaningful contents of awareness presupposes some minimal interpretation of incoming sensory data in the light of an existing ideational framework. In the first few months of life not only is the experiential basis for this framework lacking, but the necessary neuroanatomic and neurophysiologic substrate for cortical functioning is also absent. (pp. 544–545 in *Theories and problems of child development*, 1958, Grune & Stratton, Inc., by permission)

Not only must the "neuroanatomic and neurophysiologic substrate" necessary for perceptual functioning be developed in the infant through further maturation, but he must also gradually develop his *percepts* through learning from sensory experience. Recent work in perception and learning capabilities of infants, however, suggests that by the end of the first 4 to 6 months certain aspects of visual perception are readily demonstrable in infants. Eleanor Gibson (1963), for example, found that most 6-month-old babies could not be prevailed upon to crawl across an area covered with heavy glass arranged so as to give the illusion of a drop-off to a dangerous depth. The infants apparently perceived the drop-off, or "cliff," effect, which meant danger to them. As to how this learning takes place, again, is a matter of theory. Some students of perception place emphasis upon the stimulus input rather than upon the S → R relationship. From this point of view the structuring or categorizing of information furnished by the senses is the essential aspect of the perceiving function. Bruner (1957) describes the process as follows:

> Perception involves an act of categorization. Put in terms of antecedent and subsequent conditions from which we make our inferences, we stimulate an organism with some appropriate input and he responds by referring the input to some class of things or events. "That is an orange," he states. . . . On the basis of certain defining or critical attributes in the input which are usually called cues, although they should be called clues, there is a selective placing of the input in one category or identity rather than another. The category need not be elaborate: "a sound," "a touch," "a pain," are examples of categorized inputs. (p. 225)
>
> A second feature of perception, beyond its seemingly categorical and referential nature is that it can be described as varyingly veridical [true to reality]. This is what has classically been called the "representative function" of perception: what is perceived is somehow a representation of the external world. (p. 228)

IMITATION Generally, the term "perceptual learning" refers to the categorizing process as described by Bruner (1957). We come to know the outside world and its complexities through our senses, and we categorize and organize that knowledge and subsume it into our everchanging cognitive structure. But our knowing and categorizing are not limited to objects and situations. Often involved in these situations are other individuals and their acts and performances, and we not only categorize these observed performances in a cognitive sense, but in many instances we are also able, upon observing them, to reproduce those performances ourselves. This is also perceptual learning—learning in which we acquire new performance patterns by observing them in other individuals. Bandura (1962) describes this process as *response learning*

> . . . in which subjects combine fractional responses into relatively complex novel patterns solely by observing the performances of social models often without any opportunity to perform the model's behavior in the exposure setting, and without any reinforcers delivered immediately either to the models or to the observers. Here, clearly, social cues constitute an indispensable aspect of the learning process. (pp. 216–217)

Bandura also pointed out that in present-day theorizing about observational learning the many commonly observed instances of the direct and immediate taking-on of "novel" performances simply by seeing them being performed by others are generally ignored.

The accounts of learning from models, however, are usually limited to descriptions of changes in overt behavior (the learning and perfection of motor skills). In such instances, of course, the principles of operant conditioning are particularly applicable (Bijou and Baer, 1961; Skinner, 1953). Skinner's principle of *shaping* through successive approximations is assumed to be the underlying process in the acquisition of all novel performances. Accordingly, this process always involves the positive reinforcement of any element or aspect of the desired new pattern which the learner chances to approximate, while all other components of his behavior are left unrewarded. As practice continues, the standards of closeness of the approximations to the model performance which are required for reward are gradually raised until, through successive trials, the perfected pattern is achieved. Skinner's (1953) generalized description of the shaping process is as follows:

> Operant conditioning shapes behavior as a sculptor shapes a lump of clay. Although at points the sculptor seems to have produced an entirely novel object, we can always follow the process back to the original undifferentiated lump, and we can make the successive stages by which we return to this condition as small as we wish. At no point does anything emerge which is very different from what preceded it. The final product seems to have a special unity or integrity of design, but we cannot find a point at which this suddenly appears. In the same sense, an operant is not something which appears full blown in the behavior of the organism. It is the result of a continuous shaping process. (p. 91)

This is clearly the process by which skilled performances are acquired and perfected. The model performance is carefully observed, and continued efforts are made to approximate that model, and each partial success receives its reinforcement. Performance learning is often rewarded directly by the one who is setting the model, but the sense of achievement is also a rewarding consequence. Skill learning is facilitated by differential reinforcement. This, of course, is learning by observation (imitation).

But, as Bandura insists, there are many instances in common experience of direct and immediate learning through imitation which do not involve the principle of successive approximations. "It is doubtful . . . if many of the responses that almost all members of our society exhibit would ever be acquired if social training proceeded solely by the method of successive approximations" (Bandura and Walters, 1963, p. 3). Young children readily pick up simple acts which they observe in adults. In their play they often go through rather elaborate performances in imitation of the daily routine activities of their parents.

In such direct acquisition of response patterns through imitation —"solely by observing the performance"—there is no implication of an instinctive ability independent of previous learning. The imitator in these instances, through much previous practice and experience in diverse areas of motor activity, has become proficient in a great many fractional responses which he is capable of combining and structuring into any of a variety of possible performance patterns. The novel aspect of the imitated performance is the patterning of fractional responses. It should also be pointed out that these immediately imitated performances are not usually, if ever, exact copies in every respect and detail of the observed performances. They may in fact be very inaccurate copies.

Nevertheless, the reality of direct learning of overt performance patterns through the observation of models has been clearly demonstrated (Bandura, 1962; Bandura, Ross, and Ross, 1961; Bandura and Walters, 1963), and this should be taken into account in any adequate theory of social learning. But it is equally true, as we have seen, that generally in the learning and the perfection of motor skills there is much shaping of behavior through continued practice resulting in successive approximations with reinforcement. It is quite obvious that the skills of the concert violinist or the expert typist, for example, could never be acquired solely by the observation of models, no matter how expert and precise those models may be.

The influence of models is a very important factor in many areas of functional development, and particularly in social learning and personality development.

Summary

Our primary objective throughout this book is to understand as clearly as possible the nature of the processes of development in the human individual. Our interest in learning theory, therefore, stems from this developmental orientation. Learning is a process of developmental change, and the term subsumes all aspects and degrees of change in the functioning of the individual that are not the result of biological developmental processes, that is, those which come about through exercise, activity, and experience (functioning).

The infant, as we have seen, is born with a certain repertory of reflexes that are simple, ready-to-function responses to specific stimulations. No learning is necessary for the baby's performance of stimulus-response sequences, although the muscles involved undoubtedly have been strengthened through exercise prior to birth.

From the initial moment on, a complicated learning process is under way, a process too complex and involved to be explained in terms of any single simple formula. In the first place, each separate movement in each reflex produces its indigenous stimuli, thus meeting Guthrie's (1952) simultaneous contiguity requirement for strengthening the S → R connection. The reflex patterns themselves through exercise become strengthened and "shaped" (Ferster and Skinner, 1957) for more effectiveness. Out of many random responses in the total pattern certain ones are selected (Thorndike's trial and error) and receive primary reinforcement. New stimuli, both extraneous and response-produced, become associated, through "classical" conditioning, with gratification and thus become secondary reinforcers.

When semisolid and solid foods are introduced to the child he must learn through trial and error, and shaping, the way to manage food in his mouth. Food likes and dislikes are acquired through various processes of association. Throughout the developmental period the child learns to eat and to like many foods. He acquires skill in the use of tableware, and through verbal association and practice he learns the many niceties of social behavior at the dinner table. All of these learnings require not just one but a number of theoretical formulations adequately to account for them.

What is true of early functional development is even more obviously true of the acquisition of the "higher" forms of functioning. If one could trace the course of development in detail of the many motor, intellectual, and social skills that make for adequate and effectual personal functioning in our complex society, one would undoubtedly find all of the theories of learning exemplified.

SELECTED READING SUGGESTIONS

Anderson, R. C., and D. P. Ausubel. *Readings in the psychology of cognition.* New York: Holt, Rinehart and Winston, Inc., 1965. (See particularly pp. 3–17, 103–115, 116–132.)

Bigge, M. L. *Learning theories for teachers.* New York: Harper & Row, 1964.

Gagné, R. M. *Conditions of learning.* New York: Holt, Rinehart and Winston, Inc., 1965.

Hilgard, E. R. *Theories of learning.* Second ed.; New York: Appleton, 1948.

Piaget, J. *The psychology of intelligence.* Paterson, N.J.: Littlefield, Adams, 1960. (Read Chapter 3, Intelligence and perception.)

CHAPTER 9

Language Development

Communication in its broad aspects is obviously not limited to mankind. Subhuman species commonly interact with one another and influence one another's behavior by means of sounds, gestures, and other motor patterns. But what about the central or "mental" concomitants of this behavior? Does the bird issue his cry *in order to* warn others of his kind? Does the enraged beast make his ferocious roar with *intent* to frighten or discourage his adversary? Is there really any intentionality in subhuman signals, in the frightening screech of rage or alarm or the strutting and gentle cooing of birds at mating time or the clucking of the hen as she conducts her brood about the yard? Or, are these various behaviors, effective as they are in eliciting appropriate responses in others, simply "built-in" instinctive or reflexive patterns made in response to external and internal stimuli?

The bulk of the evidence suggests the latter interpretation. Although subhuman species do influence one another with their sounds and their gestures and can bring about community of action in the group as well as appropriate individual behavior, it is quite likely that communication *with purpose and deliberate intent* is limited to man.

Communication and Learning

Our present concern is with the development, in the individual human being, of the ability intentionally and voluntarily to transmit meaning and information to others through the learned, specialized functioning of bodily structures. Not only is intentional communication itself a learned function but the ability to transmit and to receive information with specialized meaning is a tremendously important factor in facilitating further learning in general.

Intentional communication obviously implies the use of a vehicle (a means of transmission). Information about things not actually present to sense is transmitted to others by means of sounds, gestures, or other signs that by common consent have come to stand for those things and the items of description concerning them. Language in the sense of elaborate systems of specialized signs and symbols for the reciprocal transmission and reception of information is a functional achievement largely, if not entirely, limited to mankind.

Clearly, it is through the medium of language that the great bulk of learning is achieved by the average human individual. Mowrer (1954) emphasized the great importance of language in the transmission of culture:

> . . . language makes it possible for its users to have *vicarious experience*, to learn through and from the learning of others— and this, as I see it, is the essence of education. Culture, in both its technological and social, regulatory aspects, is what our forebears have been taught and have confirmed or modified on the basis of their own experience, which they then pass on to us and which we in turn transmit to our children and students. While the power of example, as opposed to precept, is not to be underrated, yet there seems to be no serious dissent from the assumption that this continuous never ending flow of knowledge and belief which we call culture occurs mainly through the medium of language and that without it, the cultural stream would quickly shrink to the veriest trickle. (p. 684)

Speech and Its Acquisition

A language, in a broad sense is any means whatsoever of communicating meaning and feeling among individuals. The language of speech, however, is communication through the use of a highly evolved system of articulate vocal and related sounds. Since communication is a two-way process of interaction, speech, in a sense, is a double function: one of comprehending the meanings being expressed by another, and one of transmitting meanings to another through the use of commonly understood symbols.

Verbal behavior and its modification, as was stated earlier, is becoming an important area of interest for research psychologists. Verbal communication is the behavioral manifestation and expression of mental functioning of a rather high order. It can, therefore, be viewed in both its behavioristic and its cognitive aspects.

Students of operant conditioning are becoming quite active experimentally in the area of verbal functioning. From their point of view, verbal behavior is defined as "behavior which is reinforced through the mediation of another organism" (Skinner, 1957, p. 20). This, of course, is a statement in neobehavioristic terms of the fact that verbal language is a learned mode of psychological interaction (communication) between persons. Operant-conditioning studies have shown that, in speech learning, social reinforcement normally follows verbal responses and that social reinforcement tends to increase the frequency of the responses. Thus, when verbal functioning is viewed in its purely behavioral aspects its acquisition through learning, like the learning of any other observable and measurable form of behavior, can be studied by use of operant-conditioning methods. And, like other kinds of acquisition, verbal learning can also be investigated and analyzed in its cognitive aspects as well.

The living organism, as we have emphasized earlier, is a perpetually active organism. Its parts and various organ systems must be active and must function each in ways determined by its particular structure and organization. Earlier chapters were concerned with the functioning of certain of these systems and how they come to be interrelated and coordinated with one another to result in integrated organismic functioning. The sound-making apparatus, of course, is an organ system that is vitally important in this respect.

As with other systems, the peculiar structural nature of the organs of speech determines their functional possibilities. At first thought this organ system is a relatively simple structure, yet, from the point of view of its marvelously wide range of functional adjustments and possibilities, it becomes a very complex and intricate system.

Analysis of Speech

In simple outline the physical structures involved in speech are the lungs, the windpipe—at the top of which are the vocal folds and the glottis—the cavities of the throat, nose, and mouth with their intricate systems of muscles, the hard and soft palates, the gums, the teeth, and the lips. The marvel of speech, of course, lies in the regulation and the coordination of these various parts as they operate to produce the great variety of speech sounds.

The analysis of speech into its component sound elements is a function of the discipline of linguistics. The first great task in this process was to make an inventory of all the sound elements used in the various languages of the world. In the development of such an inventory, a system of category labels was needed. Irwin (1949) described this phase in the analysis of speech:

> For the scientific investigation of speech, the first need is a set of accurate symbols for the basic speech sounds, just as in physics and chemistry scientific progress depended upon the invention of the periodic table with precisely defined symbols for the elements. The English alphabet is not a precise scientific instrument, for one of its symbols may stand for several different sounds, and contrariwise, different combinations of letters may represent the same sound. For example, in the words father, sergeant, and hearth the symbols, a, e, and ea, respectively all are sounded in the same way, like a in ah.
>
> In the International Phonetic Alphabet, invented about 40 years ago, the speech investigator has a precise tool that makes scientific work possible. This alphabet, unlike conventional ones, has one, and only one, symbol for each elemental sound. (p. 22)

The sound inventory of the International Phonetic Alphabet, with its system of symbols, presumably includes every sound category that the human speech organ system is capable of making.

Researchers have been attempting to designate the particular anatomial parts of the speech apparatus and the particular pattern of coordinated adjustments involved in the production of each of the sound categories.

Infant Speech

The human infant comes equipped structurally to produce the full complement of possible sound categories (phones). This function, like all others however, develops through exercise (learning). The first

postnatal act the baby performs is the production of a vocal sound—
a monosyllabic cry. This sound, in terms of phonetic categories, is
usually the sound as in "fat." This particular sound constitutes about
90 percent of the baby's total vocal sounds during the first few days
of his life.

A number of studies have been made of infant crying (Aldrich,
Sung, and Knop, 1945a, 1945b; Aldrich *et al.*, 1946; Lynip, 1951;
McCarthy, 1954). During early infancy there is usually very frequent
crying, much of which is "emergency respiration." Crying is, of course,
the baby's main defense and only means of making known his discomfort. Brown (1958) emphasized that the crying mode of communication is a very imperfect one: "It has been reported that the infant's
cries of distress have the same quality whatever the nature of the
distress. If this be so, it would seem to follow that . . . children are
often fed when they need to be watered, and bounced when they need
to sleep" (p. 196). After a few months, however, the baby has learned
to use crying in a more efficient way as means of getting attention apart
from any bodily need or discomfort.

The infant's complete sound repertoire during this early period
usually consists of about eight distinguishable sounds—five vowels
and three consonants. These sounds represent about one-fifth of those
commonly used by adults (Irwin, 1949).

The baby's early vocal sounds are crying sounds. Soon, however, as
an aspect of his general undifferentiated activity, the infant begins to
make noncrying sounds as he gradually gains more control over the
parts of his mouth cavity for a greater range of vocalizing. He begins
to make the "soft cooings and utterances that delight parents" (Irwin,
1949, p. 22). Vocalizing at this level has no directed purpose or meaning. It is nothing more than a reflex air emission through the vocal
folds which are taut and can vibrate. "The infant's vocalizations,"
wrote Lynip (1951), "have no more relation to an adult's words than
his leg kickings have to a grown-up's genuflections."

Soon a new phase in sound making called babbling begins. During
this period the baby seems to enjoy exercising his vocal abilities and
he actually practices at random many of the phonetic elements of the
International Phonetic Alphabet. Regardless of race or nationality, all
babies' babbling sounds are identical. The child seems to be trying new
vowels and new consonant sounds, such as bilabials *p*, *b*, and *m*. He
repeats such sounds "over and over again on varying pitches, with
varying intensities and cadences. He mouths them, gets the kinesthetic
feel of them with lips, tongue and cheeks, and unconsciously and end-
lessly practices them" (Irwin, 1949, p. 23). He obviously enjoys his
spontaneous vocal activity. It is self-initiated when the infant is comfortable, content, dry, warm, and fed, and with reduced external

stimuli. The babbling stage is a significant period in speech development.

After about a year of babbling some approximations of words begin to appear in the baby's utterances, probably meaning that the cultural factor is becoming more important. The baby, in connection with his random practice of speech sounds (phones), now is beginning to utter and to practice the phonemes of the language of his community.[1]

Practicing phonemes simply means that the child is being influenced in his spontaneous vocalizations by what he hears. When he chances to make a sound that approximates a word, that particular sound has no more meaning to him than his purely random babbling has had. This sort of practice, however, marks a significant stage in speech development. Babbling becomes "lalling"—the repetition of *heard* sounds and sound combinations. Successful imitation of his own sounds and those of others seems also to be highly satisfying to him. His imitations improve with practice (see Chapter 8). In the process of his random sound making, he often chances to utter and to repeat a syllable which to the mother or some other adult in the situation *seems* to have meaning. Me may say "da da," for example. If the father is present, he feels sure his baby is beginning to talk and that he is calling directly to him. Daddy then is likely to respond immediately by presenting himself to the baby while repeating the baby's "da da." If the father is not present, the mother is likely to think the baby must be asking, perhaps, for the doll or the toy dog and she presents him with the object for which he seems to be asking. She is likewise quite sure her baby is beginning to talk. It is fortunate for the baby's learning that she does so believe, because what she is likely to do each time in reaction to that particular utterance is to place it in association, in the baby's experience, with the person or object to which she believes it refers. Her smiling face while repeating the baby's "ma ma," and gesturing in relation to herself, not only reinforces his tendency to repeat the utterance but also tends to invest the sound with meaning for him. He is taught in that way to use words with meaning.

The Growing Vocabulary

One indication of speech learning that has long been used is increase in the number of words used. During the first 2 months of life babies use, on the average, between seven and eight sounds. By age 2½ years the average number of sounds has increased to twenty-seven. These

---

[1] Phonemes are those phonetic elements—the vowels and consonants—which constitute a particular language. They are the smallest structural units of a particular language (Brown, 1958).

sounds are among the approximately three dozen English phonemes. This means, of course, that at age 2½ years the child is using two-thirds of the speech sounds he will be using later on.

During the early stage of speech learning, the child's comprehension vocabulary is much larger than his speech vocabulary. Very early he learns to respond to such commands as "no-no," "lie down," "come here." These words are combined with gestures and with physical guidance and demonstrations, which help to establish a rather large "passive" vocabulary.

The active, or speech, vocabulary is gradually developed through a complicated learning process. It is not until about age 10 months that the baby is likely to have the use of a single word. At age 1 year he may have three words at his command. These first words are useful to him in making known his wants. They are nouns and usually monosyllables pronounced singly, or doubled, such as "ba(ll)," "da(dog)," "ma ma," "da da." With nouns at his command, the child, in his need, begins to learn action words to combine with nouns; verbs such as "go," "come," "give," are usually among the first to come into use. By the time the baby reaches age 18 months he is likely to have an active vocabulary of twenty words, including a few adjectives and adverbs. "Good," "nice," "naughty," and "hot" are usually among his first adjectives. Other parts of speech come even later. At age 2½ years the child usually has command of some 250 words. As his concepts broaden or become more precise and specific, his word meanings grow in number.

Still another measure of language development is the child's ability to organize words into sentences. This is the child's "ultimate language problem" (Irwin, 1949). His first sentence, as we have said, is one word. He learns to make his demands with such single words as "do," "give," and "ball." Children on the average begin to use longer sentences at about age 15 months. At 2 years the average sentence length is 1.7 words. At 5 years sentences average 4.6 words in length.

Learning to Talk

The process of verbal interaction with a "tutor" is an important aspect of the process of language acquisition (Brown, 1958). The baby's own repeated utterances one by one become equivalent, in his experience, to the words he hears others speak. Through face-to-face rehearsals with his mother, the baby perfects his own approximations of these words. Through a process of identifying equivalents in speech sounds he categorizes speech elements.

Concurrently, these utterances gain referents. For example, in interaction with his mother, she (her smiling face, the sounds she makes, and the many comforts and gratifications she stands for) becomes the "referent category" associated with his own utterance of "mama" and its variations, and with the "mommy" and the "mother" he hears in the speech of others.

In the beginning, the referent category is likely to be broad and inclusive. In other words, the child's utterance of a word becomes over-generalized in its meaning for him. He may be heard to say "da da" when his father and other individuals are near. His father is naturally pleased with the idea that his baby is calling him and the usual tutoring interaction takes place. The baby at first, however, learns a generalized referent for his utterance, "da da." That is, he may say "da da" at the sight of anyone or any number of people. But with added experience he soon learns to recognize the "invariance" of the speech symbol, and at the same time the referent for his word becomes more specific and invariant. Brown (1958) has called this language-learning process the "original word game." The infant, or other learner of a language, is "the player," and the parent or teacher is the "tutor":

> Because speech has a systematic structure it is easier to learn to recognize invariance in speech than to recognize it in other behavior. For the player of the Original Word Game a speech invariance is a signal to form some hypothesis about the corresponding invariance of referent. . . . Whether or not his hypothesis about the referent is correct the player speaks the name where his hypothesis indicates that it should be spoken. The tutor approves, or corrects this performance according as it fits or does not fit the referent category. In learning referents and names the player of the Original Word Game prepares himself to receive the science, the rules of thumb, the prejudices, the total expectancies of his society. (Brown, 1958, pp. 227–228)

Thus the baby begins to learn to talk. At first his use of words with meaning constitutes a very small proportion of his vocalizations. But such use becomes rapidly more frequent. By the end of his second year meaningful words have become very prominent in his speech-sound repertory. Not only is there an increase in the number of words used but the accuracy with which the constituent sounds in the words are produced improves with practice. "Ma ma ma" becomes a distinct "momy," while "da da da" becomes "daddy," and "mi mi" first becomes "mik mik" and finally "milk." In operant-conditioning terms, the child's vocal responses become shaped through the reinforcement of his successive approximations.

The learning situation in which sound-symbols come to have meaning (gain referents) involves far more than the mere strengthening-of-a-response tendency (reinforcement). Repeated past experiences of the appearance of the mother, for example, have come to mean comfort to the baby. The sight of her, the sounds she makes, the objects she carries, the tastes, the smells, and the cutaneous and kinesthetic experiences she consistently brings to him all are a part of the formation of his rapidly developing cognitive structure. The new cognitive experience of a word-sound he makes, and which he hears his mother make, becomes another aspect of the total repeated experience of "mother." The vocal-sound combination "ma ma" gains much the same quality of meaning as the other experiences he enjoys with her.

THE RULES OF SPEECH As we have seen, during a child's first two years his language acquisition consists largely of learning to say single words and connecting these word-symbols with their referents. But, as Bruner (1964) stated, the "puzzle begins when the child first achieves the use of productive grammar" (p. 3). A profound change occurs in the child's speech behavior at about the end of his second year when he begins apparently to recognize speech invariants and to learn the "rules" of language construction. Recent research in speech learning has been concerned for the most part with the problem of how speech acquisition takes place.

The child somehow must learn the rules of speech from the generalized model presented to him in the natural language of the adults around him. He learns gradually and implicitly to follow the rules without any deliberate effort to formulate them as rules. He "may begin as a parrot imitating what others say, but he will end as a poet able to say things that have not been said before but which will be grammatical and meaningful in his community. This is the terminal achievement which a theory of language achievement must explain" (Brown and Berko, 1960, p. 1). The rules are concerned with the elementary units of meaningful sound and the patterns of their combination and arrangement in speech. These elementary units of meaning are called morphemes.

A morpheme may be a complete word or it may be a part of a word or an addition to or modification of a word that attaches an additional unit of meaning to the word. For example, the word "dog" is a morpheme referring to a single member of an animal category. By adding the sound "z" ("s"), additional meaning is attached to the word. "Dogs" has the added meaning of plurality.

Students of speech learning in children view these problems of language composition at two levels: the rules of *grammar* and the rules of *syntax*. Grammar, in this rather narrow technical sense, is concerned with the classes into which morphemes naturally fall. These classes are usually divided into two groups: the lexical classes, or *contentives*, and the functional classes, or *functors* (Brown and Bellugi, 1964; Miller and Ervin, 1964). The English contentives include the nouns, the verbs, and the adjectives, which are the words with semantic content. They make reference and give information. Each of these three contentives can also be divided into subclasses. Thus, there are three sorts of English nouns: the mass nouns, the count nouns, and the proper nouns. Verbs are transitive or intransitive. The functors include the other parts of speech: the prepositions, conjunctions, interrogatives, noun determiners, and auxiliaries. These last classes are called functors because "their grammatical functions are more obvious than their semantic content."

The rules governing the meaningful arrangements of morphemes are important concerns of grammar. Parts of speech derive their technical definitions largely in terms of these rules. Nouns, for example, are "a class of words having similar 'privileges of occurrence.' " They "can follow articles and can occur in subject and object positions and, in this respect, are distinct from such other classes of words as the verb, adjective, and adverb" (Brown and Berko, 1960, p. 2).

Rules about privileges of occurrence for individual words and phrases apparently are implicitly observed by the child. As recent evidence indicates, he playfully but deliberately practices these syntactic arrangements. Ruth Weir (1962) recorded the spontaneous utterances of her 2-year-old son while he was alone in his crib before going to sleep. Her recordings were made over a period of eighteen evenings. These recordings particularly reveal the fact that although children may not explicitly formulate rules of syntax they do concern themselves with word order in speech and with relationships among words. Young Anthony Weir must have observed the "privileges of occurrence" of different word classes and of the different positions they may occupy in sentences. He quite clearly had assimilated implicitly certain rules of word sequences in speech, and in his solitary soliloquies he practiced word placements and sequences in terms of these rules. Thus in his little sentences he tried out replacing one noun with another noun or a noun phrase or a pronoun. He interchanged adjectives, trying them out with different proper nouns. He practiced interchanging verbs. He discriminated between word classes and tried out the rules of their appropriate occurrence in speech. Excerpts from the Weir recordings will illustrate:

> Not a yellow blanket—The white—White. . . . What color—
> What color blanket—What color mop—What color glass. . . .
> Put on a blanket—White blanket—And yellow blanket—Where's

yellow blanket. . . . There's a hat—There's another—There's hat— There's another hat—That's a hat. . . . There is the light —Where is the light—Here is the light (pp 107–112)

Thus a child learns to identify and to use properly the parts of speech. He comes to identify the class to which a new word belongs by its placement in the utterance and thus to discern something of its utility in speech. This is "one of the ways in which the lawful flexibility of speech is developed" (Brown and Berko, 1960, p. 2). With the new words that he has thus "classified" the child can now create something new in his speech.

THE ACQUISITION OF SYNTAX It is clear from what we have already noted that as the child learns the different word classes and the rules of their occurrence in speech, he is learning some of the fundamentals of sentence construction. We have seen that by the time he reaches age 18 months he is beginning to use two-word sentences. By age 36 months the child can produce every variety of simple English sentence. The processes through which the child achieves this remarkable development have recently been the subject of intensive study (Brown and Bellugi, 1964; Brown and Fraser, 1964). As the study by Weir (1962) has clearly indicated, children will experiment with speech and its parts and engage in much practice during their periods of solitude. It is equally clear that the basic learning upon which this solitary experimentation and practice is based takes place as mother and child interact verbally day by day. A longitudinal study reported by Brown and Bellugi (1964) is based on recordings of such mother-child interactions.

Two children, a boy ("Adam") age 27 months and a girl ("Eve") age 18 months, were selected for intensive study. Each child was visited every second week. At the beginning of the study, the average length of Adam's utterances was 1.84 morphemes and of Eve's, 1.40 morphemes. At the end of the period of observation their averages respectively were 3.55 and 3.27 morphemes.

The development of the sentence-constructing capacity was the focus of the study. What is the nature of the learning involved as the child progresses from the one-word sentence to utterances grammatically correct of ten or more words? To what extent is it a matter of imitation of adult speech of which he hears so much and with which he interacts in dialogues with his mother?

One immediate observation of these investigators was that there was frequent imitation on the part of both mother and child. As an example of mother's "imitation," Adam, in one brief interchange, said,

"There go one" (truck), and the mother responded with "Yes, there goes one." Examples of the child's imitations were the following utterances taken from the record (Brown and Bellugi, 1964, p. 136):

MOTHER'S UTTERANCE	CHILD'S IMITATION
Wait a minute	Wait a minute
Daddy's brief case	Daddy brief case
Fraser will be unhappy	Fraser unhappy
He's going out	He go out
That's an old-time train	Old time train

A second significant observation was that in such interchanges the mother's sentences were short and similar in structure to the child's, but they were perfectly grammatical in structure with no words missing. The child's sentences, on the other hand, although generally correct in word order, were usually reduced by the elimination of certain classes of words. The child's speech, even in his direct imitations, tended to be "telegraphic" in form, not only in the sense that the number of words was reduced but also in the classes of words that were left out. In composing telegraphic messages, the adult retains the contentives (the words that carry the meaning), while many of the functors are eliminated without loss of meaning. Interestingly, the child reduces his sentences in the same manner. An important problem is to explain the significance of this tendency and how the child acquires it.

Why should young children omit functors and retain contentives? There is more than one plausible answer. Nouns, verbs and adjectives are words that make reference. One can conceive of teaching the meanings of these words by speaking them, one at a time, and pointing at things or actions or qualities. And of course parents do exactly that. These are the kinds of words that children have been encouraged to practice speaking one at a time. The child arrives at the age of sentence construction with a stock of well-practiced nouns, verbs and adjectives. Is it not likely then that this prior practice causes him to retain the contentives from model sentences too long to be reproduced in full, that the child imitates those forms in the speech he hears which are already well developed in him as individual habits? There is probably some truth in this explanation but it is not the only determinant since children will often select for retention contentives that are relatively unfamiliar to them. (Brown and Bellugi, 1964, p. 138)

Another feature of mother-child conversation, which does not support the explanation of children's telegraphic speech contained in the previous quotation, is the tendency on the part of mother to *expand* her imitations of the child's speech. The child, for example, said "Baby highchair." The mother expanded his utterance with "Baby *is in the* highchair." Other examples were "Mommy eggnog" to "Mommy *had her* eggnog," "Throw Daddy" to "Throw *it to* Daddy," and "Pick glove" to "Pick *the* glove *up.*" Mother-child conversation is largely a cycle of reductions and expansions.

The mothers expansions, to be sure, add meaning, but they are not made in accordance with any specific grammatical rule. They are made with reference to the specific situation (the specific circumstances giving rise to the child's utterance) as well as in direct response to the child's utterance. Generally these additions are functors, but such corrections and the learning that accrues from them apparently affects minimally, if at all, the child's tendency to neglect them in his utterances.

Brown and Bellugi concluded that the child's many and varied attempts at verbal expression—in conversation with mother, or in solitude—in general represent a continuing effort on his part to assimilate the regularities of English syntax. His speech development is not merely a matter of learning to say word by word and sentence by sentence what others about him say. This study and other important recent research in this area of development clearly indicate that verbal responses as such are not *all* that is learned. Speech acquisition is, rather, a matter of gradually inducing the rules and principles of language structuring that make it possible for the child to generate sentences. He thus "processes the speech to which he is exposed so as to induce from it a latent structure" (Brown and Bellugi, 1964, p. 144). Brown and Fraser (1964) were more explicit in their summary statement:

> For the present, then, we are working with the hypothesis that child speech is a systematic reduction of adult speech largely accomplished by omitting function words that carry little information. From this corpus of reduced sentences we suggest that the child induces general rules which govern the construction of new utterances. As a child becomes capable (through maturation and the consolidation of frequently occurring sequences) of registering more of the detail of adult speech, his original rules will have to be revised and supplemented. As the generative grammar grows more complicated and more like the adult grammar, the child's speech will become capable of expressing a greater variety of meaning. (p. 79)

Such a complicated process of acquisition is not wholly accounted for in terms of current learning theory. Undoubtedly, there are along the way many specific learnings that are facilitated by reinforcement. In the verbal interchanges between mother and child, for example, the latter receives rich reward for his speech achievements from the attention and approval centered upon him. His pronunciations in the course of interchange are shaped toward perfection by the process of successive approximations with their self-produced reinforcements.

As the studies of speech learning in children suggest, there is something about the over-all acquisition of speech facility that is not touched by mechanistic theory. Here, cognitive theory seems to offer an explanation. Bruner (1964) suggested that cognitive growth is the epitome of the interaction between the individual child and his culture. Also:

> Growth depends upon the mastery of techniques and cannot be understood without reference to such mastery. These techniques are not, in the main, inventions of the individuals who are "growing up"; they are, rather, skills transmitted with varying efficiency and success by the culture—language being a prime example. Cognitive growth, then, is in a major way from the outside in, as well as from the inside out. (p. 1)

Language, then, may be regarded as a "technique" provided by and made available to the child by the culture in which he grows. Language is so pervasive in his experience and in his life that he is constantly interacting with it. Modifications and additions to his cognitive structure are very largely the results of the progressive mastery of this cultural technique, which makes it possible for him not only to *represent* his experiences but also to *transform* them and thereby to generate in himself new understandings (Bruner, 1964).

Factors Affecting Speech Development

One of the striking facts about acquisition of speech in children is the wide range of individual variations in rate of achievement. Since speech development is a very complicated and involved learning process, any of the factors that, in various ways, affect learning in general may be crucial in an individual child's learning to talk.

There is much evidence, for example, that the rate of progress in mental development is a basic factor in speech facility. Studies of early speech sounds in children have led to the suggestion that the types of consonant sounds and the consonant-vowel frequency ratios in babies' babbling may prove to be the best predictors of later intelligence (Catalano and McCarthy, 1954). Children who are precocious in mental development have repeatedly shown marked linguistic superiority. Studies have also shown that the lower the intellect rating, the poorer the speech (Cruickshank and Johnson, 1958).

As with any other learned function, the various aspects of the environment in which the child develops become crucial factors in language development. In other connections we have emphasized the importance of adequate and appropriate stimulation for optimal development. Homes that provide books and other forms of appropriate literature and stimulating materials that invite constructive play, along with free access to them for the child, constitute a basically favorable environment. The number of adults with whom the child daily interacts, the extent to which he is talked with, told stories to and read to, and the number of playmates he has have been found to be important home-environmental factors affecting speech development (McCarthy, 1960).

Social Class and Language Acquisition

Research evidence clearly indicates a significant relationship between a family's social class and language development in its children (Bernstein, 1961; Deutsch, 1963, 1965; Deutsch and Brown, 1964). The social-class differences in language, however, are not limited to the purely quantitative aspects of language facility, such as size of vocabulary. According to Bernstein's (1960) study of this problem, the "differences in language facility result from entirely different *modes* of speech found within the middle-class and the lower working-class" (p. 271). Because of the difference in social organization between rather widely differing social classes, quite different emphases are placed upon language as a potential to be developed in children. "Once this emphasis or stress is placed," wrote Bernstein, "then the resulting forms of language use progressively orient the speakers to distinct and different types of relationships to objects and persons, irrespective of the level of measured intelligence" (1960, p. 271). Thus, the very nature of the child's orientations to his social and material world, as well as the form and the quality of his speech, may be significantly affected by social-class-imposed "emphasis," or attitudes toward the speech function.

Bernstein compared samples of teenage boys from middle-class and lower working-class families of England as to their performances on two types of intelligence tests: a vocabulary (verbal) test and a nonverbal test. His findings were quite revealing. Fifty-eight of the sixty-one working-class boys had language-test IQ's within the average range (90–110). The other three boys scored below IQ 90. On the nonverbal test, however, more than half of the boys (thirty-six of the sixty-one) obtained IQ's of 110 or above.

The middle-class boys, on the other hand, presented quite a different picture of the relationship between the two types of performance. On both the language and the nonlanguage tests, all of the forty-five subjects scored IQ's of 100 or above, with very similar distributions throughout.

A comparison of the mean raw scores of the two groups highlighted the same basic facts. The mean scores on the nonverbal test for the middle-class and the working-class groups were 51.4 and 47.36, respectively. On the language test the corresponding differences were 60.2 and 41.9. This difference of 18.3 is highly significant.

The results of this study quite clearly indicate that the "relational operations" required by the nonverbal test "are available to members of the working-class, whereas the concepts and principles required for the upper ranges of the verbal test are not" (1960, p. 273). For these children, language does not become an effective technique for cognitive development. It fails to become an adequate internalized program for ordering experience. Bruner (1964) suggested that the internalization of language (so that it can function effectively as a technique of cognitive development) "depends upon interaction with others, upon the need to develop corresponding categories and transformations for communal action. It is the need for cognitive coin that can be exchanged with those on whom we depend" (p. 14). The paucity of verbal interchange within the lower-class family does not provide enough "cognitive coin" of the higher denominations.

Deutsch's (1965) study of social class and language development led to essentially the same conclusions as Bernstein's. The tendency of parents of lower-class families is to answer the child's request with a perfunctory single word, "yes" or "no" or "go away," rather than with a complete sentence or an explanation:

> . . . as compared with the middle-class homes, there is a paucity of organized family activities in a large number of lower-class homes. As a result, there is less conversation, for example, at meals, as meals are less likely to be regularly scheduled family affairs. . . .
>
> In general, we have found that lower-class children, Negro and white, compared with middle-class children, are subject to what we've labeled a "cumulative deficit phenomenon" which takes place between the first and the fifth grade years. (p. 80)

Deutsch's findings indicate that language in the lower-class family tends to be used in a restrictive fashion, rather than in a fashion that would broaden the child's perspective. As Deutsch (1963) pointed out, the preschool child in the crowded lower-class apartment typically is subjected to much noise, but noise that is generally not meaningful to him. With the paucity of instructional conversation directed toward him, he is in an ideal situation to learn *in*attention. He "does not get practice in auditory discrimination, or feedback from adults correcting his enunciation, pronunciation and grammar" (p. 171).

In general, as Bernstein (1960) stated, in the lower-class family the emphasis is not placed upon language as a potential to be developed. Language is not valued as a technique to be used by the child in his cognitive and his total personal development. Consequently, no effort is made by the parent to present a good linguistic model for the child or in any other way to encourage correct and adequate speech development. Children take into themselves the attitudes and the values as well as the behavioral and speech patterns of the specific culture in which they grow up.

Minority-Group Membership

In many instances, the factor of race and ethnic group membership of a family is associated with its social class. The child of a Negro family in a lower-class slum area, for example, is doubly disadvantaged in the area of language development. The Negro community during the hundred years since slavery, has occupied, for the most part, a marginal position on the economic scale. Because of this chronic economic instability, the Negro male, particularly at the lower-class levels, has suffered continuous discouragement and feelings of inadequacy. This, of course, has contributed to family instability. The status of the father as the family head is affected adversely by his inability to provide the material needs of the family. Broken homes due to absence of the father are most frequent in this group. Hence, the lack in the family of an adequate father figure, and in many instances the complete absence of a male model of any kind in the child's home experience, would in general limit still further the adult sources of cognitive stimulation for the child and the possibilities of his learning through verbal interchange. "One can postulate on considerable evidence that language is one of the areas which is most sensitive to the impact of the multiplicity of problems associated with the stimulus deprivation found in the marginal circumstances of lower-class life" (Deutsch, 1963, p. 173).

BILINGUALISM   Another minority-group situation that creates language-learning difficulty is that of the "child of immigrant parents who at home continue to speak the native tongue and maintain most of the native customs, beliefs and value patterns" (Soffietti, 1955, pp. 224–225). In this situation *bilingualism* develops. But, the child of an immigrant family faces more than a matter of dealing with two distinct linguistic habits. He is clearly involved with two distinct cultures. During his preschool years the language of the parents has precedence, and only after entrance into the school system will the child find it essential to learn English.

Bilingualism has long been a school problem in the United States. Children do not easily lose the effects of the parental language and culture upon their own English speech. According to the findings of Smith and Kasdon (1961), during a period of twenty years (between 1938 and 1958), the Filipino and Japanese parents of Hawaii had practically ceased using their native tongues, and the language ratings of their homes indicated the Anglicizing of their speech. The children, furthermore, no longer were regarded as bilingual. Yet Smith and Kasdon found that,

> Although there has been a gain in children's command of English since 1938, the task of teaching standard English is still a major one for the kindergarten teachers inasmuch as the children in the two racial groups studied are retarded slightly more than a year in their use of oral English in terms of the measures used in this study. (p. 138)

Interpersonal relationships very early in the child's linguistic development are extremely important. For the infant to have regular intimate and nurturant contacts with a "mothering one" is especially important in this connection, because these contacts naturally involve a kind of vocal interaction from the beginning. The baby cries and the mother soothes with words and appropriate actions. When comfortable and contented, the baby gurgles and coos and the mother responds vocally to his utterances. The mother is alert to her baby's vocal sounds and soon begins to respond to them in ways that invest them with meaning for the child.

Obviously there are many ways of encouraging speech learning. In the ordinary family situation, especially where other children are present, the baby naturally gets much stimulation and encouragement. Parents can further promote speech learning by deliberately encouraging family conversation at levels at which the younger members can participate.

Speech directed specifically toward a young child stimulates and encourages vocal response. This was demonstrated in an experimental study of 3-months-old infants by Rheingold, Gewirtz, and Ross (1959). They found that by responding each time to the baby's vocalization with a "complex of social acts," including a vocal sound and a smile, the frequency of the baby's vocalizing increased significantly. Vocal speech is the natural mode of social interaction, for it can develop only through social interaction.

The Assessment of Speech Development

In view of the complexities of the process of learning to talk, the usual language achievement of the child during his early years is truly remarkable. To parents, that progress sometimes seems slow. Indeed, it is not smooth and steady. Like other aspects of development, there are discernible cyclic variations in rate of progress, periods during which the child may be consolidating his gains and periods in which other aspects of his total development presumably have pre-eminence (Jersild, 1946). Characteristically during these periods of relatively rapid progress, which are separated by "plateaus," certain specific levels of performance, or stages, in speech development are achieved. These stages have been established, together with the age at which they most frequently appear, by students of speech development. Such stages may be regarded as indicators of progress, and, when listed in their sequential order and with their respective age equivalents, they constitute a rough developmental sequence. An individual child's status in speech learning can be roughly appraised by referring his level of performance to such a scale.

Table 9.1 is a listing of stages in speech development. The age equivalents for the various levels of performance are based upon the observations of a number of different investigators (Carroll, 1960; Irwin, 1949; Lewis, 1951; Lynip, 1951; McCarthy, 1960; Nice, 1925, 1932; Simon 1957; Terman and Merrill, 1937).

The items in Tables 9.2 and 9.3 were abstracted from the developmental records of Paul and Sally 695, respectively. Some of these items were taken from their actual performance records, developmental and intelligence tests, and written analyses of the test results. The others were found in observational reports and in summaries by staff and student observers. These speech items, in each case, were arranged in chronological order, then listed with the age of the child at the time of the report. An attempt, only partially successful, was then made to identify each item with an item in the scale of speech

Table 9.1

Progress Indicators of Speech Development

INDICATORS	AGE EXPECTED (MONTHS)
I. *Pre-speech Vocalizations*	
Crying—explosive sounds, grunts, sneezes, sighs, coughs, guttural sounds	0–2
Vowel sounds—"a" as in "fat," "i" as in "fit," "e" as in "set," "u" as in "up," and "u" as in "food"	4
All speech sounds, random vocalization	
Babbling stage—sounds "uttered for the mere delight of uttering them"	8
Lalling period—phoneme practice, imitation of heard sounds, "ma ma," "da da," "ba ba"	11
II. *Speech*	
Understands assortment of action words—"drink," "go," "come," "give," "bye bye"	12
Generalized meaning of nouns—"da da" may refer to any man	12
Single-word sentences—"give," "ball," "dog"	12
Early sentence stage—nouns, verbs, and some adverbs and adjectives, "good," "nice," "hot." No prepositions or pronouns	17
Understands simple sentences—"Where is the ball?" "Give mother the spoon." "Want to go bye bye?" Active vocabulary about twenty words	18
Short sentence stage—two-word sentences, excess of nouns, lack of articles, prepositions	24
Comprehends simple requests and is able to carry them out—"Give me the kitty." "Put the spoon in the cup." Stanford-Binet Test	24
Identifies objects by use	30
Question-asking stage—questions asked mainly for pleasure of asking	36
Complete sentence stage—five-word sentences, virtually all parts of speech present	48
Counts three objects (Stanford-Binet)	60
Knows meaning of numbers	72
Knows meaning of "morning," "afternoon," "night," "summer," "winter" (Stanford-Binet)	78

development (see Table 9.1) and thus to arrive at an approximate age equivalent for it.

Paul's and Sally's progress in speech development, as appraised in this manner, are shown graphically in Figure 9.1. These plottings reflect what is quite evident in the comments on the records. Both of these children were consistently described as being "advanced," "very advanced," and "superior" in their language performance in the test situation. Recorded examples of their sentences consistently used in play also portrayed high levels of speech performance.

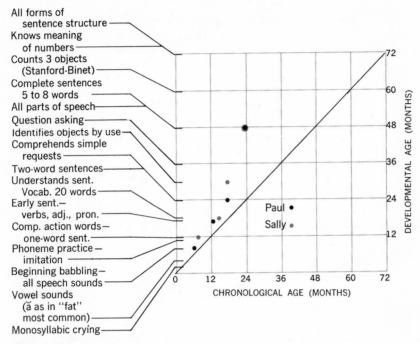

All forms of
  sentence structure
Knows meaning
  of numbers
Counts 3 objects
  (Stanford-Binet)
Complete sentences
  5 to 8 words
All parts of speech
Question asking
Identifies objects by use
Comprehends simple
  requests
Two-word sentences
Understands sent.
  Vocab. 20 words
Early sent.—
  verbs, adj., pron.
Comp. action words—
  one-word sent.
Phoneme practice—
  imitation
Beginning babbling—
  all speech sounds
Vowel sounds
  (ă as in "fat"
  most common)
Monosyllabic crying

Paul ●
Sally ●

DEVELOPMENTAL AGE (MONTHS)

72 · 60 · 48 · 36 · 24 · 12

CHRONOLOGICAL AGE (MONTHS)

0 · 12 · 24 · 36 · 48 · 60 · 72

Figure 9.1

Speech development of Paul and Sally 695 in terms of approximate age equivalents.

Table 9.2

Speech Development of Paul 695 as Appraised from Examples
in his Developmental Record and from Test Results
and Comments

SPEECH ITEM	AGE OBSERVED (MONTHS)	AGE EXPECTED (MONTHS)
"A great deal of babbling"	6.5	8
Consonants beginning to appear in his speech	6.5	
Seems to respond to his own name	6.5	
Said "bow wow" and "meow" in response to pictures	13	18
"Baa baa" in response to picture of sheep	15	18
Complete-sentence stage (five- to eight-word sentences) "Paul, Daddy, Mama, going downtown on bus." "Going to Aunt Mary's school." "Going to play with ball."	24	48
Eleven distinct words recognized by tester, two of which referred to body parts "hair" and "neck"	18	
Responded correctly to all four directions with ball	18	24

Table 9.2 (Cont.)

SPEECH ITEM	AGE OBSERVED (MONTHS)	AGE EXPECTED (MONTHS)
Named eight objects on picture cards, including "smoke" coming from chimney	18	30
Mother noted over 200 sounds "with definite associations"—not all made complete words"	18	24
Tester noted he "has command of virtually every form of sentence structure: 'I want to go to the car store to buy a big coal truck, and then I can get into it and drive it away.'"	31	72
Defines words in terms of use: "Dresses to put on ladies and little dresses to put on little girls"	38	70

Table 9.3

Speech Development of Sally 695 as Appraised from Examples
in her Developmental Record and from Test Results
and Comments

SPEECH ITEM	AGE OBSERVED (MONTHS)	AGE EXPECTED (MONTHS)
One-word sentences "da da" and "ma ma"	8	15
Chattered about the "bow wow" and "meow" as she looked at pictures	13	18
"Baa baa," pointing picture of black sheep on wall	15	18
Uses many approximations to common words, "bu bu" (button), "na na" (down), "co co" (cold, when her hands are against window pane), "woo" (shoe), "ya ya" (sock)	15	18
Carried out two verbal directions with ball on test	18	——
Named three test objects	18	——
Named five items on picture cards	18	——
Said "ball ball" when handed ball	18	——
Gives use of ball: "ball rolls"	18	30
Repeats practically everything she hears	23	——
Correcting many pronunciations as "down" in place of "na"	23	——
Long sentences, expresses original ideas	24	48
Some use of pronouns	24	——
Picture vocabulary of sixteen words	24	——
Uses nouns, verbs, adjectives, and adverbs	31	——
Many sentences of seven and eight words	41	——

Learning to Read

Very closely related to the process of learning to talk is that of learning to read. In fact, in the experience of many children these are two phases of a continuous process—the process of associating symbols with their referents. In speech acquisition, the symbol in each case is a vocal sound; in reading, the symbol is visual in nature. Both symbols have the same referant. The vocal sound "dog," for example, through repeated association comes to symbolize a class of objects: the noisy animal outside, the little wiggly animal inside, the toy animal with which the child plays. The common characteristics of this variety of objects are abstracted and together become the aspect of the referent category for which the vocal sound "dog" becomes established in the child's cognitive structure as the invariant sign.

Subsequently, or in some cases concurrently, children become intensely interested in their books containing pictures of dogs, each labeled with the printed and written symbol "dog." These visual symbols also readily become associated in the child's experience with the animal category "dog," and with the vocal sound "dog," which he hears and which he himself makes. Thus, the sight of the dog outside, along with the sound of his bark, and picture of the dog in his book, along with the associated printed word, become adequate stimuli (alone or jointly) for his utterance "dog." When he is able to say "dog" in response to the printed word, the latter has become a sign with meaning (much the same meaning as have the actually perceived animals, the pictures of the animals, and the word "dog" as heard). These all may be regarded, then, as "equivalent stimuli" (G. W. Allport, 1960) for the "meaning disposition" (Brown, 1958, p. 103)—the concept of dog. The child's cognitive organization, to that extent, has been altered and amplified. To the child, the symbol "dog" has acquired "representational properties" such that "it evokes an image, or other ideational content in the reacting subject (the child) that is cognitively equivalent to that evoked by the designated object itself" (Anderson and Ausubel, 1965, p. 64). The child has learned to read the word "dog."

Reading Readiness

As with other sorts of functional facility, we assume that acquisition always must await structural readiness. A child, it is assumed, cannot establsh connections between objects or his experiences with these objects and their representational equivalents (printed symbols) until the maturation of his organism has progressed to the point where such connections are organically possible. The question as to *when* that point of readiness in children is reached is one which has received much attention in recent decades. Tests of reading readiness have been developed, and scores on these tests have replaced the older readiness criteria of chronological age and mental age for determining at what point in the child's school experience he should be launched on the task of learning to read. In terms of readiness-test scores, some children are started in reading at age 5 years, others are not deemed ready for such learning until age 7 or later.

Clearly, reading readiness involves the capacity to perceive. The child must first become repeatedly aware of objects, persons, and relationships *as* objects, persons, or relationships. This perceiving function itself develops during the first months of the child's life through further maturation and the exercise of his sensory equipment. Then, through the many and varied perceptual experiences with objects and classes of objects, experiential backgrounds (cognitive structure) become established. Into this structure can then be assimilated the associated sounds (heard names) and the visually apprehended configurations (printed names). These latter can then become symbols for the perceived objects with which they have been associated. Symbols thus "become meaningful when they are able to evoke images that are reasonable facsimiles of the perceptions evoked by the objects they signify" (Ausubel, 1963, p. 67). Development sufficient for this level of functioning obviously is a prerequisite for learning to read.

A Complex Process

As was suggested earlier, reading, in a sense, is an extension of talking. The child first learns that certain vocal sounds and combinations of sounds are symbols representing objects, persons, acts, and relationships. The next step is to learn that certain graphic, visually apprehended symbols customarily are made to represent the sound symbols which he already comprehends and can use. As this learning task is accomplished, the printed word comes to represent the sound which stands for the object. The child is learning to read.

In a simple statement of this process, there is little to suggest the real difficulties involved in the developmental task with which the child is confronted when he enters the first grade and is expected to learn to read. Gates (1957) clearly portrayed the situation:

> Reading is probably the most difficult and subtle of all the
> scholastic abilities and skills to teach, and the critical period

comes at the very beginning of school life when the children are least experienced and most readily bewildered. It is very difficult to show a child, for example, all the tricks of working out the recognition and pronunciation of the weirdly artificial little hieroglyphics which printed words are. To be successful a child must catch on to good techniques. What is good for one word is often poor for another. To learn to recognize sound, and blend the sounds of the letters may suffice for *hat* or *bag* but be utterly confounding for *haughty* or *hippopotamus*, the former because of phonetic inconsistence and the latter because the number of letters exceeds the child's immediate memory span. (p. 531)

As Gates further pointed out, in many instances learning to read turns out to be one of the most difficult and critical learning tasks of one's lifetime. There are, of course, many possible factors which may, in various combinations and variations, contribute toward making the experience a zestful and generally happy one or one full of confusion, frustration, and anxiety. As we have already pointed out, maturational and experiential readiness are perhaps the most basic factors. With a lack of sufficient maturity and experiential background, a child's own expectations, as well as the expectations of others, may be very slow and difficult or even impossible of realization. "If he learns to read well, all is well; if he does poorly or fails, the respect of his parents and acquaintances and his own self esteem are threatened" (Gates, 1957, p. 528).

The vital importance of adequate environmental stimulation must once more be emphasized in connection with this developmental task of learning to read. Because of the close connection between talking and reading, anything that encourages the use and comprehension of speech will also facilitate reading learning. The richness of the preschool child's experience with things, places, and people, and in enjoyable language activities in connection with them, is a tremendously important factor. In stores, museums, libraries, and in his books and play materials he will see and hear things in association with their names. In a great many ways a child may be led pleasantly and naturally to learn much that is basic to meaningful reading.

Recent Research Findings

In recent years much interest has developed in the periods of infancy and early childhood. New approaches to the evaluation of early cognitive ability are being devised which are leading to certain revisions of the concept of functional readiness. Suggestions, with some supporting evidence, of infant learning capacity of an order formerly unimagined are beginning to appear in the literature. By the use of carefully designed techniques and with adequate and appropriate stimulation, very young children are being trained to discriminate and to respond differentially to visual and auditory cues. Children as young as 2 years of age have been taught to read (Fowler, 1962a, 1962b, 1964).

In view of such findings, the older concept of readiness to learn requires re-examination. Is reading readiness, for example, really a condition, a stage, of structural development which comes about through the process of biological maturation, a process whose pattern and tempo in each case are genetically determined? To what extent is it valid to assert that development cannot be "forced": that we must await the signs of readiness in the child without any effort to hurry the process; that when a child is ready to achieve sphincter control, to learn to walk, or to talk or to read, he will begin to take on those functions, and that attempts to teach or to train before the signs of readiness appear should be avoided? Do recent research findings indicate that the process of biological maturation in each instance can be modified in pattern and speeded up in tempo through environmental stimulation and manipulation, thus making it possible, for example, to produce reading readiness in children at considerably earlier ages than would be the case without such stimulation or environmental manipulation?

An alternative view of the matter, which is more in line with the current conceptions of the nature of human development, regards learning readiness as something more than a result of biological maturation alone. The experiential aspect of readiness must also be regarded as of prime importance. In the past, the young child's accumulating background of casual learning—his developing cognitive structure—has been generally neglected in the concept of readiness. Research is currently demonstrating the importance of the predominant nature the verbal interchange between the very young child and his mother in relation to his cognitive development (Bernstein, 1961; Hess and Shipman, 1965). In terms of these findings, different degrees of experiential readiness in children to acquire the early stages of vocal language are probably a function of the extent of the mothers' use of a rich, elaborative mode of communicating with them from the beginning. Likewise, the readiness with which a child acquires implicitly the use of the rules of grammar and syntax in his speech may well be a result of this type of prior cognitive structure building. Again, learning to read, which is essentially a process of relating visual cues with associated auditory sounds and their meanings, is possible of accomplishment by a child only to the extent to which he is experientially ready in terms of a background of relevant learning which has accrued from the ubiquitous experience of language sounds gradually becoming meaningful to him almost from the time of birth.

This experiential-readiness concept does not preclude the importance of the maturation process. Maturation must provide the capacity, in terms of level of structural development, for relevant learning all along the way. Two children, for example, exposed from birth to the same quality of experience and amount of environmental stimulation, may be quite far apart in their ability to read because of a difference in level of *maturational readiness*. On the other hand, a child whose mother talks to him in terms of verbal cues that "relate events to one another and the present to the future" (an elaborative mode of verbal communication) presumably would acquire an experiential readiness for language learning earlier than another child at the same level of capacity (maturation) but whose background of verbal interchange is limited, restricted, stereotyped, "lacking in specificity and exactness needed for precise conceptualization and differentiation" (Hess and Shipman, 1965, p. 871).

SELECTED READING SUGGESTIONS

Bernstein, B. Social class and linguistic development: a theory of social learning. In A. H. Halsey, Jean Floud, and C. A. Anderson (eds.), *Education, economy and society*. New York: Free Press, 1961.

Brown, R. *Words and things*. New York: Free Press, 1958.

Brown, R., and Ursula Bellugi. Three processes in the child's acquisition of syntax. *Harvard educ. Rev.*, 1964, **34**, 133–151.

Bruner, J. S. The course of cognitive growth. *Amer. Psychologist*, 1964, **19**, 1–15.

Weir, Ruth H. *Language of the crib*. New York: Humanities Press, Inc., 1962.

CHAPTER 10

Thinking

One of the most distinctively human categories of functioning is thinking activity. Thinking is a "higher" cognitive process by which knowledge is apprehended, organized, and transformed.

As a broad category of functioning, thinking includes the mental activities commonly referred to as reason, memory, imagination, fantasy, revery, and the like. The common element in all such processes is mental representation. In every case of thinking there is some kind of representation, or symbolic substitute, in consciousness of previous experience, which may be in the form of *sensory images* of previous perceptual experiences or may be in the form of *implicitly recalled words or other symbols*.

Thinking processes differ from motor functioning or perceptual apprehension in being free of time and special limitations. We can think of distant objects and of perceptually inaccessible situations. We can recall and manipulate past experiences. We can also regard the world in novel ways by transforming and manipulating our representations of previous learning.

Since much of our representation is in the form of verbal symbols, there is a close relationship between talking and thinking. The range and the richness of one's verbal competence largely define the limits of one's symbolic thinking. In terms of this kind of representation we can indulge in flights of imagination, solve problems, or creatively expand our concepts about the world. In this discussion of thinking activity, therefore, we shall be dealing mainly with the "stream of thought," with reasoning and problem solving, with creativity, and with the expansion of our conceptualizations.

Modes of Representation

Memory

The term memory in its broad sense refers to any manifestation or evidence of remaining "traces" of previous learning or any kind of revival, manipulation, or reinstatement of past experience or behavior. Traditionally, three quite different kinds of cognitive facts or processes, all referred to as memory, have been differentiated. One type of memory is *retention* of the effects of past functioning. Evidence for the existence of retention is simply the fact of learning—the observable, lasting change in some aspect of behavior. *Recall,* or remembering, is another type of memory process. An act of recall, of course, is an actual reinstatement, a consciousness, or an overt behavior which involves, in varying degrees of completeness, previous experiences or learned acts. The third memory process is *recognition,* a function especially important in perceptual learning.

RECALL   There are three forms of recall: (1) the re-enactment of learned overt behavior patterns, completely or in part, according to present needs and circumstances; (2) the reinstatement of previously perceived reality through imagery; and (3) the "shorthand" representation and manipulation of the world and its relationships in symbols. Bruner (1964) referred to these modes of representation as *enactive* representation, *iconic* representation, and *symbolic* representation. "Their appearance in the life of the child is in that order, each depending upon the previous one for its development, yet all remaining more or less intact throughout life" (p. 2).

The recall, or remembering function plays a crucial role in further cognitive development. Bruner (1964) stressed this point:

If we are to benefit from contact with recurrent regularities in the environment, we must represent them in some manner.

To dismiss this problem as "mere memory" is to misunderstand it. For the most important thing about memory is not storage of past experience, but rather the retrieval of what is relevant in some usable form. This depends upon how past experience is coded and processed so that it may indeed be relevant and usable in the present when needed. The end product of such a system of coding and processing is what we may speak of as a representation. (p. 2)

The second mode of recall—the reinstatement in consciousness in some degree of completeness and vividness of a previously experienced event, object, person, or situation which is not, at the time, present to sense—has been a difficult phenomenon to explain. The image is obviously mentalistic in nature, yet it has been explained in stimulus-response terms. Since an image comes to mind in response to some stimulus, external or internal, that stimulus must have had some associative connection with the specific stimulus or situation which gave rise to the original experience of which the image is a representation. The stimulus, whatever it may be that now elicits the image, can be thought of, therefore, as a conditioned stimulus, and the image, a conditioned response (Mowrer, 1960a; Skinner, 1953). The young child looking for the "vanished object" (Piaget, 1952), it would seem, experiences an image of the previously perceived object.

The reality of images in experience as a result of sensory conditioning has been admitted by Skinner (1953). In his words, "a man may see or hear 'stimuli which are not present' on the pattern of conditioned reflexes: he may see X, not only when X is present, but when any stimulus which has frequently accompanied X is present. The dinner bell not only makes our mouth water, it makes us see food" (p. 266).

The symbolic mode of representation is by far the most frequently used and most effective thinking facility, particularly in the more productive levels of thinking that are discussed later in this chapter. The elaborate system of sound symbols used in speech are internalized in the sense that they and their referents are readily represented in consciousness. These representations, as we shall see, are very important tools of thought.

Development of Representational Capacity

It is clear, then, that the essential element in thinking activity is representation. This means that a child is not capable of thinking until he has developed the capacity to represent (in consciousness) objects, situations, and relationships that are not, at the time, present for direct sensory experience.

Piaget (1952) referred to the first 18 to 24 months of the child's life as the sensorimotor period (see Chapter 6). Observations of children's behavior during these early months indicate that they literally live in the "here and now," that their behavior is completely dominated by immediate sensory stimulation. Their capacity for mental representation has not yet emerged.

This early period, however, is an important one in the development of representational ability. It is a period of perceptual learning. The child learns to see and to react to objects as such. In his manipulation of them he coordinates and assimilates the various sensory impressions he gets from them. He experiments with objects "in order to see."

Prevision

It is in the later stages of this sensorimotor period that the child also begins to recognize signs of immediately following events. He has experienced these sequences many times. These perceptions of movements and sequences, which Piaget calls mobile schemata, involve characteristic sounds of various kinds. A particular sound thus becomes a sign "which permits the child to *foresee*, not only an event connected with his action but also any event conceived as being independent and connected with the object" (Piaget, 1952, p. 248—italics added). Thus the child acquires a kind of "prevision." He anticipated the usual sequel from the sign.

> Thus the signs consisting of creaks of the table or of chairs, of the person rising, etc., were acquired, like most of the others, as a function of the schemata of the meal. They are henceforth utilized in any circumstance whatever. . . .
> Finally let us remark . . . that the term prevision which we have used must not create an illusion or evoke more than concrete expectation. Deduction does not yet exist, because there is doubtless still no "representation." When Jacqueline expects to see a person where a door is opening, or fruit juice in a spoon coming out of a certain receptacle, it is not necessary, in order that there be understanding of these signs and consequently prevision, that she picture these objects to herself in their absence. It is enough that the signs set in motion a certain attitude of expectation and a certain schema of recognition of person or of food. (Piaget, 1952, p. 252)

Thus Piaget distinguished between perceptual (concrete) *prevision* (an "attitude of expectation and a certain schema of recognition") and *representation* in consciousness of objects or events not present to sense and of which the child is, as yet, incapable.

Elaboration of the Object

As we have seen, the child during these early stages of intellectual development acquires the ability to see objects as objects. His deliberate reaching-prehensile ability becomes well established with fairly precise eye-hand coordination. He manipulates objects and experiments with them "in order to see." He also acquires the ability to differentiate means from ends in his experimentation. But, as Piaget (1952) pointed out, not until about the beginning of the second year of life (the onset of the fifth stage) does the child begin "a new putting into relationship of objects among themselves" (p. 263). Up to that point in his development, the child has not established relations among objects independent of his actions with respect to them. He begins now, however, to see objects in a different relationship with himself. In Piaget's words,

> . . . this kind of accommodation to things, combined with the coordination of schemata already acquired during the preceding stage, result in definitely detaching the "object" from the activity itself while inserting it in coherent spatial groups in the same way as in the causal and temporal series which are independent of self. (p. 265)

In the child's efforts to assimilate new objects into his already acquired behavior patterns, he discovers that some objects resist. He is unable to manipulate them as he wishes. He discovers that such objects have properties which cannot be reduced to the level of his available schemata. Thus, as he encounters difficulty in his efforts to assimilate things to his own purposes, he becomes curious about the unforeseen properties of the objects which underlie their resistance. He then seeks to *accommodate* to them. Accommodation becomes an end in itself. Henceforth, "accommodation exists before every assimilation" (Piaget, 1952, p. 277). The child gradually realizes the independent nature of objects as he finally becomes able to assimilate them to his purposes.

These efforts to discover constitute a kind of "empirical groping" behavior, but different from earlier groping. Now "the groping is oriented as a function of the goal itself, that is to say, of the problem

presented . . . instead of taking place simply 'in order to see' "
(Piaget, 1952, p. 288). The "problem presented" is the discovery of
"centers of force," the discovery of the nature of objects. This discovery is the process of "the elaboration of the object," a prerequisite
to mental representation.

The child's mental functioning, however, is still in the realm of
the concrete. It is in a more advanced stage of development, but
"the subject's experience remains immediate and consequently a
victim of the most naïve phenomenalism" (p. 326). Further cognitive
developments with respect to knowing the concrete world are necessary as a prerequisite to mental representation.

In this connection, Piaget (1952) pointed out more specifically
that there are two interrelated conditions prerequisite to the higher
level of mental function: (1) "Permanent" objects must be constituted
in a system of spatial and causal relations, which can occur only from
intimate experience with the objective environment. (2) "One must
place oneself among these objects and, in order thus to come out of
one's own perspective, one must elaborate a system of spatial, causal
and objective relations" (p. 327). The small child necessarily sees
objects from his own limited perspective. In order really to know
objects in their varied relationships he must experience his environment from *many* perspectives by mingling and interacting with the
objects of which his environment is composed, just as a toddler is
wont to do, with his newly developed locomotor and prehensile abilities. This mingling of self with things is also essential in the development of self-perception. The "most difficult obstacle to perceive in
everything is oneself" (p. 327).

This is the stage of "discovery of new means through active experimentation." Moreover,

> . . . this more advanced adaptation of intelligence to the real
> is accompanied by a structurization of the external environment
> into permanent objects and coherent spatial relations as well as
> by a correlative objectification and specialization of causality
> and time. (p. 330)

Invention and Representation

On the basis of the foregoing developments there is a gradual change
in the direction of greater awareness of relationships. Clearer fore-
sight and an ability of "invention operating by simple mental com-

bination" gradually develop. Now, when confronted by a novel situation, the child's reactions rather than being of the nature of empirical groping are more likely to result from sudden invention. In other words, the solution is arrived at by a priori mental combination, by foreseeing which maneuvers will fail and which will succeed, rather than by a process of overt trial and error. To quote again from Piaget:

> Henceforth there exists invention and no longer only discovery; there is, moreover, representation and no longer only sensorimotor groping. These two aspects of systematic intelligence are interdependent. To invent is to combine mental, that is to say, representative, schemata and, in order to become mental, the sensorimotor schemata must be capable of intercombining in every way, that is to say, of being able to give rise to true inventions. (1952, p. 341)

This stage of mental development is ordinarily reached sometime during the latter half of the second year of life. The emergence of the ability to represent in consciousness the possible outcomes of behavior means the emergence of the ability to think. The abstractions the child has learned and the categories he has thus formed in direct contact with objective reality he can now begin to manipulate, organize, and transform as mental representations of reality.

The Development of Concepts

The child's ability to think, then, grows directly out of his varied direct contacts and sensory experiences with his world outside. He develops the ability to represent mentally these experiences in the absence of the actual objects of sensory experience and to manipulate, reorganize, and transform them. His cognitive structure is augmented. He can now *conceptualize*.

The Nature of Concepts

It is important at this point that we distinguish clearly between the processes of perception and conceptualization. Perception is the direct and immediate awareness (knowing) of an objectively present object or situation. Perception is the "clear awareness of the properties of objects and situations" that are present to sense. It is the individual, concrete object that is perceived (see Chapters 5 and 8).

By contrast, conceptualization is an abstracting, generalizing, and categorizing process based upon sense perception. It is a process of perceptual learning. On the basis of repeated perceptual cognition of individual members of a class of objects (oranges, for example)—experiences involving the various sense modalities—certain common properties or attributes are experienced in association with the orange. Its characteristic color, spherical shape, odor, and taste, each by itself comes to mean "orange." Thus when any one of these attributes is sensed the experience is immediately categorized and the verbal label "orange" comes to mind. "It is an orange." The concept "orange" has been formed. A concept, then, is the result of abstracting from many individual perceptual experiences the common properties of an object category.

The Study of Concept Formation in Children

There is, of course, no disagreement among students of thinking as to the essential role of learning in concept formation. There are, however, different research approaches to the problem in which the specific role of learning is seen differently, and receives varying degrees of emphasis.

THE OBJECTIVISTIC APPROACH   The behavioristically inclined investigator, for example, sees the process primarily as the establishment of common responses to particular classes of stimuli, and his research approach is the experimental-learning approach. The child-subjects are placed in various controlled situations in which they learn new modes of categorizing. The factors involved in the learning process are thus studied.

To take a specific example, many different pairs of words, such as "dog" and "tree," "robin" and "truck," and "cow" and "cloud" were presented to a child. In each instance in which the child chose the animal in the pair of stimuli to respond to, he was rewarded (the animal response was reinforced). He thus learned consistently to make a common response to a *class* of stimuli. The child ultimately learns to discriminate animals in entirely new stimulus pairs belonging to that class and to respond to them correctly. Obviously this is an example of learning in a perceptual situation, one in which a concept is established. Presumably some sort of generalized representation of animal-ness arises in the subject, which leads to the appropriate response to any new stimulus of that class (Palermo and Lipsitt, 1963).

Interestingly enough, one special problem in concept formation with which objectivistic research has become concerned is the problem of mediation, or conscious representation. More specifically, the concern is with the problem of establishing definite criteria for the existence of implicit mediating responses and the accompanying response-produced stimuli, and with demonstrating the role of these in discrimination learning and categorization (Kelleher, 1956; H. H. Kendler and D'Amato, 1955; T. S. Kendler, 1963; T. S. Kendler and H. H. Kendler, 1959; T. S. Kendler, H. H. Kendler, and Leonard, 1962; T. S. Kendler, H. H. Kendler, and Wells, 1960; Spiker, 1963).

Findings from this line of research indicate that mediating responses do not appear regularly in the cognitive behavior of children before age 8 years, but that when the use of response-produced cues becomes established the phenomenon of "inference" becomes possible. T. S. Kendler (1963) summarized:

> For a substantial proportion of the older children the final integration is more dependent on self-produced cues than on the external sitmulus B. Apparently the occurrence of inference, like the occurrence of reversal shift, is dependent, on a system of covert mediating responses which occur more readily in older than younger children. It seems that the experimental study of inferential behavior in children may provide another useful vehicle for examining the development of the covert response system underlying the higher mental processes. (p. 47)

THE COGNITIVE VIEW   Investigators with the more cognitive point of view see the problem of concept development much more in terms of internal states of the organism—what is the developmental status of the organism, what is its background of learning at the time of the new learning, and so forth. Thus, while they recognize the fact that one's cognitive structure does reflect his history of learning, they are not so much concerned with the *particular* antecedents of new learning. Ausubel (1963), for example, wrote that "existing cognitive structure . . . is the major factor influencing the learning and retention of meaningful new material" (p. 26). Bruner expressed this same emphasis in a summary statement: "In any case, we know that, when people associate things with each other, they most often do it by the extension or combination of groupings previously formed" (Bruner and Olver, 1963, p. 127).

Bruner and Olver's (1963) study was concerned with the rules and strategies (procedures) people use in the associative grouping of stimuli. They described a number of strategies "that have nothing to do with the content used in the grouping." Rather, these strategies were related to what the subject "was up to" at the time. In other words, the strategy that is used depends upon the child's mental status and his previous grouping experience (cognitive structure). Such experience, of course, is related to the age and the intelligence level of the child. An interesting finding in this research was that change in classifying strategy with development proceeded, in a sense, from the complex to the simple. The words of the investigators will be helpful here:

> The development of intelligence, given intervening opportunity for problem solving in the life of the growing organism, moves in the direction of reducing the strain of information processing by the growth of strategies of grouping that encode information in a manner (a) that chunks information in *simpler* form, (b) that gains *connectedness* with rules of grouping already formed, and (c) that is designed to *maximize the possibility of combinatorial operations* such that groupings already formed can be combined and detached from other forms of grouping. In a word then, what distinguishes the young child from the older child is the fact that the younger one is more complicated than the older one, not the reverse. (Bruner and Olver, 1963, pp. 133–134)

With the growth of ability, then, perceived objects and events are classified and categorized *more* in terms of how they relate to prior groupings and progressively *less* in terms of the actual content of the things being grouped. Stated in terms of concepts, the child's representations of his perceived world become progressively more comprehensive, more flexible, and interrelatable, and they therefore constitute a more versatile and efficient facility for thinking activity.

Styles of Categorization

Currently, a number of research workers are studying the strategies children adopt in their grouping and categorizing behavior. These investigators must recognize immediately that concepts vary in degree of generality, from the broad and inclusive to the specific with very limiting boundaries. Different specific-object categories, however, share common attributes. When an assortment of objects, all different in most respects, are presented to a child with the request that he pick out those that are alike, he can usually quite readily group them in terms of what he perceives as common attributes or in terms of some other relationship he sees among them. However, the specific bases for grouping the same set of objects by different children have been found to vary with the child's past perceptual experiences and with other personal qualities (Kagan *et al.*, 1964; Sigel, 1961; Sigel, 1965). The particular strategy a child characteristically adopts in his grouping behavior is called his cognitive style.

The styles of categorization used by children have been classified and described by Sigel (1965). One of these bases for categorization is the *descriptive part-whole* abstraction. Objects are grouped and labeled as belonging together because of observed "similarity in one or more elements within the stimulus complex." For example, pictures of a policeman and a soldier are chosen as alike because "they both have shoes" or "they both have uniforms" (p. 1).

Another style for grouping is based on the *relational-contextual* abstraction. An "*interdependence* among two or more stimuli" is seen by the child as the basis for grouping. For example, a man and a woman are selected as belonging together "because the woman helps the man." A hammer and a nail are selected "because you use the hammer to bang in a nail" (p. 1).

A third basis for grouping, according to research findings, is the *categorical-inferential* quality. In these cases, the label itself "reflects an inference about stimuli grouped together." Every item grouped together by this criterion is an "instance" of the label. For example, "they are professional people," "animals," and so on. Two subclasses of this mode of grouping were also noted. One of these is the *categorical-functional*, where inference is made regarding a common function, and the second is *class-naming*, where the label itself directly reflects the inference (Sigel, 1965, pp. 1–2).

LABELING AND DAILY LIVING   Life would indeed by chaotic were it not for the human tendency to discern common features among objects and situations, to categorize them according to their common features, and to interact with the world in terms of concepts. To deal separately and individually with every stimulus that impinges upon our senses would be overwhelmingly impossible. "For us, as adults, diversity is neither distressing nor chaotic, for we have created order out of the seeming disorder" (Sigel, 1964, p. 209).

Not only do we deal with the objectively present "world" in terms of categories, but, as has already been noted, concepts become freed from the necessity for direct external stimulation. In other words, already-formed categories of objects, situations, and relationships can be represented in consciousness. As our concepts become more and more highly abstracted and can be represented with greater facility by symbols, the more important they become in our thinking function.

Some Common Concepts

The realities of life—the objects, the situations, the relationships with which human beings constantly must deal in the course of living— are so numerous and so involved as to make for utter confusion and futility were it not for the human capacity to group, or categorize, or conceptualize. With this mental facility we are able to achieve a "reduction in load" (Bruner and Olver, 1963). "Concepts function as an adaptive mechanism through which we cope with reality" (Sigel, 1964, p. 209). But concepts and their utilization in thinking, as we have seen, are joint products of maturation and learning. Among the most important developmental tasks of childhood, therefore, is the acquisition of the generalized ability to categorize, and hence to deal conceptually and relatedly with categories of experience. Early concepts are relatively simple. They usually represent concrete objects and simple situations. With development, the level of conceptualization becomes more complex and abstract.

Object Concepts

Quite naturally, object concepts are the first to develop. Concrete objects are directly and immediately experienced. The child's object categories are at first broad and loosely bounded. With added experience they become delimited and with more specific referents. The child soon begins also to learn words in association with the objects he is experiencing. Specific words become "attached" to specific categories of experience. At the same time broader category concepts also develop. The dog, the kitten, and perhaps the bear in one picture book are now "animals."

Attribute Concepts

Concepts of *attributes* of objects are more difficult to formulate, for greater demands are made upon the abilities of abstraction. According to research findings (Sigel, 1953, 1954, 1961), abstracting size attributes is a more difficult process than abstracting such attributes as color or form because the size of an object is apprehended only when it is compared with another object. Children at 3 to 5 years of age begin to acquire this ability to compare and thus to abstract and conceptualize the size attribute of objects.

Interesting research has been conducted in regard to children's concepts of the object attributes of *amount, weight,* and *volume* (Smedslund, 1961a, 1961b). Young children have difficulty keeping their concepts of weight, for example, distinct and independent from the shape of the object. In one sort of experiment, one of two identical balls of clay is changed in shape before the child's eyes. When questioned about the change the child is likely to say that the ball that is changed in shape also becomes heavier (Piaget and Inhelder, 1941). Children, according to such research findings, require the concept of the conservation of quantity at an average age of 7 or 8 years, of weight by age 9 or 10 years, and of volume not until age 11 or 12 years.

Relationship Concepts

Dealing mentally with information concerning relationships between objects, people, and situations involves another sort of concept. The idea of space, for example, usually implies objects in relationship. When we think of space it is usually space between or among things. Even the concept of "outer space" is rather incomprehensible except as it relates to something or someone.

Concepts of space and space relations have received considerable research attention as well as theoretical consideration. As in other areas of conceptual development, Piaget's work here has contributed much and has stimulated others to do research in the development of space concepts.

According to Piaget's theorizing, the child grows through a series of developmental stages which eventuate in his ability to think in terms of concepts of spatial relations. These stages all relate to the child's sensory experiences and his prehension-manipulation of objects within his reach. In the beginning, before prehension has developed, the child "is in the center of a sort of moving and colored sphere whose images imprison him without his having any hold on them other than by making them reappear by movements of head and eyes" (Piaget, 1954, p. 145).

As prehensile ability develops, the child begins to grasp the objects within his reach. The process of the "elaboration of the object" is essential at this stage of development. The child searches for an object that has just become hidden by a screening object. The desired object is identified as behind and beyond the screen. Thus, perceptions of relative distance in terms of perspective are developed. As the child pulls objects toward himself and throws them away from himself and as he stacks them one on top of another or puts them in and takes them out of containers, he experiences relative distances in space and he sees the space within the container in relation to object size. He comes to see objects together with or separate from each other as he handles them and moves them about. By age 4 years the child also sees himself as an object among objects and in spatial relationships with other objects (Meyer, 1940).

Another sort of relationship concept is the concept of *causality*. It is vital to our understanding of events (and of objects and people in relation to events) that we view them in terms of causal sequences. The ability to conceptualize cause-and-effects relationships, as with other representational abilities, is based upon earlier direct observations of the objective world. We acquire concepts of causality by directly observing causal sequences in nature. Underlying this acquisition from experience, of course, is the assumed factor of biological (functional) maturation.

Again, the thinking and the observations of Piaget (1929, 1930) set the stage for a great deal of research regarding the child's development of concepts of causality. Piaget's own observations led him to postulate a sequence of developmental stages, again taking the child through his perceptual development in relation to things in his environment. Piaget noted that very young children differ in their basic orientation to reality. He noted three sorts of orientation, each based upon the child's initial inability to differentiate between self and not-self (between his own thoughts and feelings and the aspects of physical reality which give rise to those subjective experiences).

One of the orientations giving evidence of this basic "undifferentiation" is the tendency for the children to react to their own thoughts and desires as physical entities, This tendency develops into what Piaget called realism. The second orientation postulated by Piaget is the reverse of the first; the tendency to clothe these undifferentiated physical realities with such subjective qualities as consciousness and purpose, which he called animism. The third orientation is to come implicitly to "see" the physical aspects of experience as products of human creation. Thus, every object and event in the objective world is assumed to have been made by people, hence artificialism. These three tendencies, according to the results of Piaget's experiments, precede the formation of causal concepts. The period is referred to as the precausal period.

A great deal of research was stimulated by Piaget's published material. The findings in many of the other studies failed to substantiate Piaget's conclusions. There is considerable disagreement, for example, as to the frequency with which animism is to be found in children (Deutsche, 1937; Huang, 1943; Jahoda, 1958; Russell, 1940), Sigel (1964), at the end of his brief review of research on concepts of causality, wrote:

> We can conclude that children do provide different kinds of explanations for physical and psychical phenomena, that there is a crude correspondence with age but not a one-to-one relationship, and that the existence of stages of causal explanations is still a tenable hypothesis. The invariance of these stages needs more precise and rigorous testing, assessing the role of experience and knowledge in the onset of particular stages. (pp. 235–236)

Concepts of cause and effect, along with the other relational concepts, are importantly involved in the processes of thinking.

Levels of Thinking

There are a number of motivational situations that give rise to different varieties and levels of representational functioning. We shall consider now one conceptualization of the major varieties of controlled thinking activity.

Guilford's conceptual model of intelligence has been briefly discussed earlier (see Chapter 6). The three dimensions of that model were concerned with the *operations* or functions of the intellect, the *content* with which those operations deal, and the *products* or outcomes of those functions. In other words, intelligence, from Guilford's point of view, is mental activity. Since the term thinking is in its broad sense mental activity (the functioning of the intellect) and since thinking, as we have noted, always involves content (we think about something), and since the activity eventuates in some sort of product, the Guilford model can be used as a framework for a discussion of thinking (the functioning of the intellect) (Guilford and Merrifield, 1960).

The five operations that constitute the first dimension of the model really designate five main types of thinking: *cognitive thinking, memorative thinking,* two types of *productive thinking,* and *evaluative thinking* (Merrifield, 1966).

Cognitive Thinking

Cognition involves thinking in the sense of knowing, being aware of, "having in mind," or comprehending. In this sense we "think about," or are cognisant of, what is objectively before us. Even though the object of thought (the situation) is being perceived and comprehended directly, usually also mental representation and manipulation are involved in the process of "knowing." Cognition of a totally new situation, such as that faced by a child when he first enters school, involves more than the mere awareness of individual objects and people. It would also involve some sort of discrimination and classification. The process of placing objects in classes or categories has been identified as concept formation, which is one important aspect of cognitive thinking (Bruner and Olver, 1963).

Memorative Thinking

The second category of mental operation is memory. This, of course, is thinking in which there is direct recall of past learning and experience. All types of mental reinstatement and representation may be involved in memorative thinking.

A rather large proportion of this type of functioning consists of the free flow of consciousness, or autistic thinking, the kind of representational activity that just takes place with no particular outcome or objective to be reached. It is thinking for the enjoyment of the activity itself. Much of the thinking of persons in their later years, for example, is likely to consist largely of memories of experiences and activities of their earlier, more active years, recalled in an unsystematic sequence and for no immediate purpose other than the satisfaction derived from the reliving of those experiences. Reveries of this sort, however, are likely to become embellished and exaggerated in varying degrees with repetition.

Young people are also often disposed to think autistically. However, they are more likely to live in the future, to imagine themselves in situations or activities that they have experienced only vicariously. This type of autistic thinking does not involve "true" memories. It is, however, a kind of memorative activity, involving the recall and manipulation of what has been learned through contacts with people and the various mass media.

Productive Thinking

Productive thinking generates or discovers what was not evident before; it educes, makes anew, and thinks differently from the general.

There are two types of productive thinking: *divergent production* and *convergent production*. Divergent production is original, or creative, thinking. "Creative thinking is invention, for one thing, and invention is a form of production" (Guilford and Merrifield, 1960, p. 11). This kind of production involves flexibility, originality, and imagination.

Convergent production, on the other hand, is thinking of a more contained and controlled nature. It is thinking in the direction of *the* solution or, at most, a limited number of "correct" solutions to a structured problem. The criteria for an acceptable solution are well defined. Convergent thinking is generally called problem solving. In contrast to the autistic type of conscious activity, it is mental activity with a specific purpose other than the sheer enjoyment of the activity itself. Objects, situations, relationships, and implications are manipulated symbolically in trial-and-error fashion but oriented toward the solution of a problem or the resolution of a conflict situation. Practical problems involving physically present objects or difficult environmental situations being objectively faced may be solved through the use of images or symbolic representations of one sort or another. Images of possible modifications or rearrangements of objects or of relationships among objects may be conjured up and tried out in imagination. In such instances, the objective problem situation is being faced directly, and, as thinking continues, is being perceptually surveyed. Thus, perception and mental representation are involved simultaneously. "Learning sets" previously established in the person's cognitive structure are utilized, and, in terms of "shorthand," ideational trial and error, the problem may be solved as if by sudden insight (Harlow and Harlow, 1949). Problem solving itself is a more controlled and directed kind of cognitive thinking than that which was described earlier.

In certain instances, the problem to be solved may be a purely theoretical one in which no objective environmental situation is being immediately faced. The symbols are likely to be other than direct sensory images. Highly abstract symbols representing conceived scientific entities or relationships are mentally manipulated, combined, and recombined in various ways in search of a solution. Verbal symbols, mathematical symbols, and chemical and physical notations are utilized in scientific thinking. This is the process of *reasoning*.

Even though divergent thinking is more closely identified with creativity, in the general sense of the term, convergent thinking can be equally creative. As noted above, Guilford and Merrifield (1960) stated that creativity implies invention. "There is a connotation that in invention we get away from the conventional answers, hence conclusions are not uniquely determined. All this points clearly toward the category of divergent production" (p. 11). These authors go on to say, however, that they have come to realize.

> . . . that the redefinition of abilities, which are in the convergent-production category. . . . are also of much importance in creative thinking. They represent transformations of thought, reinterpretations, and freedom from functional fixedness in the derivation of unique solutions. It may be that the transformations category rather generally makes contributions to creative thinking. (p. 11)

Evaluative Thinking

The fourth kind of thinking, as a type of operation of the intellect, is *evaluation*. "To judge, to compare correctly elements with reference to a given standard, to assign consistent values to elements in a group, to rate in terms of consensus, to leap over uncertainty and to land 'on target' " (Merrifield, 1966, p. 24) is a brief but apt description of this type of thinking. Binet saw this level of mental activity as the essence of intelligence when he wrote his oft quoted statement: "to judge well, understand well, reason well—these are the essentials of intelligence (Binet and Simon, 1916, p. 42).

Learning and Thinking

Thinking is a function of the intellect. Consequently, one's potentiality for the development of thinking ability, like all original developmental potentialities, is genetically determined (see Chapter 6). This potentiality varies widely among individuals. A person's many and varied abilities to function have developed within the limits of his inherent potential and are largely matters of learning. Hence, whatever thinking abilities one may possess have been acquired through learning, through the exercise of one's thinking (representational) apparatus.

It is also clear that the sort of environment in which the child grows up has much to do with the extent to which he exercises and thus learns each of the various types of thinking activity. The school and the quality of teaching the child receives is an important aspect of his general developmental environment. Bruner (1957, 1959) stressed the importance of what he termed generic learning, particularly in the schoolroom, in relation to the development of productive thinking. Generic learning is not merely the gaining and storing of information in the form in which it is given. Rather, it is learning that leads to the recoding of information and, hence, to the eduction of general principles (concepts) that allow the child to "cross the barrier into thinking." Thinking that results directly from generic learning, then, is thinking that "goes beyond the information given." Through insightful teaching, children can be helped to learn generically, thus enabling them to use their learning creatively (Bruner, 1959).

Cognitive Structure and Learning to Think

The concept of cognitive structure was introduced in the discussion of learning in Chapter 8. One's cognitive structure is conceived of as one's fund of knowledge which is organized in terms of hierarchical relationships and conceptual systems. It presumably results largely from generic learning. Learning in these terms involves the process of relating new material to this structure. New items of information (new knowledge) are assimilated into already organized systems in meaningful ways. In the words of Ausubel:

> . . . as new material enters the cognitive field, it interacts with and is appropriately subsumed under a relevant and more inclusive conceptual system. The very fact that it is subsumable (relatable to stable elements in cognitive structure) accounts for its meaningfulness and makes possible the perception of insightful *relationships*. If it were not subsumable, it would constitute rote material and form discrete and isolated traces. (Anderson and Ausubel, 1965, pp. 105–106)

Learning Sets

All new learnings that are functionally useful are achieved only in terms of what has been previously acquired and organized into the cognitive structure. General approaches to learning problems and learning skills are learned in this way. Acquired skills in learning are called learning sets. Thus, one learns *how* to learn. One learns generalized techniques of thinking through problems. These learning sets become incorporated into the cognitive structure as systems under which related new learnings are subsumed. In summarizing their experimental findings concerning the operation of learning sets, Harlow and Harlow (1949) wrote:

> Thus the individual learns to cope with more and more difficult problems. At the highest stage in this progression, the intelligent human adult selects from innumerable, previously acquired learning sets the raw material for thinking. . . . Thinking does not develop spontaneously as an expression of innate abilities; it is the end result of a long learning process. . . . The brain is essential to thought, but the untutored brain is not enough, no matter how good a brain it may be. An untrained brain is sufficient for trial-and-error, fumbling-through behavior, but only training enables an individual to think in terms of ideas and concepts. (pp. 38–39)

Children can learn to think, and they can be helped and facilitated in their acquisition of thinking approaches and skills. They can be helped to learn generically by being given practice in the manipulation of materials and ideas related to those materials, in problem situations that encourage the development of learning sets in both divergent and convergent thinking.

SELECTED READING SUGGESTIONS

Anderson, R. C., and D. P. Ausubel. *Readings in the psychology of cognition.* New York: Holt, Rinehart and Winston, Inc., 1965. (Read J. S. Bruner, Learning and thinking; J. S. Bruner and Rose Olver, Development of equivalence of transformations; I. Maltzman, Thinking from a behavioristic point of view; and J. S. Bruner, The art of discovery.)

Gallagher, J. J. Productive thinking. In M. L. Hoffman and Lois M. Hoffman (eds.), *Review of child development research.* New York: Russell Sage Foundation, 1964.

Harlow, H. F., and Margaret K. Harlow. Learning to think. *Scientif. Amer.*, 1949, 181, 36–39.

Kneller, G. F. *The art and science of creativity.* New York: Holt, Rinehart and Winston, Inc., 1965.

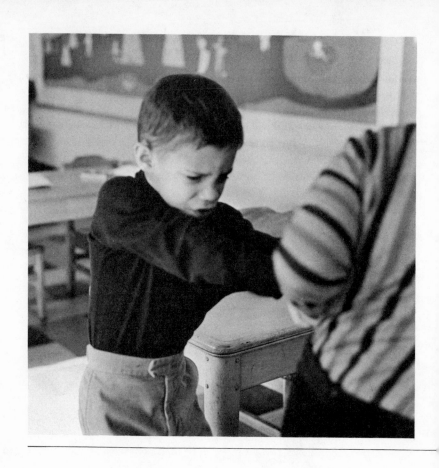

CHAPTER 11

Emotional Development

It is interesting to try to conceive of what human existence would be like without feelings and emotions. To live without ever experiencing pleasure or displeasure, delight or distress, elation or depression, love or anger, joy or sorrow is difficult to imagine. Our emotions give us motive power to live, to move, to strive. The baby nurses at his mother's breast not *just* to have a full stomach. He continues to nurse because the process as such is pleasant and gratifying to him. It is not the child's well-nourished body per se or his newly won ability to walk upright or the nature of his self-image as such that move him to further activity. It is, rather, the feeling of well-being, the joy of freedom of activity, and the gratification that comes from exploration and manipulation that activate him, make him "open to the world," and keep him striving to experience more and more of the world about him.

The Nature of Emotions

Emotionality as an area of functioning is very complex and difficult to investigate. Important as it is in our lives, when viewed objectively, it is a behavioral area which man has in common with subhuman species. Furthermore, although man's cognitive processes are importantly involved, his affective experiences and his emotional behavior are largely mediated by lower centers of the brain. These centers and the other bodily structures necessary for emotional functioning are intact and in a state of readiness at birth. The human being is born well equipped for experiencing feelings of pleasure and displeasure and for displaying emotional behavior. In that particular respect, man is more like the subhuman species. In that particular respect, also, maturational changes between birth and adulthood are relatively minor. Hence, even though emotionality is complex and multifaceted, involving, as it does, the whole organism, it is the most "primitive" major area of human functioning.

Aspects of Emotionality

Emotionality has been defined in various ways and has been seen from different theoretical points of view by students of human behavior. One of these approaches, objective in nature, is to define an emotion in terms of the external situation from the point of view of the stimulus that gives rise to it. Thus, those emotional reactions which result from situations that are judged objectively to be dangerous would be labeled "fear" or "terror." Likewise, reactions to confining or frustrating situations, would be "anger" or "rage," and so on. This was the approach used by early investigators of emotions in infants and children. Watson (1924), for example, in his efforts to account for all infant emotions, defined the three emotions "fear," "anger," and "love" in terms of the relatively few stimuli to which he found infants responsive. The infants' response to a sudden loud noise or a sudden loss of support he labeled "fear," their reactions to restraint he labeled "anger," and responses to rocking, stroking, fondling, and the like, were "love."

A second objective approach to the study of emotions closely related to the first, is in terms of the observable reactions, or measurable bodily changes, that constitute emotional behavior. Emotional behavior, from this viewpoint, is both external and internal. External behavior, of course, is quite readily observed. When the behavior is destructive or assaultive in nature it is labeled "anger" or "rage."

When it appears as less violent approach acts, it is "affection" or "love" or "lust" or even "elation." When behavior appears as retreat or flight it is "fear." Quite obviously, the mere observation of external behavior (without more information, including a knowledge of the eliciting stimuli) is not a sufficient basis for an adequate classification of emotion.

The internal responses involved in emotion are very complex and, of course, cannot be observed directly. Their effects, however, can be measured by the use of instruments. The study of the internal (visceral) changes involved in emotion has contributed much to our understanding. Complicated sequences and patterns of change involving the vascular system, the endocrine system, and the involuntary muscular system, are extremely important aspects of the complex we call emotion. These physiological reactions are controlled and regulated by the autonomic division of the nervous system. In a very general way, the "approach" and "avoidance" aspects of behavior are mediated by the parasympathetic and the sympathetic segments of the autonomic division, respectively. The internal aspects of emotional behavior, however, are always widespread and diffuse, and so far only very rough correlations with specific nervous structures have been established.

A third approach to the problem of the emotions is to regard emotion as a conscious experience. In spite of efforts on the part of some students of human behavior to avoid a consideration of the conscious aspect of emotions, no "normal" human being (including the objective psychologist himself) can doubt the reality of the consciously experienced emotion. When we *act* angry in response to an anger-provoking stimulus, we also *feel* angry.

Emotion: A Response of the Total Person

In view of these three approaches to the study of emotional behavior, an important fact stands out: Emotionality is an extremely complex area of human functioning which involves the whole organism. The stimulus aspect cannot be neglected. Cognition is always involved. There is no emotion without either the actual perception of the provoking situation or the anticipation of it in terms of images. Normally, a situation does not provoke genuine fear or anger or jealousy or joy or elation unless it is first perceived or thought of as something about which one must be fearful or angry or jealous or joyful or elated. Even in the case of irrational anxiety or worry, images or other symbols representing past cognitive experiences or imagined ones are being centrally manipulated.

The external behavioral aspects, the so-called expressive movements of emotion, are equally essential to the total complex. In full-fledged anger, for example, although actual destructive aggression may be held in check, there are, nevertheless, implicit if not overt patterns of muscular contractions and gross bodily movements that express hostility and tendency to aggression. The kinesthetic stimuli produced by these expressive behaviors give rise to sensory experiences that are important ingredients in the total experiential aspect of the complex.

Simultaneously with overt behavior come the internal responses, which are mediated by the autonomic division of the nervous system in response to cognitive awareness of the situation. The whole pattern of changes is "designed" to prepare the organism *physically* for biologically appropriate activity. In the case of fear or anger, the joint action of the autonomic nervous system and the endocrine glandular system supplies the blood with additional energy-giving blood sugar and produces changes in the pattern of blood-vessel tension so as to shunt that energy-laden blood into the skeletal muscles for greater strength in meeting the "emergency." Internal organs, like skeletal muscles, are equipped with sense receptors that are stimulated by the internal activity, thus giving rise to patterns of sensations, which add to the "unanalyzed mass" that constitutes the emotional experience.

A realization of the importance of these sensory components arising from response-produced stimuli was what led William James, in 1890, to make his famous paradoxical statement that "we do not tremble because we are afraid, but we are afraid because we tremble." According to his theory, which was also stated independently by the Danish physiologist Lange, an emotion is *the way the body feels* when in a disturbed internal state and while making various overt expressive movements. The massive, unanalyzed experience arising from the bodily processes and the expressive movements *is* the emotion, according to James.

The important point here is that an adequate consideration of an area of human behavior as complex as the emotions must deal with overt behavioral, as well as experiential, aspects and with physiological, as well as psychological, aspects. We would agree essentially with Ausubel:

> Emotion may be defined as a heightened state of *subjective experience* accompanied by skeletal-motor and autonomic-humoral responses, and by a selectively generalized state of lowered response thresholds. . . .
> The following sequential steps are involved in the instigation

of an emotional response: (a) *interpretive* phase—perception or anticipation of an event that is interpreted as threatening or enhancing an ego-involved need, goal, value, or attribute of self; (b) *preparatory reactive* phase consisting of a selectively generalized lowering of the particular response thresholds implicated in a given emotion; (c) *consumatory reactive* phase with subjective, autonomic-humoral, and skeletal-motor components; and (d) a *reflective reactive* phase involving subjective awareness of the drive state and of visceral and skeletal responses. (p. 317 in *Theories and problems of child development*, 1958, Grune & Stratton, Inc., by permission)

Positive and Negative Emotions

As is obvious and common in everyone's experience, there are two general directional types, or categories, of emotional behavior and experience. These types are so different qualitatively that they seem, subjectively, and appear, objectively, to have nothing in common. "Pleasant," "positive," and "approach" apply to the one directional type, while "unpleasant," "negative," "escape," "injure," and "destroy" apply to the other. Not only are they logical and subjective opposites but the two types of experience also involve mutually antagonistic autonomic functioning, thus mediating over-all patterns of visceral change that are quite different. Yet the common term emotion applies equally well and without conflict to both categories of experience. Both types are heightened states of subjective experience. Both are extreme deviations from the comfortable, normal internal state of affairs, both being, in a sense, emergency reactions.

As we shall see in other connections later, the relative dominance of one or the other of these two emotional types has important implications in the child's personal development. Chapter 8, for example, showed how readily new stimuli and new situations can become effective in eliciting emotional behavior. The prevailing nature of the young child's environment will have much to do with determining whether the social aspects of his life become attached to the positive or the negative categories of emotion.

The Study of Emotional Development

Emotional experiences and outward emotional behavior are matters of universal, first-hand acquaintance. Daily, we all experience a variety of emotions in ourselves, and we are constantly meeting the problem of dealing with them in others. Underdeveloped emotional capacity, uncontrolled emotional behavior, and pathological expressions of emotion are major areas of concern among those who must deal with human problems at any level, whether individual, group, national, or international. Hence, the need for greater understanding of the nature and development of emotionality.

Controlled research in this area is extremely difficult. Behavior under emotion-arousing conditions in natural settings can be observed directly and descriptions of that behavior can be recorded. But affectivity per se—what the individual is actually experiencing under those conditions—obviously cannot be observed objectively. Affectivity must be inferred in terms of the situation and the observed external behavior associated with the situation. We include in the behavior that can be observed the individual's subjective *report* of his feelings.

Our greatest insights into the nature of emotionality have come from the clinical approach. In the clinical setting, real emotional problems of individuals with widely varying backgrounds and experiences are studied. The clinician must, in each case, understand and deal with a total, unique emotional situation. Through such clinical experience has come a growing realization of the importance to healthy emotional development of understanding and respecting the child's own point of view, his "private meanings," his individual strivings and frustrations, his own self-image, and his attitudes toward himself in relation to others and the total situation.

In our studies of individual children, we hope to approximate as nearly as possible a "clinical" understanding of the child's characteristic emotional behavior patterns and to arrive at an estimate of his level of emotional development. First-hand, recorded observations of the child in his home, at school, and as he interacts with his peers and with the adults in his daily life are the primary sources of data for this understanding and evaluation. We shall return to this particular problem of appraisal in various other connections later.

Congenital Affectivity

The first breath of the newborn infant appears to be an outward aspect, or expression, of an emotional disturbance—a "protest" against intolerable conditions. The newborn apparently keeps on breathing because breathing promotes a satisfying state of affairs. It eliminates discomfort.

During the neonatal period, the baby normally shows signs of emotional excitement only when conditions, external and internal, are such as to cause him bodily discomfort or sensuous pleasure. When he feels pain from some physical disorder or external condition, when he is hungry, or when he is wet or cold or otherwise uncomfortable, he "reports" immediately with signs of distress. No condition outside his own body which does not impinge directly upon his sense organs is of his slightest concern. He is completely egocentric in that sense; he cannot be otherwise. When he senses discomfort he reacts immediately. He "demands" immediate relief from discomfort and immediate gratification of his needs with loud and insistent crying. He does not have to learn these patterns; they are already built-in.

As explained in Chapter 7, babies are not all alike. They vary widely with respect to a number of temperamental tendencies. Some are by nature highly active, others are unusually quiet; some of them almost from the beginning seem to be relatively undisturbed and calm in their new conditions of existence, others appear to be displeased and uncomfortable. Babies also vary widely in their reactivity to strong stimuli. The "excitement" pattern (reactions of startle, shock, and withdrawal), with its wide individual variation, is common in infants, particularly during the first month of life before the development of the inhibiting function of the brain.

Rather marked congenital differences in temperament were observed in Paul and Sally 695. Paul was relatively quiet, with an observant and "thoughtful" appearance, while Sally, from the beginning, was an active child, inclined toward "unevenness of disposition." She was more reactive to restrictions, with ready tears when her movements were hampered. Both babies were alert when awake and quite reactive to stimulation.

Congenital temperamental differences presumably constitute the beginnings of individual differences in later emotionality.

The Role of Learning
in Early Emotional Development

Emotional learning, however, gets under way very soon. The baby's emotional expressions begin to vary with the situation (with the particular source or locus of discomfort), and he begins to show differentiated expressive signs of pleasure from gratification as well as distress from pain or discomfort. As maturation progresses and he gains experience, he becomes responsive emotionally to a wider and wider range of stimuli. Thus, the direction of the child's emotional development and the characteristic quality of his emotional expressions are influenced by his environment, and particularly by the kind of care and handling he receives. Once again, development is a product of organism-environment interaction.

The baby's responsiveness to other human beings soon becomes pronounced, and, although evidence is not always clear, the consensus is that the quality of the attention and care he receives during this early period has much to do with the development of his later capacity to accept love and affection *from* others or to feel love *for* others. The evidence for this facet of emotional development comes largely from clinical observations. The development of the capacity for love is discussed in greater detail in a later section of this chapter.

Developmental Sequences

For an accurate assessment of developmental status in emotionality, however, just as in other functional areas, some sort of scale or sequence of stages is necessary. As is true with other generalized qualities of behavior, no completely satisfactory series of indicators has been established, although several formulations have been proposed. Probably the best known of these is the series of stages postulated by Freud.

The Freudian Stages

The series of stages in the psychosexual development of the individual adopted by many psychologists as the basic framework of personality development are the *oral*, the *anal*, the *genital* or *phallic*, the *latency*, and the *puberal* periods. Certain of these stages were briefly described in the discussion of the vital functions (see Chapter 4). We shall sketch this series of stages again specifically as an example of a sequence in the development of emotionality.

The *oral* period covers early infancy, when taking food through nursing at the breast and being made comfortable by this process are the totality of life. Much of the baby's experiences of release from tension and gratification come from or are associated with the oral activity of food taking. When gratification through nursing is not forthcoming, when tension has mounted, feelings of frustration are experienced; anxiety and the sense of insecurity arise. With gratification come pleasure and a sense of security. This period, during which emotional experience—either pleasurable or otherwise—centers around infant oral activity, lasts to about the end of the first year, thus corresponding to the period of greatest dependency.

The generalized pleasure aspects of infant oral activity, quite apart from the mere relief from hunger, is emphasized by the psycho-analytically oriented students of child behavior.

Throughout this early period, the child is rapidly learning to do things for himself. He begins now to explore more widely as he masters the ability to move about on his own power. His abilities to manipulate with his hands the objects about him appear now to be replacing the pleasure he has been deriving from *sucking* his fingers. Furthermore, as he becomes more and more able to "get into things," restrictions are placed upon him. He begins to experience new demands and pressures. The attitudes of those around him regarding order and cleanliness begin to be felt. The job of toilet training begins in earnest. Since the eliminative functions pertain to, and directly involve, his own body and its sensitivities, they are "closer" to him than are any other activities. They involve tension, release from tension, frustration, and gratification. The child's preoccupation is thus shifted from oral activity to the anal region. According to the Freudian account, the child has now reached the *anal* stage.

Certainly, this period in the child's life is extremely important from the standpoint of determining developmental trends, and it can be a very difficult period for both the child and his parents.

By the time the child has reached the age of 3 years, oral pleasures, as a rule, are no longer predominant in his life. He is also well along in achieving bowel and bladder control. Concentration upon anal activities has also lessened as his manipulative and locomotor abilities and his interests in things outside himself gain precedence. His curiosity about and interest in people also are expanding. This interest inevitably leads to questioning about sexuality and reproduction. He is now entering the *genital* or *phallic* stage. According to psychoanalytic theory, the child at about this stage tends to become especially attached emotionally to his parent of the opposite sex, and this attachment is erotic in nature. Little boys feel themselves to be the rivals of their fathers for the love of their mothers, and girls likewise become their mothers' rivals in love. These feelings, we are told, are often associated with wishes for the death of the rival. This is called the Oedipus complex.

The Oedipal situation, of course, is a very stressful predicament. It is characterized by the painful conflict between "id" demands for gratification and "ego" restraints. Strong guilt feelings are generated. The child loves his father and he strongly identifies with him, yet his father is his rival and he wishes for his father's elimination. The way out of this shameful conflict is the repression of these guilt-arousing wishes, along with the childish associations and memories connected with them. Psychoanalytic theory thus purports to account for the common lack in adulthood of memories of childhood experiences.

Freud (1938) described the whole period of infancy and early childhood as being characterized by "infantile sexuality," which reaches its height of surgency during this third, or phallic, stage. He held that the apparent loss of memory during the latency period was not "a real forgetting of infantile impressions but rather amnesia similar to that observed in neurotics of their later experiences, the nature of which consists of the memories being kept away from consciousness [repression]" (p. 582). He further maintained that "the influx of this [infantile] sexuality does not stop, even in this latency period, but its energy is deflected either wholly or partially from sexual utilization and conducted to other aims. . . . a process which merits the name *sublimation*" (p. 584).

At any rate, according to Freudian theory, the resolution of conflict and the relief from stress through repression and amnesia mark the beginning of the *latency* period, the fourth period in emotional (psychosexual) development. This period covers approximately the ages 6 to 10 years.

With the onset of puberal changes, the child experiences a period of physiological instability. During this *puberal* period (the fifth period), there is much preoccupation with the body and its changes. A step-up in interest in the opposite sex and many other changes in feelings and attitudes make this period an extremely important one developmentally. In terms of Freudian theory, pubescence sets off a reawakening, a resurgence, of sexuality that for a time has been latent.

These five periods may be taken in broad outline to represent emotional development. Theoretically, at least, they are directly related to specific stages in the maturation of the organism. The oral period is one of infant helplessness. The anal period begins as the child, through the maturation of body structures, begins to overcome his helplessness, to operate with some degree of independence, and thus to have shifted to himself some measure of responsibility for his independent acts. Thus, he must begin now to conform to the cleanliness requirements of society by gaining control of his hitherto involuntary eliminative processes. The demands of society force upon him a preoccupation with anal functions during the period when maturation is in process of bringing the body and those neural structures involved to a stage of development in which voluntary control is possible. The maturational basis for the early phallic period, however, is not so clear. Perhaps general maturation of the child's organ systems, particularly of the brain cortex and the neuromuscular systems, makes possible a shift from conscious efforts to control the eliminative processes, and a preoccupation with them to an increased interest in his parents and their relationships with each other and with him. Hence, the development of the Oedipus situation, with its tensions and conflicts.

The latency period begins with the gradual cessation of the stressful genital period. Controls have been achieved, the pressure is off, and considerable independence has been gained. The child's tensions and gratifications are no longer so largely determined by the functions of the alimentary canal and his intense relationships with his parents. They come now largely from a physically active life in an interesting world of things and people outside his home and family situation. The maturational and growth changes that characterize the puberal period are quite dramatic. They furnish an obvious basis for the many changes in interests and activities which take place during this period. Implications of puberal changes for emotional development and adjustment are profound.

A Development Sequence
Based on Infant Observation

From the point of view of practical usefulness as a scale for assessing the attained level of emotional development in a given child, the phases of psychosexual development based on psychoanalytic theory leave much to be desired. There is need for much more specific behavioral indicators of progress.

Perhaps the nearest approach to a useful series of developmental stages for the first 2 years of life comes from an investigation by Bridges (1932). In this study, based on observations of the emotional behavior from birth of sixty-two children, a careful record was made in each case of a response and the environmental conditions that preceded it. One outcome of the study was a generalized description of emotional development in terms of four kinds of change, as follows:

1. Intense emotional responses become less frequent.
2. The reaction to any given stimulus becomes more specific.
3. Emotional responses are transferred from one situation to another which did not originally evoke them.
4. Emotional responses gradually become more differentiated.

In relation to the fourth aspect of change, that is, differentiation, Bridges described, with approximate timing, the sequence that takes place from birth to 2 years of age (see Figure 11.1). From the beginning, certain kinds of stimulation give rise to a generalized, over-all excitement, which Bridges regarded as the original emotion. Infants

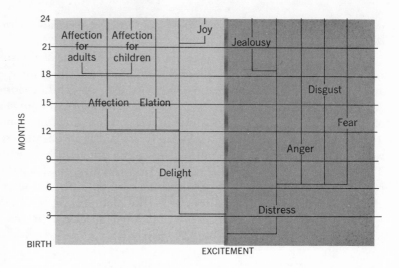

Figure 11.1

The early development of emotions. Adapted from Bridges
(1932), p. 340, by permission.

who are thus excited are described in terms of suddenly tensed muscles,
quickened breath, jerky, kicking leg movements, and wide-open eyes
gazing into the distance. This pattern was found to persist throughout
the first 2 years of life.

At about 3 weeks of age the first step in differentiation takes place.
Distress, or unpleasurable excitement, as distinct from generalized
excitement, appears. In distress there is greater muscle tension, more
interference with breathing, louder and more irregular crying at a
higher pitch. Tears may flow, the face become flushed, the mouth
distorted, and the fists clenched.

Not until the age of about 3 months does the distinctly pleasurable
sort of excitement, delight, become differentiated. This pattern involves kicking, faster breathing, opening of the mouth, crooning
sounds, and smiling. In contrast with the distress pattern, the movements in delight are free rather than restrained, the eyes are opened
rather than closed, there are smiles rather than frowns, and approach
movements rather than withdrawal.

The next differentiations in the sequence are on the unpleasurable
side. According to Bridges, at about 5 months of age the baby shows
unmistakable signs of anger, as differentiated from the more generalized distress. The clearest sign of anger is a wail, as if in protest,
without the closing of the eyes. Closely following anger comes disgust,
characterized by coughing, sputtering, and frowning while the baby is

being fed. The third differentiation from distress, according to this study, is fear, observable at about 7 months of age. The presence of a stranger is the most frequent stimulus to fear. The behavior pattern includes general inhibition of movement, tears, and steady crying, with eyes tightly closed and head bent. The body remains rigid and inactive.

At about the same time (7 months) a pleasurable emotional pattern, elation, becomes distinguishable from generalized delight. The baby smiles, takes a deep breath, and appears to express satisfaction in a sort of grunt.

By the eleventh month there are clear signs of affection for adults. The baby at this time will put his arms around the adult's neck and stroke or pat the face with obvious delight. Sometimes he will approximate a kiss by bringing his lips close to the adult's face. By age 15 months he makes an affectionate response to other children as well as to adults.

Very shortly after affection manifests itself, jealousy appears as a further differentiation of distress. It is characterized by tears, bent head, and by standing stiff and motionless. In some instances anger and aggression are part of the picture.

Finally, at about 20 to 21 months, the pattern described as joy makes its appearance.

This sequence of differentiations described by Bridges perhaps comes nearest to meeting the requirements of a series of progress indicators in emotional development. However, as we have noted, it covers only the first 2 years of life. The different behavior patterns are extremely difficult to recognize and distinguish in a baby's behavior. A given child's status in emotional development, we must therefore conclude, must be estimated mainly in terms of a general understanding of emotionality and of the changes that take place with age, rather than in terms of a definite scale of progress indicators.

Maturation and Learning in Emotional Development

As was suggested in our discussion of the Freudian sequence, maturation as well as learning is involved in the development of emotions. Freud's psychosexual stages relate directly to bodily structures and their maturation.

Emotionality in general, however, since it is so pervasive, involving as it does the functioning, more or less, of the total organism, is not so closely bound in its changes with time to the maturation of a specific bodily structure, as is the case, for example, with the development of mentality. The great diversity of emotional patterns and modes of emotional adjustment to be found among otherwise mature people must be accounted for very largely in terms of learning in environmental diversity. This, of course, is not to discount the fact that individual differences in constitutional nature have much to do with determining idiosyncrasies in reactions to given environmental situations. It appears to be true, then, that beyond the early period of affective differentiation, as described by Bridges, the role of the maturational factor in the direction and extent of emotional change is of relatively minor importance.

Planned and Incidental Learning

That significant changes in the quality and patterning of emotions do take place, particularly during childhood, there is no doubt. Earlier in this chapter, the two opposing categories of emotional experience were mentioned, and in that connection we emphasized the importance of the prevailing quality (positive or negative) of the child's home environment in determining the general nature of his emotional and social attitudes and behavior. More specifically, evidence suggests that the prevailing quality of the experience the child has with his mother during early childhood is of paramount importance.

I. D. Harris (1959), in an intensive study of a group of children and their mothers, concluded that a mother's loving care—her warm dependability and her understanding of her child's individual needs for expression—was "crucially" related to later desirable emotional and social adjustment and that the lack of such warmness and understanding were factors in later maladjustment. In the words of Harris:

> The mother can be a source of nutriment and pleasure for an infant as he feeds, but she can also be a source of pain, tension and frustration. If she is a source of pleasure, then the growing child will look upon others, and later humans as gratifiers; if she is a source of pain and tension, the growing child will react to others and to later humans as frustrating. (p. 25)

During the toddler period, when the "socialization" of the child is underway in earnest (see Chapter 8), progress in learning takes place at a rapid rate. Two general types of learning can be identified during this period particularly. First, the child, of course, learns those patterns of behavior—personal and social habits and ways of speaking and thinking—which the parents set out to teach him in order to make of him an acceptable member of society. But, while this deliberate inculcation of the culture is taking place, the child also learns things that were not deliberately planned or consciously taught by the parents. There is likely to be much *incidental emotional* learning taking place. For example, the child is likely to learn, by association, a joyful response or an indifferent one or one of dread and resentment at the appearance of his father. He may learn to react to his parents generally with positive, approaching affection, or he may learn to associate them with frustration, anger, or fear.

The sort of emotional learning that does take place, in any case, depends upon the quality of the emotional interaction that prevails between the child and his parents. And the quality of that prevailing interaction is dependent upon two sets of factors: (1) the particular personal make-up of each parent (predominant traits, attitudes, expectations, frustrations); and (2) the child's unique pattern of temperamental tendencies such as those discussed in Chapter 7 (another example of organism-environment interaction).

Imprinting versus Healthy Learning

There is another line of evidence from recent research, mainly animal research, however, which suggests a somewhat different interpretation of the relationship between learned emotional patterns and environmental stimulation (Scott, 1962). The suggested coming out of these studies is that perhaps it is not so much the pleasant quality of the emotional interaction between parent and young child as it is that there be *strong* emotional content of *some sort* in the interaction during the early critical period. In Scott's words:

> It should not be surprising that *many kinds* of emotional reactions contribute to a social relationship. The surprising thing is that emotions which we normally consider aversive should produce the *same* effect as those which appear to be rewarding. . . . [This fact] provides an explanation for certain well-known clinical observations such as the development by neglected children of strong affection for cruel and abusive parents. (p. 954)

In view of apparent conflict in the evidence cited by such investigators as Scott (1962), I. D. Harris (1959), and Diamond (1957), it is clear that a distinction must be drawn between an early emotional bond due to the imprinting process and healthy emotional adjustment and development in children. E. H. Hess's (1960) ducklings did become the more strongly imprinted to follow the mechanical model duck, the greater the effort and the *pain* they encountered in following it. Harlow's (1958) infant monkeys did crawl desperately toward their rejecting, punishing mothers, who, in their own infancy, had been reared on terrycloth dummy "mothers" instead of interactive monkey mothers. Children have been known to become emotionally attached to cruel, unloving parents. But Harlow's dummy-reared monkey mothers had not developed the normal monkey *interactive* behavior patterns in their association with and close attachment to their dummy mothers. Furthermore, in the vast majority of instances, human individuals who have been reared by neglecting and cruel parents must overcome great handicaps in acquiring the capacity to interact warmly and affectionately with others. Scott (1962) summarized the evidence as follows:

> There are demonstrable *positive mechanisms,* varying from species to species, *which bring young animals close to other members of their kind:* the clinging response of young rhesus monkeys; the following response of chicks, ducklings, and lambs, and other herd animals; social investigation, tail wagging, and playful fighting of puppies; and the visual investigation and smiling of the human infant. These are, of course, accompanied by *interacting responses* from adults and immature members of the species: holding and clasping by primate mothers, brooding of mother hens and other birds, calling by mother sheep, investigation and play on the part of other young puppies, and the various supporting and nurturing activities of human mothers. (p. 951, italics added)

These interacting responses, on the part of others, normally involve pleasurable and satisfying emotional content and make the difference between simple imprinting of an emotional bond and the establishment of the foundation for healthy interpersonal relationships and emotional adjustment. The capacity to interact warmly and creatively with other human beings is generally the product of early emotional learning in interaction with a warmly dependable and understandingly nurturant "mothering one." This kind of emotional learning is qualitatively different from, and more than, the simple imprinting of an emotional bond.

Love: A Process of Interaction

Throughout our discussion of emotionality, the active aspect of emotion (that is, the idea that an emotion is a function of the organism and that when one is emotional, a complex *process* is underway) has repeatedly come to the fore. We were also reminded of the two-directional nature of emotionality. There are emotions in which the direction of activity is away from or in opposition to the object of the emotion. These are the negative emotions. The action is individualistic, separating, alienating. One becomes angry at, fearful of, and withdraws from another.

Approach behavior characterizes the positive type of emotion. One draws near to and acts in relationship with another. Love is the prototype of positive emotion. Love is uniting, integrating, need satisfying. The action is *inter*action. Each of the two persons involved is both actor and object of the action, giver and receiver. The relationship is reciprocal. The mother, for example, holds her baby close, thus gratifying their mutual need for closeness. Her acts of love stimulate in her child reciprocal love responses. The interaction is uniting and mutually gratifying. It tends to be what Erich Fromm (1956) called "interpersonal fusion."

Emotional Deprivation

The term emotional deprivation refers to a lack, in the child's experience, of a positive reciprocal relationship with another person. It refers either to the rather precipitous loss of an accustomed relationship with a nurturing person in which his need for warm loving care has been regularly gratified or to the absence, from the beginning, of conditions that permit the formation of such a relationship. Available evidence suggests that both of these types of deprivation can have profound effects upon the development of the capacity to function in the reciprocal love relationship.

We have already noted the importance of adequate and appropriate stimulation for optimal development during infancy. Stimulus deprivation is perhaps the more appropriate term to apply to the situation of an infant lying by itself in an "institution" crib during the first few months of its life. At first, other persons, as persons, are of no significance to a baby regardless of where he may be. He spends much of his time sleeping. But when he is awake he is very responsive to stimuli both external and internal. He cries immediately at any bodily discomfort and is just as immediately comforted by being cuddled in warm and close contact with another person. He may respond with excitement to the sights and sounds of persons moving about him and particularly to being "talked to" and to the other noises people make to babies.

In the usual family situation, the baby does not want for stimulation. The baby is likely to get much patting, stroking, and fondling, particularly if there are other children in the home, and this attention along with the frequent feeding and bodily care he receives often leaves little waking time for him to be "bored." This kind of stimulation, of course, is what was lacking in the traditional "institution" as described by Goldfarb (1945), Spitz (1945, 1946), and others. Furthermore, the indications are that it is the lack of general stimulation, rather than the lack of a specific "mothering one" per se, that are responsible for the retarding effects of institution care during the early months of the baby's life. It is likely also that this retarding effect is the result of the lack of opportunity to learn, rather than an actual maturational retardation (Dennis and Najarian, 1957). In this connection, Yarrow (1964), after a careful survey of the relevant literature, summarized the situation as follows:

> . . . The institution is not simply an environment lacking in a mother-figure with whom the child has developed an attachment; institutional environments tend to be deviant in many other respects, such as in the amount, the quality, and the variety of sensory and social stimulation, and in the kinds of learning conditions provided (Goldfarb, 1955; Rheingold, 1960, 1961; Provence and Lipton, 1962; David and Appell, 1962). The low caretaker-infant ratio is associated with significant deprivation in the sheer amount of maternal care. This quantitative deprivation in maternal care, in turn is associated with inadequate kinesthetic, tactile, social and affective stimulation. (p. 99)

Although studies from a variety of sources indicate that environmental deprivation may have serious effects even on very young infants, there are very few data on the important question of how early in infancy *separation* from a mother figure begins to have an impact. Schaffer's (1958) research is one of the few studies with data directly relevant to this issue. On the basis of findings that overt protest reactions to maternal separation (such as excessive crying, fear of strangers, clinging to the mother) are not evident before 7 months of age, Schaffer concluded that separation reactions appear "relatively suddenly and at full force around 7 months of age" (p. 98). By definition, true separation reactions cannot appear until after a focused relationship with the mother has developed.

The baby soon begins to show signs of an emerging ability to perceive—to react differentially to objects as objects and to people as people. He begins to respond differently to different people. His affiliative interest increases, and he begins to relate to persons as individuals and to interact emotionally with them. The pleasures of gratification and of relief from pain and discomfort soon become associated in his experience with a particular person, usually his mother. A strong affectional bond thus becomes established between mother and baby. Thereafter, no amount of casual or impersonal stimulation can take the place of that person-to-person emotional relationship. From that point on, to have that relationship disrupted, and for the child to be denied dependable, intimate contact with the "mothering one," would be more than stimulus deprivation. The term emotional deprivation would, under those circumstances, more accurately describe the child's situation.

RESEARCH CONCERNING EMOTIONAL DEPRIVATION   Most of the early studies of maternal deprivation in institutions involved children who were separated from their mothers and placed in the institutions at ages over 1 year (Robertson and Bowlby, 1952; Roudinesco, David, and Nicolas, 1952; Spitz and Wolf, 1946). The reports of these investigations were practically unanimous in regard to the emotional damage these children suffered. The general pattern of immediate reactions to separation were crying and strong protest, followed by progressive withdrawal from relationships with people. After the immediate protest and crying came signs of despair and resignation and apathetic behavior. As a rule, these children formed no emotional attachments to any of the institution personnel and even showed very little feeling toward the parents when they visited them later on. They acted as if "neither mothering nor any contact with humans has much significance for them" (Robertson and Bowlby, 1952, p. 133).

However, there is relatively little direct research evidence regarding the long-term effects of maternal separation. Certain follow-up studies have produced suggestive evidence. Bowlby (1944), for example, in a clinical study of a group of young thieves, characterized certain of them as "affectionless characters." An analysis of the backgrounds of these individuals indicated that they had been separated from their mothers in infancy. In general, however, results of these follow-up studies have been quite varied. Different children have different experiences in relation to separation, and, due to the diversity of temperamental nature among the children, these experiences have different meanings for different children. In a summary statement, Yarrow wrote:

> The research data can be integrated with regard to their implications in terms of the following major variables: the developmental stage of the child at the time of separation; the character of the relationship with the mother prior to separation; the character of maternal care during a temporary separation or

following permanent separation; subsequent experiences, that is, experiences which are reinforcing or ameliorating of separation trauma; and individual differences in vulnerability to separation. (1964, p. 121)

The mere fact of being reared by the biological mother in the family home, of course, does not preclude the possibility of emotional deprivation. The quantity as well as the quality of mothering that babies actually experience from their mothers obviously varies through a wide range.

Emotional Problems of Childhood

Individual Differences

In Chapter 7, certain ways in which infants vary one from another by congenital temperamental nature was discussed. One of these variables is the ease of emotional arousal and upset. Some infants, it was pointed out, are generally highly reactive to intense stimulation. These infants startle easily and rather violently and are likely, therefore, to be more inclined toward the fear-withdrawal pattern than babies who are less strongly reactive to noise and other intense stimuli.

Some babies also seem, by congenital nature, to react with a sort of characteristic displeasure. They seem to be expressing a perpetual dissatisfaction and irritation with extrauterine life. At the other extreme are babies who, from the beginning, seem generally to be pleased with and contented in the world in which they find themselves. Some children also can withstand frustrating and anger-provoking situations with much greater equanimity than others. In other words, aside from the characteristic reaction of pleasure or displeasure with life in general, babies, as well as older people, differ in frustration tolerance.

Such observations indicate that an individual's characteristic moods have some basis in the sort of temperamental balance with which he is born. But these congenital emotional predispositions are only predispositions. The pattern of moods and emotional dispositions that soon come to characterize a person are largely a matter of learning, and *what* is learned depends very largely upon the nature of environment and particularly upon the interpersonal atmosphere that predominates in one's daily life.

Thus, growing out of organism-environment interaction is a wide variety of emotional problems that beset children and often continue to plague them throughout life.

Anxiety

Anxiety may develop very early in infancy in relation to the nursing situation. The tenseness and anxiety of the young mother is transmitted to her infant. "Thus anxiety is called out by emotional disturbances of certain types in the significant person—that is, the person with whom the infant is doing something" (Sullivan, 1953, p. 9). Anxiety, of course is one of the common immediate effects of separation from mother during infancy. The theory is that from these early anxiety experiences "grows the whole exceedingly important structure of anxiety, and performances that can be understood only by reference to the conception of anxiety" (p. 9).

Later in childhood the attitudes and the behavior of parents continue to be the prime causes of anxiety. Regarding parental punishment and its effects, Sullivan wrote:

> The punishments are commonly the inflicting of pain, the refusal of contact or of attention, and of course, the inducing of anxiety—a very special punishment. I know of no reason why punishment should be undesirable as an educative influence excepting it be anxiety-ladened. (p. 155, by permission)

Sullivan suggests further that anxiety at any age is an important complicating factor in learning as well as in coping effectively with the environment. "The effect of severe anxiety reminds one in some ways of a blow on the head in that it simply wipes out what is immediately proximal to its occurrence" (p. 152). It produces useless confusion and loss of effectiveness in performance. As Sigel (1964) pointed out, anxiety is an inhibiting factor in children's conceptual learning: "Children who are highly anxious tend to employ concepts dealing with the emotional aspects of the situation more than do those who are not" (p. 239).

Less severe anxiety, on the other hand, may facilitate learning. In the process of becoming "socialized," certain degrees of anxiety may help the child to distinguish anxiety-provoked situations and actions and thus to alter his activities accordingly.

Anxiety, like other human attributes and functions, is universal. Everyone experiences anxiety, but there are, of course, wide individual differences in vulnerability. It is also clear that parental care and the relationships thus established between parents and children are vital factors in the development of anxieties in children. Kagan noted that the lack of a masculine father figure with which to identify was found to interfere with sex-role identity and thus to be a cause of anxiety (Hoffman and Hoffman, 1964, p. 148).

Childhood Fears

A useful distinction between fear and anxiety is in terms of the emotion-provoking situation. The term anxiety is usually applied to a fearlike state induced by anticipated or imagined threats to one's physical or psychological well-being. The danger or threat is not immediately and objectively present to sense. Fear, on the other hand, is the emotional reaction to an objectively present situation which is perceived as threatening to one's well-being.

In our discussion of the developmental sequences in emotionality, the concept of an undifferentiated beginning stage was presented. Emotionality in the neonate, accordingly, consists of undifferentiated excitement without distinction between even the pleasant and the unpleasant. Only after some 6 months of age, according to Bridges (1932), is it possible to identify the emotion of fear as distinct from other forms of distress. At that level, of course, there are only a very few originally adequate (unconditioned) stimuli to fear. The presence or the approach of a stranger, for example, may call forth the frightened distress pattern. Loud noise and sudden lowering of his body also appear to be among the relatively few originally adequate fear stimuli. The baby is thus protected during his early months of life from a great deal of distressing fear.

The baby's cognitive abilities, however, are rapidly developing, which means that he is gaining in his ability to recognize danger and to perceive more objects and situations as threatening. Through the process of conditioning, stimuli not inherently frightening become, for the particular child, fear-provoking.

Thus, developmental changes take place in relation to children's fears. Up to the age of 23 months, according to the findings of Jersild and Holmes (1935), noise, objects that make noise, and strange objects, persons, and situations, most frequently are the causes accounting for about one-fourth of all fear experiences. During the next 2 years, these two classes of stimuli account for a smaller and smaller percentage of fear episodes (10 percent at age 4 years). By contrast, imaginary creatures, darkness, being alone, dreams, and the like, increase dramatically in frequency as fear stimuli during the same two-year period, from only about 5 percent to nearly 30 percent. Our subject Paul at age 4½ years over a period of some months had considerable trouble going to sleep at night and asked for his door to be left open. He apparently was resisting sleep because of "those animals" that came into his room. These findings of Jersild and Holmes are presented in Figure 11.2.

Changes continue to take place in the character of the threatening

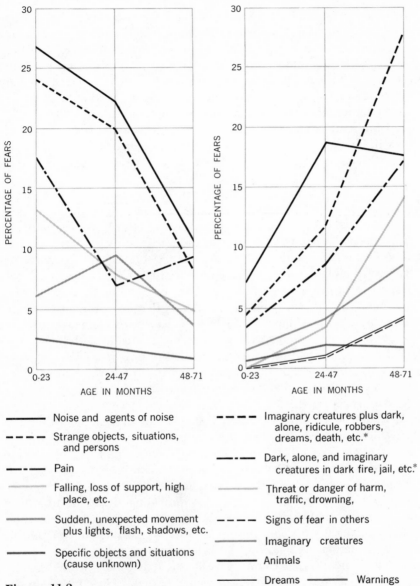

Figure 11.2

Relative frequency of fears in response to various situations reported by children or observed in children by parents or teachers. The data include 146 records of observation of children for periods of 21 days (31, 91, and 24 at the respective biyearly levels), combined with occasional records of 117 additional children (26, 27, and 23 at the respective levels). Starred items represent the cumulative tally of two or more categories that also are depicted separately. Adapted from Jersild (1960), p. 261, by permission.

situations as the child gets older. During the elementary school period imaginary, fanciful, supernatural, and remote dangers are relatively frequent fear-evokers. Children are also inclined to fear the elements, such as lightning and storms. They worry about such matters as death or injury and the recall of "scary" stories, movies, and television dramas. Some of the fears from these latter classes of stimuli, are more of the nature of anxieties (Angelino, Dollins, and Mech, 1956).

Children at these ages also worry frequently about matters related to self, for example, their own adequacy and status. They worry about possible failure about being different or being ridiculed.

COPING WITH CHILDREN'S FEARS   The problem of dealing with excessive fears in children is a difficult and sometimes distressful one for parents. Fear of the dark and fear of harmless objects and animals are among the irrational fears that most frequently concern parents. The immediate reaction of the adult to a childish fear is to try to explain it away or, as in the case of fear of the dark bedroom, simply not to "give in" to the child (turn off the light or close the door), on the theory that the child will "find out" that there is really nothing to be afraid of and thereby overcome his fear. Such methods generally are of no avail. Rational explanations to young children have no real effect upon the emotion of fear, regardless of how irrational the basis of the fear may be. Forcing a child to remain in a dark room with his fear is more likely to reinforce the fear reaction itself than to help him to overcome it.

Studies of children's fears and of methods of dealing with them have demonstrated a number of procedures that are in varying degrees effective (Jersild and Holmes, 1935; M. C. Jones, 1924a, 1924b). Among the methods tested: (1) setting up counterresources and skills that are helpful in meeting the fearful situation when it occurs; (2) promoting familiarity with the feared object by providing situations in which there is opportunity, but not coercion, to become acquainted with it; (3) arranging for the child to observe others who show no fear in the feared situation; and (4) direct reconditioning.

These methods, of course, vary in their usefulness with different types of fear situations. The acquiring of new skills, for example, might be quite a helpful approach to overcoming the fear of deep water. For the child to acquire competence as a swimmer in the relative safety of shallow water might release him from his fear of deeper water. When one knows what to do in a feared situation and how to do it, to the point of having confidence in one's ability to do it, one is not likely to continue to be terrified by it.

When a child is given the opportunity, without any pressure or coercion, to become better acquainted with a feared object or situation, his fear often subsides. In one of M. C. Jones' (1924b) experiments, a child who was afraid of rabbits lost his fear after a rabbit had been in his vicinity where he could observe it for some time. He simply became better acquainted with the rabbit, its appearance, and its activities.

The method of social imitation is in certain respects similar to the method of acquaintance. Here the child observes the behavior of his friends as they react fearlessly to the object he fears:

> Bobby was playing in the pen with Mary and Laurel. The rabbit was introduced in a basket. Bobby cried, "no, no," and motioned for the experimenter to remove it. The two girls, however, ran up readily enough, looked in at the rabbit, and talked excitedly. Bobby became promptly interested, said "What? Me see," and ran forward, his curiosity and assertiveness in the situation overmastering other impulses. (M. C. Jones, 1924b, p. 387)

Perhaps the most generally effective method of helping children overcome their fears is the method of reconditioning. In another case reported by M. C. Jones (1924a), the child had acquired an extreme fear of furry animals. The method of social imitation had been tried with him, but it had relatively little success. The procedure of reconditioning, as used with him, was described as follows:

> At lunch time the child was seated at a low table in a room about forty feet long. Just as he began to eat his lunch, the rabbit was displayed in a wire cage at a distance just far enough away not to disturb his eating. This was a very important point, for were the strong conditioned stimulus allowed to work too actively, it is quite to be expected that the positive reactions to the food would change. That is, the food might in turn become a conditioned stimulus for the fear response. To prevent accidents in this admittedly ticklish matter, the rabbit was kept in his cage during the early phases of the work. Each day the position of the cage was marked. The next day the cage and rabbit were brought somewhat closer. Eventually the rabbit could be placed on the table and even in Peter's lap. In the final stage of the experiment he ate with one hand as he stroked the rabbit with the other. We may assume from this that Peter's inner emotional response had been re-conditioned even as his outward behavior toward the rabbit had been re-directed. (M. C. Jones, 1924a, pp. 308–316)

It is clear in this account that reconditioning can be quite effective. It is also clear that it must be used with caution and by one who understands well the principles of learning involved.

In a great many instances, children, as they grow older and gain better understanding, "naturally" outgrow many of their burdensome fears.

Anger

Anger and fear, in certain respects, are rather closely related. In the first place, they are both "emergency" responses of the unpleasant variety, and consequently involve very similar patterns of change in physiological processes, changes designed to prepare the organism for immediate, strenuous, overt activity. In part, at least, because of this close correspondence in the physiological component, the two emotions are sometimes aroused simultaneously and by the same stimulus. Sometimes, also, the child vacillates between the two affective experiences. However, because ordinarily there are more anger-provoking than fear-arousing occasions in the protected life of the child in our culture, anger is a more frequent response than fear in children.

It will be recalled, however, that Bridges observed that anger, as a differentiated emotional pattern of behavior and experience, does not exist at birth. Furthermore, as the specific anger pattern emerges, there are relatively few originally adequate stimuli for its arousal. In general, the situations that do give rise to anger in early infancy are those involving pain or discomfort or bodily restraint.

The number and variety of restraining factors and situations rapidly grow. Very soon there are a great many ways in which others, even as they care for the child, interfere with his free bodily movements. His own inabilities quickly become sources of frustration. His activities are frequently interfered with or blocked. Thus the over-all situation with respect to anger rapidly changes. As Jersild (1954) put it, "The occasions that elicit anger parallel the course of development. A child's susceptibility to anger at any given maturity level is influenced by the limitations and by the urges, strivings, and activity tendencies that are characteristic of that level" (p. 883).

OVERT ASPECTS OF THE ANGER RESPONSE   The character of the overt expression of anger also changes with the age and experience of the child. Infant anger can be described generally in terms of four characteristics (Morgan, 1934). (1) The young infant may be said to be completely egocentric. As was mentioned in connection with the Freudian stages of emotional development, he becomes concerned only when conditions within and outside his own body cause him pain, discomfort, or frustration. He is completely self-centered in that sense. (2) Along with his egocentricity is his complete intolerance of bodily discomfort or restraint. When he is hungry or wet or otherwise in pain or discomfort, for example, he makes the fact known in no uncertain terms. He cries, kicks with abandon, he arches his back, struggles, and twists. (3) The young infant is exceedingly demanding. In his intolerance of discomfort, he demands *immediate relief*. He cannot defer satisfaction of his needs. (4) Finally, the baby is very explosive and violent in his anger expression.

These attributes of infant expressions of anger are not limited to early infancy. As Morgan pointed out, when such attributes are observed in the older child or the adult they are signs of so-called emotional immaturity. Violent outbursts of rage are common in young children. The preschool child is likely to express anger in much the same manner as the infant.

In the expression of anger, as in other kinds of behavior, however, there is much diversity among children. We have already mentioned the wide variation in frustration tolerance; some children can withstand anger-provoking situations with much greater equanimity than can others. The variation is undoubtedly related to original temperamental nature as well as to factors in the child's environment and the experiences he has undergone.

The family environment and the kind of training the child has had are important factors in determining the frequency as well as the explosiveness of anger expression. Socialization of the child means, among other things, bringing his aggressions under control. But the very nature of the training creates frustrations that are likely to result in angry aggressive behavior on the part of the child. "The socializer thereby becomes an instigator to the very action she is trying to change" (Levin and Turgeon, 1957, p. 304). In spite of this situation, however, mothers generally do succeed in this aspect of socialization.

The more authoritarian the parents' attitudes and approaches to discipline in their efforts to make the child's behavior conform to their conceptions of what is socially desirable, the more frequent are likely to be angry outbursts of the child (Levin and Sears, 1956). Since authoritarian procedures are more prevalent in homes of the lower socioeconomic class, children from these homes experience more thwarting and consequently display more intense and more frequent anger than do children from homes of higher socioeconomic levels.

Jealousy

As Jersild (1954) pointed out, rivalry between siblings can be a source of much thwarting, hostility, anxiety, and grief. Jealousy appears to be a combination of emotions, rather than a single, primary one. Descartes' definition of jealousy was "a kind of fear related to the desire we have for keeping some possession."

> Components of jealousy, as described by Ribot, include a pleasurable element related to something desired or possessed, an element of depressing vexation arising through the idea of dispossession or privation and destructive tendencies such as hatred and anger directed toward the real or imagined cause of this dispossession or privation. (Jersild, 1954, p. 899)

Jealousy in children usually arises from a competitive situation between siblings. Children often compete for the attention and the demonstrations of affection of parents or other significant adults in their lives. Jealousy often originates with the birth of a sibling when the child is from 2 to 5 years old, and particularly when he is the first born. He is disturbed by being displaced as the center of attention in the family. He resents the time and attention now given to the new baby, and, not receiving the amount of attention he is accustomed to, he feels neglected. He may experience anger, self-pity, grief, dejection, fear, and anxiety.

The jealous child may express his feelings in overt hostile behavior, such as a sly pinch or shove or some substitute form of attack. This anger and hostility may also be directed against the person whose affection or attention is desired. The latter may also be the recipient or reproachful remarks or appeals for sympathy.

Because of the differences in temperament, appearance, age, and other personal attributes in their chlidren, parents may actually show a disproportionate share of interest in, and give more attention to, one child than to another, without realizing that they are showing favoritism. Fathers often are more lenient and affectionate with their daughters than with their sons, whereas mothers appear to favor their sons.

Children are usually quite sensitive to these forms of differential treatment, and jealously and resentment sometimes develop, even among older children. At these older ages, jealous responses are more varied and more indirect, often taking the form of teasing or bullying. The older child may resort to "babyish" behavior or become clinging and overdemanding of the parent. He may become sulky, surly, and disagreeable or even destructive. Many instances of undesirable behavior in children, not easily understood as to origin, actually have arisen as expressions of jealousy.

Emotional Development in the Twin Subjects

As was mentioned earlier, our twins differed in temperamental nature from the beginning. Their mother quite naturally was very aware of these differences. In a questionnaire only a few months after the babies' birth she stated that Paul resembled his father in "his quiet thoughtfulness and sense of humor and that Sally was much more like her mother in her unevenness of disposition and a tendency to tears."

At age 5 months both babies gave clear evidence of their ability to differentiate between people. It will be recalled that Bridges observed fear in her infants, on the average, at about age 7 months. Paul and Sally gave clear evidence of fear when, at 5 months of age they were undressed, weighed, and measured by an examiner strange to them.

At age 7 months, the twins were subjected to their first "developmental" examination. Even though Paul was awakened for the test he accepted the strange examiner without concern and showed marked interest in the test materials. Sally "in contrast to her brother showed a very keen interest in people, paying somewhat less attention to things." There was also evidence that she was a little fearful of the strange examiner.

Throughout their development, however, Paul was more inclined to be reserved in his reactions to people. Sally was more outgoing and spontaneous in her relationships. For example, on their visit to the infant laboratory for their tests and measurements at age 13 months, it was observed that "while Sally made immediate overtures toward the examiner who came to greet them in the waiting room, Paul hung back and clung close to his mother." Paul at this visit was quite resistant to the whole procedure. Only after a period of time did he accept the tester.

Perhaps the most significant indicator of emotional difficulty in Paul was his tendency to wakefulness and some sleep disturbance which began at about 8 months of age and continued with considerable variation for some three additional years. Since the children were together much of the time, this erratic sleep pattern, to a lesser degree, was also followed by Sally. In Paul, particularly, this difficulty was accompanied by thumb sucking and bed wetting. When he was about 2½, his mother stated that his uneasiness about going to sleep seemed to be related to a fear that she might leave him. About this time he complained about his mother's frequent absence from the home. He also began to have "night fears."

There were, however, indications that he was working through his difficulties. For example, on one occasion while he was being undressed for bed, he went to the window and raised the shade, saying that he wanted to see things that he wasn't afraid anymore. His need for his blanket, which he held to his lips while he sucked his thumb, was also lessening.

Throughout the preschool period Sally was becoming increasingly outgoing. She frequently brought her girlfriends home to play with her. On these occasions, and also at nursery school, the girls began to ostracize Paul from their play. This proved to be a bit difficult for him to "take." He began objecting mildly to going to nursery school. This was of relatively short duration.

Clearly, Paul, like most children, had his adjustment diffiulties, but when an over-all view is taken of his emotional development, it becomes apparent that he "jumped his hurdles as he came to them," and made healthy progress in his affective development. Sally developed into a charming vivacious and outgoing young lady.

It will be noted in the foregoing account of affective behavior in our twins that most of the items had perhaps more to do with social behavior than with emotionality per se. The items of information in the developmental file made very little reference to the items in Bridges' developmental sequence. Consequently only two points are plotted in Figure 11.1. With adequate observational records of a child's early emotional development, Figure 11.1 would be useful as a graphic record.

Summary

This chapter has looked particularly at the "activity" aspect of emotionality. From this point of view, emotion involves certain physiological changes, but, in a more general way, it involves the total person. At the same time, the experiential aspect of emotional functioning is of vital importance in human living and interpersonal relationships. The negative and the positive behaviors give meaning to human existence.

Emotion, since it is a kind of total functioning, involves bodily structures, and these structures obviously are the result of biological growth and maturation. The structures involved in emotionality, however, are already well advanced in their development, and are, for the most part, ready for functioning at the time of birth. Postnatal

emotional development, therefore, with certain conspicuous exceptions, is very largely the product of learning from environmental
influences.

Individual developmental progress can best be traced in terms of an
established developmental sequence of stages. However, relatively
little success, thus far, has been achieved in the identification of
universal and invariable developmental stages which are adequate
to the task of tracing emotional development. The Freudian stages
of psychosexual development and Bridges' infant stages of affectivity
are perhaps the nearest approaches to such sequences.

Since environmental influences are so important as determiners of
the extent, direction, and quality of developmental change in emotionality, adequate and appropriate stimulation, particularly during
infancy and early childhood, is essential. We suggest that the kind of
stimulation a baby normally and naturally receives from the constant
care and handling by his mother is perhaps the most adequate and
appropriate stimulation for normal emotional development. Development resulting from this kind of care and stimulation is of quite a
different order than what has been referred to as "imprinting" in
animal experimentation.

Emotional "problems" in children also arise most often from environmental influences, and they can be controlled or alleviated only
by the wise manipulation of the environment or by protecting the
child from being subjected to undesirable environmental influences.

SELECTED READING SUGGESTIONS

Baller, W. R. *Readings in the psychology of human growth and development.*
New York: Holt, Rinehart and Winston, Inc., 1962. (Read Bridges,
Emotional development in early infancy; Redl and Jacobson, Help-
ing the emotionally disturbed child.)

Dennis, W. *Readings in child psychology.* Second ed.; Englewood Cliffs, N.J.:
Prentice-Hall, 1963. (Read M. Sherman, The interpretation of emotional response; Watson and Watson, Conditioned emotional reactions; Jones and Jones, Fear of snakes; and Dennis, Infant reactions
to restraint.)

Fraiberg, Selma H. *The magic years.* New York: Scribner, 1959. (Read Chapter
5, Helping the child overcome his fears; and Chapter 8, The right
to feel.)

CHAPTER 12

Personality Development

The Concept of Personality

In common usage, the term personality refers to a vaguely conceived human quality which everyone recognizes as of special importance in interpersonal relationships. It is a term frequently used in conversation, particularly when the topic involves social interaction. Individuals are spoken of as having "difficult" personalities, "charming" personalities, "pleasing" personalities, "ugly" personalities. People are also charged with having "no personality," or are said to be "full of" or "radiating" personality. We all know, in a general way, what is meant by such expressions. They convey a common meaning that is readily understood.

The Problem of Definition

Even though we do "know" in a general way what is meant by the term personality when we use it ourselves or hear it used in conversation, yet if we were asked to explain just what it means or to define it we probably would find ourselves in difficulty. Authoritative writers in the social and behavioral sciences apparently experience some of the same difficulty. There is much diversity to be found among textbook definitions of personality. It is difficult to give precise technical meaning to such a commonly used word. Usually each writer or investigator formulates his own definition, emphasizing the particular facet of the concept that suits his own disciplinary bias or that is consistent with the material he has to present.

Theories of Personality

Various theories of personality have been developed. People trained in a particular scientific discipline or in a particular professional field tend to have similar disciplinary biases and thus tend to make the same, or similar, assumptions and to formulate similar theoretical frames of reference in terms of which to interpret their observations of human behavior. For example, the sociologist or the cultural anthropologist "sees" human behavior with his particular bias and from his particular level of observation. He is likely, therefore, to observe first the behavior patterns and traits that are common to a particular cultural or ethnic group and thus to regard individual personality as largely a product or a mere "reflection" of the culture.

Most sociological definitions, however, merely put special emphasis upon the cultural factor in the development of personality. Although some of these writers go so far as to contend that personality is nothing more than the individual counterpart or expression of the culture, a fairly common contemporary point of view among students of society is expressed in the following statement by Parsons (1963):

> My view will be that, while the main content of the structure of the personality is derived from social systems and culture through socialization, the personality becomes an independent system through its relations to its own organism and through the uniqueness of its own life experiences; it is not a mere epiphenomenon of the structure of the society. There is, however,

not merely interdependence between the two, but what I call interpenetration. (p. 35)

Biologically trained observers, on the other hand, with quite different frames of reference, find the explanations of behavior and of the characteristic traits of individuals in their physiology and constitutional make-up. Thus, the biological emphasis in personality theory has developed. One outstanding proponent of this emphasis is W. H. Sheldon (1940, 1942, 1949; Sheldon, Dupertuis, and McDermott, 1954). We have reviewed certain aspects of his work in earlier discussions. He has stated his theoretical position as follows:

> It has been growing increasingly plain that the situation calls for a biologically oriented psychology, or one taking for its operational frame of reference a scientifically defensible description of the *structure* (together with the behavior) of the human organism itself. This is perhaps tantamount to saying that psychology requires a physical anthropology for its immediate foundation support. More than that, it requires a physical anthropology couched in terms of components, or variables, which can be measured and quantified at both the structural and behavioral ends—the anthropological and psychological ends—of the structure-behavior continuum which is human personality. (1949, p. xv)

Longitudinal studies of child development generally have stressed the biological factor in the personal adjustments and development of children (M. C. Jones and Bayley, 1950; M. C. Jones and Mussen, 1958; Mussen and Jones, 1957; Sontag, Baker, and Nelson, 1958).

Within the limits of a particular scientific discipline or professional group there are also differing points of view. Thus, from the general field of psychology have come many contrasting theories as to the structure and the origin and development of personality. Books have been written from these various points of view. Comparative explications of the major theories, and groupings of theories also have been published and are available to the student (G. W. Allport, 1960; Hall and Lindzey, 1957; Hunt, 1944). It is not our present purpose, therefore, to attempt a comparative discussion of these theoretical positions. Even to attempt to classify them and then adequately characterize the major groupings is not feasible here. We shall, therefore, only point briefly to certain major issues raised in the theoretical writings of students of the psychology of personality and to some of the contrasting positions held regarding those issues.

The Problem of Motivation

One of the major issues about which theories of personality differ is the nature and the sources of motivation. Obviously the motives, drives, wishes, needs, and purposes that activate people are of central importance to the understanding of how personalities develop. As to the importance of this problem, there is no disagreement among theorists. As to the source, the locus and origin of the "mainspring" of human conduct, there is currently rather basic disagreement. In order that we may see clearly the setting and the development of this issue we shall first turn briefly once more to some of the thinking of Sigmund Freud.

PSYCHOANALYTIC THEORY   Freud the famous Viennese physician is given credit for formulating the first comprehensive theory of personality. This complex theoretical framework, as it evolved in Freud's thinking, was many years in the making, undergoing changes, additions, and deletions up to the time of his death in 1939. His discoveries and his thinking have wielded a tremendous influence upon the fields of psychology and psychotherapy. His many followers are still busy expanding and, in varying degrees, modifying his formulations.

Freud's concept of the *unconscious* is basic to his theory of motivation. He conceptualized the mental activity of an individual as being very much more elaborate and complicated than that of which the individual is consciously aware. The analogy which Freud used to point up this comparison was that of the iceberg. The great mass of the floating iceberg is under the surface of the water with a relatively small proportion of it in view above the water. The visible and the submerged portions of the iceberg were analogous, in Freud's thinking, to the conscious and the unconscious portions, respectively, of human mental activity. He pictured the content of the unconscious as a great accumulation of unseen but vital forces (urges, feelings, passions, and so on), which exercise control over much of the conscious life of man. In other words, motivation, from the Freudian point of view, is very largely *unconscious*.

Not only are these mainsprings of our conduct hidden from consciousness but they continue as mainsprings throughout life. We are either born with them as "instincts" or they originate from the experiences of infancy and early childhood. Hence, Freud's *structural* and *genetic* approaches to the problem of motivation were developed.

Structurally, Freud saw the mind as consisting of three main functions, the *id*, the *ego*, and the *superego*. The id we are born with. It consists of biologically determined impulses largely sexual in nature. It is the source of drive energy which is somatic in origin. This energy arises from internal or external stimulation that upsets the homeostatic balance in the organism and thus creates tension. The id cannot tolerate tension. It counteracts increases in tension by invoking processes (primary process) to relieve the tension thus restoring equilibrium. This relief from tension is pleasurable. All of this id activity is completely unconscious. It is the original (genetic) source of a drive, which, as such, continues throughout life.

As the infant develops, out of its experience a differentiation, a change, takes place in the original (id) situation. Experience teaches that the processes of the id (reflexes and images, the primary process) are not adequate to meet the needs of the organism for relief from tension (hunger, erogenus-zone tension, and so on). To meet these needs in a real sense, transactions with the outside world are necessary. This function of relating to reality is the province of the ego, which is a differentiated portion of the id. The ego, according to Freud, has no motivating drive as such. It is only the mediator of drive gratification from the outside world.

With further experience in relating to reality, the child learns what is permitted in terms of gratification and what is prohibited. The prohibitions and the exhortations of the culture (the parents) become internalized. This is seen as a further differentiation from the original, unconscious id. This function is called the superego. The superego is sometimes portrayed as consisting of two divisions: the *conscience*, the internalized prohibitions; and the *ego ideal*, which represents the strivings toward what the parents praise (toward perfection). Freud became struck with the fact that the conscience can be as compelling and irrational in its demands as the id itself.

This structural conception of the operation of the mind, then, is the motivational system of psychoanalytic theory. Freud's conceptualization of the development of these three functions of the mind also constitute his genetic approach to the understanding of mental life. Motivation thus is infantile in origin. According to Freudian theory, then, the id, the primitive reservoir of instinctual energy, is the original and lifelong source of motivation. It remains the mainspring of conduct, and the aim of that conduct continues to be the reduction of tension and restoration of homeostatic balance.

There are, then, three aspects to this motivational issue posed by Freudian theory that have developmental implications in relation to personality. These are (1) unconscious versus conscious motivation, (2) primitive instinctual versus contemporary ego-mediated motives, and (3) the question of tension reduction as the sole aim of motivated activity. The first and second of these are so closely related that they will be considered together.

It is undoubtedly true that the neonate is activated entirely by tensions set up by internal organic conditions and by external stimuli impinging directly upon him and entirely without his conscious awareness of those stimulating conditions. It is also true, of course, *that* throughout life a great deal of one's motor activity is carried on without conscious direction, that one does many things "without thinking." Due very largely to Freudian influence, many psychologists have assumed that the "real" reasons why people do what they do most often are hidden reasons and that the consciously stated reasons are likely to be nothing more than rationalizations. This assumption has given rise to the development of many so-called projective devices and their wide use in psychological measurement.

THE IMPORTANCE OF CONSCIOUS, EGO-MEDIATED MOTIVES   G. W. Allport (1960) who decries the prevalence of the assumption of hidden reasons for people's actions, has described the general trend of psychological thinking since Freud:

> This prevailing atmosphere of theory has engendered a kind of contempt for the "psychic surface" of life. The individual's conscious report is rejected as untrustworthy, and the contemporary thrust of his motives is disregarded in favor of a backward tracing of his conduct to earlier formative stages. The individual loses his right to be believed. And while he is busy leading his life in the present with a forward thrust into the future, most psychologists have become busy tracing it backward into the past. (p. 96, by permission, copyright © 1960 by Gordon W. Allport)

Allport obviously believes in the efficacy of present desires and interests which are conscious and reportable for the understanding the healthy personality.

"Holistic" theorists such as Angyal (1941), Goldstein (1939), and Maslow (1954) also find relatively little use for the concept of unconscious motivation and are little concerned with other than contemporary drives. For this group of students of personality, the pervasive, all-inclusive human motive is self-actualization, and the various consciously experienced "drives," such as those toward the satisfaction of hunger, sex, and the need to achieve, are merely manifestations of the master motive of self-realization.

Work with the war neuroses since World War II has contributed to the development of the various self, or ego, psychologies reviving interest in and appreciation of contemporary and conscious, ego-mediated drives and motives. Carl Rogers' self-theory is an example of this contemporary orientation. His related client-centered therapy involves the mutual acceptance by client and therapist of the client's present drives, emotions, and attitudes, and his facing up to them realistically (Rogers, 1942, 1951). From several points of view, then, relatively little importance is assigned to the past as a determinant of present behavior. The "here-and-now" is sufficient unto itself. Motivation "may be—and in healthy people usually is—autonomous of its origins" (G. W. Allport, 1960, p. 29).

THE QUESTION OF AIM IN HUMAN FUNCTIONING   The Freudian concept of tension reduction as the prime source of gratification and pleasure and as continuing to be the *only* aim of the organism receives little support from present-day theorists. As was suggested earlier, the newborn infant is probably disturbed and activated only by tension-producing internal conditions and noxious stimuli, and there is no question that gratification and pleasure continue throughout life to result from relief from the basic "drive" conditions (hunger, pain, sex deprivation, and so on). But this is not to say that tension reduction remains the *only* motivational aim in life. It is a common observation that young children very early begin to seek *more* stimulation rather than simply to return to a tensionless state (Schachtel, 1959). Holistic theory holds strongly that the goal of normal, healthy people is not simply to discharge tension. On the contrary, the goal is to utilize energy, to bring it into balance, to mobilize it to the end of the greatest possible realization of individual potentiality (Hall and Lindzey, 1957, p. 303).

Theories also differ as to the role that learning plays in personality formation. Here again, it is largely a matter of emphasis. All theories would agree that learning is importantly involved. Some theories, however, are concerned mainly with the *development* of personality, and with this emphasis, personality theory in some instances becomes primarily learning theory. Other theories are concerned with the stable, persistent aspects of personality and with their modification or their resistance to modification with time, rather than with the processes of development.

There are, of course, many other special emphases regarding the nature and development of the complex and pervasive human quality we call personality. We have only felt it necessary here to point to this diversity and to suggest a few of the broader areas of difference in thinking among students of personality.

Research Approaches to the Study of Personality

There are two general research approaches to the understanding of personality which are of significance in relation to our present interest: the generalistic, or statistical; and the individualistic, or idiographic (G. W. Allport, 1937, 1942, 1960).

The great bulk of personality research has been concerned with the identification and description of *common* traits—the qualities, characteristics, and behavior traits that are presumed to exist to *some* degree in people in general—and with the development of techniques and devices for the assessment of those traits. Many variations of this general approach have been used. In recent years, however, the most effective means of identifying and describing common personality traits has come to be the method of factor analysis (R. B. Cattell, 1957; Eysenck, 1947). Statistically determined "factors" are interpreted as traits of personality, and tests and "inventories" are devised for the quantitative appraisal of those traits.

From certain theoretical points of view, however, the essence of individual personality is entirely missed by such generalized approaches. The "self" psychologists, such as Rogers (1951), Maslow (1954), and others, and those who are "personalistic" in their thinking, such as Murry (1938), are among those who are not satisfied with the general statistical approach. Since each person is unique, he must be regarded as qualitatively different from others, not just different in the amounts of the various common traits he possesses. G. W. Allport has long advocated a greater use of the idiographic approach.

But methods for individual personality study that are scientifically acceptable are relatively few in number and, perhaps because they are difficult to apply, they have not been widely used. One of the most promising methods of individual personality analysis is the Q-methodology of Stephenson (1953) referred to in Chapter 7. In this procedure a reliably large balanced sample of feelings, attitudes, or personal inclinations is sorted by the subject into categories, each item according to its relevance to *himself* and the degree to which it expresses his own self-evaluation. The results of the sorting are then analyzed and ordered, presenting one view, at least, of that person's unique personal organization.

Baldwin (1942, 1946) has also described two procedures for analyzing statistically the contents of personal documents and other material which relates to the adjustments and development of the single individual.

What We Shall Mean by "Personality"

As we shall use the term, personality is merely the quality or fact of being a person. A person is an individual human being, unique and different from every other individual. In the words of William Stern (1938), "The person is a living whole, individual, unique, striving toward goals, self-contained and yet open to the world around him; he is capable of having experience" (p. 70).

One's personality, then, is that total quality or that complex combination of qualities that makes one unique and gives one his individual identity. Personality is that to which we respond in our daily contacts and interactions with others.

It is true, of course, that in our immediate reactions to others we tend to categorize them by a system of classification. We "type" him in terms of some outstanding quality. We assign him to a place among the "dynamic" or the quiet or the extroverts or the pleasing, and so on. But if we know him well, we never confuse him with anyone else. When we relate to him or interact with him, we are relating to *his individuality*. In all interpersonal relationships we interact, in each case, with *a person*, not with a type, or a category of persons.

Personality study, from this point of view, is the study of personal uniqueness. It involves, in each case, an analysis of the combination (pattern) of qualities and attributes that characterize the individual person.

It is a fact that babies at birth are persons, each by virtue of his individual identity and uniqueness (see Chapter 2). The processes of biological heredity, except in the case of monozygotic twins, provide for no other alternative than individual uniqueness in hereditary pattern. It is, of course, the over-all pattern of attributes and traits that makes one baby different from every other baby. Millions of babies at birth may have exactly the same length as measured in inches. They are exactly alike in one attribute: length. Relatively few of these same babies would weigh exactly the same, and, as feature after feature is added to the pattern of attributes being considered, the number of like individuals would become smaller and smaller. Finally, no two of these millions of babies could be found to be exactly alike in every respect. They are alike only in that they all have the common quality of uniqueness.

Uniqueness in each case, then, results from an individual combination of attributes, qualities, and behavior patterns. Since one's personality *is* his uniqueness, in order to understand or appraise it, we must know something of its underlying variables and the dynamics of their organization and change.

Determinants of Uniqueness

Some of the factors that determine uniqueness are structural; that is, they are qualities of the physical organism. Others are behavioral (functional) in nature. The determinants of personality may be categorized as follows: (1) general morphological and physical features; (2) constitutionally based attributes of temperament; (3) abilities, talents, and facilities that make for effectiveness of personal functioning; (4) generalized and pervasively organized behavior dispositions; and (5) learned patterns of social behavior and functioning, including the various attitudes, beliefs, opinions, prejudices, and the like that affect one's interpersonal relationships.

It is obviously not possible to catalogue completely, much less to describe in its detailed relationships, the total configuration of attributes of a given individual. It is impossible to trace the development of personality except in very general terms. Some analysis is necessary. We must resort to the piecemeal procedure of "looking at" particular aspects of the total, one at a time. Our present purpose, therefore, is to examine in some detail certain of the important determining variables of personal uniqueness, tracing briefly the development of thinking and inquiry with regard to each. Some of the more important of these types of variables have been considered in other connections (see Chapters 3, 6, 7, and 10).

Physical and Morphological Attributes

As we have seen, each individual is born with a unique constitutional make-up. He possesses at birth a combination of physical features all his own, which constitute one important aspect of his individuality. As a physical being he is different, and will continue to be different, from every other individual throughout his life.

But what is more important is the possible influence his particular pattern of physical and morphological traits may have upon the development of other aspects of his uniqueness. It may, for example, have much to do with his parents' immediate reaction to him, and the kind of reception they give him as a newcomer in the family. A lusty robust baby with a loud demanding voice may inspire in his parents quite different feelings and ways of regarding and handling him than would be the case were the baby frail, delicate, and finely featured. Congenital physical attributes in their unique combination may thus be important determinants of parent-baby interaction (Blauvelt and McKenna, 1961; Levy and Hess, 1952). As we shall see, the degree and type of interaction begins immediately to operate as a factor influencing the direction of developmental change in personality.

It is clear also that physical features may continue to be important factors determining one's self concept and the quality of one's interactions with others throughout life. Preschool children's physical endowments, attractive or otherwise, strongly influence the behavior and the attitudes, expressed or implicit, toward them of the nursery school teacher and other adults who are important in their lives. Children soon begin to "see" themselves as others seem to see them. They design their self concepts in terms of their interpretations of others' attitudes and feelings toward them.

For a boy of adolescent age to be too small or too fat or lacking the usual signs of sexual maturity may be very disturbing to him particularly because of the behavior or remarks of his peers; this "disturbance" might even give rise to unfortunate social behavior patterns and attitudes. Physical features are not only important factors contributing to uniqueness in and of themselves, but they also play *crucial* roles in the development of other attitudinal and behavioral attributes of individuality.

Physique-Temperament Relationships

The importance of the various attributes that constitute physique in relation to personal adjustment and development has long been recognized. Theories concerning this relationship antedate the birth of academic psychology by several centuries. Psychologists generally, however, with certain notable exceptions, have not found evidence of relationships between types of physique and patterns of temperament or personality, although probably no student of human behavior would deny the obvious fact that to the individual adolescent, for example, his body has great significance. Most psychologists, therefore, are likely to hold that morphological features have individual and idiosyncratic, rather than common or universal, significance. Investigators, nevertheless, continue to search for more general relationships.

Chapter 3 considered the physical and morphological features of the human individual and how they develop. In that connection, Sheldon's method of studying the components of physique in particular, was presented and illustrated.

Sheldon was especially interested in the problem of the physique-temperament relationship. In an elaborate program of research (1940), Sheldon made a correlational analysis of a long list of emotional and behavioral traits as observed in young adults. The analysis resulted finally in three sets, or "clusters," of highly interrelated traits. Each of these clusters, which he regarded as components of temperament, Sheldon associated, in terms of its apparent meaning, with one of the three components of physique. Thus he labeled them respectively *viscerotonia, somatotonia,* and *cerebrotonia.*

In his detailed somatotype study of 200 men, Sheldon (1940) obtained surprisingly high correlations between the physique components and the associated components of temperament, as follows:

Endomorphy—viscerotonia   +.79
Mesomorphy—somatotonia   +.82
Ectomorphy—cerebrotonia   +.83

As a general rule, American psychologists have ignored Sheldon's findings. Certain writers (Diamond, 1957; Hall and Lindzey, 1957), however, regard them as significant and worthy of careful consideration. Such correlations do furnish evidence in support of the commonly held assumption that physique and temperament are related in a general sense.

Walker (1962, 1963) studied 125 nursery school children with the purpose of assessing the relationship between body build and behavior. The children were rated on a specially prepared behavior-rating scale by their nursery school teachers. Nine "cluster scores" were developed from the intercorrelations among the items of the rating scale. Following the procedures prescribed by Sheldon, somatotyping photographs (front, side, and rear views) were obtained for each child. Three judges independently rated the photographs for each of the three physique components on Sheldon's 7-point scale.

A number of significant relationships between physique components and specific behavior items were found. Some interesting relationships also appeared for the total cluster scores. Endomorphy, for example, showed least relationship with behavior. Only aggressive, assertive behavior in boys and cooperative, conforming behavior in girls tended slightly to be related to endomorphy. Mesomorphy, on the other hand, correlated significantly in boys with eight of the nine cluster scores. According to these correlations, boys in whom mesomorphy was a strong component tended to be aggressive and assertive, energetic, active, alert and curious, social and friendly, excitable and unstable, and cheerful and expressive, tended not to be fearful and anxious or cooperative and conforming. Mesomorphic girls also tended to be energetic and active and aggressive and assertive but tended not to be fearful and anxious. By contrast, ectomorphy in boys was positively associated with the tendencies to be cooperative and conforming and not to be aggressive and assertive; in girls ectomorphy was associated with the tendencies not to be social and friendly. Walker (1962) summarized the findings of his study as follows:

> In this group of preschool children important associations do exist between individuals' physiques and particular behavior characteristics. Further, these associations show considerable similarity to those described by Sheldon for college-age men, though the strength of the association is not as strong as he reports. It is suggested that the relations are multiply determined, arising from primary bodily conditions (e.g., strength, energy, sensory thresholds), from direct learnings concerning the efficacy of different modes of behavior and adjustment techniques, and from less direct learnings regarding expectations and evaluations accorded to different physiques by others. (p. 79)

Physique in Relation to Other Personal Attributes

A number of research studies have verified the importance of physique and its components in relation to other personal characteristics. It has been found, for example, that children with "muscular solidarity" (mesomorphic tendency) also tend to be shorter and heavier and to grow at a faster rate and thus to reach the peak of their puberal growth spurt earlier than children with more linear and delicately built bodies (Dupertuis and Michael, 1953). Sheldon's morphological types have been found to differ significantly in average physical strength (H. E. Jones, 1949). In one of the best known studies of juvenile delinquency, it was found that the sturdier body build was more characteristic of delinquents than of nondelinquents (Glueck and Glueck, 1956).

Such research evidence, of course, supports Sheldon's basic assumption that the components of one's body structure, in combination, constitute the foundation of one's inherent organismic nature and must, therefore, bear an important relationship with temperament, which is an expression or function of organismic nature.

Although the accumulating evidence indicates that certain morphological attributes do have a general significance in relation to behavior and temperament, it nevertheless seems quite clear that the most important relationships between the physical and the psychological aspects are individual and personal in nature. There is no doubt that bodily attributes in their combinations and patterning can be important factors making for uniqueness, both in an immediate, direct sense and indirectly as they influence behavior.

Temperamental Predispositions

In our discussion of the physique-temperament relationship, the term temperament is used in a very broad sense to include all the various emotional and behavioral aspects of personality. A more precise and perhaps more meaningful usage of the term is to limit its meaning to those original, emotionally toned, and constitutionally based *pre*-dispositions to respond affectively to the external world. Temperament, in this narrow sense, is congenital. Temperamental behavioral predispositions arise from the congenital nature of the individual organism.

A number of original predispositions have been observed and described by students of infancy and early childhood, and one of the striking facts invariably stressed is the wide range of individual differences among babies with respect to these "dimensions" of temperament. Crying in newborn infants, for example, has been carefully studied (Aldrich *et al.*, 1945a, 1945b, 1946). Wide variation was found in the frequency and amount of crying as well as quality and in the meaning the crying had for each infant. Some babies are much more predisposed to express discomfort and distress through crying than are others. Perhaps, because of differences in inherent constitutional nature, the ones who cry most and loudest actually experience more discomfort and distress. Having keener cutaneous and organic sense receptors, they may actually sense disturbing or painful conditions more keenly.

Certain dimensions of temperament are discussed in some detail in Chapter 7; also, their relevance to emotional development is presented in Chapter 11. The relative strengths of the various constitutionally based predispositions in each child most surely contribute to his uniqueness as a person very early in life, and, like the components of his physique, they are important factors influencing later development of personality.

General Effectiveness in Coping with Environment

The young child's rapidly developing cognitive ability is of crucial importance as a determinant of the individual quality and uniqueness of his behavior and his interaction with others. Intelligence level, therefore, even without any conscious attempt to evaluate it as such, is an extremely important variable in our everyday appraisals of personality. Chapter 6 is devoted to a rather detailed consideration of intelligence and its development. The viewpoint expressed there is that intelligence as measured and as popularly appraised in daily life is cognitive ability—the ability to know how to function effectively. It is, therefore, an important factor in over-all functional adequacy, and persons differ widely in their functional adequacy. Thus intelligence, in combination with the myriads of other ways in which individuals differ, contributes to individual uniqueness. The adequacy and effectiveness with which a person functions in meeting everyday life situations is an important aspect of his personality.

Behavioral Factors of Uniqueness

Every individual, then, is born with a pattern of constitutional and morphological features all his own. Along with his organismic uniqueness (and very largely based upon it), he is also born with certain temperamental predispositions to behave generally in characteristic ways in relation to his environment. As this unique organization of congenital qualities comes in contact with a constantly changing personal environment, "coping" reactions begin and behavioral development through learning is underway. What a person does—the patterning of his behavior—perhaps more than anything else determines his individual uniqueness.

Behavioral Change
through Direct Social Conditioning

Developmental change, both in organismic structure and its functioning, proceeds at rapid rates, and many factors influence those changes. The particular morphological features a child possesses may influence significantly the direction and quality of his behavioral development.

HABITS   A great many patterned ways of doing things and of thinking are more specifically related to the culture into which the child is born and to the specific conditions of living that surround him. Children are taught to dress themselves in certain routine ways. They are taught to behave at the family dinner table in ways that are acceptable. They learn to be polite, or perhaps they do not learn to be polite, to their elders. As they grow older, these patterns, or habits, change according to circumstances and in relation to changes in their general milieu. When they go away to college or into the army or into some other field of activity, they usually discard many of their early habits and take on many new ones. But, even though the patterns of specific habits do change from time to time, certain specific ways of doing things tend to resist change and to become characteristic of the individual. Each person at any particular time is characterized by his particular pattern of habits, his idiosyncracies of personal and social behavior.

ATTITUDES One's habitual ways of regarding and thinking about people, about manners, institutions, and life in general, develop from one's experiences, life circumstances, and the people around him. And, like other habits, attitudes can change with time and circumstances.

Many, perhaps most of our attitudes are, in each case, the immediate result of prejudgment, the distinctly human process of generalization (that is, labeling and fitting objects of the external world into categories). The conditions of human existence are too complex to be dealt with always item by item. Objects and people and situations must be classified, labeled, and categorized. The fundamental mental process of cognition appears to be largely one of naming and categorizing. A currently active area of research in cognition in young children is concerned with the styles and "modes of perceptual organization and conceptual categorization of the external environment" (Sigel et al., 1963, p. 4). "The human mind must think with the aid of categories. Once formed, categories are the basis for normal prejudgment. We cannot possibly avoid the process. Orderly living depends upon it" (G. W. Allport, 1954, p. 20). "Normal" prejudgment, then, is not to be decried. It is an extremely important process in the economy of living. Allport pointed out that our adjustments to the constant flow of daily problems are largely made in terms of preformed categories. Furthermore, as we have seen, current research concerning "styles" of categorization used by young children, and developmental changes in style produced by age, promise to underline the basic importance of the processes of labeling and prejudgment in human existence and to throw new and important light upon certain qualitative aspects of intellectual development (Sigel et al., 1963).

Throughout life, from early childhood, people, objects, situations, and circumstances of living are thus classified, labeled, and put into categories. In this process our attitudes are born. They develop and, most often, are modified through relabeling and perhaps more refined categorizing. The 8-month-old child, in his immature way, is likely to put a strange face in the category of objects to be feared. With more maturity and experience, the same face might have become shifted to quite a different category. At age 2½ years, the child might now greet that face with an attitude of joyous acceptance. Attitudes do change with experience. Prejudgment is a continuous process, upon which orderly living depends.

PREJUDICE   Prejudice, likewise, is prejudgment. It is the *non-deliberate* labeling and assignment of a person or a group or an event to a previously established category. The labeling process, in the case of prejudice, however, is not only nondeliberate but it is also emotionally charged, and the category of assignment is one high in affective value. Thus, there are "love-prejudices" as well as "hate-prejudices" (G. W. Allport, 1954), and in either case a vital personal "value" is involved in the labeling. In the absence of a personal value (a love prejudice) there could be no hate prejudice. G. W. Allport, in discussing the "normality of prejudgment," wrote:

> Now there is good reason to believe that this love-prejudice is far more basic to human life than is its opposite, hate-prejudice (which Spinoza says "consists in feeling about anyone through hate less than is right"). One must first overestimate the things one loves before one can underestimate their contraries. Fences are built primarily for the protection of what we cherish.
>
> Positive attachments are essential to life. The young child could not exist without his dependent relationship on a nurturant person. He must love and identify himself with someone or something before he can learn what to hate. (1954, p. 25, by permission)

The process of prejudgment is psychological. It is obvious that the *values* involved in the formation of categories used in everyday adjustments, and from which attitudes and prejudices arise, are personal in nature. Like any other aspect of human development, however, attitudes and prejudices develop through individual-environment interaction. In his social and emotional interchange with his parents, his larger family, and his community, the child "takes on" as his own many ready-made values. He gradually comes to share with the members of his "in-groups" many readily available classification categories and, thus, many attitudes and prejudices. As the child identifies with parents and others, their modes of labeling (prejudices) become his.

Research findings indicate that group prejudices thus adopted by the individual continue to be his as long as he remains a member of the group. Group pressures upon individual members are strong. In regard to this aspect of the problem of prejudice, G. W. Allport (1954) wrote:

> A strong argument in favor of this view is the relative ineffectiveness of attempts to change attitudes through influencing individuals. Suppose a child attends a lesson in intercultural education in the classroom. The chances are this lesson will be smothered by the more embracing norms of his family, gang, or neighborhood. To change the child's attitudes it would be necessary to alter the cultural equilibrium of these, to him, more important groups. It would be necessary for the family, the gang, or the neighborhood to sanction tolerance before he as an individual could practice it. (p. 40, by permission)

The acquisition of prejudices is thus largely a matter of incidental learning. The category labels applied to persons, groups, or institutions by parents and other significant ones in the child's life will readily and inevitably become his own labels and prejudices.

The Acquisition of Fundamental Behavior Dispositions

Perhaps the most crucial single factor in personal functional development, however, is the interaction, largely emotional in nature, between the child (with his pattern of temperamental predispositions) and the more intimate human aspects of his environment (other individuals, his parents, who care for him and exercise control over him).

Much of this interchange, generally, is gratifying and pleasant to both parent and child; sometimes it is fraught with anxiety, frustration, or rage. The prevailing nature and quality of this emotional interchange is important, and its nature and quality obviously depends upon how the inborn temperamental nature of the infant relates to the personal make-up and adjustments of the parent.

The nature of interpersonal environment changes as the child grows and changes. During infancy, the period of complete dependency, it is the "mothering one" and the quality of her nurturant care that is the all-important factor. Later, as a preschooler, the control aspects of the larger environment become relatively more important. Much of the child's learning related to his personal development, however, is identificatory or imitative in nature (Bandura, 1962). The child frequently adopts as his model his same-sex parent, identifies strongly with that parent, and thus gains an enhanced "sense of status" indirectly (Ausubel, 1958).

A number of theories regarding the underlying conditions of learning through identification have been proposed (Bandura, Ross, and Ross, 1963). One of these theories, of course is the Freudian idea of rivalry, or "status envy," in which the same-sex parent is envied as the recipient of affectional and sexual rewards from the parent of the opposite sex. The theory is that in the effort to be an effective rival the behavior and attitudes of the envied parent are taken on through imitation.

A contrasting theory of identification holds that it is the one in power, the dispenser and controller of favors and rewards, rather than the recipient of rewards, who is imitated. Accordingly, the child identifies with his father because he is the powerful one who can control and dispense favors, not because he is in the favored position to receive the rewards. The results of a recent experimental test of these theories rather strongly support the social-power theory (Bandura, Ross, and Ross, 1963). Under the conditions of the experiment, the children tended strongly to identify with (to imitate) the behavior of the controller (the dispenser of power) rather than the "consumer of resources."

To be sure, whatever may be the underlying motivation for this type of social learning, identification is an exceedingly important process in early behavioral development. It contributes significantly to personal uniqueness, since every parental model is an individual, different from every other, and the child's pattern of identification, in line with his own individuality, will be unique.

The Study of Behavior Records

Much of human behavior, of course, is directly observable. Behavioral development in children can be studied by observing and systematically recording specific items of behavior in their play and other activities at successive age levels. Here again, however, wide individual differences will appear in the behavior records of a group of children at any age level. Certain items will appear with some frequency in the records of most, but not all, children. Some items will appear as especially characteristic of some children but will occur relatively rarely in the behavior of others. In the study and analysis of such material, we can derive some understanding of the behavioral aspect of individual personalities and the patterns of their development. There are two general approaches to this problem.

The Group-Statistical Approach

The most common approach to studying behavior has been to analyze the mass of data for a group of children by means of factor analysis or some other method of "clustering" data in terms of their commonality of meaning. The factors thus derived are interpreted as representing common "traits," or dispositions to behave in consistent ways in a variety of situations. This is a "nomothetic" procedure. The traits are common traits presumably present to some degree in each child of the group. Differences are, therefore, quantitative in nature. Each child can receive a quantitative score on each of the factors.

However, the *pattern* of relative magnitudes of the various scores each child receives always turns out to be different from that of any other child. Each child's score pattern is unique although the traits making up the pattern are common to the group.

In an earlier study (Roberts and Ball, 1938), behavior of many children was observed and recorded over a period of several years by use of behavior check-lists. Rather voluminous check-list records of the play behavior and other characteristics of this group of preschool children were compiled. In a cursory examination of these records, certain relationships and affinities among specific behaviors can be discerned directly. Statistical analysis showed that certain items tended to appear together in individual children's records (Stott, 1962). The items of a "cluster" were found generally to be consistent with one another or to have meaning in common. Each cluster, therefore, was taken to represent a generalized behavior trend that characterized some children more than others.

Just as certain discrete items tended to go naturally together in describing a particular behavior trend in a child, so also did certain clusters seem to be especially congruent with one another and to be related statistically. Together, such a set of clusters was taken to represent a behavior generalization of a higher order and with greater pervasiveness than those expressed by the separate clusters. Thus, when a particular cluster of recorded items portrays a pattern of behavior characteristic of a particular child, it is likely that the patterns portrayed by the other clusters of the related group, although different, also "fit" consistently and are compatible with one another (G. W. Allport, 1960). They tend to round out a consistent characterization. There apparently develops within the child a generalized *disposition* to behave with an over-all consistency and integrity in widely different situations and with a pattern of behavior appropriate to the situation in each case. In other words, within a range of differing situations, "equivalent fields of stimulation" and "equivalent fields of response" have become established and integrated (G. W. Allport, 1960).

However, the behavior expressions of these dispositions (that is, the specific actions or equivalent responses in terms of which personality is judged) change with development and experience. For example, "shyness" as an underlying behavior disposition would be an important facet of individuality and would probably continue to be present in the individual's make-up throughout his life. But that same disposition to shyness would be expressed at age 4 in terms of 4-year-old behavior and at age 20 in behavior more appropriate for a 20-year-old.

Not only does the behavioral expression of a particular disposition change with age, but wide individual differences are found among children in the combinations of specific behavior patterns expressive of that particular disposition at any given age level. Hence, two children whose behavior patterns are equally expressive of a particular disposition may differ considerably in the specific behavior patterns they use for its expression.

Behavior dispositions in unique combination, then, are important factors of individuality. They have their basis in the very nature of the organism. They are "dynamic" in the sense that they dispose the individual to exhibit certain qualities and patterns of behavior in terms of which they (the dispositions) can be identified.

COMMON CHILDHOOD BEHAVIOR FACTORS In the study by Stott (1962), the correlations among the individual check-list items were determined statistically and in terms of the magnitudes of these intercorrelations the 220 items were grouped together into 51 clusters. Although the individual items constituting a cluster were among themselves quite different, yet each cluster as a whole conveyed the meaning of a behavior trend distinct from the rest. Scores were then derived for each of the 63 children on each of the 51 clusters. Intercorrelations among the cluster scores were then obtained and a factor analysis was made of the table of intercorrelations. A set of 13 meaningful factors were obtained.

The "children" studied by Roberts and Ball (1938) were nursery school children during the 1920s and early 1930s. More recently, another study was made which was, in a limited sense, a replication of the earlier one. A revised and abbreviated version of the original set of check-lists consisting of 168 items was the data-collecting instrument for this later study. Teachers in twenty-five nursery schools were asked to rate their children individually by use of this list. The instructions were simply to "check only those statements which you feel are *really true* of the child. Do not guess if you are not reasonably sure." Behavior ratings were obtained on 340 preschool children.

The same statistical procedure was followed as in the earlier study. The analysis resulted in a set of 8 factors. This means that the 168 specific items had finally become segregated in terms of affinity and meaning relationships into 8 groupings (factors). Each factor, as before, was interpreted as a common behavior disposition, as follows:

Factor A. Social ascendance—lack of leadership

Factor B. Personal responsibility—irresponsible impulsiveness

Factor C. Introvertive self-sufficiency—need for the presence and support of others

Factor D. Social effectiveness (sociability)—social ineptitude

Factor E. Personal attractiveness—lack of personal appeal

Factor F. Personal security; stability—emotional instability (dependency)

Factor G. Compulsive domination—compliant, retiring (adaptability)

Factor H. Dependability—nondependability

These names, of course, were arbitrarily attached to the factors in an effort to convey as clearly as possible the interpreted meaning in each case. As the names suggest, there are some rather close relationships among them. For example, Factor A, "social ascendance," would seem to be similar in meaning to Factor D, "social effectiveness." As a matter of fact they proved to be statistically correlated to the extent of $+.65$. However, even though some factors do have meaning in common, when their constituent items are examined side by side each is seen to have quite a different aura. There is justification for regarding them as two rather distinct behavior dispositions. Complete listings of the eight factors, each with its set of component clusters and separate items, are given in Appendix B.

THE SOCIAL BEHAVIOR PROFILE   Figure 12.1 contains individual behavior profiles of Paul and Sally 695 as appraised from checklist ratings when they were 4 years old. According to her profile, Sally was an outstanding leader. This "social ascendance" undoubtedly was fostered in its development more by a natural endowment of "personal attractiveness" and appeal than by her efforts to be sociable and friendly, since her rating in "social effectiveness" was only slightly above average. Sally was also outstanding in her tendency to be "self-sufficient" rather than dependent upon the presence and cooperation of others in her play. She could lead out in group play, getting the

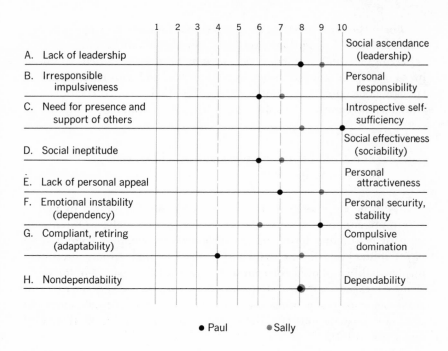

Figure 12.1

Social behavior "profiles" of Paul and Sally 695 based upon check-list ratings at age 4.

willing cooperation of other children, or she could become contentedly and happily engaged in activity by herself. Although not particularly outstanding in the other traits on the profile, she tended generally to be on the positive side.

Paul also was rated generally on the positive side of the chart. In certain respects the two patterns are similar. Both children, each in his and her own way, for example, displayed leadership behavior. Both were inclined to be socially ascendant but in somewhat different ways. Both also showed relatively little need for the presence and support of others in their play, although both fit well into cooperative play as the occasion demanded. Paul, as well as Sally, enjoyed playing with other children, but he, somewhat more than his sister, was inclined to function by himself. Paul showed considerably more emotional stability in the sense that he was slower to be aroused and more inclined to deliberate. Another disposition in which there was contrast between them was in the need to dominate. Paul was a bit on the retiring side, while Sally showed a greater-than-average tendency to control and to manipulate her playmates.

These children, as we have seen, were also well-endowed mentally. Repeated tests during their preschool and elementary school ages gave IQ ratings for both of them of 130 to 165. They were "gifted" children in that respect and, coming from a stable and constructive home environment, they were not hampered in their family relationships with serious emotional problems or unresolved conflicts.

The Complexity of the Behavioral Aspects of Personality

It should be emphasized here that a profile such as shown in Figure 12.1 represents only a very limited aspect of personality. Our discussions of personality have implied an extremely complex combination of attributes and qualities which are indeed myriad. In any assessment of personality it would, of course, be impossible to account for more than a meager sampling of the relevant variables. Other analyses of child behavior using other sources of data have portrayed somewhat different constellations of traits (Becker and Krug, 1964; R. B. Cattell and Coan, 1957).

The behavioral aspects of individuality are perhaps more meaningful, and more vitally important in human living than are the other areas of uniqueness. They are also more fluid, more subject to change, and therefore more dynamic in relation to effective personal and social adjustments. At the same time these attributes of the person are most elusive and difficult to measure. One of the difficulties often made much of is that every life situation involves a different set of behavior patterns. Although a given person may have acquired an "organization" of fundamental behavior dispositions, which, in general, characterize his functioning in all of life's situations, in terms of specific behaviors he may perform quite differently in the different areas of his life. These studied diverse behavior patterns have given rise to the concept of multiple "selves." "A man," said William James (1910), "has as many selves as there are distinct groups of persons about whose opinion he cares" (p. 179). Role theory also emphasizes the diversity of behavior from situation to situation. From this point of view, one can scarcely conceive of a behavior profile such as Figure 12.1, based as it is upon only eight traits, assessed from observations of the child in a single situation as adequately portraying the behavior aspects of his personality.

On the other hand, the concept of "behavior dispositions" implies more than is seen in purely situational behavior. In other words, even though Sally, in many respects, may have been a "different child" at home than she was in nursery school, yet in association with her peers in the home play-yard she probably would have shown the same general dispositions to be "ascendant" and also to be characteristically "self-sufficient," rather than to be dependent upon the support of other children in her play. G. W. Allport (1960) expressed this general point of view when he wrote concerning situational variability as follows:

> In the first place, some of our assessment methods have built into them a safeguard against situational variability. They explicitly vary the situation. Thus a person's disposition to be ascendant, or his aesthetic value, or his neurotic tendency is tested by a wide range of items depicting a great variety of situations commonly experienced. While some studies show that a trait measured in this way does vary, say, from the academic to the business situation, or from the athletic to the purely social, it is more common to find that the person carries with him, by and large, his typical level of anxiety, a typical amount of aesthetic interest and of ascendance, a typical aspiration level and a fairly constant degree of prejudice. (p. 116, by permission, copyright © 1960 by Gordon W. Allport)

The limited number of common behavior dispositions which we found in children as described above, to be sure, represent but a very narrow segment of childhood personalities. They probably represent, nevertheless, some rather basic variables. Certain of them are found to correspond quite closely to those identified by other investigators. For example, our Factor A, the disposition to be socially ascendant, seems to have much in common with R. B. Cattell's (1957) childhood Factor E, "dominance versus submissiveness." Likewise, the tendency to be personally stable, versus emotional instability, which came out of our analysis, corresponds rather closely to Cattell's "emotional maturity," Factor C and with a "trait of temperament" identified by Guilford (1958a) which he called "stability versus cycloid disposition." Analytical studies of personality development are constantly adding to the list of fairly well-identified common behavior dispositions in children, variables that presumably constitute the basic and relatively stable and persisting aspects of personality.

Opposition to Group Approaches to Personality

As was indicated earlier, students of personality with different theoretical points of view are often not happy with the group-statistical approach nor with the idea of common traits. The contention is that if every person is really unique, to describe a given person in terms of common traits—traits that are really composites, or distillates from the pooled behavior of many individuals—is *not* to portray his individuality.

The contrast between the two approaches becomes apparent at the very beginning of the study of personality, the point of data compilation. In the case of the common-traits approach, even though the check-list or inventory is filled in with specific reference in each case to a particular child, the items, or the behavior descriptions in terms of which that child is checked, are descriptions of behaviors that have been observed in many children, behaviors common to the population of which he is a member. They are not descriptions of him and with him and only him in mind. Hence, even though many of the items may "fit" him very well and in combination present a profile that is unique, yet it may well be that the very qualities that are peculiarly his are not at all registered on his check-list. Even though certain significant behavior dispositions in their relative strengths may be expressed quantitatively on the individual's common-trait profile, yet it probably often happens that other unique behavior dispositions may not appear on the profile. Thus, certain qualitative differences between him and others—the differences that really constitute individuality—may be entirely missed in the common-trait approach.

An Idiographic Evaluation

Since our primary interest is in the individual and his development, we attempted to portray our two young personalities idiographically. The procedure described by A. L. Baldwin (1942) was adapted to our situation and to the kinds of data that are available in the developmental records of our twin subjects. Baldwin's procedure is designed for use with qualitative material concerning personal attributes and behavior; for example, personal documents, casual descriptions of reactions in various situations, informal observational reports, and so on.

The mass of material for each subject was first divided into what Baldwin called incidents. We divided the incidents chronologically, grouping together all the personal and behavioral material, usually for a period of about a week. Some periods contained many items, others, relatively few. Then we noted by count and tabulated the number of times each particular "category" (behavior pattern or personal characteristic) was mentioned in the material within each time period. These relative frequencies for each period, and for the total, were then studied. The two important assumptions, of course, were (1) that the frequency with which an item category appeared in the mass of personal material was an indication of its importance in the child's personality, and (2) that the tendency of two behaviors to occur together was evidence of the degree of relationship between them (Baldwin, 1942).

PERSONALITY PORTRAYALS   In terms of the regularly occurring patterns of behavior, feelings, and relationships thus revealed in the table of frequencies, the following personality portrayal of Paul emerged.

1. The quality of deliberateness runs consistently through all of Paul's record. At age 20 months the unusually careful and deliberate way in which he aligned his blocks and placed them in patterns was noted. At age 20 months, also, his speech was described as "slow and deliberate." This speech characteristic was frequently noted throughout the nursery school period. At age 30 months the tester noted that Paul worked "deliberately and persistently" on the tasks presented to him. "He gets so involved in an activity that he can hardly be distracted from his work." His slow and deliberate approach to activities was again noted at age 5 years. When Paul was in the twelfth grade, as a part of our testing program he was asked to sort a set of statements about "self" in a Q-sort test (see Chapter 7). At the end of more than an hour, when twice the allotted time had elapsed, he had not finished the task. He was deliberately and critically analyzing each statement from the standpoint of its grammar, ambiguity, and other criteria.

2. The next most frequently noted quality in Paul's functioning, particularly during his preschool period, was his need for stability in his relationships with his environment. This quality, at times, appeared as rather strong negativism. He rather consistently resisted the morning inspection procedure at nursery school. He tended to resist arbitrary directions from adults which required too sudden (for him) change in activity. He was bothered by the continually changing student personnel in the nursery school. At the beginning of his nursery school experience he resisted "violently" the toileting procedure.

Another indication of this need for stability, or for the

feeling of being in control, was his need, even beyond age 4, to have with him constantly his blue blanket from his bed. This had more of the appearance of insecurity than of negativism. Paul was also much disturbed when, during the summer, as he was approaching age 4, the backyard of his family home was used as a nursery play-yard for (to him) strange children. He resented the children's presence in *his* yard and refused to participate to any extent in their play. Another disturbing factor which upset his need to keep things under control occurred when Paul and his sister were about age 4½. Sally and her girlfriends excluded him from their play for several months. Paul, during this time, frequently wanted to stay home to avoid facing the situation. It was stated in the record that Paul during this disturbing period showed more of a "sense of importance" at nursery school on days when Sally was absent with a cold.

3. A third outstanding quality in Paul was his independence and self-sufficiency. Even at age 3 years he was described as having definite ideas of his own for play. At age 4 he chose his own books at the children's section of the library. In nursery school his interests were more in relation to things and materials, and he showed unusual ingenuity in working with materials. He would go ahead with his own ideas, and as other children followed his lead he often became the center of activity. His relations with the other children were good but he rarely became involved in group play except as others joined in activities which he initiated. As a club member he often incorporated much dramatic play in the activities in which the others joined and participated.

In most respects the portrayal of Sally obtained from the analysis of her behavioral record contrasted markedly from that of her brother. In certain other areas, however, there was considerable similarity. In terms of the relatedness of the behavioral categories, five clusters appeared.

1. Sally was most frequently described as vivacious, lively, excitable, jestful, and very expressive of pleasure, particularly in relating to, and interaction with, other children and adults.

2. In her relationships with her peers she characteristically took the initiative and usually was the leader, although she could readily join a group-play situation and participate im-

mediately in cooperative play. She was usually ready to help a younger playmate in need. She was inclined, however, to be selective as to whom she would play with, and she was quite adept in manipulating the play group, or an individual playmate, toward gaining her own ends.

3. As an individual, Sally was realistically competent and independent. She was able relatively efficiently to care for herself in the toilet and washroom. She was spontaneous in her selection of play materials, with a tendency to use a wide variety from day to day. She also exhibited considerable creativity in her use of these materials. She was able to relax effectively during rest periods and she realistically accepted the morning inspection routine of the nursery school.

4. Sally was oriented toward and interested in people more than material things. She generally was very cordial and talkative with adults, and she enjoyed especially the social aspects of mealtime. She readily developed special affectional attachments to certain of the nursery school teachers, and she was inclined to "play" for their attention and approval.

5. Sally not only showed some dependence upon the attention and approval of the teachers but also some tendency to be jealous of the attention or affection they gave to others, and particularly to her brother. She expressed some hostility toward Paul by delighting in destroying his creative products. She also deliberately excluded Paul from her play with her girlfriends.

Clearly the two sets of characterizations—the common behavior-factor profiles and individual, qualitative portrayals—are in no way inconsistent or contradictory, and in certain respects they agree quite closely. The idiographic accounts however, do bring out in each case certain aspects of individuality that the check-list approach could not capture. Idiosyncracies, such as Paul's need for his blanket or Sally's jealousy of and related hostile feelings toward her brother, add bits of uniqueness to the total picture.

Summary

This chapter has outlined a very broad conception of personality. Personality is simply the "quality or fact" of being a unique person. But the attributes, the traits, the variables which, in unique combination and patterning, give one uniqueness and individuality are myriad. We arbitrarily grouped these variables under five headings: (1) morphological and physical features; (2) constitutionally-based attributes of temperament; (3) abilities that determine the level of effectiveness in personal functioning; (4) incidentally-learned patterns of personal and social behavior, including one's attitudes, beliefs, and prejudices; and (5) generalized behavior dispositions.

These groupings of variables differ widely as to origin, as to their susceptibility to change, and as to the conditions of their development. The environment plays a much greater role in determining individual differences in some characteristics than in others. Differences in external environment, for example, as a rule, has little to do with making some individuals very tall and some very short.

Every individual is also born with a particular temperamental nature. Developmental changes in the expression of that temperament, unlike changes in height, may be greatly influenced by the environment. A basic tendency to be active, to be constantly doing something, for example, is most likely to continue to characterize an individual throughout his life, regardless of whether he becomes an evangelist, a business tycoon, or a gangster. Thus the same pattern of original predispositions, in interaction with one sort of socializing environment, might give rise to quite different traits of personality (behavior dispositions) than might have developed had the socializing environment been of a different sort.

One's individuality thus persists throughout life, but its modes of expression may, nevertheless, undergo radical change. The outward manifestations of one's affective tendencies and the specific behavior patterns representing one's broadly generalized behavioral dispositions continue to adapt to changing circumstances and social expectations as one moves through the various levels of physical and personal development. With all the changes in one's "surface" behavior, which manifestly are changes in his personality, he remains basically the same person. He maintains his individuality.

SELECTED   READING   SUGGESTIONS

Allport, G. W. *Personality and social encounter.* Boston: Beacon Press, 1960. (Read particularly pages 3–66.)

Allport, G. W. *The nature of prejudice.* Reading, Mass.: Addison-Wesley, 1954.

Hall, C. S., and G. Lindzey. *Theories of personality.* New York: Wiley, 1957.

Maslow, A. H. *Motivation and personality.* New York: Harper & Row, 1954.

Moustakas, C. (ed.). *The self: explorations in personal growth.* New York: Harper & Row, 1956.

CHAPTER 13

The Origins
of Individuality

An old issue in development, for years now dead and abandoned,
involved such questions as: "Which is more important, heredity or
environment?" "Is walking a product of maturation or is it learned?"
"Is personality inherited or is it merely an individual expression of
the culture?" Such "either-or" questions now, of course, never occur
to students of human nature as questions for serious consideration.

There are, nevertheless, strong disciplinary biases in the current
literature dealing with personality and its development, and with
human development generally, concerning the *relative* importance of
the biological and the cultural factors. Progress, however, is being
made on both fronts. The mysteries of biological heredity are gradually
being unlocked. With their modern equipment for technical research,
the sciences of genetics and biochemistry are making steady progress
toward an understanding of the intracellular mechanism of hereditary

control and the processes regulating development. In the light of present knowledge, on the other hand, no one would question the essential role the environment in all aspects and phases of development. Nature and nurture in human development are, even today, important topics about which much is yet to be learned.

The generally accepted viewpoint, then, is that all development whatsoever, physical or psychological, is the result of the interaction between the organism and its environment, that is, between nature and nurture.

From the moment of conception there is implicit in the individual a development potential and a particular design in terms of which the vital interchange between organism and environment takes place. This potential and the nature of this design are determined by the particular combination of hereditary determiners that come together at the union of the original germ cells. The genetic factor thus determines the nature of and potentiality for organic response to and interchange with the environment. It lays down the over-all pattern of development and the ultimate limit of developmental achievement possible to the individual.

Of equally vital importance, of course, is the quality and the adequacy of the environment. Obviously, if the environment does not provide the essential stimulation (the necessary nourishment and nurture) for optimum response and interchange, the processes of development cannot proceed at the level of greatest potential. This chapter will focus particularly upon these two essential factors of development: biological hereditary endowment and environment.

The Mechanism of Hereditary Endowment

The development of every individual human being has its beginning with the union of an ovum, or egg, and a spermatozoon, or sperm. Each of these original cells, microscopic in size, is made up of a material called cytoplasm and a nucleus, or central body. The tiny nucleus of each cell contains twenty-three minute, active, threadlike structures called chromosomes. Careful study of chromosomes, under the most powerful magnification, has revealed that they differ considerably, one from another, each being identifiable in terms of shape and size, and that each consists of a great many gelatinous, beadlike structures called genes strung closely together. It is estimated that the chromosomes, then, with their constituent genes, all packed within the fantastically small nucleus of the sperm cell comprise all the hereditary material contributed by the father. Likewise, within the larger body of the egg cell is its nucleus containing a duplicate set of twenty-three gene-laden chromosomes, which comprise the mother's contribution to the hereditary make-up of the child-to-be. As the sperm enters the egg the two cells fuse and become one, the fertilized ovum, with a single nucleus containing the twenty-three matched pairs (forty-six in all) of chromosomes.

Thus, with the union of the two germ cells, two separate lines of heredity come together with a total of some 80,000 to 120,000 genes, each with its determining potential. The process of the development of a new individual is underway.

> The parent cells have a twofold function in reproduction. Together they initiate the most remarkable and dynamic event in nature: the assembly of a living body out of single molecules of proteins, carbohydrates and other biochemicals. In addition, the parent cells control the specific design of the body. It is a design that will follow a pattern passed along a chain of inheritance, going back to the biological roots of this family. In a sense each new life actually has no definite beginning. Its existence is inherent in the existence of the parent cells and these, in turn, have arisen from the preceding parent cells. When any two parent cells unite, they bring together a blend of the attributes of all ancestors before them. Thus, since all people are descended from a small number of early human beings they are linked by a common heritage. (Flanagan, 1962, p. 19)

To trace the development of a new individual, however, we must begin with the union of the ovum and the sperm. This fertilized egg, a single cell, divides into two new cells. In this division each of the forty-six chromosomes splits lengthwise into two parts, each an exact duplicate of the other. Thus the nucleus of each "daughter" cell contains the full quota of forty-six chromosomes with identical gene components.

This process of cell proliferation continues throughout the period of growth eventuating finally in the adult human being. Obviously a great deal of differentiation, specialization, and integration takes place as the various anatomical structures and organs of the body are formed, each for its particular specialized function. Yet at the same time, each and every single cell making up the complex organism contains a nucleus with exactly the same content (the full quota of hereditary determiners which throughout the course of development together exercise their guiding, regulating, and controlling influence). Thus from the moment of the original union of egg and sperm, by virtue of the influence of these minute regulators present in every cell, the organism is *destined* to become a human being of a specific racial origin with a particular family hereditary background. Yet by virtue of the same control mechanism, each individual is unique and different from every other in terms of the character and relative prominence of each trait, and particularly in terms of the combination and patterning of these various attributes and traits, each of which the individual possesses to some degree in common with his kind.

Inherited Individuality

In the process of physical growth, even though the nuclear content of every cell continues to be the same as that of the original fertilized egg, a great deal of cell differentiation and specialization must nevertheless take place as the different bodily structures are formed. Early in this process of specialization, a mass of cells is set aside and preserved, later to serve the function of reproduction. When a child is born these particular cells are stored safely inside the immature genital organs. There they remain inviolate until, at the time of puberty, changes in the hormonal secretions of the endocrine glands stimulate developmental activity in them. They begin to divide and thus multiply in number in the same manner as the other cells of the body divide and redivide to produce growth.

But another process of change is necessary before the "reproductive" cells become fully developed ova or sperm cells. The immature reproductive cells each contain the full quota of forty-six chromosomes. But the original sperm and egg at the time of their union each contained only twenty-three chromosomes, one member of each pair.

So, before the immature male germ cells can become mature spermatoza, their quota of chromosomes must be reduced by one-half. A "reduction division" must take place. In this type of cell division the individual chromosomes do not split into two identical halves thus providing each of the new cells with the full number of forty-six. Instead, the members of each pair of whole chromosomes separate, one going into each of the new cells. These two new cells are alike in that each possesses one of each of the twenty-three kinds of chromosomes, but they are quite different in terms of their loads of hereditary determiners, some of the chromosomes in each of them having come originally from the father and others from the mother (see Figure 13.1).

A comparable process, somewhat different in its details, occurs in the maturation of ova in the female. The same shuffle of individual chromosomes insures that each ovum will have one member of each of the twenty-three pairs of chromosomes, yet each and every ovum will be different in its combination of heritary determiners.

In view of such a mechanism of individual heredity, it is not diffi-

SPERMATOGENESIS–(IN ANIMALS)–OOGENESIS

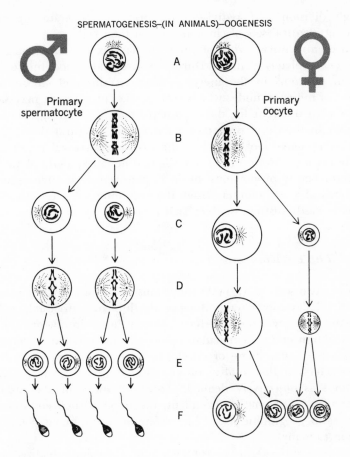

Primary
spermatocyte

Primary
oocyte

A

B

C

D

E

F

Figure 13.1

The process of reduction division in the development of reproductive cells, male and female. Adapted from A. M. Winchester
(1951), p. 49, by permission.

cult to see why children in the same family may look somewhat alike,
be similar in certain respects, or resemble the father or the mother,
or some other member of the family background in certain respects,
but at the same time be quite different from anyone else in total
make-up and pattern of characteristics.

The only possible exceptions to this rule of uniqueness are the
so-called identical twins or monozygotic twins (two individuals coming
from the same zygote, or fertilized ovum). What apparently happens
is that at the first division of the fertilized ovum the two "daughter"
cells instead of remaining attached to each other to begin the formation of a single organism, disassociate themselves. They then proceed

through division and redivision to form two separate organisms possessing identical sets of chromosomes in their cells.

But even identical twins, presumed to have exactly the same genes, are never completely identical. During the prenatal period, they occupy different positions in the uterus and the strains and stresses (the patterns of influence under which growth takes place) must necessarily be somewhat different for them, perhaps slightly "favoring" one over the other in the development of a particular structural detail. Even though they may "look alike" to the casual observer, a parent very quickly becomes aware of certain slight differences, perhaps in size, in certain bodily proportions, or in responsiveness to environmental conditions. To the mother, from the beginning, the twins are individuals, easily distinguishable, each unique in his own way.

The Environment

There are two sorts of variable conditions or factors which constitute the general developmental milieu of the human individual, and to which the term environment refers. There is the environment common to all children or to a particular segment of the population, perhaps during a particular phase of development. Environment in such instances refers to the totality of external (to the organism) living conditions as objectively defined. Thus, we speak of the prenatal environment, the home environment, the impoverished environment of a certain geographic area. The reference is to living conditions common to many.

We also use the term environment in a more individualized sense to refer to the particular constellation of conditions and stimuli, internal as well as external, that are actually affecting the development or influencing the behavior of a particular individual at a given time. This is his effective environment. The adequacy, in both the qualitative and the quantitative sense, of the child's food intake or the health care tendered him are important items in his effective environment. Attempts are often made to modify or to enhance a child's learning environment by providing demonstrations or interesting materials for him to manipulate or challenging situations with which he must cope. The lack of adequate and appropriate stimulation of the "institution" babies that have been studied, as compared with family-reared babies, appears to have been the chief deterrent to their developmental progress. They suffered "stimulus deprivation." Their individual effective environments were inadequate for optimum development. In general, the socialization of a child is a matter of regulating and manipulating his effective environment to bring about behavioral change in the desired direction. In the discussions that follow, the term environment will be used in both the general and the more individualized senses.

Prenatal Conditions of Life and Growth

The living fertilized ovum obviously could not long survive under other than its normal conditions of living. Upon reaching its destination in the uterus, a favorable environment in interaction with the genetic determiners within the cells' nuclei is necessary for continued life and growth. It is through the continuous interaction of these two factors during the embryonic stage that differentiation begins, resulting finally in the highly diversified forms and functions of cells which make up the different structures and organs of the body. The exact nature of the process of cell differentiation is, as yet, not well understood, but undoubtedly the variations in the intercellular environment (the differences in pressures and stress due to different positions cells occupy within the embryo) play a vital role in the process.

Later, during the fetal period, specific pressure and vibratory stimuli from the outside are transmitted through the medium of the uterine environment to the developing organism. These stimuli, together with stimuli intrinsic to the fetus, produce muscular activity and fetal movements and thus contribute to the development and strengthening of muscular tissues through exercise.

SPECIAL HAZARDS OF THE PRENATAL ENVIRONMENT   There are still those who hold to some of the traditional beliefs regarding prenatal influences. The belief that the thoughts, desires, and emotional experiences of the mother can influence directly, or "mark" her unborn child, of course, has no basis in fact. Since there is no neural connection between mother and fetus, there is no possibility of direct transmission of thoughts and feelings. The mother's contemplation of beauty or intense enjoyment of music and nature or her shock and terror on seeing a mouse, or a snake, or a hare, cannot of themselves influence the emotional nature or "mark" with some abnormality the child she is carrying.

During recent years, however, much has been learned about certain other maternal conditions and activities that can seriously affect the developing fetus. Just as oxygen and nourishment can be transferred from the mother's blood to that of the fetus through the placenta and the umbilical cord, so also can harmful chemical substances. There is growing evidence that chemical irregularities in the mother's blood brought about by endocrine imbalance, dietary deficiencies, or ill health may have serious effects. Maternal malnutrition often results in the unborn child being deprived of essential vitamins or nutrients necessary for its normal growth and health. Childhood abnormalities, such as rickets, nervous instability, epilepsy, and cerebral palsy, have been found to result from serious malnutrition in the mother at certain points during the period of pregnancy.

Maternal disease often constitutes a serious hazard because of its influence upon the chemical nature of the mother's blood with possible deleterious effects upon fetal development. Cretinism, for example, may result from endocrine disorders in the mother. Infectious diseases during the second and third months of pregnancy are especially damaging because it is during that period that the organs of the new body are being formed. Physical malformations, deafness, blindness, microcephaly, and motor disorders can result from such infections as syphylis, gonorrhea, poliomyelitis, and German measles.

Certain drugs, alcohol, and nicotine directly affect the mother's blood chemistry. It is quite possible, according to Montagu (1963):

> . . . that the products of tobacco entering the embryonic and fetal circulation adversely affect not only the heart and circulatory system but also many other organs. The increase in cardiac and circulatory disorders in recent years may not be unconnected, in part at least, with the smoking of pregnant mothers. (p. 108)

As previously stated, the emotional states of the mother cannot be transmitted directly to the unborn child. Severe emotional tensions continuing over long periods, nevertheless, can effect the chemical balance of the mother's blood and, by placental transmission, affect the level of fetal activity. There is some evidence that these effects may carry over into infancy in the form of adjustment difficulties.

In spite of the protection nature has afforded the human individual during its 9 months of prenatal development, there are, as we have seen, many environmental hazards to his health and welfare during that period. With greater understanding of these dangers and more awareness and care on the part of prospective mothers, much of the prenatal hazards can be avoided.

The Environment of the Infant

The so-called crisis of birth consists of the sudden, radical change in total environment to which the neonate must adapt. His living medium suddenly has become radically different. He is no longer enveloped and cradled in relative quiet and darkness in a fluid medium of constant temperature. William James described the probable immediate situation of the newborn infant as one of being caught up in a "big buzzing, blooming confusion" of air currents, pain, pressures, light, and noise. But what is important to his survival is the fact that he reacts in special ways to certain specific stimuli within that confusion, thereby initiating certain physiological functions so essential to postnatal existence. He responds, for example, to a slap on the buttocks or to a chilling air current with an inhalation and a gasp, thus initiating independent breathing.

The human neonate is the most helpless and dependent of all creatures, but he is also possessed with the greatest potentiality and capacity for adjustment and developmental change. The long process of development toward the realization of that potentiality soon gets under way as he interacts with his environment.

As previously mentioned, the amount and appropriateness of stimulation a child receives during infancy appears to be a very important matter. The evidence suggests that the ordinary family situation, with its human sights and sounds, in which the baby is taken in arms, nursed, cuddled, rocked, handed about, and talked to as he is cared for, constitutes an environment most conducive to his healthy development during his infantile dependency (see Chapter 11). Attractive objects of appropriate size for the baby to reach for, knock about, and try to grasp offer additional stimulation and exercise during periods when he is awake and by himself.

Normally, the infant's earliest "human" environment probably consists, in his experience, of shifting lights and colors, sounds, and the comforting warmth of body contact as he receives gratification and relief from bodily discomfort. His "instinctive" reaction to discomfort of any sort is crying, and he very early "learns" the connection between his crying and the gratification and relief that comes *with* these shifting shadows and sounds. Thus, he soon learns to manipulate and control his environment. This is the earliest form of social interaction. His profound helplessness and dependence thus constitutes a kind of independence. The world around him responds to his demands (Ausubel, 1958).

This volitional independence, however, diminishes as the child gradually emerges from his helplessness and acquires functional ability. His social environment, in other words, changes in relation to him as he gradually acquires the ability to do for himself. In the meantime, of course, the sights, sounds, smells, and comforts which early constitute the human aspects of his environment, have now become persons whom he identifies and responds to differentially as they facilitate or frustrate him in the pursuance of his objectives. These persons are no longer completely subservient to his will. They now restrict, frustrate, and punish, as well as facilitate the satisfaction of his needs. The child is now in the midst of what Ausubel calls the "crisis of maturation," when he must relinquish much of his volitional independence. The so-called socialization process is now under way in earnest.

The Environment of the Toddler

With the achievement of independent locomotion, the child's effective environment becomes greatly expanded. As he moves about, he is confronted moment by moment with a new array of objects, which to him are exciting and attractive—things to be reached for, grasped and manipulated. Without experience he has no basis for judgment as to what may be grasped, mouthed and manipulated, thrown down, and what may not be touched. This he must learn. It is one of the earliest learning problems in his socialization. He learns these and many other lessons of conduct through interaction with the human aspect of his environment, particularly his parents.

The effective environment of the toddler, thus, has rather precipitously become much more complex. It is two-sided. There is the world of things, which holds much promise of the gratification of an intrinsic tendency within him to seek stimulation, to "take in" his world. The other aspect of his environment, the human side, has suddenly become repressive, limiting, frustrating. In his interactions with this two-sided environment, the child learns something of the nature of reality and his own relationship with it. His ego develops.

The Socializing Environment

As a rule, parents have rather definite conceptions of what is acceptable and what is unacceptable behavior for children of different ages. They expect their children to measure up to certain preconceived standards of conduct and achievement, and the extent to which they measure up is a source of parental pride and satisfaction or of disappointment and a sense of failure. And, as we shall see, the particular patterns of behavior that are acceptable and the levels of parental expectations with regard to achievement vary from culture to culture, from social class to social class, and from family to family.

Cultural Molding

In general, children grow up stamped in many ways by the particular culture into which they are born. Babies born and reared in the United States, in all their great diversity and their individuality, turn out unmistakably to be Americans, just as those born behind the Iron Curtain turn out to be Russians in attitudes, ways of thinking, and mannerisms. And it is just as clear that this is not entirely a matter of biological inheritance. To be sure, when egg and sperm of Caucasian American parents unite, the final outcome is invariably a Caucasian human being, never a Fijian or a Chinese in color and general physical characteristics. The mechanism of heredity is the determining factor here. But if that Caucasian baby happened to be born in Fiji and was left to be reared in a Fijian family he would grow up to behave and think like a Fijian. Even though he possesses all of the morphological characteristics of a Caucasian American, he will not behave like one. Kluckhohn (1949) described an interesting example of the influence of culture in relation to behavioral traits:

> Some years ago I met a young man who did not speak a word of English and was obviously bewildered by American ways. By "blood" he was as American as you or I, for his parents had gone from Indiana to China as missionaries. Orphaned in infancy, he was reared by a Chinese family in a remote village. All who met him found him more Chinese than American. The facts of his blue eyes, and light hair were less impressive than a Chinese style of gait, Chinese facial expression, and Chinese modes of thought. The biological heritage was American, but the cultural training had been Chinese. He returned to China. (p. 19)

Within any national or ethnic culture, of course, there are many so-called subcultures. In the European and Asian countries, areas in close proximity to each other have different languages or dialects and somewhat different customs, traditions, and modes of dress. In the United States, even though there is something of a national character, there are, nevertheless, marked regional differences in ways of living, modes of dress, speech accents, manerisms. Even in this age of great mobility and powerful mass media, a child born and reared in a particular section of the United States still becomes stamped, in certain respects, with that particular subculture. He is readily recognized in young adulthood, as a Southerner, a Bostonian, a Westerner.

Then, of course, within any regional subculture, or even within any locality or community, there are social-class differences, occupational, economic, and educational differences among families. Each family as it develops establishes its own unique patterns of interaction, modes of individual role functioning, family customs, and traditions. All of these cultural influences—national, ethnic, regional, neighborhood, and family—find expression in some particular pattern of relative potency in the child's home environment.

The Influence of Social Class

In a democracy, as in any other type of social order, people tend to sort themselves and one another into categories in terms of ways of living, common social behavior patterns, and feelings of status. According to Havighurst and Taba (1949) a social class is "a group of people who think of themselves as belonging to the same social level and who generally are willing to associate intimately with one another—to visit each other in their homes, to dine with one another, to have their families inter-marry and so on" (p. 16).

Duvall (1962) described the social-class situation with respect to its self-perpetuating influences upon children:

> A child at birth is placed within society according to the social status of his parents. He may live out his life within the family status into which he was born. Or he may move up or down the social ladder as he "betters himself," or "is no credit to his family." . . .
>
> A family generally is aware of its status within the community. Others are seen as "our kind of folks," or "better than we are," or "not the kind of people we want to associate with," as families identify with those of similar status, those of higher and those of lower status respectively. Families who have social access to each other are generally considered to be of the same general social class. (p. 70, reprinted by permission from *Family Development*, Second Edition, by Evelyn Duvall, published by J. B. Lippincott Company. Copyright © 1962, 1957)

People who thus feel akin to one another tend to think alike and to share common attitudes and patterns of living. Their somewhat common attitudes and beliefs about children and how they should be "brought up" tend to resist the influences for change from outside their social realm. Thus today, even though the popular magazines and other mass media make readily available to all levels of society the popularized versions of the most up-to-date research findings, as well as the current points of view of the "authorities" in the fields of child psychology, child care, and family relations, still rather wide social-class differences remain in degree of sophistication, in attitudes about children, and in patterns of child rearing. Warner, Meeker, and Eells (1949), in their study of social class in America, found rather wide differences in average educational level among the various social classes. According to their findings, all of the children of the two "upper" classes, for example, attended high school, while only 28 percent of the "lower" class ever entered high school.

As an environmental influence upon the development and adjustments of children, Rodman (1965) clearly portrayed the factor of social class:

> A person's social class background has a pervasive influence upon his life. The lower the class background the likelier they are to have tuberculosis, to die early, to receive poor physical care, to get poor justice in the courts, to bear illegitimate children, to have unstable marital relationships, to have "less" motivation and "lower" aspirations. An excedingly wide variety of injustices and deprivations can be documented for members of the lower class of society—physical, social, occupational, legal, economic, and political. Even in affluent society like the United States, the poor are plentiful, and the injustices and deprivations they face are facts of life. (p. 213)

PATTERNS OF CHILD REARING   Martha C. Ericson (1946), in a study of child rearing in relation to social status, found some interesting differences between the middle- and the lower-class parents in their attitudes and expectations concerning their children:

> Middle-class families were generally found to be more exacting in their expectations. Training was generally begun earlier in middle-class than in lower-class families. In the middle-class families there was more emphasis on early responsibility, closer supervision of children's activities, and greater emphasis on individual achievement. (p. 191)

A more recent study by Sears, Maccoby, and Levin (1957), compared middle-class and working-class mothers as to their child-training practices. They found that the working-class mothers were significantly more severe in toilet training, more inclined to punish, scold, or shame the child for "accidents" than were the middle-class mothers. Although the working-class mothers did not begin this training earlier, they achieved results sooner. The difference in degree of severity and punitiveness was found in all areas of child guidance and training. The working-class parents tended to have less patience in relation to their children's dependency needs and to be less permissive with respect to such matters as sex play and expressions of aggression. Their method of control and training in these areas also tended to be more severe. In general, according to the findings of this study, the educational level of parents was the differentiating factor:

> The middle-class mothers, and those with higher education, seemed to impose fewer restrictions and demands upon their five-year-olds than did the working-class mothers of lesser education. Messiness at the table was somewhat less often permitted for children in the lower groups, and those children were subject to more stringent requirements about such things as hanging up their clothes, keeping their feet off the furniture and being quiet around the house. (Sears, Maccoby, and Levin, 1957, p. 429)

In comparing the results of these two studies, M. C. Ericson's, in 1946, and Sears *et al.,* in 1957, some interesting changes seem to have taken place during that eleven-year period. In the earlier study, middle-class families were the "more exacting in their expectations" and seemed generally to be more inclined to pressure their children; they began toilet training earlier, and there was "greater emphasis on individual achievement." By comparison, the middle-class mothers in the later study seemed to be more relaxed and less severe and punitive than the working-class mothers.

The extent to which these apparent differences in middle-class attitudes and practices represent a real secular change in so short a period of time, of course, is not known. The group of Chicago mothers designated as "middle-class" in 1946 may or may not correspond in terms of socioeconomic status or cultural and educational level to a group of mothers from "two suburbs of a large metropolitan area of New England" eleven years later, also designated as "middle-class." The probabilities are great, in fact, that the two middle-class groups represented quite different positions in the social-class hierarchy with respect to the lower-class mothers and the working-class mothers with whom they were respectively compared. On the other hand, social change in general, including the great increase in amount of educational literature in the popular magazines during the eleven-year period, might well have brought about real attitudinal changes. Perhaps as middle-class mothers, as a group, became better educated and gained a fuller understanding of child nature, they lost some of their tendencies to pressure their children. Perhaps they did become more relaxed and permissive. It is likewise possible that parents at the lower socioeconomic levels, with generally improved economic conditions and more leisure, became more upward-striving and thus more inclined to subject their children to "more stringent requirements" and to impose upon them more restrictions and demands in their efforts to obtain the "better things of life" for their families. At any rate, all comparative studies of social classes have found rather striking differences in attitudes of parents toward children, and in child-rearing and training practices.

SOCIAL CLASS AND EDUCATION   Studies have also consistently shown a higher educational mortality rate among the lower-class children. It has become clear that this cannot be adequately explained in terms of a class difference in intelligence level. Teachers, by and large, are middle class in origin and in their orientation. Consequently, they tend unconsciously to feel closer to and more comfortable with children from their own social level. They tend also to "handle with care" children with higher social status and to depreciate or neglect children of lower classes (Warner *et al.*, 1949). The children themselves in the school situation very early pattern their attitudes toward one another in conformity with adult social status differentiations. According to one study, regardless of the social status of their own families, children generally tend to attribute socially desirable characteristics to their schoolmates from the upper classes and to rate those from the lower-class families as not being "good looking" or as "people you would not want as friends" (Neugarten, 1946).

One of the consequences of school experiences is likely to be a general and lasting dislike on the part of lower-class children for the whole idea of education. In the past, the characteristic lower-class attitude toward school generally has been unfavorable and negativistic. The parents have often tended to encourage resistance and attitudes of hostility and rebellion in their children toward teachers and the school program generally.

Such attitudes obviously are not conducive to the kinds of learning which result in school progress. Hence, the interaction between the pupil and his teachers is not likely to be pleasant and constructive. Baller and Charles (1961) described a striking example of this kind of teacher-pupil interaction:

> But there are other children in Miss Johnson's class whose patterns of behavior are constantly at variance with what the school approves and values. Tony, for example, seems to prefer copying the English papers of other pupils to preparing the

assignments for himself. When he is reproached for his indifferent school work or his aversion to doing the lessons on his own he gives Miss Johnson further cause for disappointment by explaining that he does not like English, he does not like school, and he does not hesitate to say in the presence of his teachers that he expects someday to make more money than "educated people" by working at his father's occupation; that his father manages to do all right on an eighth grade education. The stinger in Tony's remarks is his obvious disdain for much that the school stands for. His unyielding conviction that he knows a better way of life than that which the school proclaims is painful evidence to his teachers that they have lost a battle—a battle with a style of life that is much out of harmony with what they themselves believe in and what they try hard to get children to exhibit. (pp. 177–178)

Lower-class youngsters thus may become progressively more unhappy and discouraged, and the teacher's unfavorable attitude toward lower-class children and his judgment of their school ability become reinforced. In spite of the good intentions and the democratic ideals that characterize public school teachers generally, this tends to be perpetuated, and the social-class hierarchy continues to exist as a factor not to be discounted in the molding of personality.

Family Influences

The home environment has been an object of study and analysis for many years. In 1916, the Whittier Scale for grading home conditions was published (Williams, 1916). This scale and other early measurement efforts emphasized the material possessions, the physical equipment of the home. Gradually with time, more and more attention was given to variables that were psychological in nature. Stogdill (1936) was among the first to be concerned with the measurement of parental attitudes. MacFarlane's (1938) studies of parent personality and Champney's careful "armchair factor analysis" of parent behavior and attitude (1939a, 1939b, 1941) made significant contributions. Champney's study led to the construction of the Fels Parent-Behavior Rating Scales, which were an outstanding contribution to measurement technique.

Early studies of the home environment, as well as a number of later investigations yet to be discussed, were primarily concerned with interpersonal and other environmental influences upon emotional adjustments and personality development in children. Even though the Iowa studies and others had demonstrated the significance of the environmental factor in relation to cognitive development, students of home environment generally had not concerned themselves with its possible significance in relation to the cognitive aspect of development.

Present-day national involvement with such widespread social problems as ignorance, unequal educational opportunities, and school drop-outs have contributed to the development of a new orientation in the study of the family and its influences. The researcher's concern, for example, is no longer with the over-all relation between social class and intelligence ratings and educational achievement. These facts are pretty well established. The questions now are more specific and more searching. Specifically what aspects of lower-class living are responsible for the general retardation of cognitive development? Why specifically is it that lower-class children, who are apparently born with an average intellectual potentiality equal to that of children of the middle, and upper classes, enter the public schools at age 6 with a lower average level of educability, without the cognitive skills necessary for coping with first-grade work? And why does the gap in cognitive facility continue to *widen* with age?

EARLY FAMILY EXPERIENCE AND COGNITIVE DEVELOPMENT Recent research (see Chapters 7 and 9) has attempted to find answers to questions of environmental influences on the individual (Bernstein, 1961; R. D. Hess, 1964; R. D. Hess and Shipman, 1965).

Cognitive development, like any other aspect of development, results from the interaction between the child, with his particular capacity level, and an appropriate environment. Optimal cognitive development requires an optimal quality and level of cognitive stimulation. Because of the obviously great importance of verbal symbols in the process of concept formation and in information learning generally, it is logical to assume that optimal cognitive stimulation would be some sort of verbal interchange. Research results, as we have already seen, strongly suggest that the mode of verbal communication between a mother and her preschool child is vitally important to the development of the latter's cognitive structure and hence to his later educability in school.

The findings also clearly indicate that there are wide differences among families in style, quality, and elaborateness of verbal interchange between mother and young child. Further, there is a striking difference, in this respect, between lower-, or welfare-class, mothers and mothers of the middle stratum of society. Lower-class mothers more frequently use restricted styles of verbal communication with their children. "Restricted codes are nonspecific clichés, statements, or observations about events made in general terms that will be readily understood. The basic quality of this mode is to limit the range and detail of concept and information involved" (R. D. Hess and Shipman, 1965, p. 871).

Middle-status mothers, on the other hand, more frequently use what Bernstein called elaborated codes, "those in which communication is individualized and the message is specific to a particular situation, topic and person. It is more particular, more differentiated, and more precise. It permits expression of a wider and more complex range of thought, tending toward discrimination among cognitive and affective content" (R. D. Hess and Shipman, 1965, p. 871). As a summary statement Hess and Shipman wrote:

> The picture that is beginning to emerge is that the meaning of deprivation is a deprivation of meaning—a cognitive environment in which behavior is controlled by status rules rather than by attention to the individual characteristics of a specific situation and one in which behavior is not mediated by verbal cues or by teaching that relates events to one another and the present to the future. This environment produces a child who relates to authority rather than to rationale, who, although often compliant, is not reflective in his behavior, and for whom the consequences of an act are largely considered in terms of immediate punishment or reward rather than future effects and long-range goals. (1965, p. 885)

Research workers in this area see this lack of adequate cognitive stimulation in the verbal interchange between parent and child as the basic cause of low educability among lower-class children. They also see the solution to the problem of the "welfare class" not in terms of rehabilitation at the adult level but, rather, in the long-term process of education designed to raise the level of verbal interaction between parents and their young preschool children.

SOME FAMILY-LIFE PATTERNS AND THEIR RELATION TO TOTAL PERSONAL DEVELOPMENT   Continued work at Fels Research Institute with the use of Champney's (1939b) scales furnished evidence that there are certain common patterns, or "syndromes" (combinations of interaction characteristics) in terms of which families can be characterized, and that these patterns constitute some of the most crucial aspects of the family environment in relation to over-all personal development.

In 1945, A. L. Baldwin, Kalhorn, and Breeze reported a syndrome analysis of parent behavior ratings in which the rated variables were grouped into three main clusters (syndromes) (p. 14). These three syndromes, each with its cluster of rated parental attitude variables, are as follows:

1. **Democracy in the home**
   Justification of policy
   Democracy of policy
   Noncoerciveness of suggestions
   Readiness of explanation
   Direction of criticism (approval)
   Clarity of policy
   Understanding of the child
   Nonrestrictiveness of regulations
2. **Acceptance of child**
   Acceptance of child
   Rapport with the child
   Affectionateness toward child
   Direction of criticism (approval)
   Effectiveness of policy
   Child-centeredness of the home
   Nondisciplinary friction
3. **Indulgence**
   General protectiveness
   General babying
   Child-centeredness of the home
   Acceptance of the child
   Solicitousness for welfare
   Duration of contact with mother
   Intensity of contact with mother

In the words of the investigators, "these syndromes are thought of as patterns of variables about which parent behavior may be organized and which reflect underlying emotional attitudes, philosophies or personality traits" (A. L. Baldwin, Kalhorn, and Breeze, 1945, pp. 14–15). Each syndrome was regarded as a dimension of family inter- action. A given family, therefore, may occupy any position on the continuum. Thus the uniqueness of any family situation might be reflected in the pattern or combination of positions on these three continua.

This syndrome analysis of Champney's parent behavior variables was a careful but informal and nonrigorous classification of the varia- bles in terms of their intercorrelations. Somewhat later, Roff (1949) made a factorial study of the same table of intercorrelations. The analysis yielded seven factors. Roff interpreted and labeled them as follows:

I. Concern for child
II. Democratic guidance
III. Permissiveness
IV. Parent-child harmony
V. Sociability-adjustment of parents
VI. Activeness of the home
VII. Nonreadiness of suggestion

With the exception of Factors V and VI, Roff's factors clearly involve parent-child relationships. Factor II, "democratic guidance," corresponds quite closely to the "democracy-in-the-home" syndrome of Baldwin *et al.* One item of that syndrome, "readiness of explanation," however, turned out to be the defining variable of Roff's Factor VII. Factor IV, "parent-child harmony," corresponds quite closely in variable content with Syndrome 2, "acceptance of child," while the content of Factor I, "concern for child," includes all the items of Syndrome 3, "indulgence," with the exception the "intensity of contact" item. Thus, it may be said that, in general, the factor analysis was a validation of the earlier syndrome analysis, with some regrouping and redefinition of variables. Roff regarded his Factors V and VI as referring "to characteristics of the parents without specific reference to the children" (p. 42).

In an earlier study, the reactions of teenage children to questions regarding their home situations were analyzed. Four quite distinct common patterns of family life were revealed (Stott, 1939). This study involved groups of youngsters, over 1800 in all, representing three different home settings: the urban setting, the small Midwestern town, and the farm in the open country. The questionnaire to which the youngsters responded included questions about the amount of recreation the family enjoyed both outside and in the home, expressions of affection in their relationships with their parents, the extent to which they confided in their parents, their feelings about the personal characteristics and habits—personal and social—of their parents, the health, both physical and emotional, of their parents, and the recency of parental punishment.

The responses of the three residence groups were analyzed separately by means of factor analysis. The outcome of the analysis, in each case, was a number of clusters of questionnaire items (factors), which were interpreted as family life patterns, each distinct and different from the others. Each factor could also be interpreted as representing a particular type of family environment.

A finding of interest was the fact that essentially the same factors came out of all three analyses. The following summary statement is found in the report:

Although there were differences in the corresponding total environmental, or family behavior patterns among the three general home settings, they were in most cases so similar that the same descriptive designations fit all equally well. . . . The same characteristic patterns tended to appear repeatedly when entirely different populations were used, even though each population represented quite a different general home setting and a somewhat different cultural background.

These (common factors) were (1) a pattern of intra-familial relationships which is characterized by "confidence affection and companionability," (2) a somewhat related, but less inclusive family behavior pattern of "congeniality," (3) a factor involving family discord or perhaps parental misconduct, which predisposes the adolescent child to offer criticism of his parents' behavior, which includes frequent punishment of the child in the home, and (4) a "nervous tension" factor, "nervousness," or something which the child interprets as nervousness on the part of the parents, and usually such other items as illness of parents and infrequent demonstrations of affection. (Stott, 1939, p. 156)

This investigation also showed significant relationships between family pattern and the personality adjustments of the children. For example, "self-reliance" in the sense of being independent in working

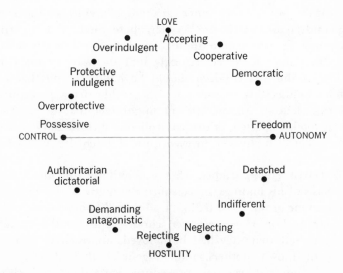

Figure 13.2

E. S. Schaefer's (1959) circumplex model for maternal behavior.

through personal difficulties and problems was associated to a significant degree with the family pattern of "confidence, affection, and companionability" in all three residence groups. A measure of "personal adjustment" bore a similarly significant relationship with that same family life factor.

More recently E. S. Schaefer (1959, 1961) used factor analysis in his study particularly of maternal attitude and behavior material. The outcome of his analyses was the suggestion that the many variables of maternal behavior can be brought into the framework of two main factors. These factors, again, are regarded as dimensions, or continua. They were interpreted as love-hostility and control-autonomy. Figure 13.2 is based on a model developed by Schaefer, which summarized his findings.

Parental Attitudes and Behavior

Young married couples usually approach parenthood with rather definite ideas about how children should be cared for and reared. Husbands and wives, however, do not always agree on such matters, and, in many instances they find themselves in the midst of the process of child rearing before their differences have been resolved. Such adjustment problems are not easily resolved because child-rearing attitudes tend to be rather firmly fixed.

ATTITUDES TOWARD CHILD REARING   Parent's attitudes about raising children are determined very largely by the kind of up-bringing they themselves experienced in their parental homes. In many instances, the parent feels very strongly that the way he was handled as a child is the way children should be handled, and that parent sets about deliberately to carry out the child-rearing procedures he or she experienced. Another parent might feel that he or she was misunderstood, neglected, or overcontrolled as a child and deliberately rear his or her own children in ways quite different from personal experiences.

I. D. Harris (1959), studied school-age children and their mothers. On the basis of his findings, he classified the mothers into three broad groupings. One group consisted of "traditional" mothers, because they had determined to rear their own children just as they had been reared; they felt that they had been loved, appreciated, and understood by their own mothers, and, in general, their desires were to follow the same patterns and procedures with their own children. Other mothers in Harris' study felt cheated because their own mothers had failed to satisfy their needs for warmth, love, and affection. This group consisted of "dependent" mothers because, as adults, they were still unconsciously seeking for fulfillment of their own needs, often to the detriment of their children. They generally had unhappy memories of their own childhood experiences and therefore determined to rear their children differently and to give them an abundance of love and affection. Some of these mothers apparently were able to carry out their determined course of action while others were not able to do so, actually following the same patterns they themselves experienced as children.

The third class of mothers were those who were also unhappy with their own upbringing but for a different reason. They felt that they had not been "understood" as individuals. They had been restricted and controlled too closely by their own mothers. This group consisted of the "rebellious" mothers. As a group, they resolved to be less restrictive and domineering with their children, but, like the dependent mothers, they were able to carry through with their resolve, in some instances while others were not able to do so, but tended to follow the familiar patterns of their own mothers, even though they consciously disliked them and rebelled against them.

Harris' findings generally support the conclusion that parents do have rather strong convictions about how children should be reared, and that these convictions arise largely from positive or negative reactions to their own childhood experiences. The further indication is that parents are not always able to function in relation to their own children in ways that are consistent with their current convictions. They often revert to patterns which they rationally have repudiated, but which nevertheless they identify with as part of their own past. At any rate, parents generally, and with varying degrees of success, set out to bring up their children according to their own feelings and beliefs as to what is appropriate behavior for children in the family setting, in public, at school, and in other areas of life. They pass on to their children their own attitudes, prejudices, and beliefs in their efforts to fashion their children in their own images of what an acceptable member of society should be like.

Emotional Behavior Dispositions in Parents

Certain parental dispositions have much to do specifically with the quality of parental behavior and thus with the particular human environment provided for the children. In the various analyses of parental attitudes and behavior which we have examined, two variables *invariably* appeared in one guise or another: (1) the disposition, or capacity to love; (2) the disposition to dominate and control, ranging from complete domination to complete relinquishment of authority and control. These two personality variables are important factors at all levels of human relationships, and, since relationships within the family by their very nature are peculiarly personal and intimate, they are of crucial importance as factors in the young child's environment.

PARENTAL LOVE Authoritative writers of the past fifty years have not always been in agreement concerning the matter of parental love. Perhaps in no other area in the study of child nature and parent-child relationships has professional thinking differed more sharply or changed more radically. Freud, in his earlier writings (1913), contended that too much "parental tenderness" spoils the child and causes difficulty for him in later life when he must be satisfied with lesser amounts of love. A few years later the American behaviorist-psychologist J. B. Watson much more strongly expressed the same point of view. In his book (1928), written specifically for parents, he devoted a full chapter to the dangers of too much mother love. Among his pronouncements were the following:

> All too soon the child gets shot through with too many of these love reactions. In addition, the child gets honeycombed with love responses for the nurse, for the father, and for any other constant attendant who fondles it. Love reactions soon dominate the child. . . . In conclusion won't you then remember when you are tempted to pet your child that mother love is a dangerous instrument? An instrument which may inflict a never healing wound, a wound which may make infancy unhappy, adolescence a nightmare, an instrument which may wreck your adult son or daughter's vocational future and their chances for marital happiness. (p. 87)

During the decade or two following Watson's manual, the pendulum of expert opinion swung to the other extreme in relation to infant care (Ribble, 1943; Spitz, 1945, 1946). A number of writers have been equally forceful in stressing the child's need for parental love and its crucial importance in the emotional development of young children.

Margaret Ribble, one of the most ardent believers in the importance of a close mother-infant relationship, stated that "invariably the child who is deprived of individual mothering shows disordered behavior, with a compensatory retardation in general alertness" (1943, p. 82).

QUALITATIVE DIFFERENCES IN PARENTAL ACCEPTANCE   Parents "accept" and love their children in widely varying degrees and also with different sorts of motivation. To rephrase, parental acceptance varies not only in the degree to which it is manifest in outward behavior but also in quality. A mother might exhibit great concern for the welfare of her child. She might "fuss" over him, insist on extreme, or unusual precautionary measures to insure his safety. She might worry a great deal about him when he is out of her sight and in other ways express in her overt behavior what appears to be great love for him, while in reality, and probably completely unconsciously, her basic feeling toward the child may be one of profound rejection. Her overacceptance, her exaggerated expressions of love and concern for him, may be unconscious compensation for or protection against her basic rejection and lack of genuine love for him (Symonds, 1939).

Pseudoacceptance of a child in some instances may be exploitative due to emotional immaturity in the parent. The manifest "love" is not genuine love for the child but rather an exploitation of the child in unconscious self-seeking efforts on the parents' part to obtain gratification of unmet emotional needs (I. D. Harris, 1959). The overt behavior of parents in relation to their children, in most instances, however, probably truly expresses, in varying degrees, genuine acceptance and feelings of love on the one hand or frank rejection on the other.

Individuals, as they become parents, do differ rather widely in the capacity and disposition to love and accept their children (Porter, 1955; Sloman, 1948; von Maring, 1955). Evidence also indicates that this capacity is determined to a large extent by the quality of the parents' own family experiences as children.

PARENTAL DOMINATION   The other personality variable in parents, which perhaps has most to do with the quality of parent-child interaction, is the tendency, or need, to dominate. When this tendency is strong, it is rooted in the individual's own early childhood experiences and is likely to remain throughout life as a fundamental personality characteristic. In a person thus strongly disposed, to be the dominant one, to be "boss," and always to be right, are, to him, vital sources of inner security. Domination is not to be understanding of another's feelings or opinions. As a parent, the dominating personality is not likely to be sensitive to his child's individual needs or to have much sympathetic understanding of childish idiosyncrasies. Parents vary widely with respect to this variable, also, from complete domination and strict and rigid control to overpermissiveness and even complete relinquishment of control.

Parental Dispositions
toward Child Care and Handling

Since parents differ widely in degree and quality of acceptance and in tendency to dominate as they interact with their children, each of these variables, as indicated earlier, may be thought of as a continuous variable, or a dimension of parental attitude. In recent research studies, the factor-analysis approach was used to demonstrate the fact that these two parental attitudes vary independently of each other (Becker *et al.*, 1959; Schaefer, 1959).

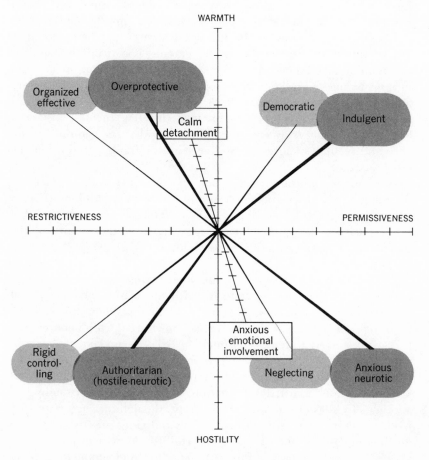

Figure 13.3

Becker's (Becker et al., 1959) hypothetical model of parental behavior, by permission.

Becker and associates (1959), on the basis of a number of factor-analysis studies, presented an alternative model in which the control variable is subdivided. Figure 13.3 shows Becker's hypothetical model. In a discussion of this figure and its interpretation, Becker (1964) wrote that they had attempted to show, "how the various concepts referring to types of parents fit into the model and point to the need for the third dimension to encompass important distinctions" (p. 174).

PATTERNS OF PARENTAL BEHAVIOR   The "love" variable, as manifested in parental behavior, may be regarded as ranging from an unwholesome, overpowering, "smothering" kind of oversolicitousness, at the one extreme, to a complete lack of any show of love, utter and frank rejection, at the other. Adequate, dependable, and wholesome love and affection fall near the center of the continuum. Likewise,

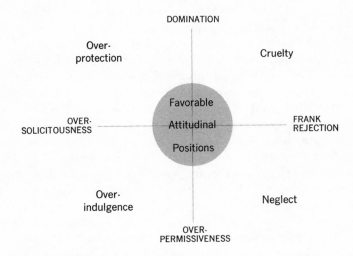

Figure 13.4

Possible combinations of, and relationships between, the domination-permissiveness and the love-rejection dimensions of parental attitude, with suggested outcomes in terms of treatment of the child.

the domination continuum would range from rigid domination and strict and unyielding control, at one extreme, to overpermissiveness and complete relinquishment of authority, at the other. Figure 13.4 is a hypothetical representation of these two dimensions of parental disposition in relation to each other.[1] The area in each quadrant of

---

[1] P. M. Symonds in an early study (1939) represented these two parental "attitude" continua and described their various combinations and some of the probable outcomes in terms of child adjustment and behavior.

this figure as in Becker's model, may be taken to represent the various possible combinations and degrees of that particular relationship. For example, oversolicitousness may be combined with domination. In the upper-left quadrant can be plotted any degree of each in relation to the other. Or, oversolicitousness might be combined with over-permissiveness in various combinations of degrees as represented by the upper-right quadrant. The area which might be described by a circle at the center of the figure represents the most desirable positions on both continua, the positions that would be occupied by the "warmly dependable" and "understanding" mother as described by I. D. Harris (1959). These mothers would give their babies abundantly adequate wholesome love, and they would neither rigidly dominate and control them nor be overpermissive but would be understanding of the children's individual needs, giving them freedom within carefully defined limits and positive guidance as they came to need it.

As is indicated in Figure 13.4, too much domination combined with oversolicitousness might be expressed in overprotective behavior toward the child, but when strong domination is combined with rejection the most likely result is cruel treatment. On the other hand, overpermissiveness and the relinquishment of control combined with oversolicitousness would mean overindulgence, while the combination of no control with frank rejection would mean complete indifference and neglect.

There are many other ways in which these dispositions toward feeling and behavior might combine in the make-up of individual parents. A hovering, "smothering" mother for example, who compulsively overwhelms her child with love, conceivably might be neither domineering nor overpermissive. It is likewise quite possible that a parent who cares not at all for her child and frankly shows her lack of feeling for him in her behavior might also occupy a middle ground on the domination versus overpermissiveness continuum.

These descriptions of the parent-child situation, of course, are oversimplifications. Normally there are two parents, each with a different pattern of attitudes and behavior dispositions in relation to others. They are not likely, therefore, to react to their children with the same quality and intensity of feeling. Both father and mother might love the child, but the *quality* of that love and its *expression* might be quite different. (One might be inclined to dominate while the other might be on the side of permissiveness.) The number and variety of interaction patterns that might develop within the triad— father, mother, and child—are indeed many. For a child to be overindulged or neglected, overprotected or treated cruelly by a mother or a father, may be deeply disturbing to him. But, in each case, the effect might be softened and partially compensated for by more healthy and constructive relationships with the other parent, or with other significant persons in his life. The interpersonal aspect of the family environment is extremely complex and variable.

Children's Incidental Learning

During the so-called socialization period children generally do learn the things their parents set out to inculcate in them. They learn good table manners. They readily acquire the habits of social behavior, the attitudes and patterns of thinking that are regarded as acceptable by their parents and in the particular subculture, the community, the social class, the religious tradition in which they live and develop. These learnings—inculcated patterns of behaving, of social interaction, attitudes, prejudices, and beliefs—all become integrated and patterned uniquely in relation to the child's individual temperamental nature and thus constitute the "surface" aspects of his personality.

But as was noted in Chapter 11, other learning occurs during this early period of socialization. All the while, the child is reacting affectively to parental persuasions and pressures, to the domination, the rewards, and punishments he is experiencing. There is much emotional interaction between the child and his parents as he identifies with or rejects the models before him, as he experiences the satisfactions and frustrations arising from his parents' socializing efforts. These affective experiences, because of the very nature of the situations giving rise to them, are sometimes positive and pleasant, sometimes quite unpleasant. The resulting incidental learning is most important because it is basic and persisting in personality formation. It is psychogenic rather than sociogenic[2] in nature.

These parental dispositions to love, to accept, and respect, to "pressure," to reject, to grant freedom, to control and restrict, to protect, to indulge, to deny, are among the more important of the many variables that determine the quality of the home environment. A truly constructive home environment involves positive parental guidance and teaching. This teaching, moreover, must be more than telling. It must present a parental model of democratic procedures. If the parent is to create an atmosphere of mutual acceptance and respect, he must himself provide the model. One basic principle in the establishment of constructive and satisfying human relationships in the home is a mutual respect for one another's dignity. Parents who fail to respect the child as a person in his own right at all levels of his development will humiliate him, enslave or exploit him, frustrate or

---

[2] See Burgess and Locke (1945, pp. 209–272) for a fuller discussion of these two factors in personality development.

overprotect him. The child, in turn, will react with disrespect toward the parent. If the parent is generally anxious and tense, tenseness is likely to characterize the family atmosphere. If the parents set the model of empathic understanding and closeness of relationships, that likewise will tend to become a common pattern in the family's inter-actions and be felt in the atmosphere of the home. Avoiding the evils of authoritarism and domination, then, is much more than the granting of complete freedom.

Outside Influences and the Family Environment

Parents generally are concerned about the welfare of their children and are conscientiously striving to provide the best possible environ-ment for them. One area of concern for some parents in their efforts to raise their children according to their own standards is the dis-crepancy between what they regard as appropriate patterns of personal and social behavior and what society commonly encourages and accepts. While the children are small and are largely confined within the limits of parental influence and teaching, the inculcation process is relatively smooth. But, as the child begins to move into the neighbor-hood and the larger community, other authority figures with their particular inculcating influences enter his life. Sometimes certain con-flicts of influence very early begin to manifest themselves in the child's home behavior.

Parental Neglect

As children emerge from the close confines of the home into the neighborhood and larger community, parents sometimes become dis-turbed by out-of-home influences to which their children are daily exposed. They see patterns of behavior which are common among the children of the neighborhood, but which, from their point of view, are outside the bounds of propriety. The lack of respect for authority, impudence, and overbrashness, and predelinquent gang activity are common neighborhood patterns.

Much of this disturbing behavior, as has been suggested at other points in our discussion, is an outcome of the neglect of parents, of the all-too-prevalent tendency to exercise, from the beginning, too little *or no* control over children and the failure to give them positive guidance. This sort of neglect is often based on the ill-advised pretext that children, for their optimal development, should be allowed freedom to express themselves without restraint. Such extreme beliefs have arisen generally from misinterpretations of concepts and principles advanced by authorities in the field of human behavior and development. The principles of acceptance and freedom, for example, with only partial understanding, have frequently given rise to patterns of extreme overpermissiveness. The notion that children must have complete and unhampered freedom of expression becomes a comfortable rationalization for the easy-going relinquishment of parental control or an unconscious compensation for a basic lack of real concern for the children's welfare.

Fredom within consistently maintained limits, which are carefully drawn and guided by the child's changing level of development, is essential to continued optimal development. The lack of parental control and guidance, on the other hand, can be a source of personal insecurity and unfortunate behavioral development in children.

In children of elementary school age, the effects of overpermissive and neglectful handling may be nothing more serious than intrusiveness, impudence, brashness, or a tendency to be overdemanding and selfish. Depending upon their temperamental natures, some children may not exhibit any particularly objectionable behavior. On the other hand, a serious lack of a feeling of personal security or a lack of a sense of direction or purpose or a need for definition of limits often develops. Such feelings may be expressed in moodiness, emotional instability, overactivity, the tendency to initiate disturbances in school, or hostility and aggression toward other children. More serious consequences may develop at later ages.

Neighborhood Influences and Social Development

The general level of parents' understanding, their attitudes, and their concern about the healthy total development of their children have much to do with social trends that are always underway. A subtle kind of exploitation of children sometimes arises in a community from certain unconscious needs of the parents. They take pride in and derive satisfaction from identifying with their children in certain forms of precocious social behavior and development. Children are pushed and perhaps overstimulated, rather than "paced," in their social development. For example, formal parties for preadolescent children, with all the adult trappings become common in some communities when, on the part of the children themselves, there could be only an artificially stimulated interest rather than a natural one at their particular level of maturation. Children are stimulated and encouraged to ape adult social behavior when they, by natural inclination, would be enjoying activities appropriate to their level of development. The public schools often play a powerful part also in encouraging this kind of trend. For healthy development, and with concern for their later satisfactions and enjoyment of life, children should be paced in their development and guided in their social activities.

A research project in which Torgoff (1960, 1961) is currently engaged is concerned with the problem of parental "pushing" versus granting freedom and independence. He conceives of these two tendencies in parents as independent variables (not as opposite ends of a single continuum), but he is particularly interested in the strength of each in relation to the other. Torgoff's A/I ratio is the ratio between the "achievement-inducing" and the "independence-granting" tendencies. Results, so far, indicate that this ratio is a more powerful factor of influence than either of the two variables considered by itself. "We have found, for instance, that the degree of obedience that middle-class parents obtain from their children, relates to the parent's A/I ratio rather than to either A or I separately" (Torgoff and Dreyer, 1961, p. 1). The stronger the parent's tendency to push in relation to his tendency to encourage autonomy, the stronger the child's tendency to strive for achievement. From these findings, one might assume, then, that the more a mother pushes her daughter in the direction of adult patterns of social behavior and dress, the stronger will be the daughter's striving to ape adult patterns prematurely and to set patterns of striving for the neighborhood.

Summary

In this chapter we have been concerned with the child's "original" nature and with his developmental milieu. His genes give him inherent individuality but the environment in which he develops is an extremely important factor in determining the outcome. At every point in the course of his development he interacts with his environment, and the nature of that interaction determines the nature and direction of change in his psychological development. The cultural factors into which he enters—racial or ethnic origin, regional location, social class, economic level, religious affiliation of his family—in combination, and each with its relative weight and importance, constitutes his broader developmental milieu and leaves its identifying marks upon him.

The most important factor of all, in influencing the child's personal development, is the predominating quality of his family relationships, particularly as they develop during the period of his socialization. In this connection, the personality of the parents, their attitudes and emotional behavior dispositions, and the climate of the home environment are crucial factors.

SELECTED READING SUGGESTIONS

Fuller, J. L., and W. R. Thompson. *Behavior genetics.* New York: Wiley, 1960.

Hoffman, M. L., and Lois W. Hoffman (eds.). *Review of child development research.* New York: Russell Sage Foundation, 1964. (The major portion of this volume deals with the factor of environment. Especially pertinent are: Caldwell, The effects of infant care; Yarrow, Separation from parents during early childhood; Becker, Consequences of different kinds of parental discipline; Swift, Effects of early group experience: the nursery school and day nursery; and Maccoby, Effects of mass media. One article deals specifically with the heredity factor: McClearn, Genetics and behavior development.)

Kluckhohn, C. *Mirror for man.* New York: McGraw-Hill, 1949.

Montagu, A. *Human heredity.* Second ed.; Cleveland: World Publishing, 1963.

Penrose, L. S. (ed.). *Recent advances in human genetics.* Boston: Little, Brown, 1960.

CHAPTER 14

Appraising
the Family in Its
"Nature and Nurture"
Functions

The family "stock" sets the hereditary limits of individual development as well as the basic patterns of biological response to and interaction with the environment. The situation into which every child is
born is a unique combination of behaving and interacting persons.
Their immediate reactions and their developing feelings and attitudes
toward him and toward one another probably constitute the most
effective environmental determiner of the direction and course of
developmental progress for that child. Since the family consists of
individuals, each of whom is undergoing developmental changes, and
since the external conditions and circumstances of living are constantly

in flux, the interpersonal relationships within the family group necessarily also change in important ways.

Patterns of interaction change because of the interaction process itself. Thus, the family as a group may be thought of as progressing along a course of development analogous to that traversed by the individual. The family is, then, a dynamic, constantly changing source of stimulation and sustenance to individual growth and development. The life processes of growth, maturation, and learning that are constantly under way within the individual are, to a great extent, dependent upon the character of the interaction processes within the other family members. At the same time, the quality of family interaction is equally dependent upon the qualities possessed by the individual family members, the levels of development they have achieved, and what is going on within them.

Accordingly, in order to understand an individual child or to account at all adequately for the course of his development, we must know something of the family group of which he is a member, of its characteristic growth trends, its composition, the circumstances under which it operates, and the changing interaction patterns and relationships that characterize it.

These developmental changes in a family, like those that take place in an individual, can be appraised only by means of a series of "stills" that are studied in relation to one another. We must study status at definite points in the family developmental cycle as if the processes involved were halted temporarily for that purpose. Then, on the basis of momentary views of the family or of its functioning, we must infer the nature of the processes under way and evaluate change over a period of time.

It is our purpose in this final chapter to consider the problem of appraising, in a particular family (Family 695), some of its features and characteristics which influence, in various and unique ways, the development of its individual members.

One of our main objectives is to consider possible ways of appraising the family environment. Certain methods and graphic devices for providing "stills" as well as "continuous" records of developmental progress will be presented as possible helps in examining and evaluating certain of the many aspects of living and of relationships within any family with which one is well acquainted.

Family Growth Trends and Characteristics

When the necessary records are available, it is often possible to note in them family characteristics and trends in development that suggest a hereditary influence. As explained in Chapter 13, the mechanism of biological heredity insures individual uniqueness. It provides that, with the exception of monozygotic twins, every individual child of a given family, in his over-all pattern of genetic attributes, will be different. However, since each child of that family comes from the same "genetic stream," similarities in developmental trends are also more likely to occur within the family than among individuals taken at random outside the family.

Two-Generation Growth Patterns

In order to note any such inherent trends in development, two-generation family development records are necessary. Such records are not available for Family 695. For our present purpose, therefore, we shall examine certain of the data from the record of Family 724 which does contain two-generation material.

The mother of this family was enrolled by her parents in the nursery school when she was 33 months of age. She remained regularly enrolled in the program to the age of 10 years 6 months. Her record of physical measurements and psychological tests thus covers a period of approximately 8 years. Some 15 years after the mother's record terminated, her two daughters, B and J, at early preschool ages, were entered into the same research series by their mother. Their developmental records, therefore, are directly comparable, age for age, to those of their mother.

Figure 14.1 (A, B, C, and D) shows graphically four sets of these mother-daughter records plotted in terms of developmental ages. A number of interesting family growth trends are suggested in these curves. Perhaps most striking is the similarity in over-all pattern, and in the characteristic course these curves assume. Even though daughter B was taller, heavier, and "more advanced" in skeletal maturation than were her mother and sister at equivalent ages, the three curves in each set correspond remarkably closely in shape and pattern.

It will be recalled that when development is plotted in terms of age equivalents (see Chapters 1, 2, and 3), the extent to which the child has maintained his relative growth status is clearly apparent in the curve. If, for example, a child's rate of growth in height, in relation to the average, is maintained, the ratio between his increasing age and his increasing height (his DQ in height) will, within normal fluctuations, remain relatively constant. This will show in the graph as a generally straight line. If his rate of growth is faster or slower than the average, and if this trend is maintained, his curve will diverge upward or downward more and more in absolute distance from the diagonal, or average (standard of reference), line. Loss in relative rate

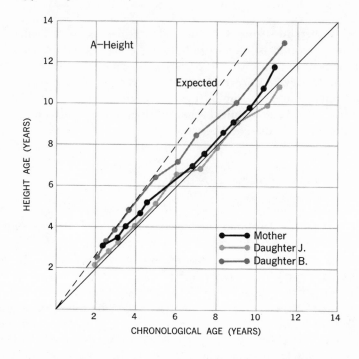

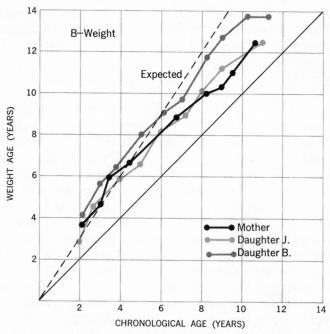

Figure 14.1

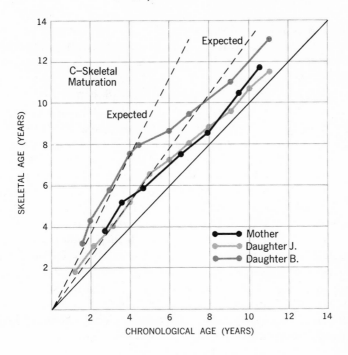

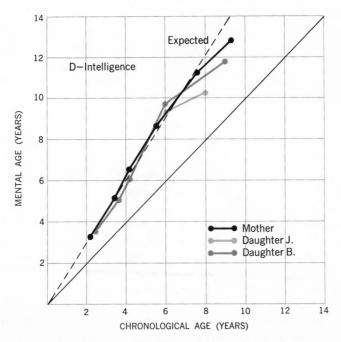

Height (A), weight (B), skeletal maturation (C), and intelligence test (D) records of Mother 724 and her two daughters J and B plotted in terms of developmental ages.

of progress, however, even though he may still remain above the average, will appear in the plotting as a bend downward toward the standard of reference and will tend to take a course more nearly parallel to the diagonal.

The characteristic growth pattern for Family 724 is particularly interesting in this respect. Their developmental curves, with the exception of those of height for mother and daughter J (see Figure 14.1A) represent rather substantial positive deviations from the average. But these curves rather consistently do not assume the "expected," proportional, or straight-line deviation. Rather, they tend to take a course generally above, but parallel to, the diagonal. In the case of skeletal maturation particularly, they even tend slightly to bend downward (see Figure 14.1C). This means, of course, that the accelerated rates of growth and maturation with which these children began were only partially maintained. Even in the mental development curves, which take a course more nearly according to general expectations, there is some decrease in ratio (IQ), particularly at the older ages (see Figure 14.1D). This, then, suggests a family developmental trend which may have been genetically influenced. In these four graphs note the straight dashed lines, which indicate the generally expected courses of "curves" that begin at accelerated rates.

Daughter B, throughout the course of her development, was taller, considerably heavier, and more advanced in bone maturation than were her mother and her sister at equivalent ages, but the shape and the course of their growth curves are remarkably similar. Other family trends portrayed in these graphs are tendencies toward larger and stockier-than-average physiques, accelerated maturation, and superior intelligence.

There are also some suggestions of genetically influenced trends in the data on Family 695. Wetzel Grid physique ratings of the paternal family line for three generations of men place them all in the more "stocky" physique channels. According to information furnished by Mr. 695, his father weighed 160 pounds and was 66 inches tall. This placed him in the A4 physique channel. Mr. 695, when these comparative data were collected, weighed 130 pounds and was 64 inches tall, placing him in channel A3. At that point in time (at age 6 years 6 months), Paul weighed 52.8 pounds and was 46.2 inches tall. This placed him in the upper portion of channel A2.

Physique ratings of the maternal line likewise suggest a familial growth trend. Again, according to available data, both of Mrs. 695's parents had physique ratings in channel A1, which is also her own physique rating. Sally's rating at age 6½ years placed her in the adjacent channel M. However, at age 14 years 2 months, her height-weight relationship placed her also in channel A1. Heredity, while it insures individual uniqueness, also perpetuates family similarities.

Environmental Factors of Growth and Health

The ways in which the home and the family might influence the development of children, of course, are so numerous and varied as to defy any attempt at complete listing and classification. These family environmental factors obviously vary in importance. For purposes of study they can be divided roughly into two classes. Some factors are more in the nature of family functions. Families vary in the extent to which the parents are aware of and are actually able and inclined to assume their responsibilities for providing the common essentials for health, growth, and personal development of family members. Other influences are of quite a different order. These include such variables as the composition, physical and social nature, and the cultural backgrounds of the family itself. Families differ structurally, for instance, in number of members, and in sex, and in age distributions of children. They also differ in physical facilities to be found in the home, in general educational level and in the adequacy of intellectual and cultural stimulation. We shall now consider the ever-changing situation of Family 695 and attempt to appraise it in relation to these two classes of family environmental factors.

Nutrition and Family Feeding

The important role of the family in providing the conditions for interchange between the developing organism and the environment has been mentioned. Food and feeding procedures in relation to the health and growth of the child are an outstanding example of such interchange. Nutrition is usually not thought of as a "family-life" topic, but certainly the adequacy or inadequacy of the food intake of a growing child depends directly, and in most cases completely, upon the family.

The problem of healthful nutrition in the family setting, however, is not a simple one. Obviously a basic obligation of the family is to provide the necessary foods in sufficient quantities and in forms suitable to the child's needs and to his ability to manage them (Rand, Sweeny, and Vincent, 1953). But another equally important family obligation is the transmission of food attitudes, preferences, and healthful dietary habits.

Moreover, the degree to which family mealtime generally is a time of relaxed and enjoyable experience, one that fosters emotional and social development and constructive family interaction and relationships, also depends upon the parents and the atmosphere they are able to establish in the feeding or eating situation.

GUIDES FOR NUTRITIONAL ADEQUACY   Nutrition has been an active research field for more than a half century. Attention has naturally centered upon the physiological and chemical aspects of the problem of determining the kinds and amounts of nutrients which would allow for the expression of optimum growth potential in children, and promote physical health and well-being in both children and adults.

The Food and Nutrition Board (1964) of the National Academy of Science and the National Research Council publishes a set of recommended dietary allowances. These allowances, first published in 1943, are revised every five years to allow for interpretations of current research findings. Allowances have been developed to be used as a guide in planning diets that will provide the kinds and amounts of nutrients needed for growth and other normal environmental stresses for groups of people.

The popular application of this research information has led to the classification of common foods into the so-called basic food groups. This device has served to simplify the problem of adequate feeding for the family, since a proper selection of food from each of the "basic four" provides the essentials of an adequate diet. In addition, many other guides to feeding children—nutritional charts, and the like— have been developed to suggest amounts of each of the basic food groups required by growing children and by adults to fulfill optimum daily nutritional requirements.

A guide with a more specific application to the caloric needs of the individual child as related to his rate of growth is included as an important feature of the Wetzel Grid. This device is described in some detail in Chapter 2 (see Figure 2.7). The individual child's weight and height are entered directly on the Grid, the relationship thus determining his present developmental level (body size). Then by following through on that level to the appropriate basal metabolism scale printed on the extreme right-hand margin of the Grid form, the child's basal metabolic needs for one day, in terms of calories, can be read directly. His approximate total caloric need for optimum growth and normal activity for the day would be *double* his basal metabolic needs, as read on the scale. The Grid form provides a separate scale for boys and for girls.

To illustrate this use of the Grid, when Paul was 6 years 3 months of age, his weight of 51 pounds and his height of 45.3 inches placed him at developmental level 55 on the Wetzel Grid. That level on the basal metabolism scale for boys is 1025 calories. Paul's total daily caloric need at that point in his life, therefore, was twice 1025, or 2050 calories.

A check on this Grid estimate may be made by referring to the table of allowances of the Food and Nutrition Board (1964, p. vii). According to those allowances, a child between ages 6 years and 9 years weighing 53 pounds and measuring 49 inches in height would require approximately 2100 calories. The difference between these two estimates is, of course, insignificant. The advantage of the Grid method is that it applies directly to the individual child.

APPRAISING THE FAMILY FEEDING FUNCTION   Guides to healthful nutritional requirements can be very helpful to the mother who wishes to maintain optimally healthy family food intake. However, in order to use these standards in the appraisal of a family's performance of its feeding function over a period of time, precise records of the food intake, both qualitative and quantitative, of each family member would be required.

Perhaps the simplest evidence of healthful family eating consists of the growth records of the individual children. In the absence of severe illness or other serious environmental vicissitudes, any interruption or significant departure from the normal course of a child's physical developmental progress is most likely to be a result of nutritional imbalance or inadequacy. As Wetzel (1943b) pointed out, the effects of malnutrition may actually be detected in an adequate appraisal of the child's growth progress "from two to five years before the clinical picture itself becomes sufficiently manifest to cause a child to be referred for treatment" (p. 209). A child's status and progress in physical growth thus may provide the most sensitive screening device for detecting nutritional imbalance or inadequate diet.

From his use of the Grid, Wetzel arrived at a general rule for differentiating between satisfactory and unsatisfactory growth. Healthy progress in a child, when plotted on the Grid, according to this rule, tends to follow along the channel of his particular body type, maintaining his specific time schedule and with preservation of his natural physique. On the other hand, the evidence for malnutrition consists of (1) a "loss" in physique as indicated by an off-channel shift of the curve downward (to the right) in the channel system, and (2) the appearance of a growth lag—the child's failure to keep up with his established schedule of progress in terms of units of body size (isodevelopmental levels) attained during a given interval of time.

The angle of departure from the normal up-channel course is called nutritional grade. "Maximum allowable departure" in healthy growth, according to Wetzel, is "—8° from the optimal gradient as represented by the pitch of the channel system." This amounts to approximately one-half channel shift in 10 developmental-level (body-size) units of advancement. Both the loss in physique (change in the direction of slenderness) and lag in rate of increase in over-all size affect this angle of departure (nutritional grade).

A rescanning of the Grid records of Paul and Sally (see Figure 2.7) reveals in each case a fairly regular up-channel course. There are no indications of serious growth lag. Neither are there any sudden, significant losses or changes in physique that suggest malnutrition. From these records we may conclude that the family of these children adequately performed its feeding function.

Provisions for Healthful Activity, Sleep, and Rest

The child is also dependent upon his parents and his home for healthful and stimulating activity and for rest and sleep. The kind and amounts needed vary with age and with the individual child. The parents' problem is to be alert to the signs that signify the individual child's varying and growing needs and to make as adequate provision as possible in the way of necessary space and facilities.

In relation to sleep and rest, as is true with eating, the cues can usually be taken from the child himself. Under favorable conditions a child will usually get the amount of sleep necessary for him.

The parents of Paul and Sally, from the beginning, took quite seriously their responsibility to provide conditions favorable for their children's development. The home always gave the impression of warmth and happiness. "Even though the rooms are small, there is adequate space. There is a nice backyard for outdoor play" (a student's home-visit report).

By the time the twins were 6 years old the family had moved three times, each time to a house with more space that could be adapted to their growing family needs. In this last home, the children had separate rooms. Each room was decorated with respect to the wishes of the occupant.

Play materials and equipment, for both outdoor and indoor play and wisely adapted to the developmental level and interests of the children, were adequately provided. Books and creative materials were always in abundance.

Figure 14.2 presents a set of subjective "ratings" of the 695 home in terms of its adequacy in providing for the recreational activities, intellectual and cultural stimulation, and the sleep and rest needs of the children. The ratings are based on home-visit observational reports. The visits were made mainly during the first 8 years of the twins' lives.

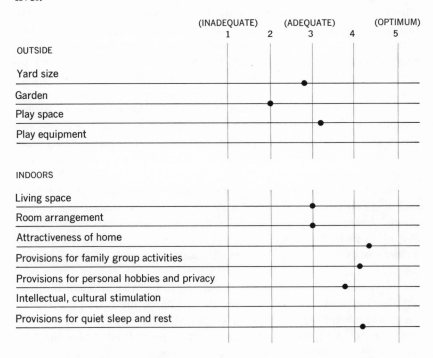

Figure 14.2

An appraisal of the recreational, esthetic, intellectual, and
sleep and rest facilities of the 695 home.

These ratings are admittedly "subjective" and are to be regarded as nothing more than a graphic summarization of the observations of a number of individuals, largely graduate students, who went into the 695 home with a "set" and a preparation to observe objectively and to report accurately. Among other observed aspects of the home situation, they noted both the backyard play space and facilities as well as any of the features of the inside of the home which might have been, in their judgment, related to the children's development, physical and psychological. The five-point scale use in these ratings was arbitrarily adopted to provide a range from a judgment of "optimum" to one of "inadequate." The four "outside" and the seven "indoors" rating variables were chosen to encompass the majority of the features of the home noted by the observers. These ratings reflect the tendency of this family to give priority to esthetic, cultural, and intellectual values.

The Family Environment and Its Appraisal

The family function of providing for the health and growth needs of family members is obviously important. But the nature of the family itself, the medium in which the individual develops, may be even more important. Here we are interested in the composition of the family or household in terms of *persons* and their cultural backgrounds. Very closely related to these factors are the social-class rating and the degree of status the family enjoys in the neighborhood and community. Economic status and the cultural level of the home environment, of course, are important factors affecting social-class rating but either of these, in and of itself, may constitute an important home environmental factor.

Matters of even greater importance are interpersonal relationships and the many and varied patterns of interaction within the family group. There are the various roles that each family member assumes and plays in terms of his own conception of what his role should be, as well as in terms of the expectations and demands of other family members.

Important as these factors are assumed to be in relation to individual development and adjustment, the available methods of studying them and objectively appraising them are relatively inadequate. Descriptions of some of the methods available and adaptable to this purpose are presented in the following sections.

Family Composition

A family identification sheet (see Figure 14.3) is useful in showing the composition of Family 695 when the twins were 6 years old. At that time the twins were the only children in the family. There was, however, the anticipation of a new baby to come into the family. Even though the arrival of the new family member was still months in the future, the anticipation of and preparations for the event constituted an important environmental factor. A written comment of a frequent visitor in the 695 home will serve to point up this fact:

> When I saw the twins shortly after Christmas, they were literally bubbling over to tell me their "news"; in great excitement, each contributing a word here and there to the sentence, they told me that they were going to have a baby brother or sister before they went back to school next fall. Their interest was further evidenced by the books they were reading, and the family talk about the coming of the new one. (family record)

FAMILY IDENTIFICATION SHEET	FATHER	MOTHER
Date of birth:	July 20, 1910	February 4, 1908
Place of birth:	Turkey	Minnesota
National extraction (1-2-3-generations):	Armenian	British
Race or races:	Caucasian	Caucasian
Religion:	No preference	No preference
Occupation:	Architect	Interior Decorator
Educational status:	Grad. New York Univ. School of Architecture	Columbia Univ. Teachers College B.S.
Date of present marriage:	September 6, 1940	September 6, 1940

CHILDREN AND OTHER PERMANENT MEMBERS OF HOUSEHOLD

Name or identifying symbol:	Paul	Sally	(Expected
Relationship in this family:	Son	Daughter	child)
Birthdate:	September 1, 1943	September 1, 1943	July 1950
Place of birth:	Detroit, Mich.	Detroit, Mich.	
Religion:			
Educational status:	1st grade	1st grade	
Occupation or school:	Noble School	Noble School	
Date of marriage:			
Date joined this household:			
Health:	Excellent	Excellent	

Figure 14.3

Family 695 when Paul and Sally were 6 years of age.

The family identification sheet also presents a limited view of the family situation in terms of background, degree of religious interest, and occupational activities and interests of the parents.

Ethnic Background

Neither parent (695) is a native of the city of their residence. The father came from a cultural background quite different from that in which their children were developing. He was born, the son of a leather merchant, in his ancestral home in (Smyrna) Turkey. His mother was a native of Istanbul. His parents had been married, by family arrangement, in their teens. Prior to the birth of Mr. 695, the family was forced to flee from their home during the Armenian uprising against the Turks. After living for a period of time in Cairo they returned to their home in Smyrna where their son, Mr. 695, was born. He was breast fed for the first 18 months of life.

Mrs. 695, by contrast, came from an American background. She was born in a small mining town in the north-central United States where her father was superintendent of schools. Her mother was a teacher. She grew up and received most of her education in a city of that area. Their mutual interest in things artistic brought the young couple, Mr. and Mrs. 695, together in New York City. These family background facts are briefly outlined in Figure 14.4.

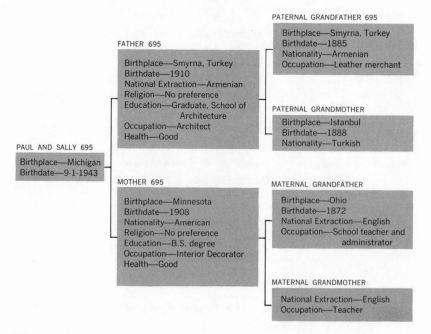

Figure 14.4

Ethnic background of Family 695.

As a general rule, family patterns tend to be carried over from one generation to the next. Grandparents from a particular cultural or ethnic group may have passed on, as a cultural heritage, certain attitudes toward children and certain patterns of parental procedure which may be very significant in the child's life, particularly in his relations with his parents and with his peers outside the home. The ways in which these two contrasting parental backgrounds were blended, harmonized, and utilized as an asset, undoubtedly constituted one of the constructive strands in the web of family influences surrounding these two children. Students from foreign countries, particularly those from eastern European countries, were welcomed as frequent visitors in their home. Interest in and appreciation of the people and the cultures similar to those of their father's background were thus stimulated in Paul and Sally. From these visitors they learned about the customs, the native costumes, and something of the culture of those countries. With these student contacts, and from occasional visits to their mother's native home area, as well as frequent visits in the 695 home of their maternal grandparents, the children became accustomed to and accepting of wide ethnic and cultural differences.

Social Status and Its Assessment

Homes of the various social classes differ considerably in the amount and nature of stimulation afforded children (see Chapter 13). Methods and patterns of child rearing, even with all the modern media of mass communication, still differ considerably at different social levels. One of the most crucial effects of social stratification is the influence it has upon the child in his school setting. Teachers, who are mostly of the middle class, tend not to understand or to be accepting of the standards and the values of their lower-class children, and consequently impose their own standards upon them. Lower-class children, receiving little support from their families, tend to become discouraged and to drop out of school.

Our present purpose is to consider means of locating a particular family in the social-class structure of a community. A considerable body of literature is concerned with the development and use of techniques for appraising the various factors that determine social class. In the past, much attention was given to appraising socioeconomic status largely in terms of material possessions and facilities, such as the number of rooms in the house, the ratio of rooms to the number of family members, the type of heating plant, whether there was a bathroom and a telephone, the number of books owned, and the number of periodicals taken. In some instances, the basic data for the ratings were obtained by questionnaire, in others through visits to the home where observations were made and questions were asked.

Later, certain groups of sociologists studied whole communities with special reference to their social-class systems. These studies indicate that families are assigned to positions in the social-class hierarchy more in terms of such factors as income, occupation, location of the home, ancestors, group memberships, and education. The economic factor is important, of course, but going with the "right" kind of people, doing the "right" things, or coming from an "old family" have even more weight in these assessments.

Typically, the people of a community are assigned to three major classes, with two subclasses for each major division: upper-upper, lower-upper, upper-middle, lower-middle, upper-lower, and lower-lower. Communities differ, however, in class structure. The age of the community, the range of economic status of the people, and the proportion of foreign-born are among the factors that apparently determine the number of social classes differentiated.

Warner, Meeker, and Eells (1949), in their study of social class in America, described two methods of measuring the social class of a given individual or family. The first of these procedures involves extensive interviews with persons well acquainted with the family and the community. From the information thus obtained the family's social class is determined in terms of such factors as the stereotyped groupings in the community to which the family members belong and the area in which they live. For our purposes the second method has more practical usefulness. It requires information on the family regarding four "status characteristics," namely, occupation, source of income, house type, and dwelling area. A family is rated in terms of each characteristic on a 7-point scale. A rating of 1 means that the family has very high status in the characteristic rated; a rating of 7 means very low status. The four status characteristics, each with its 7-point scale, are outlined below.

Occupation
1. Professionals and proprietors of large business
2. Semiprofessionals and smaller officials of large businesses
3. Clerks and kindred workers
4. Skilled workers
5. Proprietors of small businesses
6. Semiskilled workers
7. Unskilled workers

Source of income

1. Inherited wealth
2. Earned wealth
3. Profits and fees
4. Salary
5. Wages
6. Private relief
7. Public relief and nonrespectable income

House type (revised scale)

1. *Excellent houses*—includes only houses which are very large, single-family dwellings in good repair and surrounded by large lawns and yards, landscaped, and well maintained. An element of ostentation with respect to size, architecture, and general condition.
2. *Very good houses*—roughly includes all houses that do not quite measure up to the first category. The primary difference is one of size, slightly smaller but still larger than utility demands for the average family.
3. *Good houses*—may be only slightly larger than utility demands. More conventional, less ostentatious.
4. *Average houses*—wood frame and brick single-family dwellings. Conventional style, lawns well cared for but not landscaped.
5. *Fair houses*—not quite in as good condition as those of (4) above. Also includes smaller houses in excellent condition.
6. *Poor houses*—size less important than condition in determining evaluation. Badly run down but not to point where they cannot be repaired. Suffer from lack of care.
7. *Very poor houses*—deteriorated so far that they cannot be repaired. Considered unhealthy and unsafe. Building not originally intended for dwellings. Shacks overcrowded. Halls and yards littered with junk. Bad odor.

Dwelling area

1. *Very high*—"Gold Coast," "North Shore," etc.
2. *High*—the better suburbs and apartment house areas, houses with spacious yards.
3. *Above average*—areas all residential, larger than average space around houses; apartment areas in good condition.
4. *Average*—residential neighborhoods, no deterioration in the area.

5. *Below average*—area not quite holding its own, beginning to deteriorate, business entering area, and so forth.
6. *Low*—considerably deteriorated, run-down, and semislum.
7. *Very low*—slum.

An over-all index of status characteristics can be obtained by multiplying each of the four ratings by its particular weight and then adding these four weighted ratings. The weights assigned to the four status characteristics are:

STATUS CHARACTERISTIC	WEIGHT
Occupation	4
Source of income	3
House type	3
Dwelling area	2

The total rating score assigning the highest possible status to a family is 12. In that case each characteristic would have a rating of 1 and when multiplied by their respective weights would add up to 12. Similarly, four ratings of 7 would give a total score of 84, the index of the lowest possible status.

The validity of the ratings in any instance depends upon the adequacy of the information regarding the status characteristics and the care taken to assign the proper ratings. For example, it is important to understand the various subclassifications for each occupational group in order accurately to assign the proper rating to a family. Anyone about to attempt a set of ratings should first become familiar with the method. It is equally important to have accurate information about the family.

This index of status characteristics is clearly an index of socio-economic status. However, in use it has proved to be highly correlated with strictly social-class placement. In the words of Warner, Meeker, and Eells (1949), "the principles of evaluation are nationwide; their application varies from community to community. However, the variation is not very great because these basic essentials do not change radically from community to community" (p. 226).

Family 695 was rated in terms of these status characteristics when Paul and Sally were 6 years of age. By this time, Mr. 695 was well launched on a successful professional career. Table 14.1 shows the total rating score (index of status) and the relative weights of the four status characteristics in determining that index. Mr. 695's occupation contributed heavily to the family's social-status rating. Both the house type and the dwelling area were rated at the center of the scale in each case. (Both the house and the area would be regarded as middle-class.) The index of 33 places this family, at that stage in its development, in the upper portion of the upper-middle class.

The Economic Factor

As we have seen, the economic level of the family has much to do with the social-class placement of a family in its community. Occupations are rated roughly in the order of level of income associated with them. The type of dwelling a family is able to live in, as well as the type of neighborhood (dwelling area) in which it is located, also depend largely upon the level of family income. When we have achieved a valid index of social class, therefore, we have dealt with the factor of economic status as it determines, in combination with other factors, the family's placement in the social-class hierarchy.

However, economic level, *as such*, may profoundly affect family life and relationships in ways quite independent of any social-status rating the family may enjoy or suffer. It is probably not uncommon for a family to be hard-pressed financially despite high status in the community accorded by its occupational ratings, house type, dwelling area, or by being one of the oldest families. Such a financial situation may be a source of worry, irritation, and family friction. The family economic situation can affect family life in various ways, depending upon the personalities involved and the pattern of circumstances.

Table 14.1

Social Status Rating of Family 695 in Terms of the Index of Status Characteristics

STATUS CHARACTERISTIC	RATING	WEIGHT	SCORE
Occupation	1	4	4
Source of income	3	3	9
House type	4	3	12
Dwelling area	4	2	8
Total score (index)			33

Accordingly, it would seem important to make an appraisal of the economic status, as such, of any family being studied in relation to a developing child. This appraisal can best be made in terms of income, but income must always be considered in relation to many other factors, such as size of family, housing situation, financial obligations, and savings.

At the time these ratings were made (Paul and Sally were age 6 years), the family was relatively stable financially. They had an adequate house with living and play space, both outside and inside, and they were gradually remodeling and rearranging the interior to suit their needs and tastes. Although Paul and Sally were, as yet, the only children in the family a third child was being expected (see Figure 14.3). The family at that point was not well-to-do financially; they were living comfortably and without economic stress.

The Cultural Factor

Cultural level also bears some relationship to social-class rating. However, like the economic situation of the family, the cultural aspect may exert an important influence on the development of the children, quite independently of the family's social-class placement in the community. For example, a family in which the father is a semiskilled worker whose wages provide few luxuries and which lives in a deteriorating neighborhood may, nevertheless, achieve in the home an intellectually and esthetically satisfying cultural atmosphere. The value system, education, and interests of the parents would determine the success of the family's cultural exposure.

We have seen in other connections the importance of visual, auditory, and tactile stimulation to the mental and social development of infants. At virtually no expense, an environment rich in such stimulation can be provided by any interested and discerning mother. As the child begins to move about and to grasp and manipulate objects, carefully selected items, such as colorful food containers, boxes, and cans usually will be of great interest to the child. The words, letters, and pictures printed on such objects, along with much "conversation" with mother about them, can facilitate both learning to talk and learning to read (see Chapter 9).

The kind of language spoken and read in the home is inevitably the language the child will learn. If he is surrounded from the beginning with "pulp" magazines, cheap novels, and comic books, that will be the level of his literature appreciation. On the other hand, if his picture and story books are selected from the many excellent ones available, these will influence the development of his reading interests and social attitudes. Similarly, the type of music he constantly hears will have much to do with the level of music appreciation the child will develop. It is not the family income or the kind of house or neighborhood lived in but, rather, the interests and tastes of the parents and the quality of their concern for their children that constitute the intellectual, educational, and cultural environment of the home.

The kind of use the family makes of the resources in the neighborhood and larger community can also be an important factor in the child's development. In the case of Family 695, one of its outstanding features was its interest in and concern with the artistic, intellectual, and cultural aspects of living. As previously mentioned, the family took full advantage of valuable learning experiences for their children by having frequent visitors in their home with university-level students from foreign countries. Other students and professional people also were frequent visitors in the home. Mr. 695 was a member of a local chamber-music group as a cello player. This group often played in the 695 home. This was undoubtedly a factor in the development of the twins' interest in music. Paul played the violin in the school orchestra.

Both parents were, of course, artists in a professional sense. The mother, in addition to her professional work as an interior decorator, was a sculptress of considerable ability. The parents' tastes in things artistic was an added cultural aspect of the home. Also, the fact that both parents, each in his or her own right, enjoyed professional status contributed to a superior cultural home environment.

The Family Role Pattern

The individual members of a family function in relation to one another in a number of more or less distinct capacities, or roles. Some of the more typical of these roles may be indicated as follows: The man of the family functions in the capacity of

1. A person,
2. A husband,
3. A companion,
4. A provider and protector,
5. A partner,
6. A father;

The woman of the family functions in the capacity of

1. A person,
2. A wife,
3. A companion,
4. A homemaker and family manager,
5. A partner,
6. A mother;

The child functions in the capacity of

1. A person,
2. A son or daughter,
3. A brother or sister occupying a particular ordinal position.

Functioning in each of these roles gives rise to certain felt needs and developmental strivings and involves the assumption of responsibilities peculiar to the role. Even though these matters are largely family determined, the nature of one's needs, the pattern of one's strivings, and the responsibilities one assumes are modified in varying degrees by traditional cultural tendencies in thinking, feeling, and behaving with respect to this particular role at the particular stage reached in the family cycle.

Under the various environmental conditions of family living, the possible number and variety of patterns and combinations of individual needs, goals, and responsibilities are myriad. The habitual attitudes and tendencies to think, feel, and act in relation to the various family roles are likewise without limit. Many combinations of such factors constitute situations and relationships that favor human growth and satisfaction; others may result in individual frustration and family disharmony. Thus the particular role pattern that characterizes a family can constitute an important aspect of the home environment.

The character of the specific role-relationships between the parents is presumed to be of vital importance. Their relationship as husband and wife is basic, and probably influences the general level of family interaction more than any other of their role relationships. If this relationship is sound, the chances are good that the functioning of the couple in their roles as parents, providers, and homemakers will also favor the development of a wholesome home atmosphere.

The quality of the role relationships of a married couple depends ultimately upon the two personalities involved. For example, the capacity realistically to accept one's self as one is, without inner conflict and undue sensitiveness, is an extremely valuable asset. A healthy concept of self frees one from the preoccupation with self that often hampers creative and satisfying relationships with another.

Thus, if we are to evaluate a family situation from the point of view of its favorableness to child development and adjustment, we must gain some insight into the personalities of the parents and the role relationships between them. Such insight and the information on which it is based are difficult to obtain. However, the discerning interviewer or home visitor can observe much that is significant regarding the personalities and relationships within the family. This type of information and observations must always be interpreted with great care.

Appraising family role relationships   Figure 14.5 represents an attempt to summarize the available "information" about the parents of Family 695 in the form of a set of ratings or evaluations of some of their common role relationships. Before we can make a set of

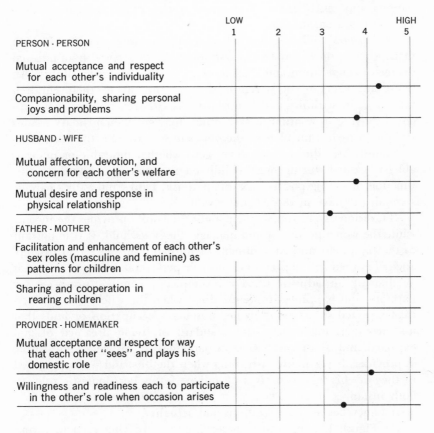

Figure 14.5

> Ratings of role relationships of Parent 695. Subjective judgments based on family records, longitudinal series.

ratings, we must carefully consider and judge a number of specific individual dispositions and qualities of pair-interaction in the couple. First of all, is each person accepted by the other as a person in his own right? To what extent is each able to recognize, accept, and respect the other in his right to be "just himself"? Also, important in the person-to-person relationship is the ability and inclination on the part of each to be "companionable," to share each other's personal joys, hopes, aspirations, and problems. From all the available information and the impressions obtained from contacts with this couple, they ranked relatively high, in general, in their person-to-person interactions.

Second, in interacting with each other in their reciprocal roles of husband and wife, again judging from available evidence, these parents apparently enjoyed a somewhat closer-than-average relationship with mutual devotion.

As "father" and "mother" to each other, a role relationship with many aspects, they reared and cared for their children with an unusual degree of cooperation and sharing of authority and responsibility. An important function of parenthood is to present to their children models of masculinity and femininity. As children observe their parents behaving in relation to each other, they get their primary lessons in how to treat a member of the opposite sex. Indeed, the most effective family-life education one ever gets, whether desirable or undesirable, is gained during one's childhood in one's own home. In this function of setting positive sex-role patterns, Paul's and Sally's parents seem also to have succeeded pretty well.

Traditionally, of course, the man of the family provides the income while the woman cares for and manages the household. It is important to the happiness and contentment of husband and wife that discrepancies between role expectation and role performance not be too great or difficult an adjustment. For example, a couple's prospects for harmony and happiness are jeopardized when the wife senses a lower-than-expected status value in her husband's occupation or finds that his income is inadequate to a standard of living dreamed of and expected, and, as a result, speaks disparagingly of his work and his role as provider. It is equally disturbing when the husband is disappointed in the way his wife conceives of and performs her domestic role. In both instances there is lack of ability or willingness to adjust to a discrepancy between expectations and actuality.

As Figure 14.5 indicates, these parents were able each to accept the other's conception and performance of his or her domestic role, and also to respect and take pride in each other in this role relationship.

Reliable information about the manner in which a couple actually play their family roles and about the quality of interaction and relationships growing out of functioning in these roles is extremely difficult to obtain. The impressions one gets in planned and casual contacts with the family may often be clearly indicative and quite valid. Again, however, interpretations in this area should be made with extreme caution. Since there is reason to assume that family roles and the patterns of relationships growing out of the performance of them are of considerable significance in relation to the emotional and social adjustments and development of children, it is one objective of research to test this assumption and appraise these relationships.

The Family Situation

Figure 14.6 illustrates another device for coordinating and summarizing various observations and impressions about a family situation, showing how the family functions in its interpersonal relationships. This form consists of a set of rating scales (spokes radiating out from the center), each representing a variable in family interaction, grouped as to represent four areas: interpersonal attitudes and feelings, emotional climate of the home, mutuality of interests and activities, and parental guidance. A number of the component variables of these four areas correspond quite closely to the parent-behavior variables identi-

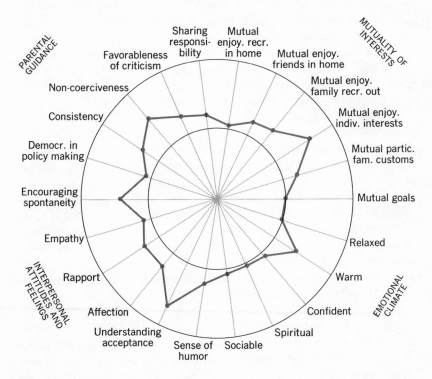

Figure 14.6

An appraisal of the psychological environment of Family 695.

fied by Champney (1941), and analyzed by A. L. Baldwin *et al.* (1945) and Roff (1949). These studies were described in Chapter 12.

The following listing presents brief definitions of the family-life variables represented on the family-situation form, grouped under the four area headings.

Interpersonal attitudes and feelings

1. Understanding acceptance—accepting and approving attitudes toward one another; each person feels that he is accepted and valued as he is and for himself.
2. Affection—felt affection freely expressed and received.
3. Rapport—feeling of "closeness" to one another without undue possessiveness. Tendencies to share (with freedom not to share) confidences, joys, troubles, triumphs, failures.
4. Empathy—sensitivity to one another's feelings.

Emotional climate of the home

5. Generally relaxed, lack of tension.
6. Generally warm and friendly
7 Atmosphere of confidence—faith in selves and others and in the ultimate goodness of life.
8. Spiritual atmosphere—presence of a deeper sense of values and satisfactions other than materialistic.
9. Generally sociable—atmosphere of welcome to neighbors and others in the home.
10. Sense of humor.

Mutuality of interests and activities

11. Mutual sharing of responsibility and work activities of family living.
12. Mutual enjoyment of family recreation in the home.
13. Mutual enjoyment of friends and others in the home.
14. Mutual enjoyment of out-of-home recreational activities.
15. Mutual enjoyment and encouragement of individual interests and activities.
16. Mutual participation in family customs and traditions.
17. Mutual goals, life-values, ideals.

Parental guidance

18. Encouragement of spontaneity—children's natural curiosity fostered and guided constructively so as to encourage an inquiring attitude, open-mindedness, freedom to learn.
19. Democracy in guidance policy making; children share in the formation of guidance policy and in the definition of limits

in accordance with their level of development and degree of readiness.

20. Consistency (without rigidity) in carrying out policy and in maintaining limits as defined and understood by the child.

21. Noncoerciveness; suggestions are offered rather than orders issued.

22. Favorableness of criticism; parental reactions couched in positive terms rather than in terms of disapproval.

After a review of the records of Family 695, centering particularly around the time when the children were beginning their public school experiences, the family-situation form was used to summarize the empressions gained regarding this family's functioning in general (see Figure 14.6). The lines connecting the rating points enclose an area in the center of the figure. The size of this area may be interpreted to represent roughly the goodness, or favorableness, of the family situation in relation to the developing children. In general, the situation was judged to be a favorable one. In the general area of parental guidance, there was evidence of much genuine concern and wise handling. Also, in the area of sharing interests and activities, the family was rated somewhat higher than average urban, middle-class families. There seemed, however, to have been a very common limiting factor here: available time during which the family could function as a unit. Both parents were very busy professionally at this point in their lives, and the children likewise were beginning a period in which their time was rather closely scheduled for participation in the usual organized out-of-home activities.

Family Development

A family, like an individual, usually passes through a series of changes that can be thought of as developmental in nature. In the beginning the family unit has only two persons, a man and a woman. The period from marriage to the birth of the first child constitutes the first phase in the family developmental cycle, the *family establishment phase*. During this phase the role structure is relatively simple. The couple must establish themselves, each with the other, as persons, take on in some form the roles of provider and homemaker, and establish mutually satisfactory relationships around these roles. But their primary concern and preoccupation are with their marital roles and relationship. They are primarily husband and wife to each other.

When pregnancy occurs, a new factor enters the situation. In terms of family personnel there are still only two people, but they begin now to "try on" new roles. They begin to think of themselves not only as husband and wife but also as parents-to-be; they begin actually practicing the father-mother role relationship with each other. This *expectancy phase*, then, is in certain important respects different from the earlier establishment phase. Because this phase is different and somewhat more complicated, some couples find it difficult, depending upon how long a period of time they have had to become adjusted to their earlier roles and the degree of readiness they have achieved for the new role pattern to which they must adjust.

The period of *child bearing and rearing* is the next major period in family development. Beginning with this period, especially, the over-all family developmental pattern varies greatly from family to family. Expansion of every aspect of family life is, however, the typical and outstanding characteristic of this period. The family group grows in size. With the addition of each child the pattern of role relationships becomes rapidly more complex. In addition to the earlier role relationships there is also the father-mother relationship between the man and the woman, and a whole constellation of parent-child relationships (father-son, father-daughter, father-eldest child, father-baby, and so on) rapidly develops. The possible family interaction patterns thus increase as the family group grows.

The *maturing family phase* is usually characterized by a gradual reduction in the size of the family unit as each child goes away to college, marries, or enters independent employment. Finally only the parents, the man and woman who first established themselves as a beginning family unit, remain, and the *empty nest phase* of the family life cycle is reached.

Each family, of course, is unique and different from every other in many respects, and details of its changes in roles, relationships, and interaction patterns are peculiar to it. It is extremely difficult to gain access to sufficient data and information about a particular family to allow insight into the processes of change that have operated to produce the particular family situation observed at any given time.

A Family Development Chart

For an over-all view of some of the broader aspects of family development in its time relationships, the Family Development Chart shown in Figure 14.7 has some value. This chart represents some of the available data concerning the development of Family 695, including the premarital period of the parents' lives. The top horizontal line relates to the family as a whole, showing roughly the different periods and phases of family development and certain circumstances that

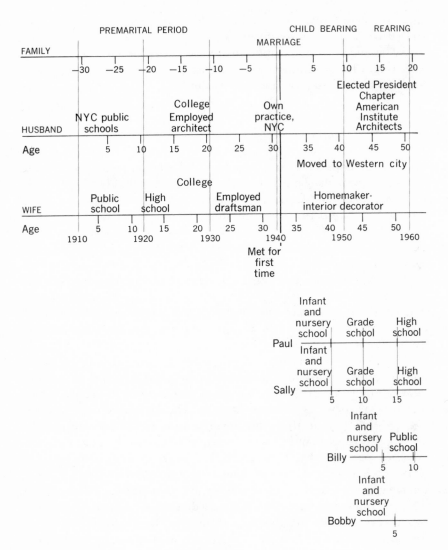

Figure 14.7

Family development of Family 695.

affected the family as a whole. This line also serves as the general time scale and time reference line for the whole figure, for it is marked in terms of actual calendar years and in terms of the years of age of the family, with marriage as the zero point on the scale.

The life span of each individual member of the family is also represented by a horizontal line, each drawn with reference to the general family time scale. The parents' lines indicate that the wife was approximately 2 years older than the husband and that they were 32 and 30 years of age, respectively, when they were married. Periods of school attendance and employment history are briefly indicated on each line. Changes in family size are easily seen in relation to other events and circumstances and in terms of time.

The Community

Many other important aspects of the total environment, both within and apart from the family, profoundly influence the development of the individual. The school, the church, and the neighborhood, with their web of interpersonal relationships, are among the more obviously important ones.

The Family and the Industrial-Economic System

The industrial-economic institutions of the community play tremendously important roles in the lives of children; they interact with and influence the family and its functioning, varying in extent (Waller, 1951). In fact, the behavior of family members toward one another is greatly influenced by their experiences and relationships outside the family. The economic system itself is an institution with which family members, particularly the provider and the homemaker, must deal. The provider goes forth in the morning, works all day for the means of supporting his family, and returns to the family group in the evening. The fact that he must, in our time, spend so much of his working time away from his family in order to provide for them renders family life, its relationships, and its pattern of roles quite different from what they were a hundred years ago, when the family's support was usually derived from a joint family enterprise in which each family member participated in some way, under the direct supervision and management of the head of the family.

Similarly, the homemaker must go forth into the world outside the home to purchase the family necessities, always within the limits of the income provided. She thus brings the family into another sort of intimate relationship with the economic system. The family and the industrial-economic system of the culture are thus vitally interdependent.

Family 695 lives in a residential area within the city. The father is a professional man who daily goes to his office and ordinarily remains all day engaged in his work. While the twins were small, his activity outside the home probably held little interest for them. It was his homecoming and the short periods of time he could spend with them that were significant. However, the fact that he was gradually growing in prestige in his profession, with a gradual increase in economic income, undoubtedly gave the parents the sense of security and satisfaction so important in determining the quality of home atmosphere.

The Significance of Place of Residence

The size of a family's income determines its economic status and level of living, which, in turn, determine the general character of the dwelling area where the family will live. The family's place of residence influences the lives and development of its children.

Race and ethnic origin in many instances have much to do with where a family will live. Discrimination against minorities, for example, often limits residence to certain relatively undesirable areas. Some ethnic groups, not necessarily affected by discriminative attitudes, often voluntarily take up residence in relatively compact areas of a large city. They also tend to perpetuate the customs, ways of living, food patterns, and even the language of their native land. Thus, for them, living in America means quite a different way of life than it does to other segments of the population.

Religious background and affiliation affect the family's adjustment to its place of residence. It is up to the family to take advantage of the facilities and resources offered by neighborhood groups. To belong to a particular church, for example, and participate in its activities, thus enjoying its fellowship, undoubtedly has much to do with the degree to which a famliy feels at home in its community.

To the family, perhaps one of the most significant factors of all is the sense of belonging which comes from a long family history of residence in the same general area. The feeling of "being at home" is at the core of the experience of living in a place that is the center of family history and tradition; the surroundings are warmly familiar, associated with one's earliest memories and with the anecdotes of one's parents and relatives.

Thus the factors that affect the conditions of living in a particular place also determine the nature of the feelings and attitudes toward it. Feelings of at-homeness or strangeness, content or discontent, security or insecurity, make the place of residence a factor of great importance to human well-being and development.

In the case of Family 695, the over-all effect of their dwelling place was "favorable." The parents, at the time of the birth of the twins, had only recently moved to the city. Since Mr. 695 was a native of

Armenia, he lacked the sense of being "at home" during the establishment phase of his family's development. Mr. 695, however, was unusually successful early in his professional career and was able quickly to gain recognition and prestige in his field. This helped his family to gain a sense of belonging to their community. They quickly became familiar with the advantages and special resources the city offered. There were no cultural restrictions in their way, and they were positively oriented and favorably disposed toward the use of those resources. These factors grew out of the community situation as the 695s related to it, and all these factors undoubtedly played a significant role in the development of the children. Unfortunately, we have no quantitative way of appraising the actual significance of the factors and the extent to which they actually operated.

The primary factor, to be sure, was the family and the quality of its relationships. The developmental potentiality with which the twins were endowed came from the family. The home which the family provided and the factors of growth and health for which the family was responsible were significant. But of vital importance were the feelings, attitudes, and other traits that characterized the parents. The family roles and relationships that emerged from these basic personal qualities and the general patterns of family interaction made up the cultural medium in which Paul and Sally developed. Good intra- and interpersonal processes never take place in a vacuum. They can develop and proceed only in the larger physical and cultural setting. The processes of family living and the processes of the community at large are vitally interdependent. In a broad sense, the family and the community present two different but interrelated aspects of the same stream of human existence.

Summary

Our review of the course of development of Paul and Sally as well as a look at the outcome in terms of developmental status at age 17 suggests a good heredity and a healthily nurturant environment throughout their lives. It is interesting to note, however, that had a prognosis been made of the success of this family—its marriage and its child-rearing function—on the basis of parental background alone, probably it would not have been a very optimistic one. Here was a man of Armenian extraction and culture, born in Turkey and reared in an Armenian family in New York City, married at age 30 to a woman, age 32, who was born and reared in the family of a school teacher in rural America. One very intriguing thing about this couple was the fact that they were able to make something of an asset out of this

initial handicap of background difference, if indeed it really constituted a handicap in their case.

Certainly, there were a number of favorable factors in their relationship. They met as students in a mutually congenial atmosphere
and with common interests and professional aspirations. They either
had from the beginning, or quite readily developed, other common
interests and points of view. There seems to have been concensus
between them about children and the kind of home atmosphere they

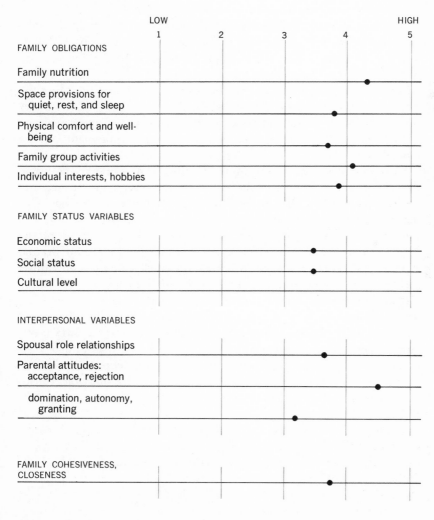

Figure 14.8

Summary profile of the family environment of Family 695.
Ratings based on an observational report in the family record.

wished to provide for them. They, as a couple, seemed able to adapt readily to unusual circumstances. Thus, when the twins were born, the living and dining areas of their small apartment were, without ado, converted to provide for the living needs of one of the babies. The tendency to give priority to family functional requirements and to the personal needs of the family members characterized this family.

Figure 14.8 is designed to represent a kind of concensus, or a composite of impressions, of a number of individuals who knew the family well, or who made special observational studies of the twins and their family situation in relation to their development.

The nutritional and health requirements of the children were always a real concern, but not a matter of anxiety on the part of Mrs. 695. She cooperated fully with her pediatrician and the Infant Service in a study of "self-demand" breast feeding of her two lusty babies. Throughout their growth period, professional guidance regarding the nutritional needs of the children was sought when needed. Even under the cramped circumstances of a small apartment, adaptations were made adequate for the activity, rest, and sleep requirements of the family.

There was no ostentation in the family's economic level of living in terms of housing. The family took pride, however, in the functional practicality and livability of their home and its internal arrangements. They cared for the intellectual and cultural developmental needs of the children. "Probably one of the most outstanding qualities of the 695s is their interest in encouraging spontaneity in an intellectual direction. Parental guidance in other areas is of equally high caliber with the possible exception of the 'coerciveness' factor. . . . As in the case of other areas, overt expressions of sociability are somewhat reserved. One gains the impression that their humor is bleached by a sense of intellectual obligation. Their joking generally requires a certain degree of sophistication which tends to deny the two younger boys the pleasure involved" (from a graduate student's report).

In general, the 695s are a close-knit family whose functions constitute a growth-promoting environment for children.

SELECTED READING SUGGESTIONS

Bandura, A. Social learning through imitation. In M. R. Jones (ed.), *Nebraska symposium on motivation*. Lincoln, Neb.: University of Nebraska Press, 1962.

Bronfenbrenner, U. Toward a theoretical model for the analysis of parent-child relationships in a social context. In J. C. Glidewell (ed.), *Parental attitudes and child behavior.* Springfield, Ill.: Charles C Thomas, 1961.

Stott, L. H. *The longitudinal study of individual development.* Detroit: The Merrill-Palmer School, 1955. (See Part IV, Factors that condition individual development.)

Bibliography
and References

Aldrich, C. A., M. A. Norval, Catharine Knop, and F. Venegas. The crying of newly born babies, IV: a follow-up study after additional nursing care had been provided. *J. Pediat.*, 1946, **28**, 665–670.

Aldrich, C. A., C. Sung, and Catharine Knop. The crying of newly born babies. *J. Pediat.*, 1945a, **26**, 313–326.

Aldrich, C. A., C. Sung, and Catharine Knop. The crying of newly born babies, II: the individual phase. *J. Pediat.*, 1945b, **27**, 89–96.

Allport, F. L. *Social psychology.* Cambridge, Mass.: Riverside, 1924.

Allport, G. W. *Personality: a psychological interpretation.* New York: Holt, Rinehart and Winston, Inc., 1937.

Allport, G. W. *Personality and social encounter.* Boston: Beacon Press, 1960.

Allport, G. W. *The nature of prejudice.* Reading, Mass.: Addison-Wesley, 1954.

Allport, G. W. *The use of personal documents in psychological science.* New York: Social Science Research Council, 1942.

Ames, Louise B. The sense of self of nursery school children as manifested by their verbal behavior. *J. genet. Psychol.*, 1952, **81**, 193–232.

Ames, Louise B. The sequential patterning of prone progression in the human infant. *Genet. Psychol. Monogr.*, 1937, **19**, 409–460.

Anderson, J. E. Child development: an historical perspective. *Child Develpm.*, 1956, **27**, 181–196.

Anderson, J. E. The limitations of infant and preschool tests in the measurement of intelligence. *J. Psychol.*, 1939, **8**, 351–379.

Anderson, R. C., and D. P. Ausubel (eds.). *Readings in the psychology of cognition.* New York: Holt, Rinehart and Winston, Inc., 1965.

Angelino, H., J. Dollins, and E. V. Mech. Trends in the "fears and worries" of school children as related to socioeconomic status and age. *J. genet. Psychol.*, 1956, **89**, 263–276.

Angyal, A. *Foundations for a science of personality.* New York: Commonwealth Fund, 1941.

Aries, P. *Centuries of childhood.* Trans. by R. Baldick. New York: Knopf, 1962.

Ausubel, D. P. Cognitive structure and the facilitation of meaningful verbal learning. *J. teacher Educ.*, 1963, **14**, 217–221.

Ausubel, D. P. *Theory and problems of child development.* New York: Grune & Stratton, 1958.

Baer, D. M. A technique of social reinforcement for the study of child behavior: behavior avoiding reinforcement withdrawal. *Child Develpm.*, 1962b, **33**, 847–858.

Baer, D. M. Laboratory control of thumbsucking by withdrawal and representation of reinforcement. *J. exp. anal. Behav.*, 1962a, **5**, 525–528.

Baer, M. J., I. H. Torgoff, and Donna J. Harris. Differential impact of weight and height on Wetzel developmental age. *Child Develpm.*, 1962, **33**, 737–750.

Baldwin, A. L. Personal structure analysis: a statistical method for investigating the single personality. *J. abnorm. soc. Psychol.,* 1942, **37,** 163–183.

Baldwin, A. L. The study of the individual personality by means of the intra-individual correlation. *J. Pers.,* 1946, **14,** 151–168.

Baldwin, A. L., J. Kalhorn, and F. Breeze. Patterns of parent behavior. *Psychol. Monogr.,* 1945, **58,** 1–73.

Baldwin, B. T. Physical growth of children from birth to maturity. *University of Iowa Studies in Child Welfare,* 1921, 1 (No. 1).

Baller, W. R. (ed.). *Readings in the psychology of human growth and development.* New York: Holt, Rinehart and Winston, Inc., 1962.

Baller, W. R., and D. C. Charles. *The psychology of human growth and development.* New York: Holt, Rinehart and Winston, Inc., 1961.

Bandura, A. Social learning through imitation. In M. R. Jones (ed.), *Nebraska symposium on motivation.* Lincoln, Neb.: University of Nebraska Press, 1962.

Bandura, A., Dorothea Ross, and Sheila Ross. A comparative test of the status envy, social power and the secondary reinforcement theories of identification learning. *J. abnorm. soc. Psychol.,* 1963, **67,** 527–534.

Bandura, A., Dorothea Ross, and Sheila Ross. Transmission of aggression through imitation of aggressive models. *J. abnorm. soc. Psychol.,* 1961, **63,** 575–582.

Bandura, A., and R. H. Walters. *Social learning and personality development.* New York: Holt, Rinehart and Winston, Inc., 1963.

Bayley, Nancy. Consistency and variability in the growth of intelligence from birth to eighteen years. *J. genet. Psychol.,* 1949, **75,** 165–196.

Bayley, Nancy. Factors influencing the growth of intelligence. 39th Yearbook of the National Society for the Study of Education, Part II, 1940b, 49–79.

Bayley, Nancy. Individual patterns of development. *Child Develpm.,* 1956, **27,** 45–74.

Bayley, Nancy. Mental growth in young children. 39th Yearbook of the National Society for the Study of Education, Part II, 1940a, 11–47.

Bayley, Nancy. On the growth of intelligence. *Amer. Psychologist,* 1955, **10,** 805–818.

Bayley, Nancy. Size and body build of adolescents in relation to rate of skeletal maturing. *Child Develpm.,* 1943, **14,** 51–90.

Bayley, Nancy. *The California first year mental scale.* Berkeley, Calif.: University of California Press, 1933.

Bayley, Nancy. The development of motor abilities during the first three years. *Monogr. Soc. Res. Child Develpm.,* 1935, **1,** 1–26.

Becker, W. C. Consequences of different kinds of parental discipline. In M. L. Hoffman and Lois W. Hoffman (eds.), *Review of child development research.* New York: Russell Sage Foundation, 1964.

Becker, W. C., and R. S. Krug. A circumplex model for social behavior in children. *Child Develpm.*, 1964, **35**, 371–396.

Becker, W. C., D. R. Peterson, L. A. Hellmer, D. J. Shoemaker, and H. C. Quay. Factors in parental behavior and personality as related to problem behavior in children. *J. consult. Psychol.*, 1959, **23**, 107–118.

Bellugi, Ursula, and R. Brown (eds.). The acquisition of language. *Monogr. Soc. Res. Child Develpm.*, 1964, **29** (No. 1).

Berko, Jean, and R. Brown. Psycholinguistic research methods. In P. H. Mussen (ed.), *Handbook of research methods in child development.* New York: Wiley, 1960.

Berlyne, D. E. Recent developments in Piaget's work. *Brit. J. educ. Psychol.*, 1957, **27**, 1–12.

Bernstein, B. Language and social class. *Brit. J. Sociol.*, 1960, **11**, 271–276.

Bernstein, B. Social class and linguistic development: a theory of social learning. In A. H. Halsey, Jean Floud, and C. A. Anderson (eds.), *Education, economy and society.* New York: Free Press, 1961.

Bigge, M. L. *Learning theories for teachers.* New York: Harper & Row, 1964.

Binet, A., and T. Simon. *The development of intelligence in children.* Trans. Elizabeth S. Kite. Baltimore: Williams & Wilkins, 1916.

Bijou, S. W. Patterns of reinforcement and resistance to extinction in young children. *Child Develpm.*, 1957, **28**, 47–55.

Bijou, S. W., and D. M. Baer. *Child development.* New York: Appleton, 1961.

Bijou, S. W., and D. M. Baer. Some methodological contributions from a functional analysis of child development. In L. P. Lipsitt and C. C. Spiker, *Advances in child development and behavior.* New York: Academic Press, Inc., 1963.

Bijou, S. W., and R. Orlando. Rapid development of multiple-schedule performances with retarded children. *J. exp. anal. Behav.*, 1961, **4**, 7–18.

Blair, A. W., and W. H. Burton. *Growth and development of the preadolescent.* New York: Appleton, 1951.

Blauvelt, Helen, and J. McKenna. Mother-neonate interaction. In B. M. Foss (ed.), *Determinants of infant behavior.* London: Methuen, 1961.

Bloom, B. S. *Stability and change in human characteristics.* New York: Wiley, 1964.

Bowlby, J. Forty-four juvenile thieves. *Int. J. Psychoanal.*, 1944, **25**, 1–57.

Bowlby, J. The influence of early environment. *Int. J. Psychoanal.*, 1940, **21**, 154–178.

Brackbill, Yvonne. Extinction of the smiling response in infants as a function of reinforcement schedule. *Child Develpm.*, 1958, **29**, 115–124.

Breckenridge, Marion E., and Margaret N. Murphy. *Growth and development of the young child.* Seventh ed.; Philadelphia: Saunders, 1963.

Breckenridge, Marion E., and E. Lee Vincent. *Child Development*. Fifth ed.; Philadelphia: Saunders, 1965.

Bridges, K. M. B. Emotional development in early infancy. *Child Develpm.,* 1932, **3**, 324–341.

Brodbeck, A. J., and O. C. Irwin. The speech behavior of infants without families. *Child Develpm.,* 1946, **17**, 145–156.

Brody, S. *Patterns of mothering*. New York: International Universities, 1956.

Bronfenbrenner, U. Toward a theoretical model for the analysis of parent-child relationships in a social context. In J. C. Glidewell (ed.), *Parental attitudes and child behavior*. Springfield, Ill.: Charles C Thomas, 1961.

Brown, R. *Words and things*. New York: Free Press, 1958.

Brown, R., and Ursula Bellugi. Three processes in the child's acquisition of syntax. *Harvard educ. Rev.,* 1964, **34**, 133–151.

Brown, R., and Jean Berko. Word association and the acquisition of grammar. *Child Develpm.,* 1960, **31**, 1–14.

Brown, R., and C. Fraser. The acquisition of syntax. In Ursula Bellugi and R. Brown, The acquisition of language. *Monogr. Soc. Res. Child Develpm.,* 1964, **29** (No. 1), 43–79.

Bruner, J. S. Going beyond the information given. In H. E. Gruber, K. R. Hammond, and R. Jessor (Cognition Symposium Committee), *Contemporary approaches to cognition*. Cambridge, Mass.: Harvard University Press, 1957.

Bruner, J. S. Learning and thinking. *Harvard educ. Rev.,* 1959, **29**, 184–192.

Bruner, J. S. The course of cognitive growth. *Amer. Psychologist,* 1964, **19**, 1–15.

Bruner, J. S., and Rose R. Olver. Development of equivalence transformations in children. *Monogr. Soc. Res. Child Develpm.,* 1963, **28** (No. 2), 125–141.

Burgess, E. W., and H. J. Locke. *The family*. New York: American Book, 1945.

Burnside, L. H. Coordination in the locomotion of infants. *Genet. Psychol. Monogr.,* 1927, **2**, 284–372.

Burt, C., E. Jones, E. Miller, and W. Moodie. *How the mind works*. New York: Appleton, 1934.

Caldwell, Bettye M., L. Hersher, E. L. Lipton, J. B. Richmond, G. A. Stern, Evelyn Eddy, R. Drachman, and A. Rothman. Mother-infant interaction in monomatric and polymatric families. *Amer. J. Orthopsychiat.,* 1963, **33**, 653–664.

Cameron, N. A., and Ann Magaret. *Behavior pathology*. Boston: Houghton Mifflin, 1951.

Carmichael, L. (ed.). *Manual of child psychology*. New York: Wiley, 1954.

Carroll, J. B. Language development. In *Encyclopedia of educational research*. Third ed.; New York: Macmillan, 1960.

Casler, L. Maternal deprivation: a critical review of the literature. *Monogr. Soc. Res. Child Develpm.,* 1961, **26** (No. 2).

Catalano, F. L., and Dorothea McCarthy. Infant speech as a possible predictor of later intelligence. *J. Psychol.,* 1954, **38,** 203–209.

Cattell, Psyche. *The measurement of intelligence of infants and young children.* New York: The Psychological Corporation, 1940.

Cattell, R. B. *Personality and motivation structure and measurement.* New York: Harcourt, 1957.

Cattell, R. B. *The IPAT test of G: culture free, scale I.* Champaign, Ill.: Institute of Personality and Ability Testing, 1950.

Cattell, R. B., and R. W. Coan. Personality factors in middle childhood as revealed in parents' ratings. *Child Develpm.,* 1957, **28,** 439–458.

Cavan, Ruth S., E. W. Burgess, R. J. Havighurst, and H. Goldhammer. *Personal adjustments in old age.* Chicago: Science Research, 1949.

Champney, H. C. *Measurement of parent behavior as a part of the child's environment.* Doctoral thesis on file, Ohio State University Library, 1939a.

Champney, H. C. *The Fels parent-behavior rating scales.* Yellow Springs, Ohio: Antioch Press, 1939b.

Champney, H. C. The variables of parent behavior. *J. abnorm. soc. Psychol.,* 1941, **36,** 525–542.

Chess, S., A. Thomas, and H. Birch. Characteristics of the individual child's behavioral responses to the environment. *Amer. J. Orthopsychiat.,* 1959, **27,** 791–802.

Conel, J. L. *The postnatal development of the human cerebral cortex,* vol. I: *The cortex of the newborn.* Cambridge, Mass.: Harvard University Press, 1939.

Conel, J. L. *The postnatal development of the human cerebral cortex,* vol. II: *The cortex of the one-month infant.* Cambridge, Mass.: Harvard University Press, 1941.

Conel, J. L. *The postnatal development of the human cerebral cortex,* vol. III: *The cortex of the three-month infant.* Cambridge, Mass.: Harvard University Press, 1947.

Conel, J. L. *The postnatal development of the human cerebral cortex,* vol. IV: *The cortex of the six-month infant.* Cambridge, Mass.: Harvard University Press, 1951.

Conel, J. L. *The postnatal development of the human cerebral cortex,* vol. V: *The cortex of the fifteen-month infant.* Cambridge, Mass.: Harvard University Press, 1955.

Conel, J. L. *The postnatal development of the human cerebral cortex,* vol. VI: *The cortex of the twenty-four-month infant.* Cambridge, Mass.: Harvard University Press, 1959.

Cooley, C. H. *Human nature and the social order.* New York: Scribner, 1922.

Cruickshank, W. M., and G. O. Johnson. *Education of exceptional children and youth.* Englewood Cliffs, N.J.: Prentice-Hall, 1958.

Dashiell, J. F. *Fundamentals of objective psychology.* Boston: Houghton Mifflin, 1928.

David, M., and G. Appell. Etude des facteurs de carence affective dans une pouponniere. *Psychiat. Enfant,* 1962, 4.

Dennis, W. A description and classification of the responses of the new born infant. *Psychol. Bull.,* 1934, 31, 5–22.

Dennis, W. Causes of retardation among institutional children: Iran. *J. genet. Psychol.,* 1960, 96, 47–59.

Dennis, W. Infant development under conditions of restricted practice and of minimum social stimulation: a preliminary report. *J. genet. Psychol.,* 1938, 53, 149–158.

Dennis, W. *Readings in child psychology.* Second ed.; Englewood Cliffs, N.J.: Prentice-Hall, 1963.

Dennis, W. The role of mass activity in the development of infant behavior. *Psychol. Rev.,* 1932, 39, 593–595.

Dennis, W., and P. Najarian. Infant development under environmental handicap. *Psychol. Monogr.,* 1957, 71, 1–13.

Deutsch, M. P. The disadvantaged child and the learning process: some social, psychological and developmental considerations. In A. H. Passow (ed.), *Education in depressed areas.* New York: Teachers College, 1963.

Deutsch, M. P. The role of social class in language development and cognition. *Amer. J. Orthopsychiat.,* 1965, 35, 78–88.

Deutsch, M. P., and B. Brown. Social influences in Negro-white intelligence differences. *J. soc. Issues,* 1964, 20, 24–35.

Deutsche, J. M. The development of children's concepts of causal relations. *University of Minnesota Institute of Child Welfare Monographs,* 1937, 13.

Diamond, S. *Personality and temperament.* New York: Harper & Row, 1957.

Dixon, J. C. Development of self recognition. *J. genet. Psychol.,* 1957, 91, 251–256.

Dupertuis, C. W., and N. B. Michael. Comparison of growth in height and weight between ectomorphic and mesomorphic boys. *Child Develpm.,* 1953, 24, 203–214.

Duvall, Evelyn M. *Family Development.* Second ed.; Philadelphia: Lippincott, 1962.

Ellis, N. R., C. D. Barnett, and M. W. Pryer. Operant behavior in mental defectives: exploratory studies. *J. exp. anal. Behav.,* 1960, 1, 63–69.

Ericson, Martha C. Child rearing and social status. *Amer. J. Sociol.,* 1946, 52, 190–192.

Erikson, E. H. *Childhood and society.* New York: Norton, 1950.

Escalona, Sibylle. Emotional development in the first year of life. In M. J. E. Senn (ed.), *Problems of infancy and childhood.* New York: Josiah Macy, Jr., Foundation, 1953.

Escalona, Sibylle, and Grace M. Heider. *Prediction and outcome: a study in child development.* New York: Basic Books, 1959.

Escalona, Sibylle, and A. Moriarty. Prediction of schoolage intelligence from infant tests. *Child Develpm.,* 1961, **32,** 597–605.

Eysenck, H. J. *Dimensions of personality.* London: Routledge, 1947.

Fantz, R. L. Pattern vision in young infants. *Psychol. Rec.,* 1958, **8,** 43–47.

Fantz, R. L. Pattern vision in newborn infants. *Science,* 1963, **140,** 296–297.

Fantz, R. L., J. M. Ardy, and M. S. Udelf. Maturation of pattern vision in infants during the first six months. *J. comp. physiol. Psychol.,* 1962, **55,** 907–917.

Ferster, C. B., and B. F. Skinner. *Schedules of reinforcement.* Appleton, 1957.

Fischer, L. K. Psychological appraisal of the "unattached preschool child." *Amer. J. Orthopsychiat.,* 1953, **23,** 803–814.

Flanagan, Geraldine L. *The first nine months of life.* New York: Simon and Schuster, 1962.

Flavell, J. H., *Developmental psychology of Jean Piaget.* Princeton, N.J.: Van Nostrand, 1963.

Food and Nutrition Board. *Recommended dietary allowances.* Sixth revised ed.; Washington, D.C.: National Academy of Science and National Research Council, 1964.

Fowler, W. Cognitive learning in infancy and early childhood. *Psychol. Bull.,* 1962a, 116–152.

Fowler, W. Structural dimensions of the learning process in early reading. *Child Develpm.* 1964, **35,** 1093–1104.

Fowler, W. Teaching a two-year-old to read: an experiment in early learning. *Genet. Psychol. Monogr.,* 1962b, **66,** 181–283.

Fraiberg, Selma H. *The magic years.* New York: Scribner, 1959.

Frank, L. K. Tactile communication. *Genet. Psychol. Monogr.,* 1957, **56,** 209–243.

Freud, S. Fragment of an analysis of a case of hysteria. Standard Edition, **7,** 1905.

Freud, S. (1905). Three contributions to the theory of sex. In *Basic writings of Sigmund Freud.* New York: Random House, Inc., 1938.

Freud, S. (1913). *Totem and taboo,* vol. XIII. London: Hogarth, 1955.

Fries, Margaret E. National and international difficulties. *Amer. J. Orthopsychiat.,* 1941, **11,** 562–573.

Fries, Margaret E. Psychosomatic relationships between mother and infant. *Psychosom. Med.,* 1944, **6,** 159–162.

Fries, Margaret E., and B. Lewi. Interrelated factors in development. *Amer. J. Orthopsychiat.,* 1938, **8,** 726–752.

Fries, Margaret E., and P. J. Woolf. Some hypotheses on the role of the congenital activity type in personality development. In *Psychoanalytic study of children,* vol. VIII. New York: International Universities, 1953, 48–62.

Fromm, E. *The art of loving.* New York: Harper & Row, 1956.

Fuller, J. L., and W. R. Thompson. *Behavior genetics.* New York: Wiley, 1960.

Gagné, R. M. *Conditions of learning.* New York: Holt, Rinehart and Winston, Inc., 1965.

Gallagher, J. J. Productive thinking. In M. L. Hoffman and Lois M. Hoffman (eds.), *Review of child development research.* New York: Russell Sage Foundation, 1964.

Gardner, D. B., G. R. Hawkes, and L. G. Burchinal. Development after noncontinuous mothering. *Child Develpm.,* 1961, **32,** 225–234.

Gardner, E. *Fundamentals of neurology.* Fourth ed.; Philadelphia: Saunders, 1963.

Gates, A. I. What we know and can do about the poor reader. *Education,* 1957, **77,** 528–533.

Gesell, A. *The mental growth of the preschool child.* New York: Macmillan, 1925.

Gesell, A., and Catherine S. Armatruda. *Developmental diagnosis.* New York: Hoeber, 1941.

Gesell, A., and Catherine S. Armatruda. *The embryology of behavior.* New York: Harper & Row, 1945.

Gesell, A., H. M. Halverson, Helen Thompson, Frances L. Ilg, B. M. Castner, and Louise B. Ames. *The first five years of life.* New York: Harper & Row, 1940.

Gesell, A., Frances L. Ilg, and Glenna E. Bullis. *Vision: its development in infant and child.* New York: Hoeber, 1949.

Gibson, Eleanor J. Perceptual development. Yearbook of the National Society for the Study of Education, Part I, 1963, **62,** 144–195.

Gibson, Eleanor J., and R. R. Walk. The "visual cliff." *Scientif. Amer.,* 1960, **202,** 2–9.

Gilmer, B. V. H. An analysis of spontaneous responses of the newborn infant. *J. genet. Psychol.,* 1933, **42,** 392–405.

Glidewell, J. C. (ed.). *Parental attitudes and child behavior.* Springfield, Ill.: Charles C Thomas, 1961.

Glueck, S., and Eleanor Glueck. *Physique and delinquency.* New York: Harper & Row, 1956.

Goldfarb, W. Emotional and intellectual consequences of psychologic deprivation in infancy: a re-evaluation. In P. Hoch and J. Zubin (eds.), *Psychopathology of childhood.* New York: Grune & Stratton, 1955.

Goldfarb, W. Infant rearing as a factor in foster home replacement. *Amer. J. Orthopsychiat.,* 1944, **14,** 162–166.

Goldfarb, W. Psychological privation in infancy and subsequent adjustment. *Amer. J. Orthopsychiat.,* 1945, **15,** 247–255.

Goldfarb, W. The effects of early institutional care on adolescent personality. *J. exp. Educ.,* 1943, **12,** 106–129.

Goldstein, K. *The organism.* New York: American Book, 1939.

Goodenough, Florence L. New evidence on environmental influence on intelligence. 39th Yearbook of the National Society for the Study of Education, Part I, 1940.

Gorman, J. J., D. G. Cogan, and S. S. Gellis. An apparatus for grading the visual acuity of infants on the basis of optokinetic nystogmus. *Pediatrics,* 1957, **19,** 1088–1092.

Govatos, L. A. A proposal for a more realistic approach in studying children's motor skill development. Inter-Institutional Seminar in Child Development, *Collected Papers,* 1960, 132–137.

Govatos, L. A. Relationships and age differences in growth measures and motor skills. *Child Develpm.,* 1959, **30,** 333–340.

Greene, J. S. *Learning to talk.* New York: Macmillan, 1946.

Greulich, W. W., and S. Idell Pyle. *Radiographic atlas of skeletal development of the hand and wrist.* Second ed.; Stanford, Calif.: Stanford University Press, 1959.

Guilford, J. P. A revised structure of intellect. *Reports from the Psychological Laboratory.* Los Angeles, Calif.: University of Southern California, 1957 (No. 9).

Guilford, J. P. A system of primary traits of temperament. *Indian J. Psychol.,* 1958a, 135–150.

Guilford, J. P. A system of psychomotor abilities. *Amer. J. Psychol.,* 1958b, **71,** 164–174.

Guilford, J. P. Three faces of intellect. *Amer. Psychologist,* 1959, **14,** 469–479.

Guilford, J. P. The structure of intellect. *Psychol. Bull.,* 1956, **53,** 267–293.

Guilford, J. P., and P. R. Merrifield. The structure of intellect model: its uses and implications. *Reports from the Psychological Laboratory.* Los Angeles, Calif.: University of Southern California, 1960, (No. 24).

Guthrie, E. R. Conditioning: a theory of learning in terms of stimulus, response and association. 40th Yearbook of the National Society for the Study of Education, Part II, 1942, 17–60.

Guthrie, E. R. *The psychology of learning.* Revised ed.; New York: Harper & Row, 1952.

Gutteridge, Mary V. A study of motor achievements of young children. *Arch. Psychol.,* 1939 (No. 244), 178.

Haimowitz, M. L., and Natalie R. Haimowitz. *Human development: selected readings.* New York: Crowell, 1960.

Hall, B. F. The trail of William Freeman. *Amer. J. Insanity,* 1848, **5,** 34–60.

Hall, C. S., and G. Lindzey. *Theories of personality.* New York: Wiley, 1957.

Halverson, H. M. An experimental study of prehension in infants by means of systematic cinema records. *Genet. Psychol. Monogr.,* 1931, **10,** 107–286.

Halverson, H. M. A further study of grasping. *J. genet. Psychol.,* 1932, **7,** 34–64.

Harlow, H. F. The formation of learning sets. *Psychol. Rev.,* 1947, **56,** 51–65.

Harlow, H. F. The nature of love. *Amer. Psychologist,* 1958, **13,** 673–684.

Harlow, H. F., and Margaret K. Harlow. Learning to think. *Scientif. Amer.,* 1949, **181,** 36–39.

Harris, D. B. (ed.). *The concept of development.* Minneapolis: University of Minnesota Press, 1957.

Harris, I. D. *Normal children and mothers.* New York: Free Press, 1959.

Harris, J. A. *The measurement of man.* Minneapolis: University of Minnesota Press, 1930.

Havighurst, R. J., and Hilda Taba. *Adolescent character and personality.* New York: Wiley, 1949.

Hebb, D. O. *A textbook of psychology.* Philadelphia: Saunders, 1958.

Henle, Mary. Some effects of motivational processes on cognition. *Psychol. Rev.,* 1955, **62,** 423–452.

Hess, E. H. Effects of drugs on imprinting behavior. In L. Uhr and J. G. Miller (eds.), *Drugs and behavior.* New York: Wiley, 1960.

Hess, R. D. Educability and rehabilitation: the future of the welfare class. *J. Marriage fam. Living,* 1964, **26,** 422–429.

Hess, R. D., and Virginia C. Shipman. Early experience and the socialization of cognitive modes in children. *Child Develpm.,* 1965, **36,** 869–886.

Hilgard, E. R. *Theories of learning.* New York: Appleton, 1956.

Hoerr, N. S., S. Idell Pyle, and C. C. Francis. *Radiographic atlas of skeletal development of the foot and ankle: a standard of reference.* Springfield, Ill.: Charles C Thomas, 1962.

Hoffman, M. L. Power assertion by the parent and its impact on the child. *Child Develpm.,* 1960, **31,** 129–143.

Hoffman, M. L., and Lois W. Hoffman (eds.). *Review of child development research.* New York: Russell Sage Foundation, 1964.

Hollenberg, E., and M. Sperry. Some antecedents of aggression and effects of frustration in doll play. *Personality,* 1951, **1,** 32–43.

Hooker, D. *The prenatal origin of behavior.* Lawrence: University of Kansas Press, 1952.

Hotelling, H. Analysis of a complex of statistical variables into principal components. *J. educ. Psychol.,* 1933, **24,** 417–520.

Huang, I. Children's conceptions of physical causality: a critical summary. *J. genet. Psychol.,* 1943, **63,** 71–121.

Hull, C. L. *Principles of behavior.* New York: Appleton, 1943.

Hunt, J. McV. *Intelligence and experience.* New York: Ronald, 1961.

Hunt, J. McV. (ed.). *Personality and the behavior disorders.* New York: Ronald, 1944.

Hurlock, Elizabeth B. *Child development.* New York: McGraw-Hill, 1964.

Inhelder, B., and J. Piaget. *The growth of logical thinking from childhood to adolescence.* New York: Basic Books, 1958.

Irwin, O. C. Infant speech. *Scientif. Amer.,* 1949, **181,** 22–24.

Irwin, O. C. The amount and nature of activities of newborn infants under constant external stimulating conditions during the first ten days of life. *Genet. Psychol. Monogr.,* 1930, **8,** 1–92.

Jackson, R. L., and H. G. Kelly. Growth charts for use in pediatric practice. *J. Pediat.,* 1945, **27,** 215–229.

Jahoda, G. Child animism, I: a critical survey of cross-cultural research. *J. soc. Psychol.,* 1958, **47,** 213–222.

James, W. *Principles of psychology.* New York: Holt, Rinehart and Winston, Inc., 1890.

James, W. *Psychology: briefer course.* New York: Holt, Rinehart and Winston, Inc., 1910.

Jersild, A. T. *Child development and the curriculum.* New York: Teachers College, 1946.

Jersild, A. T. *Child psychology.* Fifth ed.; Englewood Cliffs, N.J.: Prentice-Hall, 1960.

Jersild, A. T. Emotional development. In L. Carmichael (ed.), *Manual of child psychology.* New York: Wiley, 1954.

Jersild, A. T. *In search of self.* New York: Teachers College, 1952.

Jersild, A. T., B. Goldman, and J. Loftus. A comparative study of the worries of children in two school situations. *J. exp. Educ.,* 1941, **9,** 323–326.

Jersild, A. T., and F. B. Holmes. *Children's fears.* New York: Teachers College, 1935.

Jones, H. E. *Development in adolescence; approaches to the study of the individual.* New York: Appleton, 1943.

Jones, H. E. Development of physical abilities. Yearbook of the National Society for the Study of Education, Part I, 1944, **43,** 100–122.

Jones, H. E. *Motor performance and growth; a developmental study of static dynamometric strength.* Berkeley, Calif.: University of California Press, 1949.

Jones, H. E. Physical ability as a factor in social adjustment in adolescence. *J. educ. Res.,* 1946, **40,** 287–301.

Jones, Mary C. A laboratory study of fear: the case of Peter. *Ped. Sem.,* 1924a, **31,** 308–316.

Jones, Mary C. The elimination of children's fear. *J. exp. Psychol.,* 1924b, **7,** 382–390.

Jones, Mary C. The later careers of boys who were early- or late-maturing. *Child Develpm.,* 1957, **28,** 113–128.

Jones, Mary C., and Nancy Bayley. Physical maturing among boys as related to behavior. *J. educ. Psychol.*, 1950, **41**, 129–148.

Jones, Mary C., and P. H. Mussen. Self-conceptions motivations and inter-personal attitudes of early-and-late maturing girls. *Child Develpm.*, 1958, **29**, 491–501.

Jourard, S. M. *The transparent self.* Princeton, N.J.: Van Nostrand, 1964.

Kagan, J., H. A. Moss, and I. E. Sigel. Psychological significance of styles of conceptualization. *Monogr. Soc. Res. Child Develpm.*, 1963, **28**, 73–112.

Kagan, J., Bernice L. Rosman, Deborah Day, J. Albert, and W. Phillips. Information processing in the child: significance of analytic and reflective attitudes. *Psychol. Monogr.*, 1964, **78.**

Kanner, L. Early infantile autism. *J. Pediat.*, 1944, **25**, 211–217.

Kelleher, R. T. Discrimination learning as a function of reversal and non-reversal shifts. *J. exp. Psychol.*, 1956, **51**, 379–384.

Kelley, T. L. *Essential traits of mental life.* Cambridge, Mass.: Harvard University Press, 1935.

Kendler, H. H., M. F. D'Amato. A comparison of reversal shifts and non-reversal shifts in human concept formation behavior. *J. exp. Psychol.*, 1955, **49**, 165–174.

Kendler, T. S. Development of mediating responses in children. *Monogr. Soc. Res. Child Develpm.*, 1963, **28**, 33–48.

Kendler, T. S., H. H. Kendler, and B. Leonard. Mediated responses to size and brightness as a function of age. *Amer. J. Psychol.*, 1962, **75,** 571–586.

Kendler, T. S., and H. H. Kendler. Reversal and non-reversal shifts in kindergarten children. *J. exp. Psychol.*, 1959, **58**, 56–60.

Kendler, T. S., H. H. Kendler, and D. Wells. Reversal and non-reversal shifts in nursery school children. *J. comp. physiol. Psychol.*, 1960, **53**, 83–87.

Kessen, W., and A. M. Leutzendorff. The effect of non-nutritive sucking on movement in the newborn. *J. comp. physiol. Psychol.*, 1963, **56,** 69–72.

Kluckhohn, C. *Mirror for man.* New York: McGraw-Hill, 1949.

Kneller, G. F. *The art and science of creativity.* New York: Holt, Rinehart and Winston, Inc., 1965.

Koffka, K. *The growth of the mind: an introduction to child psychology.* New York, Harcourt, 1924.

Kohler, W. *The mentality of apes.* New York: Harcourt, 1925.

Kretschmer, E. *Physique and character.* New York: Harcourt, 1925.

Krogman, W. M. A handbook of the measurement and interpretation of height and weight in the growing child. *Monogr. Soc. Res. Child Develpm.*, 1948, **13,** (No. 3).

Krogman, W. M. The physical growth of children: an appraisal of studies 1950–1955. *Monogr. Soc. Res. Child Develpm.,* 1956, **20** (No. 1).

Krogman, W. M. The physical growth of the child. In M. Fishbein and R. J. R. Kennedy (eds.), *Modern marriage and family living.* New York: Oxford, 1957.

Kuhlman, F. A revision of the Binet-Simon system for measuring the intelligence of children. *J. Psychol. Asthen.,* 1912.

Lansing, A. I. (ed.). *Problems of aging.* Third ed.; Baltimore: Williams & Wilkins, 1952.

Lecky, P. *Self-consistency: a theory of personality.* New York: Island Press, 1951.

Leuba, C. Images as conditioned sensations. *J. exp. Psychol.,* 1940, **26,** 345–351.

Levin, H., and R. R. Sears. Identification with parents as a determinant of doll-play aggression. *Child Develpm.,* 1956, **27,** 135–153.

Levin, H., and V. F. Turgeon. The influence of the mother's presence on children's doll-play aggression. *J. abnorm. soc. Psychol.,* 1957, **55,** 304–308.

Levine, S. A further study of infantile handling and adult avoidance learning. *J. Pers.,* 1956, **25,** 70–80.

Levine, S. Infantile experience and resistance to physiological stress. *Science,* 1957, **126,** 405.

Levine, S. Stimulation in infancy. *Scientif. Amer.,* 1960, **436,** 81–86.

Levy, D. M., and Audrey Hess. Problems in determining maternal attitudes toward newborn infants. *Psychiatry,* 1952, **15,** 273–286.

Lewin, K. *Field theory in social science.* New York: Harper & Row, 1951.

Lewin, K., R. Lippitt, and R. K. White. Patterns of aggressive behavior in experimentally created "social climates." *J. soc. Psychol.,* 1939, **10,** 271–299.

Lewis, M. M. *Infant speech: a study of the beginnings of language.* New York: Humanities Press, Inc., 1951.

Locan, J. Some reflections on the ego. *Int. J. Psychoanal.,* 1953, **34,** 11–17.

Lynip, A. W. The use of magnetic devices in the collection and analysis of preverbal utterances of an infant. *Genet. Psychol. Monogr.,* 1951, 44, 221–262.

McCammon, R. W., and A. W. Sexton, Implications of longitudinal research in fitness programs. *J. Amer. med. Ass.,* 1958, **168,** 1440–1445.

McCarthy, Dorothea. Language development. *Monogr. Soc. Res. Child Develpm.,* 1960, 25 (No. 3), 5–14.

McCarthy, Dorothea. Language development in children. In L. Carmichael (ed.), *Manual of child psychology.* Second ed.; New York: Wiley, 1954.

MacFarlane, Jean W. Studies in child guidance, I: methodology of data collection and organization. *Monogr. Soc. Res. Child Develpm.*, 1938, 3 (No. 6).

McGraw, Myrtle B. *Growth: a study of Johnny and Jimmie.* New York: Appleton, 1935.

McGraw, Myrtle B. Neural maturation as exemplified in the reaching-prehensile behavior of the human infant. *J. Psychol.*, 1941, 11, 127–141.

McGraw, Myrtle B. *The neuromuscular maturation of the human infant.* New York: Columbia University Press, 1943.

Mann, I. *The development of the human eye.* New York: Grune & Stratton, 1950.

Maslow, A. H. *Motivation and personality.* New York: Harper & Row, 1954.

Meredith, H. V. Body size in infancy and childhood: a comparative study of data from Okinawa, France, South Africa, and North America. *Child Develpm.*, 1948, 19, 179–195.

Meredith, H. V. The rhythm of physical growth. *University of Iowa Studies in Child Welfare*, 1935, 11 (No. 3).

Merrifield, P. R. *An analysis of concepts from the point of view of the structure of intellect.* In H. J. Klausmeier and C. W. Harris (eds.), *Analyses of conceptual learning.* New York: Academic Press, Inc., 1966.

Merry, Frieda K., and R. V. Merry. *The first two decades of life.* New York: Harper & Row, 1950.

Meyer, E. Comprehension of spatial relations in preschool children. *J. genet. Psychol.*, 1940, 57, 119–151.

Millard, C. V. A comparison of organismic concordance-discordance rating with projective appraisals of personal adjustment. *Merrill-Palmer Quart.*, 1957, 3, 198–210.

Miller, N. E., and J. Dollard. *Social learning and imitation.* New Haven, Conn.: Yale University Press, 1941.

Miller, W., and Susan Ervin. The development of grammar in children. *Monogr. Soc. Res. Child Develpm.*, 1964, 29 (No. 1), 9–34.

Montagu, A. *Human heredity.* Second ed.; Cleveland: World Publishing, 1963.

Montagu, A. The sensory influences of the skin. *Texas Reports on Biology and Medicine, II,* 1953.

More, D. M. Developmental concordance and discordance during puberty and early adolescence. *Monogr. Soc. Res. Child Develpm.*, 1953, 18 (No. 1).

Morgan, J. J. B. *Keeping a sound mind.* New York: Macmillan, 1934.

Moustakas, C. (ed.). *The self: explorations in personal growth.* New York: Harper & Row, 1956.

Mowrer, O. H. *Learning theory and behavior.* New York: Wiley, 1960a.

Mowrer, O. H. *Learning theory and the symbolic processes.* New York: Wiley, 1960b.

Mowrer, O. H. The psychologist looks at language. *Amer. Psychologist,* 1954, **9**, 660–694.

Munn, N. L. *The evolution and growth of human behavior.* Boston: Houghton Mifflin, 1955.

Munroe, Ruth L. *Schools of psychoanalytic thought.* New York: Holt, Rinehart and Winston, Inc., 1955.

Murphy, G. *Human potentialities.* New York: Basic Books, 1958.

Murphy, Lois B. *The widening world of childhood-paths toward mastery.* New York: Basic Books, 1962.

Murry, H. A. (and collaborators). *Explorations in personality.* New York: Oxford, 1938.

Mussen, P. H., J. J. Conger, and J. Kagan. *Child development and personality.* Second ed.; New York: Harper & Row, 1963.

Mussen, P. H., and Mary C. Jones. Self-conceptions, motivations and interpersonal attitudes of late- and early-maturing boys. *Child Develpm.,* 1957, **28**, 243–256.

Nelson, W. E. (ed.). *Textbook in pediatrics.* Philadelphia: Saunders, 1954.

Neugarten, Bernice L. Social class and friendship among school children. *Amer. J. Sociol.,* 1946, **51**, 305–311.

Nice, M. M. An analysis of the conversations of children and adults. *Child Develpm.,* 1932, **3**, 240–246.

Nice, M. M. Length of sentences as a criterion of a child's progress in speech. *J. educ. Psychol.,* 1925, **16**, 370–379.

Noll, V. H., and Rachel P. Noll (eds.). *Readings in educational psychology.* New York: Macmillan, 1962.

Olson, W. C. *Child Development.* Second ed.; Boston: Heath, 1959.

Olson, W. C. Pupil development and curriculum. Ann Arbor, Mich.: University of Michigan Bureau of Educational Reference and Research, 1937.

Olson, W. C., and B. O. Hughes. *Tables for the translation of physical measurements into age units.* Ann Arbor, Mich.: Child Development Laboratories, University of Michigan Elementary School, 1938. Mimeographed.

Olson, W. C., and B. O. Hughes. The concept of organismic age. *J. educ. Res.,* 1942, **36**, 525–527.

Orlando, R., and S. W. Bijou. Single and multiple schedules of reinforcement in developmentally retarded children. *J. exp. anal. Behav.,* 1960, **3**, 339–348.

Orlansky, H. Infant care and personality. *Psychol. Bull.,* 1949, **46**, 1–48.

Osgood, C. E. A behavioristic analysis of perception and language as cognitive phenomena. (Symposium) *Contemporary approaches to cognition.* Cambridge, Mass.: Harvard University Press, 1957, pp. 75–118.

Palermo, D. S., and L. P. Lipsitt (eds.). *Research readings in child psychology.* New York: Holt, Rinehart and Winston, Inc., 1963.

Parsons, T. Social structure and the development of personality: Freud's contribution to the integration of psychology and sociology. In N. J. Smelser and W. T. Smelser, *Personality and social systems.* New York: Wiley, 1963.

Parsons, T., and E. A. Shils. *Toward a general theory of action.* Cambridge, Mass.: Harvard University Press, 1951.

Pavlov, I. P. *Conditioned reflexes.* London: Oxford, 1927.

Pease, Damaris, and D. B. Gardner. Research on the effects of non-continuous mothering. *Child Develpm.,* 1958, **29,** 141–148.

Peiper, A. *Die Eigenart der Kinderlich Hirntaetigheit.* Leipzig, Germany: Theime, 1949.

Penrose, L. S. (ed.). *Recent advances in human genetics.* Boston: Little, Brown, 1960.

Piaget, J. How children learn mathematical concepts. *Scientif. Amer.,* 1953, **189,** 74–79.

Piaget, J. *The child's conception of physical causality.* New York: Harcourt, 1930.

Piaget, J. *The child's conception of the world.* New York: Harcourt, 1929.

Piaget, J. *The construction of reality in the child.* New York: Basic Books, 1954.

Piaget, J. *The origins of intelligence.* Trans. by Margaret Cook. New York: International Universities, 1952.

Piaget, J. *The psychology of intelligence.* Paterson, N.J.: Littlefield, Adams, 1960.

Piaget, J., and B. Inhelder. *Le développement des quantités chez l'enfant.* Neuchâtel: Delachaux et Niestlé, 1941.

Pinneau, S. R. The infantile disorders of hospitalism and anaclitic depression. *Psychol. Bull.,* 1955, **52,** 429–452.

Porter, B. M. The relationship between marital adjustment and parental acceptance of children. *J. home Econ.,* 1955, **47,** 157–164.

Prentice, W. C. H. Some cognitive aspects of motivation. *Amer. Psychologist,* 1961, **16,** 503–511.

Pressey, S. L., and F. P. Robinson. *Psychology and the new education.* New York: Harper & Row, 1944.

Provence, S., and R. Lipton. *Infants in institutions.* New York: International Universities, 1962.

Pyle, S. Idell, and N. L. Hoerr. *Radiographic atlas of skeletal development of the knee: a standard of reference.* Springfield, Ill.: Charles C Thomas, 1955.

Rand, Winifred, Mary E. Sweeny, and E. Lee Vincent (revised by M. E. Breckenridge and M. N. Murphy). *Growth and development of the young child.* Fifth ed.; Philadelphia: Saunders, 1953.

Rheingold, H. L. The effects of environmental stimulation upon social and exploratory behavior in the human infant. In B. M. Foss (ed.), *Determinants of infant behavior.* New York: Wiley, 1961.

Rheingold, H. L. The measurement of maternal care. *Child Develpm.,* 1960, **31,** 565–573.

Rheingold, Harriet L., J. L. Gewirtz, and Helen W. Ross. Social conditioning of verbalizations in infants. *J. comp. physiol. Psychol.,* 1959, **52,** 68–73.

Ribble, Margaret. *The rights of infants.* New York: Columbia University Press, 1943.

Ripin, R. A comparative study of the development of infants in an institution with those in homes of low socio-economic status. *Psychol. Bull.,* 1933, **30,** 680–681.

Roberts, Katherine E., and Rachel S. Ball. A study of personality in young children by means of a series of rating scales. *J. genet. Psychol.,* 1938, **52,** 79–140.

Robertson, J., and J. Bowlby. Responses of young children to separation from their mothers. *Courr. Cent. int. d'Enfance,* 1952, **2,** 131–142.

Rodman, H. (ed.). *Marriage, family and society: a reader.* New York: Random House, Inc., 1965.

Roff, M. A factorial study of the Fels parent behavior scales. *Child Develpm.,* 1949, **20,** 29–45.

Rogers, C. R. *Client-centered therapy: its current implications and theory.* Boston: Houghton Mifflin, 1951.

Rogers, C. R. *Counseling and psychotherapy: newer concepts in practice.* Boston: Houghton Mifflin, 1942.

Rogers, C. R., and Rosiland F. Dymond (eds.). *Psychotherapy and personality change: coordinated research studies in the client-centered approach.* Chicago: University of Chicago Press, 1954.

Rostan, L. *Cours elementaire d'hygiene.* Second ed.; Paris: Bechet Jeune, 1824.

Roudinesco, J., M. David, and J. Nicolas. Responses of young children to separation from their mothers, I: observation of children ages 12 to 17 months recently separated from their families and living in an institution. *Courr. Cent. int. d'Enfance,* 1952, **2,** 66–78.

Russell, R. W. Studies in animism, II: the development of animism. *J. genet. Psychol.,* 1940, **56,** 353–366.

Salzinger, Suzanne, K. Salzinger, Stephanie Portnoy, Judith Eckman, Pauline M. Bacon, M. Deutsch, and J. Gubin. Operant conditioning of continuous speech in young children. *Child Develpm.,* 1962, **33,** 683–695.

Sarbin, T. R. A preface to a psychological analysis of the self. *Psychol. Rev.,* 1959, **59,** 11–22.

Scammon, R. E. The measurement of the body in childhood. In J. A. Harris, *The measurement of man.* Minneapolis: University of Minnesota Press, 1930.

Schachtel, E. G. *Metamorphosis.* New York: Basic Books, 1959.

Schaefer, E. S. A circumplex model for maternal behavior. *J. abnorm. soc. Psychol.,* 1959, **59,** 226–235.

Schaefer, E. S. Converging conceptual models for maternal behavior and for child behavior. In J. S. Glidewell (ed.), *Parental attitudes and child behavior.* Springfield, Ill.: Charles C Thomas, 1961.

Schaffer, H. R. Objective observations of personality development in early infancy. *Brit. J. med. Psychol.,* 1958, **31,** 174–183.

Schour, I., and M. Massler. The development of human dentition. *J. Amer. dent. Ass.,* 1941, **28,** 1153–1160.

Scott, J. P. Critical periods in behavioral development. *Science,* 1963, **13** 949–957.

Sears, R. R., Eleanor E. Maccoby, and H. Levin. *Patterns of child rearing.* New York: Harper & Row, 1957.

Sears, R. R., J. W. M. Whiting, V. Nowlis, and P. S. Sears. Some child-rearing antecedents of aggression and dependency in young children. *Genet. Psychol. Monogr.,* 1953, **47,** 135–234.

Sheldon, W. H. *The varieties of temperament.* New York: Harper & Row, 1942.

Sheldon, W. H. (with collaboration of E. M. Hartl and E. McDermott). *Varieties of delinquent youth: an introduction to constitutional psychiatry.* New York: Harper & Row, 1949.

Sheldon, W. H. (with collaboration of S. S. Stevens and W. B. Tucker). *The varieties of human physique: an introduction to constitutional psychology.* New York: Harper & Row, 1940.

Sheldon, W. H., C. W. Dupertuis, and E. McDermott. *Atlas of men: a guide for somatotyping the adult male at all ages.* New York: Harper & Row, 1954.

Shirley, Mary. *The first two years: postural and locomotor development.* Minneapolis: University of Minnesota Press, 1931.

Sigel, I. E. *Cognitive style and personality dynamics.* Interim progress report for National Institute of Mental Health, 1961.

Sigel, I. E. Sex and personality correlates of styles of categorization among young children. *Amer. Psychologist,* 1963, **18,** 350.

Sigel, I. E. *Styles of categorization in elementary school children: the role of sex differences and anxiety level.* Paper read at Biennial Meeting of the Society for Research in Child Development, 1965. Mimeographed.

Sigel, I. E. The attainment of concepts. In M. L. Hoffman and Lois W. Hoffman (eds.), *Review of child development research.* New York: Russell Sage Foundation, 1964.

Sigel, I. E. The developmental trends in abstraction ability of young elementary school children. *Child Develpm.* 1953, **24,** 131–144.

Sigel, I. E. The dominance of meaning. *J. genet. Psychol.,* 1954, **85,** 201–207.

Sigel, I., P. Jarman, and Helen Hanesian. *Styles of categorization and their perceptual, intellectual and personality correlates in young children.* Detroit, Mich.: Extension of paper read at annual meeting, American Psychological Association, 1963. Mimeographed.

Simmons, Mae W., and L. P. Lipsitt. An operant-discrimination apparatus for infants. *J. exp. anal. Behav.,* 1961, **4,** 233–235.

Simon, C. T. The development of speech. In L. E. Travis (ed.), *Handbook of speech pathology.* New York: Appleton, 1957.

Simpson, B. R. The wandering IQ: is it time to settle down? *J. Psychol.,* 1939, **7,** 351–367.

Skeels, H. M., and E. A. Filmore. Mental development of children from underprivileged homes. *J. genet. Psychol.,* 1937, **50,** 427–439.

Skeels, H. M., R. Updegraff, Beth L. Welman, and H. M. Williams. A study of environmental stimulation: an orphanage preschool project. *University of Iowa Studies in Child Welfare,* 1938, **15,** No. 4.

Skinner, B. F. *Cumulative record.* New York: Appleton, 1959.

Skinner, B. F. *Science and human nature.* New York: Macmillan, 1953.

Skinner, B. F. Teaching machines. *Science,* 1958, **128,** 969–977.

Skinner, B. F. *The behavior of organisms.* New York: Appleton, 1938.

Skinner, B. F. *Verbal behavior.* New York: Appleton, 1957.

Skodak, Marie. Children in foster homes: a study of mental development. *University of Iowa Studies in Child Welfare,* 1939, **16** (No. 1).

Sloman, Sophie S. Emotional problems in "planned-for" children. *Amer. J. Orthopsychiat.,* 1948, **18,** 523–528.

Smedslund, J. The acquisition of conservation of substance and weight in children, I: introduction. *Scandanav. J. Psychol.,* 1961a, **2,** 11–20.

Smedslund, J. The acquisition of conservation of substance and weight in children, II: external reinforcement of conservation of weight and of the operations of addition and subtraction. *Scandanav. J. Psychol.,* 1961b, **2,** 71–84.

Smedslund, J. The acquisition of conservation of substance and weight in children, III: extinction of conservation of weight acquired "normally" and by means of empirical controls on a balance scale. *Scandanav. J. Psychol.,* 1961c, **2,** 85–87.

Smith, G. M. *A simplified guide to statistics for psychology and education.* Third ed.; New York: Holt, Rinehart and Winston, Inc., 1962.

Smith, Madorah E., and L. M. Kasdon. Progress in the use of English after twenty years by children of Filipino and Japanese ancestry in Hawaii. *J. genet. Psychol.,* 1961, **99,** 129–138.

Snygg, D., and A. W. Combs. *Individual behavior: a new frame of reference for psychology.* New York: Harper & Row, 1949.

Soffietti, J. P. Bilingualism and biculturalism. *J. educ. Psychol.,* 1955, **46,** 222–227.

Sontag, L. W., C. T. Baker, and Virginia L. Nelson. Mental growth and personality development: a longitudinal study. *Monogr. Soc. Res. Child Develpm.*, 1958, **23** (No. 2).

Sontag, L. W., and E. L. Reynolds. The Fels composite sheet, I: a practical method for analyzing growth processes. *J. Pediat.*, 1945, **26**, 327–335.

Spearman, C. General intelligence objectively determined and measured. *Amer. J. Psychol.*, 1904, **15**, 201–293.

Spearman, C. *The abilities of man.* New York: Macmillan, 1927.

Spearman, C. The theory of two factors. *Psychol. Rev.*, 1914, **21**, 101–115.

Spence, K. W. *Behavior theory and learning.* Englewood Cliffs, N.J.: Prentice-Hall, 1960.

Spiker, C. C. Verbal factors in the discrimination learning of children. *Monogr. Soc. Res. Child Develpm.*, 1963, **28**, 53–69.

Spitz, R. A. Hospitalism: a follow-up report. In *Psychoanalytical studies of the child, 2.* New York: International Universities, 1946, 113–117.

Spitz, R. A. Hospitalism, an inquiry into the genesis of psychiatric conditions in early childhood. In *Psychoanalytical studies of the child, 1.* New York: International Universities, 1945, 53–74.

Spitz, R. A. Motherless infants. *Child Develpm.*, 1949, **20**, 145–155.

Spitz, R. A. Anaclitic depression. In *Psychoanalytic studies of the child, 2.* New York: International Universities, 1946, 313–342.

Staats, A. W. *Human learning.* New York: Holt, Rinehart and Winston, Inc., 1964.

Staats, A. W. Verbal and instrumental response hierarchies and their relationship to human problem solving. *Amer. J. Psychol.*, 1957, **70**, 442–446.

Staats, A. W. Verbal habit families, concepts and operant conditioning of word classes. *Psychol. Rev.*, 1961, **68**, 190–204.

Staats, A. W., and Carolyn B. Staats. A comparison of the development of speech and reading behavior with implications for research. *Child Develpm.*, 1962, **33**, 831–846.

Staats, A. W., and Carolyn B. Staats. *Complex human behavior: a systematic extension of learning principles.* New York: Holt, Rinehart and Winston, Inc., 1963.

Staats, A. W., and Carolyn B. Staats. Meaning and M: correlated but separate. *Psychol. Rev.*, 1959, **66**, 136–144.

Stephens, J. M. *The psychology of classroom learning.* New York: Holt, Rinehart and Winston, Inc., 1965.

Stephenson, W. *The study of behavior: Q-technique and its methodology.* Chicago: University of Chicago Press, 1953.

Stern, W. *General psychology from the personalistic standpoint.* Trans. by H. D. Spoerl. New York: Macmillan, 1938.

Stern, W. L. *The psychological methods of testing intelligence.* Trans. by C. M. Whipple. Baltimore: Warwick & York, 1914.

Stoddard, G. D. *The meaning of intelligence.* New York: Macmillan, 1943.

Stogdill, R. M. Experiment in the measurement of attitudes toward children: 1899–1936. *Child Develpm.* 1936, **7**, 31–36.

Stolz, H. R., and Lois M. Stolz. *Somatic development of adolescent boys.* New York: Macmillan, 1951.

Stott, L. H. Identification of four childhood personality traits as expressed in the social behavior of pre-school children. *Merrill-Palmer Quart.,* 1959, **5**, 163–175.

Stott, L. H. *The longitudinal study of individual development.* Detroit: The Merrill-Palmer School, 1955.

Stott, L. H. The nature and development of social behavior types in children. *Merrill-Palmer Quart.,* 1958, **4**, 62–73.

Stott, L. H. Personality at age four. *Child Develpm.,* 1962, **33**, 287–311.

Stott, L. H. Some family life patterns and their relation to personality development in children. *J. exp. Educ.,* 1939, **8**, 148–160.

Stott, L. H., and Rachel S. Ball. Infant and preschool mental tests: review and evaluation. *Monogr. Soc. Res. Child Develpm.,* 1965, **30** (No. 3).

Stuart, H. C., and D. G. Prugh (eds.). *The healthy child: his physical, psychological and social development.* Cambridge, Mass.: Harvard University Press, 1960.

Stutsman, Rachel. *Mental measurement of preschool children.* New York: Harcourt, 1931.

Sullivan, H. S. *Conceptions of modern psychiatry.* Washington, D.C.: William Alanson White Psychiatric Foundation, 1947.

Sullivan, H. S. *The interpersonal theory of psychiatry.* New York: Norton (London: Tavistock), 1953.

Symonds, P. M. *The psychology of parent-child relationships.* New York: Appleton, 1939.

Tanner, J. M. *Education and physical growth: implications of the study of children's growth for educational theory and practice.* London: University of London Press, 1961.

Terman, L. M. *The measurement of intelligence.* Boston: Houghton Mifflin, 1916.

Terman, L. M., and M. A. Merrill. *Measuring intelligence.* Boston: Houghton Mifflin, 1937.

Thomas, A., H. G. Birch, S. Chess, and L. C. Robins. Individuality in responses of children to similar environmental situations. *Amer. J. Psychiat.,* 1961, **117**, 798–803.

Thomas, A., and S. Chess. An approach to the study of sources of individual differences in child behavior. *Quart. Rev. Psychiat. Neurol.,* 1957, **18**, 347–357.

Thomas, A., S. Chess, H. Birch, and M. E. Hertzig. A longitudinal study of primary reaction patterns in children. *Comprehen. Psychiat.,* 1960, 103–112.

Thomas, A., Stella Chess, H. G. Birch, Margaret E. Hertzig, and S. Korn. *Behavioral individuality in early childhood.* New York: New York University Press, 1963.

Thoms, H., and B. Blevin. Life before birth. In W. R. Baller (ed.), *Readings in the psychology of human growth and development.* New York: Holt, Rinehart and Winston, Inc., 1962.

Thorndike, E. L. *Education.* New York: Macmillan, 1912.

Thorndike, E. L. *Educational psychology,* vol. 1. New York: Columbia University Press, 1913.

Thorndike, E. L. *Educational psychology,* vol. 3. New York: Columbia University Press, 1914.

Thurstone, L. L. A method of scaling psychological and educational tests. *J. educ. Psychol.,* 1925, **16,** 433–451.

Thurstone, L. L. *The vectors of the mind.* Chicago: University of Chicago Press, 1935.

Thurstone, L. L., and L. Ackerson. The mental growth curve for the Binet tests. *J. educ. Psychol.,* 1929, **20,** 569–583.

Thurstone, L. L., and Thelma G. Thurstone. Factorial studies of intelligence. *Psychometr. Monogr.,* 1941, No. 2.

Todd, T. Wingate. *Atlas of skeletal maturation.* St. Louis: Mosby, 1937.

Tolman, E. C. *Purposive behavior in animals and men.* New York: Appleton, 1932.

Torgoff, I. *Parental developmental timetable: parental field effects on children's compliance.* Paper presented at the 1961 Meetings of the Society for Research in Child Development. Mimeographed.

Torgoff, I. *Synergistic parental role components: application to expectancies and behavior—consequences for child's curiosity.* Paper presented at the 1960 convention of the American Psychological Association. Mimeographed.

Torgoff, I., and A. S. Dreyer. *Achievement-inducing and independence-granting—synergistic parental role components: relation to daughters' "parental" role orientation and level of aspiration.* Paper presented at the American Psychological Association meeting, 1961.

Torrance, E. P. *Constructive behavior: stress, personality, and mental health.* Belmont, Calif.: Wadsworth, 1965.

Trainham, G. Pilafian, J. Grace., and Ruth M. Kraft. A case history of twins breast-fed on a self-demand regime. *J. Pediat.,* 1945, **27,** 97–108.

Viola, G. *Le legge de correlazione morfolagia dei tippi individuali.* Padova, Italy: Prosperini, 1909.

von Maring, F. H. Professional and non-professional women as mothers. *J. soc. Psychol.,* 1955, **42,** 21–34.

Waelder, R. *Basic theory of psychoanalysis.* New York: International Universities, 1960.

Walker, R. N. Body build and behavior in young children, I: body build and teachers' ratings. *Monogr. Soc. Res. Child Develpm.*, 1962, **27** (No. 3).

Walker, R. N. Body build and behavior in young children, II: body build and parents' ratings. *Child Develpm.*, 1963, **34**, 1–23.

Waller, W. *The family: a dynamic interpretation.* Revised by R. Hill. New York: Holt, Rinehart and Winston, Inc., 1951.

Warner, W. L., Machia Meeker, and K. Eells. *Social class in America.* Chicago: Science Research, 1949.

Warner, W. L., Machia Meeker, and K. Eells. *Social class in America.* Second ed.; New York: Harper & Row, 1960.

Watson, J. B. Behaviorism. In C. Murchison (ed.), *The psychologies of 1925.* Worcester, Mass.: Clark University Press, 1926.

Watson, J. B. *Psychology from the standpoint of the behaviorist.* Philadelphia: Lippincott, 1924.

Watson, J. B. *The ways of behaviorism.* New York: Harper & Row, 1928.

Weir, Ruth H. *Language of the crib.* New York: Humanities Press, Inc., 1962.

Welman, Beth L. Growth in intelligence under different school environments. *J. exp. Educ.*, 1934, **3**, 59–83.

Welman, Beth L. Mental growth from preschool to college. *J. exp. Educ.*, 1937, **6**, 127–138.

Welman, Beth L. The intelligence of preschool children as measured by the Merrill-Palmer performance tests. *University of Iowa Studies in Child Welfare*, 1938, **15**, No. 3.

Welman, Beth L., and H. S. Coffey. The role of cultural status in intelligence changes for preschool children. *J. exp. Educ.*, 1936, **5**, 191–202.

Wetzel, N. C. Assessing physical fitness in children, I: case demonstration of failing growth and the determination of "par" by the grid method. *J. Pediat.*, 1943a, **22**, 82–110.

Wetzel, N. C. Assessing physical fitness in children, II: simple malnutrition: a problem of failing growth and development. *J. Pediat.*, 1943b, **22**, 208–225.

Wetzel, N. C. Assessing physical fitness in children, III: the components of physical status and physical progress and their evaluation. *J. Pediat.*, 1943c, **22**, 329–361.

Wetzel, N. C. The baby grid: an application of the grid technique to growth and development in infants. *J. Pediat.*, 1946, **29**, 329–454.

Wetzel, N. C. Physical fitness in terms of physique: Development and basal metabolism. *J. Amer. med. Ass.*, 1941, **116**, 1187–1195.

White, B. L., P. Castle, and R. Held. Observations on the development of visually-directed reaching. *Child Develpm.*, 1964, **35**, 349–364.

Williams, J. H. Whittier scale for grading home conditions. *J. Delinq.*, 1916, **1**, 271–286.

Winchester, A. M. *Genetics.* Boston: Houghton Mifflin. 1951.

Witkin, H. A., H. B. Lewis, M. Hertzman, K. Machover, P. B. Meissner, and S. Wapner. *Personality through perception.* New York: Harper & Row, 1954.

Wolff, P. H. Observations on newborn infants. *Psychosom. Med.,* 1959, **21**.

Woodrow, H. H. *Brightness and dullness in children.* Philadelphia: Lippincott, 1919.

Wyatt, G. L. *Speech and interpersonal relations.* New York: Free Press, 1959.

Wylie, Ruth C. *The self-concept: a critical survey of pertinent research literature.* Lincoln, Neb.: University of Nebraska Press, 1961.

Yarrow, L. J. Maternal deprivation: toward an empirical and conceptual reevaluation. *Psychol. Bull.,* 1961, **58**, 459–490.

Yarrow, L. J. Separation from parents during early childhood. In M. L. Hoffman and Lois W. Hoffman (eds.), *Review of child development research.* New York: Russell Sage Foundation, 1964.

Yearbook Committee, 1962, Association for Supervision and Curriculum Development. *Perceiving, behaving, becoming: a new focus for education.* Washington, D.C.: National Education Association, 1962.

Zachry, Caroline B., and M. Lighty. *Emotion and conduct of the preadolescent.* New York: Appleton, 1940.

APPENDIX A

*Some
Statistical Concepts
and Operations*

Relatively little direct use is made here of statistical methods in the usual sense, since our concern in this text is the study of a single individual. However, in evaluating the developmental status of a child at any given time during his period of growth or in estimating his rate of developmental progress, one must refer to norms, or standards of reference. Some standard means of evaluating the extent of the child's deviations from these norms is also essential. These norms and measures of deviation from or conformity to the characteristic pattern are statistical values based upon data from large numbers of individuals.

Since the relative developmental status and progress of the individual are stated and evaluated at least partially in terms of these statistical values, it is important that the student have some notion of the nature of these values and the concepts they represent. The brief statistical introduction that follows is limited to these essentials.

Probability Theory

When chance alone is operating to determine whether or not a certain event will take place, for example, turning-up the head of a penny when flipped, the event (heads) will happen about as often as not over a large number of repetitions. If the penny is flipped 1000 times, with pure chance alone operating, the number of times that the head will appear will be very near 500.

Now suppose that, instead of one, ten coins are cast each time. As was true of the single penny, each of the ten pennies will have a fifty-fifty chance of turning up heads at each cast. That being true, it is highly probable that about half will turn up heads on any given cast. It is possible, of course, for all ten on any trial to turn up heads. It is likewise possible for no heads to turn up. The probability of either of these events occurring, however, is relatively remote, just as are the chances of obtaining heads on each of ten successive flips of a single coin. The range of possibilities for the number of heads up would be 0 to 10, with a strong tendency for the number of heads to be at or near 5. This tendency is called the central tendency.

In such a chance situation, however, there will always be variability about the central tendency (that is, deviations away from it), from trial to trial. If the number of heads per cast for a large number of casts are tallied on the scale 0 to 10, the plotted frequency distribution would approximate the smooth curve (dashed line) shown in Figure A.1.

The many factors, genetic and environmental, that determine the magnitude of almost any human trait or characteristic, for example, height, seem to operate in much the same fashion as the ten coins. That is to say, each determining factor seems to act as if it were subject to the laws of chance. The probabilities are fifty-fifty that that factor will favor tallness. Thus, taken together, all the various factors determining body height in a given individual act like a series of coins and together determine his height.

In a group of individuals of the same population, genetic and environ-

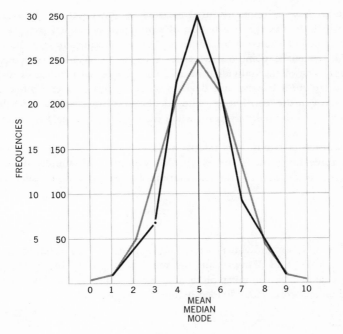

Figure A.1

Frequency curves representing the distribution of numbers of heads theoretically to be expected from tossing ten coins 1024 times (gray line), and an actual distribution from 100 casts (black line).

mental factors set a certain range of variability, with a tendency for most individuals to be near the middle of the complete range. Accordingly, when a large number of people, children or adults, are measured or tested with respect to a particular trait, the obtained scores, when tallied in terms of magnitude, usually take a bell-shaped, or normal, form like the curves shown in Figure A.1.

Measures of Central Tendency

In order to describe a group of individuals in terms of measurements or test scores or to evaluate the status of a particular member of a group, it is necessary first of all to indicate rather precisely the central tendency point on the range of possible scores. There are three commonly used measures of central tendency. Simplest is the *mode*, which is the score made by the greatest number of people (the number of heads of the ten pennies that turned up most often). It is the highest point on the distribution curve. A very rough measure obtained by inspection of the distribution, the mode requires no calculation.

The *median,* a commonly used measure, is the point on the scale (the score) which divides the distribution of scores into two equal parts. It is the score attained or exceeded by, 50 percent of the total group and thus marks the 50th percentile point on the scale. Since the median is not affected by the magnitude of the individual measurements, it is most useful in instances where there are a few extreme deviates in the group or where other irregularities exist in the distribution. The calculation of the median is reached by counting up to the half-way point when the cases are arranged in order from lowest to highest scores.

Where the distribution is relatively normal, the most stable and reliable of the three measures is the *mean* ($\overline{X}$), which is the simple arithmetical average of all the scores in the distribution. The formula for its calculation is

$$\overline{X} = \frac{\Sigma X}{N}$$

in which X is an individual score, the symbol Σ (sigma) stands for "the summation of," and N represents the number of people, or, in the penny-casting example, the number of throws. The mean, then, is the sum of all the individual scores (ΣX) divided by the number of cases (N).

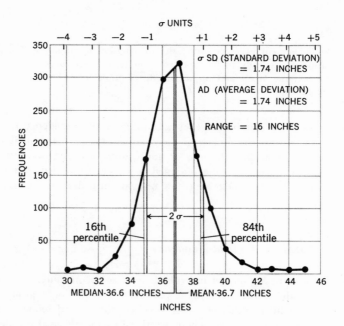

Figure A.2

> Frequency distribution of heights of 1258 three-year-old white boys, showing measures of central tendency and variability. Adapted from Woodbury (1922), p. 42, by permission.

Figure A.2 represents the distribution of heights for a group of 3-year-old white boys. The locations (on the range of heights) of the mean and median are shown. Since this distribution approaches the normal probability curve, these two measures of central tendency fall very closely together on the scale.

Measures of Variation

In studying and evaluating developmental measurements of a given individual, it is important to have a point of reference, that is, a point on the scale where members of the group or population tend most frequently to fall. This point of reference, of course, is the central tendency as designated in one of the ways described in the preceding section. But we need also a means of evaluating the individual's *deviation* from that point of reference. Is the difference between the individual and the average, or central tendency point, unusually large? Or is it a frequent difference and therefore not particularly differentiating? An index of variation about the central tendency for the group as a whole provides the needed measure.

Among the various measures of variability, four are most commonly used, namely, the *range*, the *percentile*, the *average deviation*, and the *standard deviation*.

We have already had occasion to refer to the range, which is simply the difference between the lowest obtained score and the highest. It is a very rough indication of the degree of variability. Lacking anything more precise, however, one can note the location of a given child's score within the total range of scores and thus get a rough idea of the child's relative deviation.

When the median (the 50th percentile) is taken as the index of central tendency, as is often done when dealing with the more unstable human traits (such as weight), other percentile points on the scale may be used to give the appropriate measures of variability. For example, in a distribution of weights of a group of 9-year-old boys, the median of 56.7 pounds is taken as the measure of central tendency. The 25th and the 75th percentiles fall at 52.0 pounds and 61.4 pounds, respectively. Thus 50 percent of the 2168 boys in the sample weighed between 52 and 61.4 pounds. These three percentile points, the 25th, the median (50th), and the 75th, may be taken as reference points for appraising the weight of an individual child in the group. We know, for example that a boy who weighs only 53 pounds and is therefore 8 pounds lighter than the average of his group, is well within the normal range. He is one of the middle 50 percent.

Sometimes the 16th and 84th percentiles are used as reference points on the scale, since they include between them the middle 67 percent of the individual measurements. The middle two-thirds is most frequently referred to as being within the so-called normal range of variability.

Another measure of variability, the average deviation (AD), is simply the arithmetical average of the differences between individual scores and the mean, the median, or the mode. It is easily computed and may often be substituted for the more rigorously defined measures of variability. The formula for computing it is

$$AD = \frac{\Sigma/x}{N}$$

in which Σ/x represents the absolute sum (disregarding signs)[1] of deviations from the measure of central tendency selected, most commonly the mean, or arithmetic, average.

In studying the growth status of an individual, the AD is commonly used to evaluate deviation from the central tendency. For example, it was found in a study of the heights of one population of children that the mean height of 1258 3-year-old boys was 36.7 inches, with an average deviation of 1.34 inches (see Figure A.2). Suppose that we have a special interest in one of these boys, and wish to assess his height. We find that his height is 43 inches. He is thus 6.3 inches taller than the average of his group. Is the difference great enough to be considered exceptional? To answer this question we may use the AD to evaluate the difference. We find that the deviation is more than 4 AD units, which means that his height deviates from the mean four times as much as the average or expected deviation. He must, therefore, be regarded as unusually tall for his age.

The standard deviation (SD) is statistically a more stable and reliable measure of variability than any of the other three and is ordinarily used when greater accuracy is important and when the mean is used as the measure of central tendency. It may be defined as the square root of the average of all individual deviations from the mean, squared. The general formula for the calculation of SD is

$$SD = \sqrt{\frac{\Sigma x^2}{N}}$$

in which Σ is the sum of, x is the difference between the score of the individual (X) and the mean $(\overline{X})$ of all the individual scores, and N is the number of individuals in the group.

The meaning of the standard deviation may be made clearer by referring again to Figure A.2. The total range of scores in a fairly normal distribution usually covers about 8 SD units, 4 below the mean to 4 above (-4 SD to $+4$ SD). The central portion of the range from -1 SD to $+1$ SD accounts for about two-thirds of all individual scores in the distribution, with one-third divided between the two extreme ends of the range of scores. In other words, -1 SD would coincide approximately with the 16th percentile and $+1$ would fall near the 84th percentile.

In the study of an individual child, SD is the most frequently used measure of deviation from the average to describe the child's developmental status

---

[1] Individual measures that are less than the central tendency are said to deviate negatively, and a minus sign ($-$) is attached to the difference. The plus sign ($+$) is attached to the difference when a score is greater than the average.

in relation to his group. For example, the 3-year-old boy mentioned above was 6.3 inches taller than the average of 36.7 inches for his group. The SD of the distribution of heights was 1.74 inches. His deviation (x) of 6.3 inches is thus 3.6 SD units above the mean. The point on the range marked by +3.5 is approximately the 99th percentile. Thus, there was only one 3-year-old boy in one hundred of the group studied, who was as tall as this one.

The Standard Score

A height of 43 inches for a 3-year-old boy takes on real meaning when examined in relation to the mean and SD of the group of which he is a member. We must first compare his height with the mean height for the group. The boy was 6.3 inches taller than the average, and we expressed that difference in SD units: 3.6 SD units. The boy's standard score (SS), therefore, is +3.6. A standard score is an individual's position on the measurement continuum stated in terms of SD units above or below the mean for the group. The formula for its computation is

$$SS = \frac{X - \overline{X}}{SD}$$

in which X is the individual's raw measurement or score, and $\overline{X}$ is the mean of these raw values for the group.

The SS is perhaps most frequently used when comparable measures of several different human characteristics or aspects of growth are desired. SS's for a child are directly comparable with one another, even though the original measurements were made with very different measuring instruments and in terms of units that are not directly comparable.

Percentile Scores

Another common method of making raw measurements comparable and meaningful is to convert them into percentile scores. The percentile concept has already been discussed. Its use in this connection involves simply the expression of each raw value in the series in terms of the percentage of individuals in the group who measured at or below that value. For example, a percentile score of 20 is the point on the scale of measurement values which marks off the lowest 20 percent of the group from the remaining 80 percent.

The Developmental Age Concept

The general idea of developmental age presumably was first conceived in connection with early attempts to assess mental ability. Woodrow (1919) reported that as early as 1828 a man by the name of Esquirol compared feeble-minded and normal children on the age basis. B. F. Hall (1848), in describing the trial of a man accused of killing four persons unknown to him, quoted Dr. Dimon, a psychiatrist, as saying that the accused "in point of knowledge was equal to a child of two or three years."

It was Alfred Binet, however, who, in connection with his intelligence scale of 1908, clearly formalized the concept of mental age, which since has come into common use in the testing of mental ability. In relatively recent years the concept has been expanded to apply to any measurable aspect of development, hence the broadened concept of developmental age. This concept is fully discussed in Chapters 1, 2, and 3.

*An Approach
to the Study of
Social Behavior
in Young Children*

The outcome of an analysis of the check-list ratings of the social behavior of 340 children in urban nursery schools was a set of eight meaningful factors. These factors were interpreted as social behavior dispositions (see Chapter 12).

The listings that follow give the tentative names of the eight factors, each with its compliment of item-clusters. Following each cluster label is its factor loading in that particular factor. The specific items listed under each cluster name are those which were found to be highly correlated with one another but not related significantly to the items of any other cluster.

Factor A: Social Ascendance versus Lack of Leadership

Positive Clusters: Social Ascendance

  29. *Leadership behavior 0.76*
    Dominates other children through his wealth of ideas
    Dominates other children through his ability to talk effectively
    Usually has his own ideas for activity
    Usually takes the initiative
    Gets willing cooperation easily
  8. *Managerial tendency 0.74*
    Can organize activities of the group to carry out a definite project
    Definitely schemes to get others to carry out his plans
  1. *Vigor 0.71*
    Vigorous and energetic in his attack on a project
    (Does not) attack work with little vigor; gentle
  12. *Originality 0.70*
    Original and inventive reactions
    Original in play
    (Does not) merely copy other children's reactions
  9. *Dominance in group 0.68*
    Occasionally dominates a group
    Usually leads a small group
    Is a follower in one specific group only
  23. *Zest 0.66*
    Eager to try new things
    Seems to have a plan for every minute
    Brimming over with ideas for activity
    Makes suggestions cooperatively
    Imaginative
    (Is not) slow to adjust to a novel situation
  26. *Self-reliant behavior 0.54*
    Independent of adults in overcoming difficulties

Independent of adults in having ideas about or in planning
  work or play
(Not) dependent upon adults to solve difficulties
39. *Talkativeness 0.54*
Talks to other children a great deal
(Not true) seldom talks to other children

Negative Clusters: Lack of Leadership

4. *Inefficiency −0.54*
Gives up easily, lacks persistence
Helpless unless someone organizes activity for him
Wanders around aimlessly
Dependent upon praise from adult to do his best
(Does not) nearly always accomplish tasks in spite of difficulties
2. *Fatiguability −0.51*
Becomes fatigued easily
(Does not) resist fatigue
3. *Cautious withdrawing behavior −0.51*
Overcautious
Retiring; wishes to be in the background—repressed, restrained
Does not defend his own rights with other children
(Not) rough and ready
(Not) impatient with other children

Factor B: Personal Responsibility versus Irresponsible Impulsiveness

Positive Clusters: Personal Responsibility

25. *Cooperative behavior 0.69*
Always cooperates in trying to keep the schoolroom neat and
  clean
Takes good care of school property while using it
Responds without undue delay to authority
Cooperative and responsible
(Does not) pretend absorption to evade suggestion
6. *Concentrative 0.64*
Concentrates well on this task
Absorbed, self sufficient in his activity
Is businesslike and systematic in endeavoring to carry out routine
  tasks
(Not) poor in concentration
(Not) easily distracted from task at hand

24. *Conforming behavior 0.64*
    Adjusts immediately to the daily routine
    Always goes through the daily procedure willingly
    Quietly enjoys routine activities
    Accepts the routine as a matter of course
    Responds readily to direction in the day's routine
    Likes to assist the adult in routine tasks
    (Does not) have to be urged constantly to carry out routine activities
    (Does not) take a long time to adjust to the daily routine
21. *Empathy 0.57*
    Thoughtful of others
    Sympathetic nature
    Polite
    Forgiving nature
    (Is not) inconsiderate of others
33. *Unselfishness 0.57*
    Does not take possessions of other children without permission
    Gives up equipment to other children as soon as finished with it
    (Does not) want to keep a piece of equipment if not using it
34. *Responsible behavior 0.57*
    Extreme sense of property rights and has a keen desire to see this enforced
    Takes good care of the possessions of others
    Takes good care of his own possessions
27. *Really-oriented behavior 0.51*
    Quietly accepts success
    Knows when he has done a task well
    Does not lose his sense of reality even in imaginative play
    Truthful
    A "good sport"
    Meets situations in a quiet, matter of fact manner
    Accepts necessary facts as a matter of course
    Does the best he can with what he has
    Recognizes and accepts the superiority of another child's performance
    Is a good sport when he loses to another child

Negative Clusters: Irresponsible Impulsiveness

18. *Impulsive behavior −0.60*
    Easily led into mischief
    Mischievous
    Attention from others leads him to show off or act "silly"
    Often shows off or acts "silly"

Factor C: Introvertive Self-sufficiency versus Need
for Presence and Support of Others

Clusters

36. *Self-containedness 0.79*
So absorbed in his own ideas and activities that he pays no
attention to other children
Does not respond readily to friendly advances
(Not) unhappy if he is not playing with other children
26. *Self-reliance 0.37*
Independent of adults in overcoming difficulties
Independent of adults in having ideas or planning work or
play
(Not) dependent upon adults to solve difficulties
14. *Resourcefulness 0.33*
Resourceful in dealing with difficult situations
Brave when hurt
(Does not have) haphazard methods of work and play
(Does not) dawdle to avoid a difficult task

Factor D: Social Effectiveness (Sociability)
versus Social Ineptitude

Positive Clusters: Social Effectiveness

19. *Social ease 0.65*
Unaffected, spontaneous, natural
Nearly always smiling
Unusually pleasant facial expression
(Does not) lack self-confidence
(Not) almost never smiles or laughs
35. *Friendly behavior 0.62*
Makes friends easily with other children
Makes friends with any child who happens to be near
(Does not) find it difficult to approach other children and make
friends
37. *Social sensitivity 0.62*
Contributes to the ideas of the group though not the leader
Usually pleasant with other children
Is not hesitant in making suggestions to other children
Has a pleasant manner of securing cooperation from the children

Factor E: Personal Attractiveness

Clusters

31. *Personal bearing 0.70*
    Looks very healthy
    Stands erect
    Walks with ease and grace
32. *Pleasant voice 0.65*
    Soft musical voice
    Soft musical laugh
20. *High physical endowment 0.51*
    Smile lights up his whole face
    Has an unusually good sense of humor
    Has a way of making an appeal with his eyes
    Beautiful features
    Expressive eyes
    Beautiful smooth skin

Factor F: Personal Security (Stability) versus Emotional Instability (Dependency)

Clusters

22. *Independence of adults 0.65*
    Proceeds as usual with routine in the presence of visitors
    Pays no attention to visitors
    (Does not) bid for attention of adults
40. *Emotional maturity 0.63*
    Accepts just criticism willingly
    Generous in letting other children share activities and possessions
    Not jealous if other children play with his particular friends
    (Does not) find it difficult to accept just blame
28. *Unself-consciousness 0.56*
    Perfectly natural in the presence of adults
    Matter-of-fact in his relations with adults
    (Not) self-conscious
    (Does not) crave affection from adults but is afraid to show it
16. *Affective stability 0.34*
    Even tempered
    Seldom disturbed; sudden changes in mood infrequent
    Seldom cries
    Very stable
    Seldom quarrels with other children over trivial matters
    (Not) frequently disturbed; easily upset by the disagreeable or
        exciting

(Not) very stubborn
(Not) often abrupt and surly with other children
(Does not) quarrel over trivial matters
(Does not) cry easily in playing with other children

Factor G: Compulsive Domination versus Compliant, Retiring (Adaptability)

Positive Cluster: Compulsive Domination

10. *Bossiness 0.44*
     Decides who shall participate in a group activity
     Gives commands with an air of finality
     Fights for his place as leader
     Insists that others do as he wishes
     Submits to another only after a struggle to dominate
     (Does not) hesitate to initiate activity
     (Does not) usually follow the ideas of others for activity
     Will push the issue in case of opposition

Negative Clusters: Compliant, Retiring

7. *Submissive behavior —0.70*
    Submits to any child who takes the initiative
    Submits to children of his own age
    (Does not) dominate children of his own age
16. *Affective stability —0.42*
     Even tempered
     Seldom disturbed; sudden changes in mood infrequent
     Seldom cries
     Very stable
     Seldom quarrels with other children over trivial matters
     (Not) frequently disturbed; easily upset by the disagreeable or
       exciting
     (Not) very stubborn
     (Not) often abrupt and surly with other children
     (Does not) often quarrel over trivial matters
     (Does not) cry easily in playing with other children
3. *Cautious withdrawal —0.41*
    Overcautious
    Retiring; wishes to be in the background, repressed, restrained
    Does not defend his own right with other children
    (Not) rough and ready
    (Is not) impatient with other children

Factor H: Dependability versus Nondependability

Positive Clusters: Dependability

38. *Decisiveness 0.76*
Has strong likes and dislikes for other children
(Not) placid attitudes toward other children; neither likes nor dislikes them

30. *Affectionateness 0.34*
Gives physical demonstrations of affection
Affectionate toward other children
Assumes protective attitude toward other children
Is sympathetic toward other children
Tries to help smaller children
Forgiving of other children who have hurt him or taken his belongings
(Does not) try to get even with a child with whom he is angry

34. *Responsibility 0.33*
Extreme sense of property rights and has desire to see this enforced
Takes good care of possessions of others
Takes good care of his own possessions

Negative Cluster: Nondependability

11. *Evasive behavior −0.37*
Lags in following suggestions
Regresses to babyish behavior in the face of difficulty
(Does not) concentrate his energies to accomplish a difficult task

Children's Behavior Check-List

Name_____ School or Agency_____
Age_____ Grade_____ Sex_____ Time of Day_____
Birthdate_____ Checker_____

Directions: Check only those statements which you feel are *really true* of the child. Do not guess if you are not reasonably sure.

1. (   ) Vigorous and energetic in his attack on a project
2. (   ) Overcautious, not venturesome, afraid to attempt the untried
3. (   ) Nearly always accomplishes task in spite of difficulties
4. (   ) Voice animated, alive
5. (   ) Does not become fatigued easily

6. (   ) Poor in concentration
7. (   ) Merely copies other children's reactions, not original
8. (   ) Concentrates well at his task
9. (   ) Original and inventive reactions
10. (   ) Curious and questioning
11. (   ) Expresses himself well for his age
12. (   ) Resourceful in dealing with difficult situations
13. (   ) Poor use of language for his age
14. (   ) Patient
15. (   ) Absorbed; self-sufficient in his activity
16. (   ) Restless; a certain dissatisfaction with his own activity
17. (   ) Retiring; wishes to be in the background
18. (   ) Even-tempered
19. (   ) Frequently disturbed; easily upset by the disagreeable or exciting
20. (   ) Seldom disturbed; sudden changes in mood infrequent
21. (   ) Slow to adjust to a novel experience
22. (   ) Original in play
23. (   ) Is easily distracted from task at hand
24. (   ) Gives up easily, lacks persistence
25. (   ) Submits to any child who takes the initiative
26. (   ) Dominates children of his own age (either sex)
27. (   ) Will submit to a specific child only
28. (   ) Submits to a leader only after a struggle to dominate
29. (   ) Is a follower in one specific group only
30. (   ) Occasionally dominates a group
31. (   ) Usually leads a small group
32. (   ) Decides who shall participate in the group activities
33. (   ) Can organize the activities of a group to carry out a definite purpose
34. (   ) Leads or follows as the occasion demands
35. (   ) Neither leads nor follows; plays alone
36. (   ) Dominates other children through his ability to talk effectively
37. (   ) Dominates other children through their love or admiration for him
38. (   ) Dominates other children through his wealth of ideas
39. (   ) Definitely schemes to get others to carry out his plans
40. (   ) Gives commands with an air of finality
41. (   ) Helpless unless someone organizes activity for him
42. (   ) Hesitates to initiate activity
43. (   ) Usually follows the ideas of others for activity
44. (   ) Usually has his own ideas for activity
45. (   ) Usually takes the initiative
46. (   ) Does not push the issue in case of opposition
47. (   ) Fights for his place as leader
48. (   ) Insists that other children do as he wishes
49. (   ) Does not defend his own rights with other children
50. (   ) Easily led into mischief by others
51. (   ) Fails to secure cooperation when he tries to direct activities

52. (   ) Gets willing cooperation easily
53. (   ) Almost never laughs or smiles
54. (   ) Has an unusually good sense of humor
55. (   ) Has a way of making an appeal with his eyes
56. (   ) Has a pleasing manner of speech
57. (   ) Thoughtful of others
58. (   ) Moderately selfish
59. (   ) Sympathetic nature
60. (   ) Inconsiderate of others
61. (   ) Polite
62. (   ) Mischievous
63. (   ) Brave when hurt
64. (   ) Truthful
65. (   ) Seldom cries
66. (   ) A good sport
67. (   ) Rough and ready
68. (   ) Forgiving nature
69. (   ) Wanders around aimlessly
70. (   ) Self-conscious
71. (   ) Intelligently cooperative
72. (   ) Often shows off or acts silly
73. (   ) Makes pleasant conversation with adults
74. (   ) Unaffected, spontaneous, natural
75. (   ) Imaginative
76. (   ) Lacks imagination
77. (   ) Eager to try new things
78. (   ) Seems to have a plan for every minute
79. (   ) Brimming over with ideas for activity
80. (   ) Plays or works vigorously
81. (   ) Haphazard methods of work or play
82. (   ) Lacks self confidence
83. (   ) Adjusts immediately to the daily routine
84. (   ) Always goes through the daily procedure willingly
85. (   ) Has to be constantly urged to carry out routine activities
86. (   ) Takes a long time to adjust to the daily routine
87. (   ) Responds readily to direction in the day's routine
88. (   ) Proceeds as usual with routine in the presence of visitors
89. (   ) Is businesslike and systematic in endeavoring to carry out routine activities
90. (   ) Dawdles over routine activities
91. (   ) Always cooperates in trying to keep the schoolrooms neat and clean
92. (   ) Perfectly natural in the presence of adults
93. (   ) Matter of fact in his relations with adults
94. (   ) Independent of adult in overcoming difficulties
95. (   ) Dependent upon adult to solve difficulties
96. (   ) Independent of adult in having ideas about or planning work or play activities

97. (   ) Resents aid from adults
98. (   ) Pays no attention to visitors
99. (   ) Bids for attention from adults
100. (   ) Craves affection from adults but is afraid to show it
101. (   ) Beautiful features
102. (   ) Unusually pleasant facial expression
103. (   ) Expressive eyes
104. (   ) Stands erect
105. (   ) Walks with ease and grace
106. (   ) Does not take possessions of other children without permission
107. (   ) Takes good care of school property while using it
108. (   ) Wants to keep a particular piece of equipment even if not using it himself
109. (   ) Gives up equipment to other children as soon as finished with it
110. (   ) Extreme sense of property rights and keen desire to see this enforced
111. (   ) Shows extreme consideration for school property
112. (   ) Shows extreme consideration for possessions of others
113. (   ) Takes good care of his own possessions
114. (   ) Takes good care of the possessions of other children
115. (   ) Adds cooperatively to suggestions.
116. (   ) Lags in following suggestion
117. (   ) Responds without undue delay to authority
118. (   ) So absorbed in his own thoughts that does not comprehend
119. (   ) Cooperative and responsible
120. (   ) Makes friends with other children easily
121. (   ) Finds it difficult to approach other children and make friends
122. (   ) Makes friends with any child who happens to be around him
123. (   ) Resents interest shown by other children; wants to be left alone
124. (   ) Does not respond to friendly advances
125. (   ) Tries to make entry into group of children but fails
126. (   ) Unhappy if he is not playing with other children
127. (   ) So absorbed in his own ideas that he pays no attention to other children
128. (   ) Contributes to the ideas of the group though not a leader (co-operative companion)
129. (   ) Hesitant in making suggestions to other children
130. (   ) Assumes a protective attitude toward other children
131. (   ) Usually pleasant with other children
132. (   ) Often abrupt and surly with other children
133. (   ) Has a pleasant manner of securing cooperation from other children
134. (   ) Has strong likes and dislikes for other children
135. (   ) Rather placid attitude toward other children; neither likes nor dislikes them to any degree
136. (   ) Quarrels with other children often over trivial things
137. (   ) Seldom quarrels with other children over trivial matters
138. (   ) Rough and mean with other children

139. (   ) Hurts other children often due to carelessness
140. (   ) Impatient with other children
141. (   ) Very critical of other children
142. (   ) Is a good sport when he loses to some other child
143. (   ) Is sympathetic toward other children
144. (   ) Affectionate toward other children
145. (   ) Tries to help the smaller children
146. (   ) Resents aid from other children
147. (   ) Forgiving of other children who have hurt him, taken his belongings
148. (   ) Tries to get even with a child with whom he is angry
149. (   ) Talks to other children a great deal
150. (   ) Seldom talks to other children
151. (   ) Cries easily in playing with other children
152. (   ) Generous in letting other children share activities and possessions
153. (   ) Attention from other children leads him to "show off" or act silly
154. (   ) Not jealous if other children play with his particular friends
155. (   ) Faces the issue squarely
156. (   ) Concentrates his energy to accomplish a difficult task
157. (   ) Meets situations in a quiet, matter-of-fact manner
158. (   ) Dawdles to avoid a difficult task
159. (   ) Accepts necessary facts as a matter of course
160. (   ) Does the best he can with what he has
161. (   ) Recognizes and accepts the superiority of another child
162. (   ) Accepts just criticism willingly
163. (   ) Finds it difficult to accept just blame from his faults
164. (   ) Regresses to babyish behavior in the face of difficulty
165. (   ) Quietly accepts success
166. (   ) Knows when he has done a task well

Scoring Instructions

The letters A to H on the key for each page of the check-list designate the factor, or factors, for which the items are scored. The x or its absence, in the case of each item, is the key to its scoring. Items on a given child's check-list are counted for the factors indicated when they are checked or not checked, according to this key. The total factor score in each case is the simple count of the items designated for that factor that agree with the key. These raw scores must then be converted into modified standard scores in order to make them comparable and meaningful. This can be done by use of Table B.1.

Scoring Key

1. (x) A	43. ( ) G	85. ( ) B	126. ( ) C
2. ( ) A D G	44. (x) A	86. ( ) B	127. (x) C
3. (x) A	45. (x) A	87. (x) B	128. (x) D
4. (x) D	46. ( ) G	88. (x) F	129. ( ) D
5. (x) A	47. (x) G	89. (x) B	130. (x) D H
6. ( ) B	48. (x) G		131. (x) D
7. ( ) A	49. ( ) A G	91. (x) B	132. ( ) F (x) G
8. (x) A B	50. ( ) B	92. (x) F	133. (x) D
9. (x) A	51. (x) G	93. (x) F	134. (x) H
10. (x) D	52. (x) A	94. (x) A C	135. ( ) H
11. (x) D	53. ( ) D	95. ( ) A C	136. ( ) F (x) G
12. (x) C	54. (x) E	96. (x) A C	137. (x) F ( ) G
13. ( ) D	55. (x) D E		138. ( ) D
14. (x) B	56. (x) D	98. (x) F	139. ( ) B
15. (x) B	57. (x) B	99. ( ) F	140. (x) G
16. ( ) B		100. ( ) F	141. ( ) D
17. ( ) A D G	59. (x) B	101. (x) D E	142. (x) B
18. (x) F ( ) G	60. ( ) B	102. (x) D	143. (x) D
19. ( ) F (x) G	61. (x) B	103. (x) D E	144. (x) D
20. (x) F (x) G	62. ( ) B	104. (x) E	145. (x) D H
21. ( ) A	63. (x) C	105. (x) E	146. ( ) D
22. (x) A	64. (x) B	106. (x) B	147. (x) D H
23. ( ) B	65. (x) F ( ) G	107. (x) B	148. ( ) D H
24. ( ) A	66. (x) B	108. ( ) B	149. (x) A D
25. ( ) G	67. ( ) D (x) G	109. (x) B	150. ( ) A D
26. (x) G	68. (x) B	110. (x) B H	151. ( ) F (x) G
27. (x) G	69. ( ) A	111. (x) B	152. (x) F
28. (x) G	70. ( ) F	112. (x) B	153. ( ) B
29. (x) A	71. (x) D	113. (x) B H	154. (x) F
30. ( ) A	72. ( ) B	114. (x) B H	155. (x) H
31. (x) A	73. (x) D	115. (x) A	156. (x) H
32. (x) G	74. (x) D	116. ( ) H	157. (x) B
33. (x) A	75. (x) A	117. (x) B	158. ( ) C
34. (x) D	76. ( ) A	118. (x) C	159. (x) B
35. (x) C	77. (x) A	119. (x) B	160. (x) B
36. (x) A	78. (x) A	120. (x) D	161. (x) B
37. (x) A	79. (x) A	121. ( ) D	162. (x) F
38. (x) A		122. (x) D	163. ( ) F
39. (x) A	81. ( ) C	123. ( ) D	164. ( ) H
40. (x) G	82. ( ) D	124. (x) C	165. (x) B
41. ( ) A	83. (x) B	125. ( ) D	166. (x) B
42. ( ) G	84. (x) B		

Table B.1

Table for Converting Raw Scores into Modified Standard Scores

MODIFIED STANDARD SCORE EQUIVA- LENT	RAW FACTOR-SCORE RANGE							
	A (1)	B (2)	C (3)	D (4)	E (5)	F (6)	G (7)	H (8)
1	0–1	0	——	0–7	——	0	0	0
2	2	1	0	8	——	1	1	1
3	3–6	2–5	1	9–11	——	2–3	2–3	2
4	7–9	6–10	2	12–15	0	4–6	4–6	3
5	10–13	11–16	3	16–19	1	7–8	7–9	4–5
6	14–17	17–21	4	20–23	2	9–11	10–11	6
7	18–21	22–26	5	24–26	3	12–13	12–14	7
8	22–25	27–32	6	27–30	4	14–15	15–17	8–9
9	26–29	33–37	7	31–34	5	16–18	18–19	10
10	above 29	above 37	above 7	above 34	above 5	above 18	above 19	above 10

The eight derived modified standard scores may then be plotted together on a profile form (see Figure B.1), giving a social behavior profile for the child (see also Figure 12.1).

NAME_____ AGE_____ RATER_____

	1 2 3 4 5 6 7 8 9 10	
A. Lack of leadership		Social ascendance (leadership)
B. Irresponsible impulsiveness		Personal responsibility
C. Need for presence and support of others		Introspective self-sufficiency
D. Social ineptitude		Social effectiveness (sociability)
E. Lack of personal appeal		Personal attractiveness
F. Emotional instability (dependency)		Personal security, stability
G. Compliant, retiring (adaptability)		Compulsive domination
H. Nondependability		Dependability

Figure B.1

The behavior profile form for portraying eight variables of childhood personality.

APPENDIX C

*Developmental
Record Abstracts*

Developmental Record Abstract of Don 723

The Parents and Their Background

Mr. 723 was born into a Midwestern, lower-middle-class family, "but of good, decent, healthy stock." His parents' desire was to give their children good educations and a better start in life than they themselves had had. The father had been a post office clerk for twenty-five years. He seems to have been a quiet, industrious man with few interests outside his family and his work.

The mother was of German extraction, American born. She worked as a seamstress for five years. She apparently showed no strong religious preference. She was a kind and friendly person with a devotion to family and friends. She enjoyed good health.

Mr. 723 had the usual education in the schools of his native city. He was an honor student in high school and was awarded a scholarship to attend college. Again, in college he was an honor student. He graduated with a bachelor of science degree and later with a Master's degree in mechanical engineering. He then entered the Chrysler Institute of Engineering, specializing in automotive engineering. He has continued his connection with Chrysler Corporation, Engineering Division.

By contrast, Mrs. 723 was born in Bulgaria of Bulgarian parents, members of the East Orthodox Church. Her father was well educated, having graduated from a Bulgarian university. He was a kind, understanding man, very loyal to his friends. His prime interests were his family, literature, and current events. Mrs. 723's mother was trained as a teacher at which occupation she worked for thirty years. She was reported by her daughter to have been a "good natured," kind, and friendly person, willing to sacrifice for her family or friends if need be. Little is known as to how the Communist regime in Bulgaria might have changed these people's lives. Apparently, the mother was able to continue her work as a teacher, but the father's export business very likely was limited to dealings with other satellite countries.

Mrs. 723 received her education in the Bulgarian schools. She graduated from college with a degree in social work. She also was an honor student and won a scholarship to come to America to study. She attended a large Midwestern university as a graduate student and there obtained a Master's degree in social work.

Fate brought these two young people together in marriage at ages 27 and 22. They have much in common. Highly intelligent, they both took honors in school and college. They are both sociable, friendly, and outgoing. They enjoy together such recreational activities as folk dancing and the theater. They are devoted to their family, now consisting of three children, Don, Jimmy, and Susan, and they believe in devoting time to their children and to family activities. They are also united in their interest in community affairs.

The 723s belong to the Society of Friends. Formerly, Mr. 723 was a Catholic, but his wife had no particular religious preference. As members of the Society of Friends they are not ardent churchgoers, but they apparently live their religion and try to practice the love-thy-neighbor philosophy.

Approximately three years after their marriage, Don was born. The evidence indicates that Don was eagerly wanted by both parents. All factors considered at the time of his birth, this child was born into a very favorable family situation.

Table C.1

Physical Growth Data of Don 723

AGE (YEARS-MONTHS)	WEIGHT (POUNDS)	HEIGHT (INCHES)
Birth	7.8	20.0
0-3	13.5	23.5
0-8	18.0	27.2
1-0	20.7	29.0
1-3	22.8	30.2
1-8	25.0	32.5
2-0	26.2	33.7
2-4	28.2	34.8
3-0	31.7	37.5
4-0	34.1	40.2
5-0	39.5	42.5
6-0	44.0	45.2
8-0	52.0	49.4
9-0	59.0	51.5
10-0	65.5	53.6
11-0	72.3	55.4
12-0	81.8	57.5
13-0	92.5	59.5
14-3	98.3	61.3
15-0	101.2	62.2
16-4	113.1	64.8
17-2	133.0	67.1
19-2	159.0	71.3

Table C.2

Skeletal Maturation Data of Don 723

AGE (YEARS-MONTHS)	SKELETAL AGE
0-3	0-2
0-9	0-11
1-0	1-2
1-8	1-8
2-0	1-10
2-9	2-4
3-0	2-9
4-0	3-2
5-0	3-10

Table C.2 (continued)
Skeletal Maturation Data of Don 723

AGE (YEAR-MONTHS)	SKELETAL AGE
8-0	6-2
9-1	7-6
10-0	8-3
11-0	9-1
11-9	10-0
12-0	10-2
13-0	11-0
14-9	13-0
15-0	13-10
16-0	14-3

Table C.3
Mental Test Data of Don 723

AGE (YEARS-MONTHS)	TEST	DA OR MA	DQ OR IQ
0-9	Gesell Developmental	0-10[a]	122[a]
1-0	Gesell Developmental	1-4[a]	133[a]
2-1	Cattell Infant	3-0	144
2-9	Stanford-Binet	4-6	164
3-3	Stanford-Binet	5-0	154
4-1	Stanford-Binet	5-10	143
5-0	Stanford-Binet (test not scored for lack of cooperation)		
7-0	WISC	——	138
9-1	WISC	——	140

[a] Estimated average values.

Table C.4
Developmental Chronology of Don 723

AGE	ENVIRONMENTAL EVENTS AND CIRCUMSTANCES	DEVELOPMENT (PHYSICAL, BEHAVIORAL, COGNITIVE, SOCIAL)
Birth	Duration of labor, 7 hours 46 minutes; term, 39 weeks; low forceps used.	Birth weight 7 pounds 18 ounces; condition at birth "good"
10 days	Mother enjoyed nursing time	Nursed well, rarely cried

Table C.4 (continued)
Developmental Chronology of Don 723

AGE	ENVIRONMENTAL EVENTS AND CIRCUMSTANCES	DEVELOPMENT (PHYSICAL, BEHAVIORAL, COGNITIVE, SOCIAL)
0-3	Breast fed on demand, four-feeding pattern	Physically normal in every respect, medium length, medium physique
0-8	Milk now given in bottle, occasionally glass or cup, pablum as cereal	Can drink from cup; uses spoon but "dumps" on way to mouth Sometimes sucks thumb Bowel elimination regular Unties shoe, takes off; pokes with index finger; good thumb and first finger opposition Sits alone indefinitely Gets from sitting to prone; stands with hands held Responds to own name; combines consonants with vowels, as "da da" "ba ba"—mothers report: associates "da da" with "Daddy" "Accepted" two strange adults in laboratory
0-9	All chopped foods, toast, and cookies, fruits Appropriate arrangements for adequate night- and daytime sleep Gesell Developmental Schedule administered "A happy, relaxed mother who is proud of her son"	Good progress in achievement of bowel control Cutting teeth; has 6 teeth—2 lower and 4 upper incisors *High average* in use of large muscles—stands and cruises at rail; *average* in small muscle use *High average* in adaptive behavior Removed cube from cup and put cube into cup after demonstration without release; picked up pellet At least average in language development; says "bye bye" "Advanced in personal-social behavior; cooperates in dressing; friendly with everyone Can feed self alone but requires much time
1-3	Mother away over weekend Father puts him to bed regularly, often takes care of him all day on Saturday (mother working on thesis)	"Seemed a little shy" Says "baby," "bow wow," "daddy," "mama," "tick tock" and "bib"; points to or shows tongue, nose, hands; has total of 9 or 10 words Can squat in play and re-erect without losing balance
1-8	Mother has developed overconcern about Don's eating; cannot be convinced that he is eating enough	All indications are that his nutrition is adequate

Table C.4 (continued)

Developmental Chronology of Don 723

AGE	ENVIRONMENTAL EVENTS AND CIRCUMSTANCES	DEVELOPMENT (PHYSICAL, BEHAVIORAL, COGNITIVE, SOCIAL)
	Mother sewed up end of right pajama sleeve to prevent thumb-sucking	Sucked his right thumb a good deal Don seems to be a little overdependent upon his mother; asks for attention and demands her participation in his play Sits in small chair backward; walks up and down stairs holding rail Vocabulary of 81 words plus 13 names Mother thought he was cutting his molar teeth
2-1	Parents very much interested in Don's mental progress; both parents came in to discuss this with tester Few young children for Don to play with; has a 4-year-old friend Parents always allowed other adults to help with child Mr. 723 does not know where child got idea of asking for permission	Now has a vocabulary of 89 words and 16 names; uses pronouns "I," "me," "my" correctly; mother reported he is not satisfied with "yes" or "no" answers—wants fuller explanation; asks involved questions; looks at pictures in magazines; can entertain self this way; knows nursery rhymes; plays records; tested with an MA of 3-0 Don is very sociable; accepts care of other people readily Asked permission to put thumb in his mouth
2-9	Stanford-Binet test administered First day at nursery school; mother present Mother said Don had been promised he might stay for lunch so he did so although it had not been so planned	"Performed on test with great interest and good attention" No refusals. Basal age -3-6. Passed one test item at 6 year level. MA = 4-6, IQ = 164. Accepted nursery school situation as a matter of course; cooperated willingly in all activities; rode tricycle, played in sandbox, climbed ladder, used slide, went to toilet willingly Recognizes letters of alphabet as "my letter" (D) "Jimmie's letter (J)
3-0	Light switch in Don's bedroom convenient for him to turn on	Gets up by himself, turns on light, goes to bathroom without disturbing family
3-3	Stanford-Binet test administered	Performed on test with self-confidence; tended to pass the same test items with added suc-

Table C.4 (continued)

Developmental Chronology of Don 723

AGE	ENVIRONMENTAL EVENTS AND CIRCUMSTANCES	DEVELOPMENT (PHYSICAL, BEHAVIORAL, COGNITIVE, SOCIAL)
	Suggestions by nursery school staff that unconscious parental pressure is having an effect; parents very concerned during interview about Don's receiving sufficient intellectual stimulation	cesses, as on test at age 2-9, rather than succeeding at different types of test items. MA $=$ 5-0, IQ $=$ 154 Very independent at toilet Needs help in dressing Plays well with other children Easily embarrassed Active and enthusiastic in outdoor play Cries easily but not for long
3-10	Regular attendance at the nursery school Mother inclined to "manage" to exert subtle pressure	Talks easily about many things, very few questions on "why" of things; not a leader; does not use "subtle methods" to gain his point; rather he resorts to hitting to gain possession or to express his will; tends to throw blocks or knock them down; often enjoys knocking down other's buildings (from a student observer's report)
4-1	Stanford-Binet test administered Mother pregnant with third child, a possible disturbing factor Mother strongly inclined to tell child what to do, how to do it Father seemed to be more sensitive to Don's needs than mother, gave him more personal support; mother rather "overwhelming" to child Strong pressure toward "intellectualism"	Examiner felt that results did not represent Don's capacity or usual functional level MA $=$ 5-10, IQ $=$ 143. Don expressed some aggression, showed considerable restlessness; refused (did not fail) the items of the comprehension tests Vocabulary advanced Some loss of weight shift to slenderer channel on Grid Difficulty in emotional adjustments; moments of calm judgment alternating with high tension and shrieking Showing marked reluctance to do anything on his own; seems to have developed a feeling of inadequacy Outside home, interacted happily with others until pressure is applied, then he resists and tests limits
5-0	Don's final period of nursery school; it is no longer challenging to him; staff making special effort to meet his needs	Inclined to reject other children because they do not function at his level A kind of teasing hostility and aggression Boisterous behavior In test situation "testing of limits" behavior; refused to go for test, tester agreed, Don then went along; throughout test much

Table C.4 (continued)

Developmental Chronology of Don 723

AGE	ENVIRONMENTAL EVENTS AND CIRCUMSTANCES	DEVELOPMENT (PHYSICAL, BEHAVIORAL, COGNITIVE, SOCIAL)
	Parents anxious about transfer to kindergarten Overconcern about what it can offer Don Younger sibling, Jimmy, who has "knack for gaining center of attention" now a threat to Don Stanford-Binet test administered	refusal; said "I can't do that" or "I won't do that"; high points of performance were in "comprehension," "rhymes," and numbers— if tests were scored quantitatively MA and IQ would be much too low to represent his capacity.
7-0	Stanford-Binet test administered with younger brother in room; Jimmie somewhat of a distraction	Not highly motivated in test, showed little interest; "it was a thing he had to do" Performance on memory and numbers tests especially outstanding MA $= 9$-8, IQ $= 138$
9-0	WISC psychological test administered	Responses tended to be impulsive; speed at the expense of quality and accuracy of response; shows strong verbal-conceptual orientation. Did not do so well on performance portions of test; verbal scale IQ $= 144$, performance scale IQ $= 125$
15-0	Home situation now judged to be "good"; mother still inclined to "manage"; Don's relationship with brother and sister normal	A "slow grower"; no signs of onset of puberty —a source of real concern to Don; strong dissatisfaction with "physical self"; Highly motivated intellectually

Developmental Record Abstract of Judy 730

Judy's Parents and Their Background

Both of Mr. 730's parents came from Russia and were of Jewish heritage. The father was a smallish man, 5 feet 4 inches and 150 pounds. He had completed two years of college work in Russia. He was a grocer by occupation. The mother finished high school in Russia. She had no occupation other than that of wife and mother.

Mr. 730 was born in Minneapolis, Minnesota. At the early age of 19 he became manager of a market, and later he was advertising manager of a manufacturing firm. It was at this time that he met and married his life partner.

About a year after marriage Mr. 730 entered the United States Army and began training to be a pilot.

Mrs. 730s father was a Polish immigrant who graduated with honors in mechanical engineering from an American college. Her mother ended her formal education with high school graduation. Her parents were inclined to be strict and not to demonstrate affection.

Mrs. 730 graduated from college with a bachelor of science degree in education. She also did some work toward an advanced degree. At the time of her marriage she was teaching health education. During her husband's aviation training she did some additional graduate work in vocational education.

At maturity, Mrs. 730 was just under 5 feet tall and weighed 125 pounds.

Judy arrived at the end of a full-term, normal pregnancy. Her father, who had been serving overseas, was on a 30-day leave at the time of her birth.

The period following Judy's birth undoubtedly was a rather trying time for Mrs. 730. Having to care for and manage her first baby without the presence and support of her husband, she found her situation rather difficult. She was living in the home of her parents who gave her no support or encouragement in her desire to try "new" methods of child rearing about which she had been reading.

When Judy was about 4 months old, Mr. 730 was released from the service to return to his family. For some time the young family continued to live with Mrs. 730s parents while the couple looked for a place of their own.

Immediately, Mr. 730 began sharing in Judy's physical care. This young couple felt that it was important that their baby should be helped to be acquainted and to feel equally "at home" with both parents.

Table C.5

Physical Growth Data of Judy 730

AGE (YEARS-MONTHS)	WEIGHT (POUNDS)	HEIGHT (INCHES)
Birth	6.5	18.7
0-2	10.1	21.3
0-4	13.7	23.7
0-6	17.0	25.0
0-8	19.2	26.5
0-10	21.5	27.4
1-2	23.2	29.5
1-4	23.5	30.5
1-6	24.2	31.2
1-8	25.9	32.2

Table C.5 (continued)

Physical Growth Data of Judy 730

AGE (YEARS-MONTHS)	WEIGHT (POUNDS)	HEIGHT (INCHES)
1-10	26.2	32.8
2-3	28.7	34.3
2-8	30.7	36.4
3-4	34.1	38.5
3-8	36.3	39.5
4-4	38.8	41.4
4-10	42.1	42.1
5-7	45.3	44.6
6-6	52.5	47.0
7-6	66.9	49.3
9-3	96.5	53.8
9-9	95.3	54.9
10-3	103.8	55.9
10-9	109.5	56.7
11-3	109.8	57.8
11-9	117.7	59.3
12-6	121.8	68.8
13-8	132.0	62.6
14-9	134.6	63.1
16-7	138.6	63.4

Table C.6

Skeletal Maturation Date of Judy 730

AGE (YEARS-MONTHS)	SKELETAL AGE
0-4	0-4
0-6	0-6
0-9	0-9
1-3	1-2
1-6	1-6
2-3	2-3
2-6	2-6
3-6	3-6
4-3	4-2
4-6	4-6
4-10	4-11
5-6	5-7
5-9	5-9
6-6	6-7
7-6	7-8
8-6	8-8
9-3	9-6
9-9	10-2
10-3	10-8
10-9	10-11

Table C.7

Mental Test Data of Judy 730

AGE (YEARS-MONTHS)	TEST	DA OR MA	DQ OR IQ
0-6.5	Gesell Developmental	0-8	123[a]
1-3	Gesell Developmental	1-6	120[a]
2-3	Gesell Developmental	3-0	134[a]
2-10	Stanford-Binet	3-8	129
3-7	Stanford-Binet	4-6	126
9-3	WISC	——	109

[a] Estimated average values.

Table C.8

Developmental Chronology of Judy 730

AGE	ENVIRONMENTAL EVENTS AND CIRCUMSTANCES	DEVELOPMENT (PHYSICAL, BEHAVIORAL, COGNITIVE, SOCIAL)
Birth	Full-term; labor 27 hours, spontaneous delivery	"Good" condition at birth Birth weight 6 pounds 7 ounces, length 18.7 inches
0-2	Breast milk gave out, baby put on formula; now on self-demand, four-feeding schedule Father away, but two uncles very fond of Judy	Plays with hands; has rolled from prone to supine Responds with smiles to adult advances Pushes self up from stomach
0-4	Father now at home; "roughhouse" with father or uncles Family still living with mother's parents	Can roll from supine to prone; crawls backward; reaches with right hand for object "Squeals, gurgles, bubbles, coos"
0-6	Now in home of their own Mother a happy, relaxed kind of person—keen interest in children	Now starting to creep; raises self to hands and knees; pulls to sitting position "A friendly, happy baby"
0-8	Many visitors on Sundays	Picked up block—pincer grasp; creeps all over house Says "da da," "ma ma," imitates barking dog Some shyness
0-9	Parents play with Judy in bed	

Table C.8 (continued)

Developmental Chronology of Judy 730

AGE	ENVIRONMENTAL EVENTS AND CIRCUMSTANCES	DEVELOPMENT (PHYSICAL, BEHAVIORAL, COGNITIVE, SOCIAL)
1-3	Gessell Developmental Test Mr. 730 showed some concern about Judy's terrific destructiveness Had been left one week with maid	"Very advanced" in gross motor coordination; walks and runs easily; squats in play; "high average" fine motor coordinations "High average" in language and adaptive behavior Advanced in personal-social area
1-6	Gessell Developmental Test Overstimulation at times at home; visitors—uncles and grandparents; mother concerned about Judy's wakefulness at night	*Advanced* in gross motor; walks up and down stairs without assistance High average in fine motor coordinations, adaptive behavior, and language; mother reports vocabulary of more than 20 words; uses 3 and 4 word sentences Very advanced in personal-social development; Feeds self completely
1-8	Practically no toilet training up to now	Beginning of voluntary urinary control on Judy's part
1-10	No pressure or much effort made to train Judy in elimination control	Now "very reliable" in using nursery seat for urination; seems also to be "taking over" bowel control
2-0	Family temporarily at home of grandparents; have acquired a dog Judy accepted for nursery school Parents left for two weeks	
2-3	Family back to own home Mother upset by a friend, a "lay analyst," visiting in home who said Judy seemed to be bothered by "some deep-seated frustration"—cause of her temper tantrums Gesell Developmental Test	Judy able to "act for herself" on her own decision Both affectionate and aggressive toward other children; much "emotional energy," healthy, energetic, curious At times wanted what other child had, at other times much affection shown for other children Skilled motor coordinations, advanced language; advanced in all areas, particularly personal-social

Table C.8 (continued)

Developmental Chronology of Judy 730

AGE	ENVIRONMENTAL EVENTS AND CIRCUMSTANCES	DEVELOPMENT (PHYSICAL, BEHAVIORAL, COGNITIVE, SOCIAL)
2-4	Entered nursery school; new glasses bothered Judy Stanford-Binet test attempted, not completed Mother concerned about Judy's sleep pattern Parents now allow her to remain with them when she comes to their bed Neighborhood playmate with blond hair is much admired by adults to Judy's neglect; she also hears adults remark that "it's a crime" that Judy must soon wear glasses; mother tries to make wearing of glasses a more attractive prospect	Goes to parent's bed many times during night; apparent "insecurity feeling" about mother; protests mother leaving her at nursery school Judy in nursery school was observed to pull the light, curly hair of two children
2-7	Many interesting activities at home— ice skating with father, finger painting A recent period of illness Mother pregnant— hopes to get Judy into a good sleep routine before new baby arrives	Has trouble with new glasses at nursery school Has given up diapers at night; wet only one night in recent weeks; bladder "accidents" rare during daytime Poor appetite since illness "Whimpered a few tears" when mother left her at nursery school
2-9	Baby brother born	
2-10	New baby in the home Broken glasses— appears to have difficulty seeing any distance	Judy delights in helping care for baby

Table C.8 (continued)

Developmental Chronology of Judy 730

AGE	ENVIRONMENTAL EVENTS AND CIRCUMSTANCES	DEVELOPMENT (PHYSICAL, BEHAVIORAL, COGNITIVE, SOCIAL)
	Mother concerned about Judy's "adjustment" at nursery school; thinks child is emotionally disturbed, suggests getting help from a psychiatrist	Judy's arm "broken out with eczema"; became ill with temperature of 103°; earache
	"Often looks ragged and neglected, underwear sometimes dirty, seems unbathed" (staff report)	Very active at play when at nursery school, enjoys other children
	Stanford-Binet Test, child handicapped without glasses	Attention span brief; some irritable refusals in test, MA = 3-8, IQ = 129; results of test somewhat indecisive because of refusals
	Judy's total situation at this time appears to be one of stress	
3-3	Beginning new nursery school year	Engages in more cooperative play at nursery school than formerly
	Now has breakfast with family	Becoming more ambivalent toward little brother; some regressive behavior—sucked on a bottle for two days, said "I wanted to be a baby"
	Mother pregnant again	
	Father absent on business trip	
	House hunting	
	Comments about coming of new baby	
3-5	Having play therapy interviews	Seems to be overcoming some of her emotional difficulties
3-7	Stanford-Binet test; neglect at home? (looks uncared for, clothes seem to be "thrown together," hair not well cut or combed)	Judy gives impression of toughness both physically and psychologically; she whined and complained about tasks of the test—MA = 4-6, IQ = 126
3-9	New baby in the home	In nursery school Judy is now more absorbed in social contacts with children, less clinging

Table C.8 (continued)

Developmental Chronology of Judy 730

AGE	ENVIRONMENTAL EVENTS AND CIRCUMSTANCES	DEVELOPMENT (PHYSICAL, BEHAVIORAL, COGNITIVE, SOCIAL)
	Family now living in a more adequate home	to teachers; often shows qualities of leadership; generally "more relaxed, smiling, and prettier than we have ever seen her" (staff report)
4-3	Beginning of new nursery school term Mother reported that parents had tried to make past summer "especially for Judy"; many pleasant home activities—trips, getting wood for fireplace, making jack-o-lanterns	
4-7	Certain "leaders" in nursery school, and those she regards as important, wield much influence upon Judy	Plays almost exclusively with children she admires; sometimes engages with them in nonconforming activities Expresses definite likes and dislikes for her peers; very expressive in her feelings—cries when hurt, laughs when happy, frowns when irritated, refuses to participate when not interested Occasionally irritable and "out of sorts," expresses this in hitting or asking another child to do the hitting for her; "nothing seems to satisfy her" Has planned her own sleeping schedule at home Objected to wearing her glasses—"look ugly"
5-0	Joined a special, older group for her final nursery school period; this was an especially important change for Judy Now makes the noon meal a social occasion Was accepted as the fourth member of a little subgroup with whom Judy is especially congenial	Judy gives impression of being "stocky"—somewhat shorter and heavier than other children but is now extremely skillful in handling her body Is always busy and must be involved in every activity More independent; no longer irritable, seems completely freed for happy activity

Table C.8 (continued)

Developmental Chronology of Judy 730

AGE	ENVIRONMENTAL EVENTS AND CIRCUMSTANCES	DEVELOPMENT (PHYSICAL, BEHAVIORAL, COGNITIVE, SOCIAL)
5-8	Baby sister born Now a member of recreational club; club leaders see Judy as one who needs help and support in art work and other activities	Judy enters vigorously into hostile activities against club leader (locking her in closet)
6-0	At home, children are free to express their feelings Grandmother living in the home, often does not approve	Mother feels that Judy has "regressed" since birth of sister In competing for leadership among neighborhood children Judy is at times inclined to use bribery
6-6	Occupies a middle position in club as to age Leader tries to give Judy extra attention	Personality was not particularly pleasing in comparison with others in club; not as pretty Demands considerable attention; becomes impatient, irritable if not given immediate attention More of a follower than a leader Did not relate strongly to any one member of group
7-6		Judy's personality described as "not very attractive, but refreshing"; tends to be aggressive, outspoken, demanding, and impatient; "frustration threshold" low Appears to be leader of group by making plans, but gives directions in an autocratic manner; children resist this (report of a club leader)
8-0		Judy is pretty well balanced though she has her problems Stands up for her rights, not shy Will also defend the rights of others; inclined to assert herself Independent and self-reliant most of the time
9-3	WISC administered Interviewed on food likes and dislikes	Described as "short heavy girl"; talks in a loud voice, says things emphatically Made loud protestations that test items were too hard Responded well to reassurance and praise; full scale IQ = 109 Concerned about her weight and size, and so on

Indexes

AUTHOR INDEX

SUBJECT INDEX